The Oratory School

* 0 0 0 0 4 8 1 8 *

The Life and Opinions
of
MAXIMILIEN ROBESPIERRE

ORATORY SCHOOL LIBRARY

CLASS .... 92 ROB

BOOK No. 14234

D1343073

Also by Norman Hampson

La Marine de L'An II

A Social History of the French Revolution

The Enlightenment

The First European Revolution

A Concise History of the French Revolution

Danton

Will and Circumstance

Prelude to Terror: The Constituent Assembly and the Failure of Consensus, 1789 – 1791

The Life and Opinions
of
MAXIMILIEN ROBESPIERRE

Norman Hampson

Basil Blackwell

Copyright © Norman Hampson 1974

First published in this edition 1988

Basil Blackwell Ltd
108 Cowley Road, Oxford, OX4 1JF, UK

Basil Blackwell Inc.
432 Park Avenue South, Suite 1503
New York, NY 10016, USA

Published by arrangment with Gerald Duckworth & Co. Ltd

All rights reserved. Except for the quotation of short passages for the
purposes of criticism and review, no part of this publication may be
reproduced, stored in a retrieval system, or transmitted in any form or
by any means, electronic, mechanical, photocopying, recording, or
otherwise, without the prior permission of the publisher.

Except in the United States of America, this book is sold subject to the
condition that it shall not, by way of trade or otherwise, be lent, re-
sold, hired out, or otherwise circulated without the publisher's prior
consent in any form of binding or cover other than that in which it is
published and without a similar condition including this condition
being imposed on the subsequent purchaser.

ISBN 0-631-16226-7

Printed in Great Britain by Hobbs the Printers Ltd, Southampton

To Jacqueline

Contents

Robespierre was liberty's most energetic champion . . . he represented democracy in its purest, its most noble and its most elevated sense. There never lived a greater friend of justice and humanity.

E. Hamel

The most hateful character in the forefront of human history since Machiavelli reduced to a code the wickedness of public men.

Lord Acton

I feel he is a man of meticulous probity and rare disinterestedness.

Babeuf, 1786

There are two Robespierres, the one a genuine *patriote* and man of principle, up to the 31st of May [1793] and since then the man of ambition, the tyrant and the deepest of villains.   *Babeuf, 1794*

Robespierre might well claim that he alone was able to steer the Revolution to its true goal.   *Babeuf, 1796*

Of no one of whom so much has been said is so little known.

J. W. Croker

Our revolution has made me feel the full force of the axiom that history is fiction.   *Robespierre*

Preface

I suspect that most readers, like myself, are inclined to ignore prefaces, especially long ones. Nevertheless, if they are not going to dismiss the somewhat unusual form of this book as a pretentious search for originality at any price, a decent respect for their opinion calls for some explanation of why facts should be submitted in this way to an all too candid world.

When historians are discussing their craft among themselves, many of them agree that historical judgments are subjective, unlikely to command the universal assent of contemporaries and almost certain to be set aside by future generations. When we come to write, it is a different matter. Whatever our doubts, however conscious we may be that we have only expressed one of the various possible points of view, we pronounce with what purports to be Olympian finality.

There are good reasons for this. Most of the best history has been written by men convinced of the objective validity of their judgment. Even when the reader no longer shares their point of view he often feels that the unrecognised assumptions in the historian's mind have acquired historical interest in themselves, as representative of their age. This has already led, to the writing of books about books about events and there is no logical reason why the series should not be prolonged *ad infinitum*.

Historians being human, it is hard to admit, even to one's self, that what one would like to regard as a final verdict can aspire to permanence only as the expression of transient personal or social attitudes. We all accept that this is true of lyric poetry and do not believe that everyone must always be as dejected as Shelley once claimed to be over Naples. History, however, seems different. Historians, even while they deny that their work can ever be scientific, still feel that it ought, somehow or other, to be objective. It is, after all, supposed to be about facts. The historian can neither invent his own evidence nor ignore inconvenient circumstances that disprove what he would like to believe. This leaves him with more scope than one might expect. His necessary selection of only part of the evidence, his rejection of one source in favour of a conflicting one and his inference of motive from what actually happened, give him more freedom of interpretation than he would always like. Anyone who doubts this has only to sample what has been written about Robespierre.

This view of the nature of history and the rôle of the historian is, inevitably, itself historical in the sense that it seems demonstrably true – at least to some people – at some periods and quite absurd at others. Most societies have been confident that they knew why things happened and they have set their historians the task of illustrating the operation of historical laws that everyone knew to be true, whether these reflected the will of God, freedom broadening down from precedent to precedent, dialectical materialism or any other teleology. The historical agnostic like myself may envy those who have kept the faith, but having tasted scepticism, he is exiled from all their various Edens. They know what life is about and what history is for and he knows neither. If he hopes that his material itself will somehow or other provide him with the answers, he soon learns better. Grappling with historical problems, he discovers his own limitations, as a scholar, a writer and a man. We are betrayed, not merely by what is false, but by what is inadequate within. Reading history seriously brings the same kind of self-awareness and realisation that history is a mirror rather than a telescope. Whether learning one's limitations helps one to transcend them is another matter. If not, it should at least help one to live with them.

The book that follows is a reluctant admission of these truths. It arises from an unsuccessful attempt to write something entirely different. Having been baffled and exasperated by Robespierre for many years I yielded to the illusion that the only way to make up my mind about him was to write his biography. I should, of course, have known better. Greater familiarity with the evidence merely provided new support for each of the conflicting opinions that I had hoped it would reconcile. It did at least convince me that to approach this tormented and self-contradictory man with urbane impartiality is to deprive one's self of any chance of understanding him at all. Whatever one makes of him he deserves more than that. Failing to answer any of my questions, I had no alternative but to try to find room for them all and the reader will encounter not one view of Robespierre but several. The book that follows therefore takes the form of an exposition by a narrator who keeps as closely as he can to what he considers the most important factual evidence, punctuated by the objections and opinions of three other people who have positive viewpoints of their own, although they depend on the narrator for their information. To help the reader to familiarise himself with these people, they are introduced as a civil servant (the man from the ministry), a Communist (the party member) and a clergyman (the reverend). Once their identity is established they use each other's names: Ted, Mac and Henry respectively. These characters are not arbitrary inventions; they personify attitudes which I share, which prevent me from arriving at a unitary view of Robespierre. Whatever the awkwardness of my approach, I could not honestly have adopted any other and I hope that it will at least preserve the reader from the temptation to accept what he is told and encourage him to join in the dialogue for himself.

Robespierre is both a good and a bad subject for biography. He was a man of obvious importance who exercised considerable influence over some of the most significant events in modern history. At the same time the man himself remains more enigmatic than almost any comparable figure in history. Few people have been so adulated and reviled, both by contemporaries and by posterity. There is no mountain of unpublished 'Robespierre papers' to encourage the illusion that the evidence will do the historian's work for him. To compensate for this, the completion in 1967 of a very fine scholarly edition of virtually all Robespierre's known writings, speeches and newspaper articles puts at the disposal of his biographer a mass of material that was previously so scattered as to be virtually inaccessible. Despite all this he remains as elusive as ever. Very little indeed is known of his private life during the Revolution. His speeches, like those of any other statesman, were intended to persuade others rather than to expose himself. Everything requires interpretation. That penetrating and sensitive historian, J. H. Huizinga, singled out Robespierre in his inaugural lecture at Groningen in 1905. 'The need for intuition is the greater, the more unusual is the character one is trying to understand. A psychological enigma such as Robespierre, who does not at all lend himself to analysis, can yet be brought to life by a good writer. What matters here are the echoes that are awakened in our own hearts.' I am not so naïve or presumptuous as to imagine that I can satisfy Huizinga's criteria but

I have tried to face up to his problem and I would vigorously endorse his view that the reader's own verdict will depend on the qualities of both mind and heart that he himself brings to his reading.

Finally, it is a pleasure to acknowledge a few of my many debts: to my old tutor, the late J. M. Thompson; to Richard Cobb, not merely for his generosity in putting his incomparable knowledge of the Revolution at my disposal but because, over the years, he has given me more insights into the period than either of us could enumerate; to Graham Daniels, for opening my eyes in all kinds of ways. I owe a special debt to Eugène Vinaver, both for his unfailing help and encouragement and for showing me, in his own writings, most notably in *A la recherche d'une poétique médiévale,* what I myself was trying to say. My wife's onslaughts on my prose have spared the reader a good deal of unnecessary suffering.

Without the generosity of the trustees of the Leverhulme Foundation and the kindness of Newcastle University in granting me a year's leave of absence, the book could never have been written at all.

I The Nature of the Evidence

I will tell you, I said, all about Robespierre.

I suppose, said the man from the ministry, you mean that you will tell us all you know about Robespierre.

What he means, said the party member, is that he will tell us what he wants us to think about Robespierre.

If you go on like this, I replied, I won't tell you anything at all. I certainly don't intend to tell you all I know because a lot of it is of no interest to anybody. But, as far as I can, I'll tell you everything that I think you'd like to know and if you think I'm hiding anything you can always ask.

That's assuming we know what we don't know, said the man from the ministry.

Well, it's the best we can do. You've got to take something on trust and I'll undertake not to leave out anything I think you might think important, even if I don't. Where would you like to begin?

Leave out the ancestors, said the party member. I'm supposed to be descended from Charles II but it tells you more about him than about me.

All right. But if you don't mind I'll start four months before he was born because that's when his parents got married, on 2 January 1758. His father, who was 26, had qualified as a barrister two years before and begun to practise in Arras. His mother was a brewer's daughter and the Robespierres – or de Robespierres or Derobespierres, they used all three names – seem to have thought it a bad match since they didn't go to the wedding. Maximilien was born, then, on 6 May 1758, his sister Charlotte in February 1760, another sister, who died in her teens, in December 1761, a brother, Augustin, in January 1763 and a fifth child, who died almost at once, in July 1764. Maximilien's mother herself died a few days later when he was only six.

If we go on at this rate we'll have the whole family extinct in another ten minutes, said the man from the ministry.

I thought you wanted some facts. There aren't many about his early life. For instance, what happened to his father is very

1

obscure. He seems to have left Arras about four months after his wife died, but he kept coming back from time to time. He was there in December 1765 and again in the following spring, when he borrowed 600 livres (about £30) from one of his sisters. He next reappeared in October 1768 when he borrowed again from his widowed mother, renouncing his own and his children's claims on her estate. He spent several months in Arras in 1772 when he appeared in fifteen cases at the local bar.[1] Then he seems to have disappeared for good. He died in Munich in 1777.[2]

And what did Maximilien make of all that?

Before we can look at that I'd better tell you something about our sources. Almost everything we know about his early years comes either from his sister, Charlotte, or from the abbé Proyart who was the vice-principal of Robespierre's school in Paris and then came to Arras as a cathedral canon just before the Revolution.[3] Charlotte did not see a great deal of Maximilien as a young girl but she lived with him from his return to Arras in 1782 until the Revolution. Her 'Memoirs' consist of recollections taken down and edited by Laponneraye, an admirer of Robespierre's, in the 1830s. She joined in the hero-worship and there isn't a word of criticism from start to finish. The whole family appears in a most edifying light, with Maximilien in particular as a youthful Galahad. Proyart complements Charlotte in the sense that she is precise about Arras and vague about school life at Louis-le-Grand whereas he knows comparatively little about Arras but a good deal about his pupil. But for Proyart the child Galahad was an absolute monster. He said that his book was 'a portrait whose frightful original was before our eyes only too long'.[4] Charlotte and Proyart contradicted each other so explicitly that they might almost have been doing it on purpose.

---

1. G. Walter, *Robespierre*, Paris, 1946 edition, p. 16.
J. M. Thompson's argument (in *Robespierre*, Oxford, 1939 edition, pp. xxi-xxii)
2. *Ann. hist. Rév. fr., no.* 152 (1958), p. 97.
3. L. Jacob, *Robespierre vu par ses contemporains*, Paris, 1938, p. 42n1. that Proyart was not the a.thor of *La vie et les crimes de Maximilien Robespierre* by 'Le Blond de Neuveglise', printed at Augsburg in 1795, is not convincing. All the internal evidence points in the opposite direction and Thompson's opinion is not shared by any of Robespierre's other biographers. I have therefore referred to 'Le Blond' as Proyart.
4. p. 17.

Robespierre was 'naturally gay; he knew how to tease and sometimes laughed till he cried'.[5] 'He never laughed and hardly ever smiled.' His character was 'gentle and fair, which made him loved by all'. He was 'universally loved . . . everyone was jealous to count him amongst his friends'. 'He was incapable of friendship and had not a single friend.' 'He loved us (his brother and sisters) tenderly and lavished his care and caresses on us.' 'He was as harsh as a tyrant towards his brother and sisters.' 'He was less concerned to encourage [a litigant] to plead than to reconcile him with the opposing party.' 'He would have been furious if he had prevented a lawsuit by reconciliation.' 'My brother's friendliness towards women won him their affection.' 'His character and the kind of life he led kept him completely apart from women.'[6]

About the only points on which Charlotte and the abbé agree is that Maximilien had more application than natural ability, that he nevertheless did well at school and that he was not very sociable by nature. On almost everything else they demolish each other's evidence. And yet most of the things that historians have written about these years can be traced back to one or the other. Thompson, for instance, was impressed by a rather critical description of Robespierre, since he thought it was written by his friend, Devienne. Thompson took this from the nineteenth-century historian, Paris. But the passage in question is actually taken word for word from Proyart.[7]

The two most important nineteenth-century biographies of Robespierre, by Paris and Hamel, follow Proyart and Charlotte respectively. For the former he was all black and for the latter all white. Neither makes him sound at all credible, but each of them contributes some evidence one can't find elsewhere and they can't be disregarded. If anything, the polemic got fiercer in the first half of the twentieth century, when Aulard attacked Robespierre in order to praise Danton and Mathiez took over from Hamel. Neither ventured on a biography of Robespierre. The two men who did, Walter and Thompson, hoisted a flag of truce. Walter said in his introduction, 'I have forced myself, as far as was

5. *Mémoires de Charlotte Robespierre*, ed. H. Fleischmann, Paris, n.d., p. 200.
6. Charlotte, pp. 189, 198, 202; Proyart, pp. 67, 61, 22, 55, 63.
7. Thompson, p. 20; J. A. Paris, *La jeunesse de Robespierre et la convocation des Etats Généraux en Artois*, Arras, 1870, p. 76; Proyart, p. 67.

3

humanly possible, to efface myself.'[8] His claim to be describing Robespierre rather than judging him didn't save him from the broadsides of outraged Robespierrists; understandably so, since he showed more enthusiasm for demolishing the myths that favoured Robespierre, than the other sort. Thompson rather optimistically believed that 'there is a growing consensus of informed opinion, establishing conclusions which will not easily be upset'.[9] Perhaps this is why his work tends to be disregarded in France and his excellent biography has never been translated. Since the Second World War the fighting has shifted to another front, with a new generation of historians tending to regard Robespierre as 'petit-bourgeois' and to transfer their allegiance to less gentlemanly revolutionaries. So far as we are concerned, we have the Charlotte school, the Proyart school and the would-be neutrals who have challenged a good deal of the evidence offered by the first two.

I believe we were talking about Robespierre's childhood, said the man from the ministry.

His peculiar family circumstances must have had some effect on him, perhaps a very great effect. But there isn't a single reference to either of his parents in any of his surviving writings. So we have either to make what we can of Charlotte's evidence or to write off the first ten years of his life as a complete blank.

I don't think you have any option. Otherwise you are going to make one or two assumptions, based on evidence you know to be unreliable, throw in some inferences from his later life and before you know where you are you'll be using this as firm evidence on which to base more assumptions. What do you think, reverend?

I'm not sure, replied the reverend. I see your point, but one doesn't have to be a Freudian to think that these were probably vital years. He must have had mixed feelings about this very odd father.

A French historian has made out a persuasive case for Maximilien's having developed a love-hate relationship towards his father which led him to strive for acceptance as a model of orthodox propriety while at the same time feeling guilty because he was rejecting his father.[10]

The party member seemed to be getting rather impatient: if

8. p. 7.   9. p. lv.
10. M. Gallo, *Maximilien Robespierre, histoire d'une solitude*, Paris, 1968.

you've got any evidence, produce it. If not, let's get on till you find some. You can't psycho-analyse a man just because you don't know enough about him to discuss him in any other way.

It all depends on what you mean by evidence, said the reverend. If we don't accept what's only probable I suspect that we aren't going to get very far. Maximilien's grandfather must have been an unusually charitable man if he didn't say some unkind things about this lawyer who had seduced his daughter and then abandoned the children.

And Maximilien would have had plenty of opportunities to hear them, I said, since the grandfather brought up the two boys. Charlotte said that the death of their parents – she concealed her father's peculiar behaviour as well as she could – transformed Maximilien from a careless, rowdy boy to a grave and hard-working future head of the family.[11] She maintained that in later life he was very moved whenever they talked about their mother but she gives no hint of what he thought about his father.

For all we know, said the man from the ministry, he may have written him off as an old rogue. If you haven't got any outside evidence we'll have to leave it at that.

There are two comments about his early days in Arras, both second-hand and very late. They don't help much. One man said he was *ce que l'on appelle un bon enfant* and the other that he was a *boeser tückischer knabe* (a nasty underhand boy).[12] Unless someone finds new evidence, I think we're at a dead end here.

At all events, the family disasters didn't prevent Maximilien from getting a good education. He went to the local school until he was eleven and then a canon who was a friend of the family got him a scholarship to Louis-le-Grand in Paris, which had as high a reputation as any school in the country. A fair amount has been written about the humilation of Robespierre, the scholarship-boy, mixing – or refusing to mix – with wealthy boys who were a good deal less intelligent and hard-working than he was, but it's almost all conjecture. He was certainly not well off: Proyart quotes a letter in which Robespierre asked him for money so that he could get some decent clothes to see the bishop of Arras who was visiting Paris. On the other hand there were 200 scholarship

11. pp. 188-9.   12. Jacob, op. cit., pp. 40-1.

boys in the school so there must have been plenty of others in the same boat. Proyart obviously knew him well there but he only valued the most conventional professions of Catholicism and he denounced any sign of social, political or religious unorthodoxy as moral turpitude. Robespierre said in 1793 that he had been a pretty poor Catholic since his school days and that would have been enough, quite apart from Proyart's political antagonism.[13] At least he presents a consistent picture of Robespierre as a boy consumed by intellectual pride, jealous of anyone else's success, addicted to forbidden literature – which probably meant the *philosophes* rather than pornography, not that Proyart would have recognised the distinction – and unpopular with the other boys. It could be true, but there are all kinds of reasons for a boy keeping to himself and a good many of us were pretty insufferable as precocious sixth-formers.

If you're looking in my direction, said the man from the ministry, I wouldn't disagree. But aren't there any comments about him from Old Boys?

Several of them went on to play an active part in the Revolution but most of them don't seem to have said anything about the old days at Louis-le-Grand. When they do, it's all predictable. Desmoulins appealed to his old school friend when he was trying to get Robespierre's political support. Fréron, soon after he had helped to get him overthrown and executed, described him in much the same terms as Proyart: 'gloomy, irascible, jealous of the success of his comrades', etc.[14]

It looks significant to me, said the man from the ministry, that the people who disliked him said much the same things about him and the only evidence to the contrary comes from Charlotte who didn't know what he was like at school.

I don't want to seem awkward, replied the reverend, but it's not ten minutes since you wanted to reject partisan evidence, especially when it came from a later period. I think we're all in danger of making up our minds about him before we know what we're talking about.

I could quote another school acquaintance, Beffroy de Reigny, who later edited a literary review called *Les lunes du Cousin*

13. Speech at the Jacobin Club on 21 November.
14. *Papiers inédits trouvés chez Robespierre, Saint-Just, Payan etc.*, Paris, 1828, vol. I, p. 154.

Jacques. When Robespierre sent him a couple of his works in 1786, he replied that he wasn't at all surprised by their 'elegant style and ingenious ideas'. 'The young orator would have had to deteriorate a long way to produce anything mediocre. The author of the Lunes has a very clear recollection of his agreeable contemporary's rôle at college; talent like his is not made to be forgotten.' De Reigny did not review either of Robespierre's works though, and perhaps he was only being polite.[14a] There are a few facts we do know about his school career. Between 1771 and 1776 he won three second prizes and six mentions, which suggests that he was a good scholar, if not an outstanding one.[15] Unless Proyart invented the whole story for dramatic effect, which seems unlikely, Robespierre was chosen to deliver a Latin address to Louis XVI as part of the coronation celebrations in 1775.[16] He was not, of course, allowed to compose it himself and we have no idea what he thought when he knelt in the rain before the king and queen who didn't reply or leave their coach. If he had any disloyal thoughts at the time they didn't prevent him from praising the king in the warmest terms in some of his pre-revolutionary writings. Perhaps the best evidence of what the school thought of him is the fact that when he left in 1781 it took the unusual step – by a unanimous decision – of making him a grant of 600 livres on account of his 'good conduct over a period of twelve years and his success in the course of his studies'.[17] This certainly suggests that he was not disliked by his teachers. Proyart had probably left by then. Robespierre himself left Louis-le-Grand a qualified lawyer and returned to Arras.

All I've got out of this so far, said the party member, is that he was a young meritocrat whose family connections allowed him to overcome the difficulties of being an orphan. He went to a good school, worked hard and climbed back on to the bourgeois ladder.

There's perhaps an element of truth in that; I mean about his going back to a safe career in Arras. A lot of bright young men were leaving the provinces to try their luck in Paris where most of them made a mess of things and led a demoralising life as

14a. W. Krauss in *Ann. hist. Rév. fr.*. no. 161 (1960), p. 306.
15. *Ann. hist. Rév. fr.*, no. 157 (1959), pp. 270-1.
16. Proyart, p. 48.
17. E. Hamel, *Histoire de Robespierre,* Paris, 1865, vol. I, pp. 19-20.

Grub Street pamphleteers.[18] Desmoulins was one of them. It may have been his temperament or his sense of family responsibility or a combination of both that led Robespierre to choose the obscure respectability of the Arras bar. It paid off in 1789 and there was perhaps a touch of bitterness in Desmoulins' letter to his father announcing Robespierre's election to the Estates General, when he said that Robespierre 'had the good sense to practise law in his own province'.[19] He managed to transfer his scholarship to his younger brother and Charlotte came to keep house for him. His other sister had died while he was at Louis-le-Grand so, in one way or another, he was now looking after the whole family.

He certainly got off to a good start in Arras. He had only appeared in one or two very minor cases when, in March 1782, he was appointed to succeed the doyen of the Arras bar as one of the five judges in the bishop's court.

Clerical influence again, put in the party member.

I disregarded this. There seems to be a curse on all the early evidence about him. We have what looks like something solid when an Arras lawyer wrote to a young friend in Paris on 22 February 1782 to say that Robespierre 'has just made his début here in a famous case which he pleaded in three audiences so as to frighten anyone who felt like following him in the same career. They say, for I didn't hear him myself, that he leaves far behind him, by his manner of speaking, his choice of language and clarity of style, the Liborels, the Desmazières, the Brassarts, the Blanquarts and even the famous Dauchez.'[20] This is rather too much of a good thing. His correspondent seems to have taken it at its face value but, if the date is correct, Robespierre had appeared only in one very minor and hopeless case, which he had lost. If the letter is ironical, it *could* imply that Robespierre had made rather a fool of himself by taking himself too seriously.

Back to square one, said the man from the ministry.

But not for long, I said cheerfully. We reach some reasonably firm ground in 1783 when he appeared in the lightning-conductor

18. See R. Darnton, 'The high Enlightenment and the low life of literature in pre-Revolutionary France', *Past and Present*, May 1971.

19. G. Le Notre, *Vieilles maisons, vieux papiers*, 1st series, Paris, 1932 edition, p. 13.

20. Jacob, op. cit., pp. 21-2.

case. A man called de Vissery was appealing to the Conseil d'Artois against a court order to dismantle his lightning-conductor on the ground that this newfangled invention might divert the lightning on to his neighbours' houses.[21] This was just the kind of case that allowed the paladins of the Enlightenment to go crusading against superstitious obscurantism and they made the most of it. De Vissery was represented by Buissart, an Arras lawyer with a keen interest in physics, who became a close friend of Robespierre. Buissart had already been working on his defence of lightning-conductors for a year or so. He had consulted Parisian scientists and compiled a substantial memoir which he got Robespierre to present in court. Maximilien was not responsible for the scientific argument but he seems to have argued his case with skill and conviction and he won his verdict. Everyone then set about gaining the maximum publicity for this new victory of Reason. Buissart got his memoir reviewed in the *Mercure de France*, which concluded by saying, 'Monsieur de Robespierre, a young lawyer of rare merit, displayed in this business, which was the cause of the Sciences and the Arts, an eloquence and wisdom which give the highest impression of his knowledge'. Robespierre persuaded de Vissery to pay for the publication of his *plaidoyers*. He sent copies to the *Mercure de France* – which didn't give it another review – and to Franklin. Hostile critics have suggested that he tried to give Franklin the impression that he was responsible for the whole scientific argument, but since Buissart and de Vissery also wrote to the champion of lightning-conductors and republicanism and Robespierre probably knew that Buissart had sent Franklin a copy of his memoir, one doesn't need to assume any intention to deceive.[22] It was perhaps in honour of this famous victory that Robespierre was elected to the Arras Academy later in the year.[23]

Soon after he had won his case, Robespierre made a short trip to Carvin, where some of his family lived. He wrote an account

21. See V. Barbier and C. Vellay, *Oeuvres complètes de Maximilien Robespierre*, Paris, 1910, vol. I, pp. 19-119, for Robespierre's *plaidoyer*. There is a good account of the case as a whole in C. Vellay, 'Robespierre et le procès du paratonnerre', *Annales révolutionnaires*, vol. II (1909), pp. 25-37, 201-19.

22. Walter, p. 37; C. Vellay in *Revue historique de la Révolution française*, vol. V (1914), p. 137.

23. A study of Robespierre's rôle in the Academy is being prepared by L. N. Berthe, who published a biography of its secretary, *Dubois de Fosseux*, Arras, 1969.

of it to Buissart and this has become another source of controversy. Walter takes his letter to be a confession of injured pride because he was not recognised by the tax officials at the gates of Arras. Walter reads quite a lot into Robespierre's comment, 'I have always had an enormous amount of *amour-propre*; this sign of contempt cut me to the quick and put me in a vile temper for the rest of the day.' This really is preposterous. The whole letter is an attempt at the mock-heroic, and quite an amusing one too. Robespierre begins, 'I know an author who travelled five leagues and celebrated the fact in verse and prose. But what is his enterprise compared to mine? I didn't merely cover five but six, and long ones too which, in the opinion of the locals are equal to seven ordinary leagues.' He keeps up the same style all the way through: 'The car which bore us left the city gates just as the sun's chariot sprang from the bosom of the Ocean' and he concludes with a poem in praise of jam tarts. The British historian, Lewes, who first published the letter, recognised it as an exercise in juvenile high spirits and it seems perverse to take it in any other way.[24]

I'm glad that my juvenilia are safe from the attention of some of your historians, said the reverend.

It was towards the end of the same year – 1783 – that Robespierre got involved in his first major controversy, the Deteuf case. The case itself was clear enough: a Benedictine monk who was subsequently found guilty of peculation, accused of theft a man called Deteuf, the brother of a girl who had refused his advances. Deteuf in turn sued the monastery for substantial damages, with Robespierre as his lawyer. Robespierre, although he began by disclaiming any anti-clerical intentions and paid tribute to 'the virtues that shine forth from so many monasteries', was very sharp indeed in his denunciation of this one. There was a curiously political edge to his attack when he said that the Benedictines of Anchin were accountable to the public for their actions and concluded with a plea for the punishment of calumny in the name of 'all those who glory in the name of citizen'.[25] He also took the unusual step of publishing his *mémoire* before the verdict, presumably in the hope that public opinion would put pressure on the

24. G. H. Lewes, *The Life of Maximilian Robespierre*, London, 1849, pp. 48-9.
25. Barbier and Vellay, vol. I, pp. 120-59.

court. The Benedictines were defended by Liborel, who had presented Robespierre to the Arras bar only two years before. Liborel counter-attacked violently, accusing Robespierre of 'the most atrocious diffamation' and demanding that he be censured by the court.[26] According to Walter, the case divided Arras society, with the liberals, Buissart, Dubois de Fosseux and le Gay taking Robespierre's side and a good many of the older magistrates supporting Liborel.[27] It was perhaps more complicated than that, if the accused monk was right in believing that the bishop was behind his misfortunes. Clerical rivalries bit deep. It would certainly be wrong to think that Robespierre had broken with the Church as a whole: two years later the Oratoriens who directed his old school at Arras invited him back to give the boys a lecture on Henry IV, which seems to have met with general approval.[28]

All the same, said the party member, this looks like some sort of a turning-point.

It certainly didn't take him long to turn on the man who had launched his career.

That's hardly fair, I objected. Liborel was only doing the job for which he was paid. At all events we have to be careful about following Gallo and presenting Robespierre as a man who was now in revolt against the social conformity that had ensured his popularity. We don't know enough. He may just have got himself involved in a local faction fight. It's true that the number of his cases fell off – but not until 1785 and they picked up again in 1787. What we can say is that he had shown himself to be a caustic polemicist. This was going to get him into trouble before long. It could be that, now that he was well enough established to satisfy his very modest needs, he was beginning to feel rather frustrated with the life of a provincial lawyer, but he was certainly no radical as yet.

In 1784 he decided to compete for an essay prize offered by the Academy of Metz. Since Rousseau made a reputation overnight by winning the Dijon prize in 1749 this sort of competition had appealed to obscure provincials who aspired to become Parisian men of letters. Metz had chosen as its subject *les peines infamantes,* or 'corruption of the blood', which extended to the criminal's

26. Walter, p. 52.   27. p. 52.
28. Baron Despatys, *La Révolution, la Terreur, le Directoire, 1791–99, d'après les mémoires de Gaillard,* Paris, 1909, p. 160.

family a share of his own guilt. Robespierre's essay, which he published in 1785, is an interesting example of eighteenth-century
academic writing which shows him still completely dominated by
the influence of Montesquieu's *De l'Esprit des Lois*.[29] The first
part of his argument was virtually a paraphrase of Montesquieu:
all states were of two kinds, monarchies, which rested on their
subjects' acceptance of the code of honour and republics, whose
principle was *vertu*, or civic sense. Unlike Montesquieu, who maintained that the British constitution was a near-perfect form of
balanced monarchy, Robespierre thought it was really republican.
The division between the socially conservative upholders of honour
and the egalitarian, or at least meritocratic republicans, underlay
most of the political argument of the late eighteenth century and
the Revolution.[30] Robespierre came down squarely on the conservative side. His fellow-member of the Arras Academy, Carnot,
who was to become his colleague in the Committee of Public
Safety, took a much more radical line in a paper he read to the
Academy in 1787.[31] Robespierre didn't merely take the existence
of monarchical values for granted and dismiss republican *vertu* as
an unattainable ideal, as Montesquieu had tended to do. Like
Fielding, Smollett and Goethe, he attacked *vertu* as totalitarian,
since it would oblige the citizen to do such dishonourable things
as denouncing guilty members of his own family. After a good
deal of this fairly conventional stuff he suddenly changed his tone
to protest that *peines infamantes* applied only to bourgeois and not
to nobles. 'This cruel opinion took root without difficulty in ages
of barbarism when it struck at will against an enslaved people
despised by a powerful clergy and a proud nobility who oppressed
it.'

After this flash of anger he went on to argue that something
contrary to morality and natural law could not be defended on
grounds of public utility, making the typical eighteenth-century
claim that '*Vertu* produces happiness as the sun produces light'.

29. Bib. Nat. F 43567.
30. N. Hampson, 'The French Revolution and the nationalisation of honour',
in *War and Society: Essays in memory of John Weston* (ed. M. R. D. Foot),
London, 1973.
31. Discovered by L. N. Berthe, who published it, with M. de Langre in
*Maximilien Robespierre: Les droits et l'état des bâtards et Lazare Carnot, Le
pouvoir de l'habitude*, Arras, 1971, pp. 133-58.

He claimed that it was the need of families to protect themselves from dishonour that was mainly responsible for *lettres de cachet*, by which offenders could be imprisoned without trial. He didn't seem very concerned about *lettres de cachet*, indeed at one point he seemed to be complaining that their price put them beyond the reach of the poor, and he didn't refer at all to their use by Ministers to silence political opposition. In his final section he discussed what could be done to improve the situation. He recognised the limitations of legislative action in removing what was not merely a legal penalty but also a social stigma. He was confident, though, that 'prejudices are invincible only in times of ignorance'. He thought his own age 'an enlightened century when everything is weighed, judged and discussed'. He advanced one or two practical suggestions, which included taking a more sympathetic attitude towards illegitimate children, although he was against giving them any legal claim on their parents' estate. This scandalised Proyart who regarded bastards as the legitimate targets of divine wrath and accused Robespierre of advocating polygamy![32]

There's an interesting sign of emerging class consciousness in the middle bit, said the party member and I noted that he was only worried about discrimination against bourgeois and not against commoners in general. Obviously he wanted to be a proper gentleman. But the rest of it is pretty wishy-washy academic stuff.

I think we ought to remember the time when it was written, said the reverend – and also the audience he was trying to please, cut in the man from the ministry.

That's what makes his attack on the clergy and nobility rather interesting, the party member came back. I don't suppose that was calculated to appeal to the academic gentlemen at Metz.

He was referring to the Middle Ages, I objected, and I don't think you ought to make too much of the class argument.

What I was saying, continued the reverend, is that he could only be expected to see things in contemporary terms. All the same, there seems to be a logical flaw somewhere. He begins by accepting honour as more humane than *vertu* and then he goes on to say that morality is more important than social utility and to imply that one can't be happy without *vertu*.

That's an interesting point. Montesquieu was in much the same

32. p. 54.

13

dilemma. He said – and Robespierre repeated him – that the honour of which he approved was a 'bizarre' quality that didn't correspond to true morality. But he couldn't help criticising contemporary society in terms of what he obviously thought were absolute moral standards. It just shows how closely Robespierre followed Montesquieu.

Do we care all that much, asked the man from the ministry. We look like getting bogged down in a not very interesting example of twentieth-century academic argument.

Well, the jury probably cared, I replied and I'm more concerned with their verdict than yours. They put Robespierre's essay second and, although they didn't usually give second prizes, they liked it enough to award him a gold medal. He got into the *Mercure de France* again, in December 1785, and this time it was a long review, even if a rather patronising one, written by Lacretelle, the man who had won the first prize.

He never quite brought it off, did he? All those second prizes at school and now this one.

He was doing pretty well. After all, it was his first attempt and he was only 26. At least he wasn't discouraged from having another try at Amiens in the following year. The subject this time was a eulogy of Gresset, a local man and a minor poet. It's interesting that Robespierre should have picked on this when there were more political subjects going elsewhere. For once everyone is agreed that he made a very poor job of it.[33] He soon gave up trying to say polite things about Gresset's verse and spent most of his time praising him as a man who had abandoned the pursuit of fame in Paris and the meretricious pleasures of the capital, to live in honourable obscurity in his own province.

Perhaps a touch of fellow-feeling there.

It doesn't sound like it. The whole essay reads as though Robespierre wasn't interested in it himself. It's not without interest for us, though. Once again he takes a very conservative line. 'It was the destiny of the Church at Amiens to be governed by a succession of bishops who were created to show a corrupted century the spectacle of virtues that shone forth in happier days.' He praised Gresset's protector, the bishop Lamothe, who had played an active part in the condemnation and execution for sacrilege of

33. Bib. Nat. Ln[27] 9117.

the chevalier de la Barre, which had provoked one of Voltaire's most famous campaigns against *l'infâme*. What matters most to us though is Rousseau – because of what's not there. In a moving passage, probably written in 1789, Robespierre claimed to have seen Rousseau, who died while he was still at Louis-le-Grand.[34] There is no evidence that Rousseau saw him, but this did not prevent one of Robespierre's more imaginative biographers from giving a long verbatim account of their conversation.[35] Maximilien wrote in 1789, 'While I was still young you taught me to appreciate the dignity of my own nature and to reflect on the great principles of the social order.' This is certainly true of a later period but he doesn't seem to have become a convert to Rousseauism until just before the Revolution. If he had been a devotee of Jean-Jacques in 1785 he could scarcely have missed the opportunity offered by Gresset to sing the praises of another man who preferred rustic simplicity to the false values of Paris – and he could always have propitiated the more conservative members of the Amiens jury by dissociating himself from Rousseau's radicalism. There were so many sides to Rousseau that almost everyone could appreciate some of them. Robespierre did refer to the parallel between Rousseau and Gresset and to the quarrel between Rousseau and his former allies, but he refused to take sides. 'It is not for me to decide between those *philosophes* who attacked the theatre and those who praised it.' This refers to the conflict about whether or not it would do the Swiss good to have a theatre at Geneva, which estranged Rousseau from Voltaire and d'Alembert. Even if Robespierre had thought discretion the better part of prize-winning in this particular context, he could still have got in something about *vertu* somewhere else.

Maybe, said the man from the ministry. But he seems to have put on whatever uniform he thought the occasion demanded and I'm still looking for evidence that he had any principles of his own.

It's not the Rousseau business that interests me, said the party member, but that stuff about a corrupted century and happier days. Compare it with what he was telling them at Metz the year before about this being an enlightened century when everything

---

34. Text in Fleischmann, op. cit., pp. 290-2.
35. M. Graterolle, *Robespierre*, Paris, 1894, pp. 24-9.

was weighed, judged, and discussed. He deserved to succeed when he tried so hard.

The reverend wondered if we were being quite fair. At Metz he was talking about cruel prejudices while at Amiens he was condemning the immorality of sophisticated city life. I think I could do you a reasonable sermon on either, he said, and I'm not sure that he contradicted himself as much as you two think.

All the same, said the man from the ministry, it's just as well he didn't send the right sentiments to the wrong people. What did they make of it in Amiens?

Not much. They didn't award any prize at all that year. Historians used to think that discouraged him and it may have done, for he didn't actually compete again, but he did write another essay – on illegitimacy, which Metz set as its subject in 1786. He didn't submit it to Metz but he read it to the Arras Academy.[36] The text was unknown until it was discovered a few years ago by L. N. Berthe. The style is much more incisive than that of his earlier essays and one can see emerging some of the ideas that he repeated during the Revolution. For instance, he thought there was a social need for religion, not so much to protect property as to afford consolation to those whose life was all suffering. 'The true statesman appreciates the need to call it to his help . . . Philosophy is alien to the people; religion alone can protect it against its wretchedness and its passions and restrain it amidst the shadows.' 'Politics itself is nothing but public morality.' 'Poverty corrupts the morals of the people and degrades men's souls. It disposes them to crime by stifling the germs of honour within them together with men's natural sentiment of their own dignity.' There is more than a hint of Rousseau there. All the same, he was still thinking along the old lines. Social values exist and can't be changed by legislation. So one has to live with them and harness them as far as one can to such reforms as are possible. 'Let us call honour to our aid and we shall overcome many obstacles.' He conceded that there was no hope of persuading public opinion to see anything dishonourable in men having liaisons which might produce illegitimate children, but he saw nothing incompatible with honour in the father being legally obliged to contribute to the upkeep of his offspring. He therefore

36. Berthe and de Langre, op. cit., pp. 55-100.

suggested making failure to provide for one's children a criminal offence, in the hope that public opinion would eventually come to regard it as not merely illegal but dishonourable. Since honour had more force than law, there would eventually be few cases where the latter would need to be invoked. Robespierre was still a long way from repudiating the values on which his society rested or from thinking that they could be substantially altered by legislation.

None the less, there was a good deal more warmth to this essay than to the two earlier ones. He was beginning to see people as people rather than as cases. But he was still very careful not to offend. When he criticised celibacy as bad for public morality, he insisted that he was referring only to servants – the conventional target of moralists – and to soldiers. He went out of his way to disclaim any intention of criticising ecclesiastical celibacy or of submitting 'to my reasoning, considerations that should excite only my reverence'. Perhaps thinking of the Deteuf case, he said that he was not going to make any specific reference to monks.

If he really had been a pretty poor Catholic since his college days, put in the man from the ministry, that passage about exciting his reverence was rather good.

He did imply rather timidly that he agreed with what other people had written against the monastic orders. But I agree that there was nothing here that need have given any concern to his old protector, the bishop of Arras.

A point of interest is his extravagant praise of Necker, 'a great man who seems to have been shown to the people merely for them to glimpse the full extent of the happiness they might enjoy, whose elevation was a triumph for genius, virtue and the nation and whose retirement was a public calamity'.[37] Necker, a Genevan Protestant banker, had been in charge of French finances from 1777 to 1781. When he withdrew from office on being refused a seat on the royal Council, he defied convention by constituting himself a kind of unofficial opposition. This was one of the indications that a monarchy which was still nominally autocratic was beginning to move in a constitutional direction. Politics was coming to mean rather more than merely serving the royal administration. Necker maintained his popularity by publishing books on financial policy and built up an influential network of supporters

37. p. 61

whose full extent was not to be revealed until 1787. We shouldn't read too much into Robespierre's references to Necker but they do at least show his interest in what was emerging as a public debate on government as well as his sympathy for the unofficial opposition rather than the king's ministers.

Although there is a good deal in the essay that is significant as a pointer to his future attitudes and despite the fact that it was certainly his best performance to date, it was still a rather cautious and conventional piece. He even referred to birth control as a greater crime than abandoning unwanted children.[38] The man who actually won the prize at Metz, a military engineer like Carnot, was more forthright in his language and more radical in his ideas. He adopted Rousseau's viewpoint that the institution of private property had destroyed the natural social order. Like Robespierre, he advocated the legalising of adoption, but he proposed that adoptive parents should be paid by the state and he even went on to recommend family allowances for all children, legitimate or not. He was subsequently captured by the Prussians at Verdun in 1792, transferred his allegiance and was killed defending Danzig against the Napoleonic armies in 1807.[39] I think that should be a warning to us against attaching too much importance to what anyone thought before the revolutionary crisis broke. All the options were still open and everything was still fluid. Men whose ideas at the end of the Ancien Régime had a good deal in common developed in very different directions when the political crisis forced them to make definitive choices.

I suppose we should all read the essay for ourselves, said the man from the ministry. There's obviously a good deal in it. As I said at the start, we can only know what you choose to tell us. I'm not impugning either your honesty or your competence, but if Mac were to read it, I imagine he might give a different account of it.

That's probably true, agreed the party member. I've certainly got no clear idea at the moment. I mean, he's against sin and all that, but he still sounds a bit like the pious do-gooder of Amiens. Lord Bountiful of Arras – except that all he was offering was good advice instead of hot soup.

I really don't think we can all read it now, said the reverend rather regretfully. It's getting late and we don't even seem to be

38. p. 57.   39. pp. 101–29.

within sight of the Revolution. Perhaps you're right and what people thought then wasn't all that important. But I certainly do mean to read it for myself and I'll come back to it if I think it might help.

I don't want to keep you all out of your beds, I went on, and I won't take you as far as the Revolution tonight. I should just like to look at one more legal case, that of a Madame Page who was accused of usury. At first sight it wasn't promising material, which is perhaps why Robespierre decided to broaden the issues until he seemed to be challenging the entire legal system.[40] He was very eloquent about the danger to the accused in an eighteenth-century French trial. 'A feeble and timid creature . . . may turn pale, stammer and contradict himself . . . and still be innocent.' 'At the sight of so many scaffolds steaming with innocent blood . . . I hear a powerful voice within me crying out to abjure for ever that fatal tendency to convict on presumption alone.' He attacked 'the frightful labyrinth of criminal procedure' and the ignorance of judges in seigneurial courts and looked forward to what he called the 'happy revolution' in the judicial system that he said a wise government was preparing. When it actually came, by the way, in May 1788, he joined his colleagues on the bench of the bishop's court in condemning it as ministerial despotism.[41] He got Madame Page acquitted but the court ordered the deletion from his *mémoire* of all the remarks that impugned the authority of the law and jurisprudence or criticised the judges. It is worth noticing that, even in this case, he referred three times to prosecution witnesses coming from the 'dregs of the people'. He had said much the same in the lightning-conductor case and he referred again to the *lie du peuple* in 1788 and in 1789.

What is rather curious about the Page case is the contrast between the care he took to avoid offending academic juries and his cavalier disregard for the susceptibility of the Arras judges. This was more a political speech than a legal defence and it says a lot for the judges that his client got off.

I'm beginning to think he was a thoroughly nasty little man, said the man from the ministry. He changed his line whenever it suited him and if you compare this solicitude for the defence with what was going to happen during the Terror —

40. Barbier and Vellay, vol. I, pp. 274-352.   41. Thompson, p. 41.

I can't allow you to do anything of the kind, I said firmly. If you call in the future to condemn the past you'll merely end up by confirming your own prejudices. You've got to keep to contemporary evidence.

I don't accept that. The only point in ploughing through all this pettifogging stuff about his not very distinguished youth is that it might throw some light on the future and if that's valid in one direction it must hold good in the other.

But we haven't looked at his future yet and for all you know I might persuade you that it isn't what you think.

I don't agree with Ted anyway, said the party member. After all, what Robespierre said was presumably true, which is what matters. If he sticks to this line he'll be a lot more convincing than when he drools on about virtue down on the farm.

Perhaps, said the reverend, we could have a look at how they took it in Arras.

I wish we knew. They certainly didn't make him a social outcast. There may have been a reform movement among the younger lawyers that welcomed this sort of thing. Early in 1788 de Beaumetz, the new president of the *Conseil d'Artois,* organised a number of meetings to discuss legal reform, to which he invited twenty of the local barristers. One of them who wasn't invited wrote a bitter *Lettre adressée par un avocat au Conseil d'Artois à son ami, avocat au parlement de Douai,* complaining of the restricted opportunities for young lawyers in Arras. He signed this with his initials – M.R. – and most historians have assumed this meant Maximilien Robespierre.[42] I'm inclined to think he would have called himself M. de R. or M.D. Barbier and Vellay, who edited Robespierre's legal works, argue strongly that it's not in his style. 'L' – who may have been Robespierre's old opponent, Liborel, published a venomous reply, accusing the author of the letter of being motivated only by 'sordid self-interest (and) base greed'. Now even Proyart recognised Robespierre's disinterestedness – that and hard work were the only qualities he did recognise. So it certainly seems rash to assume that Robespierre wrote the letter. The only evidence that he was excluded from these legal conferences is that the writer himself wasn't invited, so if Robespierre didn't write it we have absolutely nothing to go on.[43]

42. e.g. Thompson, p. 58; Walter, p. 55.   43. op. cit., pp. 476-501.

Outside purely legal circles he certainly doesn't seem to have been unpopular. He was made director of the Academy in 1786. In this capacity he welcomed a minor literary luminary, Mademoiselle de Kéralio, with a somewhat conventional speech in praise of women's influence rather than of women's rights. It did include a reference to 'degraded humanity which seemed obliterated under the infamous yoke of feudal tyranny'.[44] There were tensions in the Academy. Buissart and Robespierre threatened to leave if Le Gay were elected but Buissart seems to have been more involved in this than Robespierre and it looks as though the secretary, Dubois de Fosseux, managed to smoothe things over.[45]

Another sign that Robespierre still had friends was his election, apparently in June 1787, to the *Rosati*.[6] This was a rather exclusive literary club which met every year to drink to the rose in *vin rosé* and to celebrate the members' merits in verses *à l' eau de rose*. None of their poetry to survive – and it includes a few of Robespierre's own productions – is in any way remarkable, but even Hamel doesn't pretend that he was a major poet. He could at least hold his own in the *Rosati*. I don't suppose any of them had any pretensions to poetic fame. They were essentially a light-hearted social club. They liked to tease each other and their activities seem to have been entirely concerned with entertainment. The fact that Robespierre was not merely considered a suitable recruit, but that he thought it worth his while to join, when France was visibly being drawn into a political crisis, indicates that there were more sides to his character than his professional activities and academic aspirations might suggest.

Could you let us sample his poetry for ourselves, asked the reverend.

Here is one stanza, on a typical *Rosati* theme.

> O mes amis, tout buveur d'eau,
> Et vous pouvez m'en croire,
> Dans tous les temps ne fut qu'un sot,

---

44. Summarised in Hamel, vol. I, pp. 60-1; see also the article by H. Duval in *Rev. hist. de la Rév. fr.*, vol. v (1914), pp. 323-5.
45. L. N. Berthe, *Dubois de Fosseux*, p. 145.
46. L. N. Berthe, *Dictionnaire des correspondants de l'Académie d'Arras au temps de Robespierre*, Arras, 1969, p. 183. Hamel gives the date as 1782.

> J'en atteste l'histoire.
> Ce sage effronté,
> Cynique vanté,
> Me paraît bien stupide,
> O le beau plaisir!
> D'aller se tapir
> Au fond d'un tonneau vide.[47]

If Charlotte is to be believed, this anti-Diogenes, on his home ground, liked plenty of water in his wine, but perhaps we can leave it to his more ponderous critics to accuse him of literary hypocrisy. There are signs that the growing tensions of the outside world broke in on the idylls of the *Rosati*. Robespierre was introduced to the fraternity by Le Gay, the man he tried to exclude from the Academy.[48] The *Rosati* are said to have broken up in 1788 because of political quarrels.[49] They may possibly have been rather more progressive and less aristocratic than the members of the Academy. Only one of the fifteen was arrested during the Terror whereas thirteen of the thirty academicians went to gaol.[50] Here again one gets a hint that Arras society was being disrupted by the political tensions that were splitting the country as a whole. This is a subject that needs investigating and the story of the political and personal animosities in the town would probably help towards an understanding of where Robespierre stood.

I can see your problem, said the reverend, and I've no doubt you've done what you could, but I feel we've been on the surface all the time and we've probably got things badly out of perspective because we know so little of Robespierre's everyday life. That's why the *Rosati* business seems important to me, precisely because it was so trivial.

We may never know much more, since many of the local records were destroyed in 1915.

Which makes it all the more important not to be in too big a hurry to condemn Robespierre on mere presumption, as he said in the Page case.

If that's intended for me, Henry, said the man from the ministry, I'm with you up to a point. But it only means that we

47. H. Fleischmann, *Robespierre et les femmes,* Paris, n.d., p. 331.
48. ibid., p. 46. 49. ibid., p. 45n[2].
50. Paris, op. cit., pp. 157n.[1], 188n.[1]

suspend judgment, not that we assume he must have been a good chap merely because we're a bit short of evidence to the contrary. You can apply as much Christian charity as you like to the evidence, but not to what's not there.

I'll try, I said, to give you a summing up of where he stood in 1788, even if it is very tentative. He had made quite a reputation as a forceful lawyer, and rather more than that. He does seem to have been regarded – not merely by Charlotte – as a poor man's lawyer. A hostile contemporary, Alissan de Chazet, writing after his death, when he was everyone's scapegoat, said this about his life in Arras: 'One must be fair to everyone, even to Robespierre; one must admit that he was never motivated by a love of money. On the contrary, he was quite exceptionally disinterested. He gave unpaid consultations for several years and disliked taking fees from his clients even when he had won their cases for them, even though he had no patrimony and was so hard up that he had to borrow clothes.'[51] Proyart was probably saying much the same in his inimitable way – he didn't share Chazet's inhibitions about having to be fair even to Robespierre – when he wrote, 'He welcomed dishonest litigants and made himself the patron of shameful cases with which his colleagues did not wish to defile their chambers.'[52] Babeuf, the future socialist, wrote to Dubois de Fosseux about him in 1786, 'M. de Robespierre is no doubt regarded as one of the leading lights of your bar. I feel that he is a man of meticulous probity and rare disinterestedness. I have heard M. le marquis de Creny, M. l'abbé de Saint-André and M. l'avocat Desmazières extol his talents in the highest terms. The last of these said, "None of our colleagues has a greater right to be called the defender of the widow and the orphan. M. de Robespierre is not interested in making money; he is and will always remain only the lawyer of the poor".'[53] This is high praise, and Babeuf implies that his own view was widely shared. Since Robespierre was a controversial man, the absolute unanimity about his disinterestedness is all the more striking. At the same time his penchant for aggressive pleading had already got him into trouble and presumably made enemies. If Arras society was beginning to split into rival factions, he was the kind of man to be a vigorous

51. Jacob, op. cit., pp. 194-5.   52. p. 53.
53. V. Daline, 'Robespierre et Danton vus par Babeuf', *Ann. hist. Rév. fr.*, no. 162 (1960), pp. 389-90.

23

partisan. A letter to de Fosseux in February 1789 refers to an obscure incident in which a colleague who was the worse for drink had thrust his fist under Robespierre's nose and called him a rascal and a *moutaquin*. As a result of this the *gouvernance* refused to sit with Robespierre.[54] The Arras bar as a whole seems to have taken Robespierre's side and decided to boycott the *gouvernance* in its turn. Once again one has the impression of a little world of allegiances and enmities at Arras which determined what everyone thought and said about everyone else.

Despite his reputation, Robespierre never had many cases, only 26 in his best year. He had certainly not built up a thriving practice but in view of what everyone said of his disinterestedness, this could have been a matter of choice. He had presumably not fulfilled himself in his profession but we have no evidence that he was feeling frustrated or thinking of leaving Arras – unless one assumes him to have been the author of the letter about Beaumetz's discussion group. On the contrary, in the spring of 1789 he was being considered for the post of *procureur du roi* in the *maréchaussée* court, which suggests that neither he nor the authorities regarded him as a revolutionary.[55] If there had been no political crisis he might easily have settled down to a leisurely life, appearing from time to time at the bar, gradually accumulating minor offices, a member of the Academy and a highly-respected local worthy.

Charlotte presents his home life as orderly and methodical, but he was certainly no recluse – his membership of the *Rosati* is proof enough of that. We know very little indeed about his contacts with women. He was approaching the age when men of the professional classes married and there is nothing improbable in the claim of the loyal Charlotte that he could have taken his choice amongst the local heiresses. She said that for two or three years he had been paying court to a relative, Mlle Deshorties, whom he would have married if he had not gone to Paris in 1789. Her complaint that the young lady, after promising never to marry anyone else, took a husband within a year of Robespierre's departure and that this affected her brother very deeply, may or may not be true, but sounds a little less likely. One or two of his letters to women have survived, all rather stilted in their awkward gallantry.

54. Jacob, op. cit., p. 24.   55. *Ann. hist. Rév. fr.*, 1930, p. 76.

In each case he sent them copies of his legal *mémoires* which was scarcely what one would have expected from a future member of the *Rosati*. No one accused him of any sexual liaisons. This deprived the virtuous Proyart of a golden opportunity but, ingenious as ever, he managed to turn it to Robespierre's disadvantage, explaining that he was chaste only because he was afraid of catching pneumonia if he indulged in any nocturnal adventures.[56] Hamel, more plausibly, claims to have talked to an old lady who said that Robespierre was her mother's habitual dancing-partner. 'He had a serious air but he was a very good man.'[57]

I think that's just about as far as the evidence will take us, I concluded, and I haven't left out anything I think you might consider important.

Not light, but darkness visible, said the reverend cheerfully. I'm glad I'm not a historian.

You seem to have changed your tune at the end, said the party member, when you brought in all those certificates of good conduct.

Not to mention your skilful use of Proyart to put us all on Robespierre's side.

I don't think any of us knows where he stands now.

Which is just as it should be, I replied briskly. I'm not standing anywhere in particular. All I really wanted to show you was that the first five-sixths of Robespierre's life are something of a mystery and I hope you'll agree that I've done that. From now onwards, or at least after he was elected to the Estates General, we've got much more evidence from his own pen and things should get a good deal clearer.

I wonder, said the reverend.

56. p. 63.　57. p. 45.

II The Nature of the Vocation

I've been looking at that essay about the illegitimate children,
said the reverend, and I agree that if it was all we had to
remember him by, we should have forgotten Robespierre a long
time ago. All the same I liked his approach. He does give the
impression that he cared. And although he recognised a moral
problem when he saw one, he didn't think it would go away if
you preached at it. He's got a healthy scepticism about do-gooders;
in fact, he's very sensible about what the law can do and what
it can't. But if one couldn't change attitudes overnight, he saw
that something could be done – and had to be done – to protect
the children, whatever one thought about the morals of their
parents. He doesn't visit the sins of the fathers upon the children
and he doesn't think that you can solve moral problems by Acts of
Parliament – though you do need the Acts of Parliament since
it won't do to leave everything to the good intentions of individuals. He's got common sense and humanity and he's not without
imagination: I liked his warning about the danger of bringing
up children in institutions. But what surprised me was his moderation: I think a lot of people might do well to remember 'an
idea of absolute perfection and purity can only be a source of
error in politics'.[1] No, I wouldn't say it was a distinguished
piece of work, but it reads as though it was written by a good
man.

Well I think we're all agreed that it didn't make much difference to his career, I said, and if we're going to understand how
that career took shape in 1789 you'll have to let me tell you something about the state of the country.[2] The monarchy had been
drifting towards bankruptcy for a long time and in 1787 the
Finance Minister, Calonne, tried to shoot himself out of trouble.
He prepared a whole programme of economic and fiscal measures
which he hoped would give the absolute monarchy a new lease of

---

1. p. 74.
2. For a general survey of this period see J. Egret, *La pré-révolution
française*, Paris, 1962.

life.[3] Knowing the weakness of the king, he didn't try to persuade
Louis XVI to impose this by force, but summoned a meeting of
Notables – leading men from the Church, the law courts and
local government – in the hope of winning their support. What
they actually did was to bargain for political concessions – they
wanted a constitutional monarchy more or less along British lines.
They persuaded the king to get rid of Calonne, whose place was
taken by the leader of the opposition, Brienne. He in turn found
that he would have to raise additional taxation and the continuing
opposition forced him to agree to summon the Estates General in
1792.

The Estates General was a kind of medieval parliament that had
not met since 1614. Clergy, nobility and commoners, or third
estate, met separately, each Order having a veto. The royal
Ministers would obviously have preferred to do without it and
Brienne hoped to restore solvency before it met, so that he could
dismiss it if it gave any trouble. But he found himself up against
the concerted resistance of all the collective bodies: the sovereign
courts like the Conseil d'Artois that registered the floating of
loans, provincial Estates in the regions where these had survived
and the General Assembly of the clergy. By May 1788 the Government had made very little headway and it fell back on force. A
coup d'état – which contemporaries referred to as a 'revolution' –
transformed the French judicial system, drastically curtailing the
powers of both the sovereign courts and the feudal judges. This
produced an outcry from both the nobility and the legal world. In
later years Robespierre always claimed that he had joined in the
opposition at Arras. He probably sympathised with the measures
against the seigneurial courts but by now everyone saw the conflict
in political terms and the opposition claimed to be fighting for the
rights of the nation against what it called 'ministerial despotism'.

The summer of 1788 produced the first political crisis in modern
France. The new legal system provoked a judicial strike by the old
courts and open revolt in some of the areas that retained their local
Estates – though not in Artois. In July Brienne appealed for the
support of the professional classes as a whole by asking the public
for advice on the organisation of the Estates General. This was

3.   A. Goodwin, 'Calonne, the Assembly of French Notables of 1787 and the
origins of the "révolte nobiliaire" ', *English Historical Review*, vol. LXI (1946),
pp. 204, 329.

taken to mean the end of political censorship and the result was a quite unprecedented outbreak of pamphleteering which threw educated people – and probably a fair number of the uneducated as well – into heated political speculation. During the second half of 1788 the arguments became more radical. Rousseauist conceptions of popular sovereignty replaced appeals for a return to what was considered, in the tradition of Montesquieu, to have been the constitution of the good old days.[4] At the same time there was a tendency for the educated members of the third estate to detach themselves from the rest of the opposition and make bitter attacks on the social privileges of the nobility. The convocation of the Estates General was brought forward to 1789 and in August 1788 Brienne was replaced by Robespierre's hero, Necker. From then until the actual meeting of the Estates in May 1789 there was a continuous atmosphere of political crisis. Since anyone who paid direct taxes was entitled to vote, the excitement spread right down to the villages. The point to remember is that this was not just an election, as elections were known in England. In France it was something entirely new. For a lot of people it was to be the occasion when the nation as a whole was to draw up a new social contract and for some of them it was to be the beginning of the millennium.

I should imagine, said the man from the ministry, that a good many hoped it would also be the beginning of a career. What you were saying last week made Arras sound like Barchester and I don't suppose it was the only town in France where ambitious young men felt their talents weren't sufficiently recognised. For a man like Robespierre it must have seemed a providential chance to make up on the political swings for what he'd failed to gain on the academic roundabouts.

True to form, Ted, replied the party member: if a lawyer goes in for politics that's careerism; if Lord Tomnoddy graciously consents to run the country that's social service.

I wouldn't say the one was more disinterested than the other but he doesn't have the same need to intrigue his way up to the top.

What's interesting, said Mac, ignoring this last remark, is this emergence of a middle-class protest. It must have meant that

---

4. N. Hampson, 'The *recueil de pièces importantes pour servir à l'histoire de la révolution en France* and the origins of the French Revolution', *Bulletin of the John Rylands Library*, vol. XLVI (1964), pp. 385-410.

they'd been bottled up by the censorship. As soon as real politics became possible the real issues emerged.

My old tutor once said to me, observed the reverend, that anyone who said 'it must be' meant 'I hope it is but I can't prove it'. You're both doing it. All we've got to go on so far is that there was a political crisis. I suggest we do go on.

Thank you. But before we put the hustings up at Arras there are one or two things I'd like to look at. First of all I want to tell you about Robespierre's last case, in 1789.[5] He was appearing for a man called Dupond who had deserted from the French army many years before. When he returned to France to claim his share in a legacy the rival claimants managed to put him in gaol by means of a *lettre de cachet* and he'd been in prison for twelve years. It wasn't a political case, but during the crisis of 1787–8 the courts had made a great issue of the abuse of *lettres de cachet* to silence political opposition, so it gave Robespierre a golden opportunity. He opened his plea with an attack on 'this horrible system'. This led him on to refer to the events of 1788 and to 'a sovereign, escaping from a frightful conspiracy against his justice and taking refuge in the bosom of his peoples'.

Very eloquent, said Ted, but I seem to remember that he saw *lettres de cachet* rather differently in 1784, when he wasn't hoping to get elected to anything more than a gold medal at Metz.

He'd seen the light since then, said the party member.

Like most of his contemporaries, he thought the 'revolution' had been the ministerial coup d'état which had been defeated. France 'alone among all the peoples of the world, without any fatal revolution, without any catastrophe, by reason of its own magnanimity and the virtuous character of its king, has recovered the sacred and imprescriptible rights that have been violated through the centuries'. This led him on to a very personal definition of the new contract that would have to be negotiated. 'This social contract of which so much is talked . . . is anything but a free convention deliberately willed by men. Its fundamental conditions, laid down by heaven, were determined for all time by that supreme

5. Barbier and Vellay, op. cit., pp. 573-681. Thompson, in a very unusual lapse, refers to Dupond as Dupont and Duport and says that the case was tried in 1788: op. cit., pp. 35, 38.

legislator who is the sole source of all order, all happiness and all justice.'[6]

Amen, said the man from the ministry. I don't think Rousseau would have liked his way of juggling with the social contract and natural law. Does it mean *anything*?

That perhaps depends on us, said the reverend.

He made a very striking attack on contemporary society. After denouncing war, he turned on the court: 'Behold, underneath all that imposing luxury and pretended public wealth that dazzles the eyes of administrators blind to *vertu,* the enormous wealth of a few citizens founded on the ruin and wretchedness of all the rest . . . Behold above all, that lowest class – the most numerous of all – which pride thinks to stigmatise with the name of *people* – a name so sacred and majestic to the eye of reason – see it virtually forced by the excess of its poverty to disregard human dignity and moral principle, so that it comes to regard wealth as the first object of its worship and devotion.'[7]

Ted would probably call that naïve, said the party member, and it certainly reads rather oddly, but you can't deny that there's a real social conscience behind it.

It should have been said in the pulpit, said the reverend. The kingdom he has in mind is not of this world.

Whether or not it's naïve, it's certainly important, said the man from the ministry. It doesn't sound like the argument of a man who was simply trying to win a case. I agree with Henry that, whatever it is, it isn't politics, though he may not have realised it. In the first place, given an eighteenth-century economy, there was very little that anyone could do for the poor. But he's not really thinking of social justice as an end. It's only a means to something he thinks more important. You don't agree with him as much as you think you do, Mac.

It's certainly true, I continued, that he saw the future essentially in moral terms. This is how he addressed the king: 'The glory of procuring for us all the treasures of plenty, of embellishing your reign with all the sparkle and delight of luxury; successes like these, which seem to common politicians the most wonderful masterpiece of human wisdom, these are certainly not the vital part of the august mission entrusted to you by heaven and by your

6. Barbier and Vellay, pp. 661-2.
7. id., p. 675.

own soul. To lead men to happiness through *vertu* and to *vertu* by laws founded on the unshakeable principles of universal morality, designed to restore to human nature all its rights and all its primal dignity; to re-forge the immortal chain that must bind man to God and to his fellow-men by destroying all the forces of oppression and tyranny which fill the earth with fear, suspicion, pride, baseness, egoism, hatred, greed and all the vices that draw men far from the goals assigned to society by the eternal legislator; this, *Sire*, is the glorious enterprise to which he has called you.'

'This is perhaps the single moment vouchsafed to us by the bounty of the all-powerful being who presides over the destiny of empires. If we allow it to escape, it is perhaps written that henceforth his light will guide us only to days of trouble, calamity and desolation.'[8]

That's a good deal more sinister, said Ted. If it wasn't merely intended as political propaganda, it has all the marks of fanaticism. The new Jerusalem is opening its doors. There's a unique opportunity and a divine mission – and what stands in the way is not economic reality or inevitable human muddle but a coalition of all the vices. It's only a matter of time before he's going to attach that long string of abstractions to specific people. The whole thing is riddled with a kind of moral totalitarianism.

You can see how much he had now come under the influence of Rousseau, I said.

The reverend was inclined to disagree. The accent may be Rousseau's – the moral basis, the fervour and emotive language – but I don't think Rousseau saw God as intervening like this. That's where I think the danger lies; anyone who disagrees becomes an instrument of the Devil. But perhaps we shouldn't dissect his words too closely; after all, he wasn't writing a philosophical treatise.

He did publish it, I said. And these weren't his only references to God. He said that belief in an after-life was the only consolation for anyone oppressed in this. His references to the tutelary deity that watched over France may have been only classical rhetoric but he may have taken them literally. He said quite explicitly at one point, 'It is time that this idea of God, employed for so long by flatterers to secure monstrous and unlimited powers

8. Barbier and Vellay, pp. 670, 673.

for the heads of empires, should serve at last to remind us of the imprescriptible rights of man. It is time to recognise that the same divine authority which orders kings to be just, forbids peoples to be slaves.'[9]

There are some more explicitly political references at the end. He claimed that the heroic resistance to the king's Ministers of the Paris Parlement surpassed anything in antiquity. He praised Necker again, called him the new Sully and made a calculated reference to the 'cabals of a corrupt court' against the original Sully.[10] Proyart said, for what his evidence is worth, that Robespierre was sending his *mémoires* to Necker and showing people proofs of his 'flattering correspondence' with Necker's wife.[11]

What happened to Dupond, asked the man from the ministry.

I've forgotten. I only quoted the case at this length because it shows a new Robespierre emerging. Whatever Henry may think, it does look to me as though he'd experienced a sort of conversion to Rousseau. The same thing happened to Madame Roland. His style was quite different from what we've seen before. Neither the style nor the attitude behind it were going to change very much during the Revolution and this is the best definition we've got of what Robespierre thought the Revolution was about. It may have been around this time, since he refers to the 'perilous career that an unheard-of revolution has just opened before us', that he wrote his dedication to the spirit of Rousseau which was not published until long after his death.[12] This is all the more significant since it is one of the few surviving things by Robespierre that was not intended for the public. In the semi-religious language of his *mémoire* for Dupond, he swore to follow what he considered to be Rousseau's example. 'The reward of the virtuous man is his confidence that he has willed the good of his fellow-men; after that comes the recognition of the nations, which surrounds his memory, and the honours given to him by contemporaries. Like you, I should like to buy these rewards at the price of a laborious life, even at the price of a premature death.'

Haven't we had rather a surfeit of noble sentiments?

9. ibid., pp. 618, 664, 677. 10. ibid, pp. 681, 678-9. 11. p. 68.
12. Reprinted in H. Fleischmann, *Mémoires de Charlotte Robespierre*, pp. 290-2. I have disregarded the eulogy of Dupaty by M.R. which was published in 1789 since its attribution to Robespierre is doubtful.

You don't really believe, Ted, that anyone can forget himself and only think of a cause, said the party member.

I must confess to a little scepticism about people who have to remind themselves to forget themselves. I suppose there's no harm in that so long as they remember the others too and don't turn every political controversy into a Punch and Judy show.

The reverend wondered whether Ted was not in danger of trying to tread the narrow path between righteousness and sin. Of course it may not be easy to tell which is which.

And to leave things as they are suits those who are all right as they are, said Mac.

I don't want to interrupt, I said, but it might not be a bad idea if we got back to Robespierre, or at least to Arras. If you're going to understand the very complicated circumstances in which he came to be elected to the Estates General, I'll have to say something about local politics first.

Artois had been annexed to France as recently as 1659 and it had kept its own Estates. These consisted of the usual three Orders: clergy, nobility and third estate. The membership of each was traditional – no one was actually elected – and most members of each of the Orders were excluded. The First Estate consisted of the two bishops together with 29 representatives of abbeys and collegiate churches. None of the several hundred parish priests was included. Only men with six generations of nobility who were also local seigneurs were admitted to the Second Estate. This let in about 120 and excluded something like 300. The composition of the Third Estate was the oddest of all. It consisted of the mayor and nine councillors from Arras together with representatives from nine other towns, making 32 people in all.[13] Not merely was the countryside totally unrepresented; the towns themselves did not elect their own councillors. They had enjoyed this right in the past but when it had been taken away by the crown the Estates of Artois had bought it back. So it was the standing committee of the Estates which nominated the councillors who, in turn, formed the Third Estate. Not surprisingly, it tended to

13. *Almanach historique et géographique de l'Artois pour l'an de grâce 1789*, Bib. Nat. Lc[39] 17. The editors of the *Oeuvres de Maximilien Robespierre* (vol. VI, p. 6) seem to be mistaken in saying that there were only ten representatives of the Third Estate. Each councillor from Arras was entitled to vote but the other towns had only one vote each.

choose the cream of local society. The mayor of Arras, who was himself a member of the *noblesse entrante* (those entitled to sit as representatives of the nobility), described the Arras councillors, or *échevins*, as 'retired lawyers and the most notable inhabitants of this town'.[14] In addition to himself, at least two of the nine *échevins* were noble. One of them was Robespierre's friend, the secretary of the Academy, Dubois de Fosseux.

That must have made everything very cosy, said the party member. One can see why the nobility in the country as a whole were so keen on working through the Estates General, if it was going to be anything like Arras.

The Estates of Artois were convened on 29 December 1788 to vote taxes. They paid what was asked of them but they took advantage of the opportunity to tell the Ministers a few home truths, which they published in the local paper.[15] The fact that there *was* a local paper – it had only been launched at the end of 1788 – and that it was being used as a political instrument, was something quite new. After drawing attention at some length to all the 'unconstitutional and incoherent' measures of the previous summer that they said they were forgetting, the Estates turned to the future. In the name of 'true patriotism' they denounced 'the remains of a destructive system [this was 'ministerial despotism' cropping up again] born out of feudal anarchy'. They looked forward to what they called 'equality' but made it clear that this referred only to the abolition of fiscal privileges and not to 'those legitimate distinctions which the honour of a name or the brilliance of rank and birth' conferred on the more fortunate.

Everyone was thinking more about the coming elections to the Estates General than about local politics – or rather, the national crisis gave them new grounds for dissatisfaction with the local situation. The peculiar composition of the Estates of Artois became a matter of violent disagreement as soon as the provincial body claimed the right to nominate representatives to the Estates General. This set off a local dress rehearsal of the crisis that was to explode at Versailles in the spring.

The Third Estate demanded an increase in its voting strength,

14. Arch. Nat. B³ 15.
15. Arch. Nat. H. 38; printed in the *Affiches d'Artois*, Bib. Nat. Lc⁹ 18(4). For a good account of the crisis in Arras see Paris, op. cit., pp. 201-10.

together with the right to hold genuine elections in the towns. The nobility replied that they could accept any return to old customs – such as the election of councillors – but they could not authorise any change in the number of representatives of the Third Estate. To do so would jeopardise all the claims of the province to the protection of its traditional privileges.

The most serious conflict, however, was within the nobility. The *non-entrants* realised that to maintain the status quo might deprive them of any prospect of being elected to the Estates General. A petition for their right to attend the provincial Estates was published in the *Affiches d'Artois* and attracted 127 signatures.[16] This petition was taken to Versailles by a deputation that included Dubois de Fosseux. The *entrants* replied that there could be no question of suspending the constitution of the province for the special purpose of choosing deputies to the Estates General. An anonymous letter of 8 January informed the king's Ministers that one-third of the nobility were 'reasonable, mature and experienced men'. The remaining hot-heads included many who were very young. These extremists, who had succeeded in intimidating the minority, were disinclined to accept even fiscal equality and they had already agreed upon the three *têtes sulphureuses* whom they proposed to send to the Estates General.[17]

The partisans of the status quo seemed to have the upper hand in Arras but they were defeated at Versailles. The Minister of War, Puységur, told the Estates on 7 January that they did not represent the province.[18] On 10th Necker himself ordered the *entrants* to stop opposing the royal will and a few days later the king ordered the admission of the *non-entrants*.[19] On 17 January a new protagonist entered the field when the royal *bailliage* court of Arras denied the right of the Estates to elect deputies at all, demanding that Artois should follow the rest of France in making the *bailliages* its constituencies.[20] This was naturally challenged by the Estates but on 19 February the Government, which must have been heartily sick of Artois and its feuding, decided to overrule the Estates and ordered election by *bailliages*.[21] The standing com-

---

16. Arch. Nat. C. 12.
17. Arch. Nat. B.III 11, fol. 234-40; another copy in Bª 15.
18. Arch. Nat. B.III 11, fol. 202; also in Bª 15.
19. Arch. Nat. B.III 11, fol. 206; C. 12.
20. Arch. Nat. Bª 15.   21. ibid.

mittee of the Estates grumbled that the king had no right to destroy provincial privileges that his ancestors had sworn to maintain. It claimed that Artois could not be bound by any decisions made in its name by illegal representatives and asserted that no taxation could be levied in the province except with the consent of the Estates.[22] No one seems to have been impressed.

The result of all this was that local society was torn apart well before the elections to the Estates General were held in April. Throughout January and the first half of February the nobility in particular were engaging in shrill polemics which they tried to wrap up in terms of political theory. The *non-entrants* said that their opponents' appeal to prescription was out of date. 'Thirty years ago we had not such clear ideas about the rights of man, considered as man and as citizen. Reason has progressed in the last thirty years. Are we not Frenchmen? Are we subjects of Louis XVI? . . . What is the use of being noble if one is no longer a citizen?'[23] A conservative complained that the province was being inundated with calumniatory pamphlets and pompous talk of natural rights. As time went on it became obvious that when the *non-entrants* talked about natural equality what they meant was equal privileges for all nobles. The *cahier* of grievances that they eventually drafted for the Estates General was an exceptionally conservative one containing fourteen clauses about the preservation of noble privilege. If we are to see Robespierre's activities in perspective we have to remember both the bitterness on all sides and the tendency of everyone to dress up the claims of his own party in grandiloquent language.

We haven't seen much of him lately, in or out of perspective, said the man from the ministry. Where did he stand in all this?

He wasn't directly involved at first since he wasn't an *échevin*, and he didn't sit in the provincial Estates. When the Governor of Artois, the duc de Guines, visited Arras to preside over the meeting of the Estates, he attended the Academy on 9 January and agreed to become its patron. He was welcomed by de Fosseux and Robespierre who 'made a speech in which he gave M. le duc de Guines an account of the advantages which the province of Artois could expect from the virtues and exceptional talents of a Citizen Governor who had already brought it distinction before being

22. Arch. Nat. C. 12.   23. Arch. Nat. B⁴ 15.

entrusted with its administration as a reward for the many touching proofs it had given him of its affection and confidence'.[24] This seems harmless enough and it sounds as though he hadn't yet got involved in the political battle and he and de Fosseux were still on speaking terms.

He first staked out a claim for himself with a pamphlet, *A la nation artésienne,* whose title suggests that he too was still thinking in provincial terms. It is not known when this was published, or even what was in the first edition. The second edition – the only one in the Bibliothèque nationale – seems to have been amplified between 20 and 26 April.[25] The pamphlet consists mainly of a criticism of the composition and past record of the Estates of Artois. Robespierre's complaint about the indifference of the public could suggest that it was written before tempers rose in January. On the other hand, the occasional violence of his language is very different from the report of his speech to the Academy on the 9th. Perhaps a date in late January or early February is as likely as any. This might explain why so much of the pamphet echoes the language of his *mémoire* for Dupond, on which he was probably working at the same time.

He began by stressing the uniqueness of the crisis, as he had done in the Dupond case. 'We are approaching the moment that must decide for ever our liberty or our servitude.' 'While the dangerous enemies in this province are vigilant to perpetuate their rule, we are still asleep, weighed down by the chains they have given us. It is time to warn the Artesian nation of the deadly snares with which it is beset.'[26] As in his *mémoire,* he spoke of Providence offering this one opportunity for salvation. He repeated his complaint that the poor were barred by their poverty from an awareness of their basic human rights. The pamphlet, as one would expect, was more aggressive than the *mémoire.* 'Everywhere you will see the vassal sacrificed to the lord, the useful farmer to the idle and wealthy monk, the citizen of the third estate to the noble, the modest pastor to the haughty priest.'[27] The conclusion once again praised 'that Minister on whose genius and *vertu* our salvation depends' and referred to the 'august and moving' voice of the king.[28]

24. *Affiches d'Artois.* This seems to be the only record of the speech.
25. Bib. Nat. Lb[39] 6607, p. 68n[1]. The second edition consisted of 83 pages, the first contained only 50. Paris, pp. 245-7.
26. pp. 3-4.   27. p. 38.   28. p. 82.

It's all black and white, said the man from the ministry, as it was in the Dupond case, but we seem to have moved another step along the road to the extermination of the unrighteous.

There's perhaps something in that, I agreed, but you have to put things in context. People were making similar speeches all over France. Sieyès, in his pamphlet, *What is the Third Estate?* described the nobility as a malignant disease eating away the flesh of the nation. Plenty of other people were as violent as Robespierre; what's peculiar to him is this emphasis on Providence and the very poor. But let's look at the actual elections to the Estates General.[29]

The clergy and nobility held only one meeting each but things were very complicated where the third estate was concerned, because there were so many voters. In the case of Arras, each of the corporations met separately to choose representatives to a town meeting. The town meeting then sent 24 representatives to the *bailliage* and the *bailliage* in its turn sent men to join those chosen by the seven other *bailliages* that went to make up the province. At each stage a *cahier* of grievances was drafted and passed up to the next higher meeting. Any member of the third estate who wanted to get elected to the Estates General itself had four hurdles to clear.

The various corporations of Arras met on 23 March. Robespierre drafted the *cahier* of one of the humblest of them, the *cordonniers mineurs* or cloggers. Mainly concerned with professional grievances, it also contained a complaint about the egoism and harshness of the rich and an attack on the *échevins* who despised their humbler citizens 'when the first duty of those who govern the people is to elevate its character as far as they can, to inspire it with the courage and virtues that are the sources of social well-being. They would not dare to treat the wealthier citizens so badly. What right have they to behave like this to the poor, who are precisely those most entitled to protection, concern and respect?'[30]

I hope the city fathers were duly impressed by such articulate cloggers, said the man from the ministry.

Robespierre's question still needed answering, replied the party member.

Robespierre himself, I went on, attended the meeting of those

29. Paris, op. cit., pp. 255-412; E. Lecesne, *Arras sous la Révolution*, Arras, 1882, vol. I, chap. 1; *Oeuvres de Maximilien Robespierre*, vol. VI, pp. 5-21.
30. Paris, pp. 281-2.

who belonged to no professional guild. This was crowded – the *Affiches d'Artois* said there were 600 present – and noisy. The *échevins* tried to organise everything in their own way but they were brushed aside. The opposition to them was led by Ansart, a doctor who, like Robespierre and de Fosseux, was a member of the Academy. The twelve deputies chosen to go on to the town meeting included Robespierre, in sixth place. The man who represented the Third Estate on the standing committee of the Estates of Artois was eliminated in this first round.

The town meeting began on the 26th with an unsuccessful attempt by the *échevins* to disqualify those chosen by the 600. When their claim to a vote each, by virtue of their office, was rejected they resigned – but announced that they would continue in office until replaced. On the 29th the meeting discussed the future composition of the provincial estates. Robespierre, opposing a motion to postpone any change until the term of office of the present *échevins* had expired, said that 'the austere duty imposed on the Defenders of the People could allow of *no delay, no concession, no weakness,* that they had no right to single out a particular man towards whom they might feel inclined on grounds of obligation or personal friendship. They must think only of the people whose interests were in their care, of the People, wretched and oppressed for so long by every kind of abuse.' Dubois de Fosseux had no doubt where this one was aimed and he persuaded the meeting to record its censure of Robespierre's remark about the *peuple malheureux opprimé depuis longtemps.*[31] The mayor, the baron d'Aix of the *noblesse entrante,* who was in the chair, de Fosseux and Robespierre were all members of the Academy. With Robespierre attacking de Fosseux and de Fosseux leading the campaign against the *entrants,* one has some impression of the extent to which the social life of Arras had broken down.

Very tactfully put, said the man from the ministry. What I see is some rather sickening hypocrisy. I've no use for these people who ask you to admire their principles while they're serving their self-interest, and I'd be more impressed by these latter-day Spartans if their principles ever worked to their own disadvantage.

Perhaps they will, said the reverend. I can sympathise with

31. *Les ennemis de la patrie démasqués,* Arras, 1789, Bib. Nat. Lb[39] 11095, pp. 41-3.

Robespierre's objection to de Fosseux demanding full representation of all nobles in the meetings of the Second Estate while trying to hang on to his own privileged position in those of the Third.

Besides, Ted's off the point. I don't suppose Robespierre was thinking of standing for the Arras council so he wasn't trying to further his own interests.

He was talking a lot of nonsense to try and persuade himself that attacking his friend was not merely legitimate but positively virtuous.

I don't think either of you are allowing enough for situations and temperaments, said the reverend. One takes a lot of things for granted until the possibility of change comes along and then what seemed to be part of the order of things looks intolerable. Perhaps it *has* become intolerable, but that still doesn't mean that people who still take the old view are villains. But some people find it hard to see things that way. The more angry they get – and from their point of view they're right to be angry – the harder they find it to be fair to those who are still standing where they themselves were standing the day before.

Very charitable, Henry; but I'm still suspicious of crusaders who are getting a free trip to the Holy Land.

I think we're straying from the point, I said. It was obviously a very divided meeting and, as the mayor reported to Versailles, 'the anti-municipal party did not have things all its own way.'[32] The *échevins* got six of their nine members elected to the 24 representatives of the town. Robespierre came 14th, behind his old opponent Liborel.[33] He tried to get the artisans present at the meeting reimbursed for the four days' wages they had lost but the *échevins*, although they accepted the principle, created difficulties about implementing it. Robespierre was still in the running but he wasn't doing very well and the next hurdle was more difficult since the 24 men from Arras were swamped by over 500 from the other parts of the *bailliage*. Proyart said that Robespierre mobilised country cousins whom he had previously neglected and sent his brother out to canvass the country districts for him.[34] That sounds quite likely and, if one discounts Proyart's bias, not particularly reprehensible. Proyart of course, like Ted, thought he was flattering the populace in order to get elected.

32. Arch Nat. B⁸ 15.
33. Paris, p. 292. The *Affiches d'Artois* put him 12th.   34. pp. 69-70.

I didn't quite say that, objected Ted, who perhaps didn't like my putting him in such company. He may very well have seen himself in the rôle of people's champion without realising that his real motive was to make a name for himself.

His worst moment came when a committee of 49 was chosen to draft the *cahier* and he came 36th with Liborel up at No. 4. But when the men from the *bailliage* of Arras picked 184 to represent them at the final meeting of the province, Robespierre had moved up to tenth. There were only going to be eight deputies chosen to go to Versailles and the *bailliage* of Arras had only 184 votes out of 488 so his prospects still didn't look very bright. There was an interval of almost three weeks before the final meeting, on account of Easter, and during this time Robespierre published another pamphlet, *Les ennemis de la patrie démasqués*. Like the previous one, it came out anonymously, but its style makes its authorship virtually certain and this was recognised at the time.[35]

In his opening sentence Robespierre denounced a conspiracy on the part of the ambitious men who controlled the municipal and provincial administration. This was followed by a fifty-page account of the electoral manoeuvring of the previous month. This naturally reflects Robespierre's own point of view but where it can be checked from official sources it keeps closely to the facts. Towards the end, Robespierre suddenly changed his tone: 'Mighty God, let us turn our eyes from these sinister premonitions and instil into all the citizens that spirit of rectitude, of truth, of courage, of disinterestedness and that heavenly love of humanity, that holy passion for the public good, on which depend the happiness of peoples and the salvation of empires.' The present crisis was 'a fight between prejudice and reason, between humanity, honour and patriotism against pride, vanity and self-interest. What is the prize in this combat? The salvation, glory and happiness of the present generation and of the future race, or their humiliation, their servitude, their eternal misery.'[36]

The man from the ministry was whistling 'Tell me the old, old story' to himself.

There was something new to follow – an extraordinary passage in which he more or less presented himself as an example of courage, generosity and disinterestedness. 'Is it to subject the gener-

35. Jacob, op. cit., p. 34.   36. pp. 52-4.

ous impulses of lofty spirits to timid caution, concerned only with personal well-being, that the Eternal Founder of human society has endowed men's hearts with a generous feeling that sends them without hesitation to the help of the oppressed, with courage un-shaken in the midst of dangers, calm in the eye of the storm, in a word, with all those divine virtues that make them worthy to sacrifice their all for the glory and happiness of their country?

'O citizens, the nation is in danger! Domestic enemies, more dangerous than foreign armies, are secretly plotting its ruin . . . What does it matter to me that . . . they are already considering the martyrdom of all the defenders of the people?

'Who is the citizen who, if his enchanting aspirations for the relief of humanity and the triumph of the nation were dis-appointed, would complain of being destined to suffer with it, of being spared the misfortune of surviving its ruin? Ah, may the tears of friendship mingle on his tomb with those of the poor people he helped. May his memory be dear and precious to all men of goodwill, while his soul goes to the immortal home of order and justice, to enjoy the happiness that the tyranny and injustice of men have banished from the earth . . .! His destiny, beyond a doubt, will be more enviable than that of his fortunate persecutors.'[37]

That's positively paranoid, said the man from the ministry. What it seems to mean is that if our Maximilien manages to get elected there's still a chance for suffering humanity – but he's already wallowing in the joys of martyrdom before he even knows whether he's going to be defeated. It would be heaven help his enemies if he didn't get defeated. Anyone who voted for a man like that deserved what was coming to him.

Was he actually in any danger, asked the reverend.

None that I know of. I suppose his mud-slinging and his addic-tion to the *argumentum ad hominem* could have led to a duel. Charlotte made some vague remark about his election rescuing him from the hands of his enemies, but there's certainly no evidence that his life was in danger.

It is strange. Of course it fits, in a way – all the emphasis on ethics; seeing everything in black and white; the passion for martyrdom that he hinted at in his eulogy of Rousseau. But this is

37. pp. 55-8.

so extreme. Of course, everyone was excited, but I should have thought they would be full of optimism at the thought of all the good the Estates General might do.

Most of them were.

It's like something dreamed up in his garret by an unsuccessful Romantic poet. I suppose he got some of it from Rousseau – but he was only thirty and nothing had gone wrong yet. It's very hard to understand. Even if that's how he felt, to publish it . . . I suppose that shows a certain kind of sincerity . . . the need to expose one's self as proof of one's purity. But the effect, in a place like Arras . . .

One can understand the man who wrote to de Fosseux about this time to say that a lady in London had asked him for Robespierre's pamphlets but that he didn't intend to send her such maudlin sermons (*capucinades*).[38] Robespierre's friend Buissart said that his election made a lot of people envious, but he must have shocked a good many more.[39]

Well, for once we seem to be unanimous, said the man from the ministry, looking at Mac.

I'm not really bothered. The man who broke out of the cosy circle and exposed the rackets was unlikely to be the sort of man who was afraid of ruffling a few feathers and it's no wonder he got worked up. I expect all his friends were tut-tutting away and Charlotte was begging him to make it up with that nice M. de Fosseux. It would have been enough to make anyone fly off the handle. But I'm not really interested in his *états d'âme*. What mattered was which side you were on. Ted suspects he was only saying this sort of thing to get himself elected. If he's right we'll soon find out. If he really meant it, I don't much mind if he saw himself as a reincarnation of Joan of Arc.

No one else seemed to want to speak so I went on. The meeting of the representatives from the whole province opened on 20 April. There was trouble in each of the Orders. When the clergy took their first ballot there were two more votes than voters. The upper clergy – there were about 175 of them – said that the whole meeting was being rigged by a caucus of the parish priests, and walked out. The *curés* then elected the bishop of Arras as their first deputy. When he refused they picked four *curés*.[40] It would be a mistake to

38. Jacob, p. 34.   39. ibid., p. 38.   40. Arch. Nat. B* 15 and C. 14.

think this was necessarily a victory for enlightenment and progress; one *curé* sent off to the king a *cahier* of his own complaining that heretics were making converts and crime was increasing every day. Some of the heretics had 'won God's creatures for the devil by the passion of lust; even worse, they boast of eating meat on Fridays and Saturdays.'[41]

The nobles split over the question of whether or not to demand the reform of the provincial Estates in their *cahier*. De Fosseux – who had already drafted the *cahier* of his parish besides helping to draft that of Arras, now posed as a man of the Left. He invoked 'the most sacred rights of citizenship' and argued that, since all nobles were equal, a meeting of the nobility was sovereign and not bound by any constitution. The *noblesse entrante* offered a compromise. When this was rejected they went back to their extreme position and the comte de Cunchy said that the admission of the *non-entrants* would infringe the property rights of the rest; even the Estates General had no power to change the constitution of Artois and any taxes not voted by the local Estates would be illegal.[42] The *entrants* then walked out and the others chose their four deputies, who included the 'liberals', Charles de Lameth and Briois de Beaumetz.

The representatives of the three Estates had held a joint opening meeting in the cathedral with the duc de Guines presiding. When the clergy and nobility had been applauded for offering to renounce their fiscal privileges the Orders separated. The chairman of the Third Estate – another member of the Academy – suggested that a vote of thanks to the other two Orders would be appropriate. According to Guines's official report, 'A lawyer stood up and said that no thanks were due to people who had done no more than renounce an abuse. This motion was adopted by a majority vote. This Order is badly constituted on the whole. It is expected to create obstacles to the union one would like and the meeting looks like going on for a long time.'[43] In the Jacobin Club on 28 August 1792, Robespierre claimed that he was the lawyer in question.

I suppose it was one way of drawing attention to himself, said Ted.

Of course, one doesn't know the feeling of the meeting, said the

41. Arch. Nat. B.III 12, fol. 168.   42. Arch. Nat. C. 14.
43. Arch. Nat. Bª 15.

reverend. It wasn't the kind of remark to encourage a spirit of compromise but perhaps there was no chance of that anyway. I'm not defending Robespierre but the Third Estate had had to put up with quite a lot from people who were trying to rig the elections and I don't suppose all the faults were on one side.

At all events, Robespierre wasn't one of the three men from the *bailliage* of Arras who were put on the committee to draw up the *cahier*. When this had been approved on 23 April the representatives of the province began electing their deputies to the Estates General. The first two chosen were a farmer and a lawyer from Arras, Brassart. On the 25th they picked another lawyer. Robespierre and Vaillant, the Keeper of the province's Seals, competed for fourth place. Neither got a majority on the first ballot but Vaillant won the run-off. According to Proyart, Robespierre had been trying to trade support with other candidates – which should not have been difficult since the deputies were elected one at a time – and had managed to enlist the help of a man who had already been elected. On the 26th his agents supplied the voters with slips of paper carrying his name, while Robespierre made a speech attacking the local authorities.[44] All Proyart's evidence is suspect but Robespierre's reference, in the second edition of *A la nation artésienne,* to grievances which men from the *bailliage* of Artois 'have brought to this meeting' could indicate that the speech was, in fact, a reading of the pamphlet.[45]

One way or another he got himself elected in fifth place, the last three deputies chosen being two more farmers and a merchant from Arras. It had been an uphill struggle. Artois was a bad constituency to fight since the presence of electors from eight different *bailliages* meant that lawyers from the main town had relatively little influence. This may have led Robespierre to resort to more vigorous electioneering than was considered respectable. Lenglet, a colleague in the Academy, wrote that he intrigued his way into the Assembly – but that was just after his overthrow in 1794 and we can perhaps disregard it.[46]

It's what one often says about one's successful opponents, said the party member.

On the day before Robespierre's election what he had been say-

44. pp. 72-4.   45. Bib. Nat. Lb^{39} 6607, p. 68n^1.
46. Jacob, p. 48.

ing about the sufferings of the poor was sharply confirmed by a food riot in Arras when some women tried to force down the price of grain. Troops were called in. Guines himself went to the scene, bought the grain himself at the farmer's price and distributed it at the price the women had tried to impose. The municipality, scarcely living up to the black picture that Robespierre had painted, ordered the bakers to keep the town supplied with bread, imposed price controls and made a small reduction for the poor, on production of a certificate from their priest.[47]

For what happened during Robespierre's last days in Arras we are again dependent on Proyart. Robespierre, according to the abbé, had been saying that humble people would soon be taking over the local government. De Fosseux remarked ironically that no doubt Robespierre's influence would one day get *l'Anguillette* (the nickname of a particularly proletarian citizen) made mayor. At a party the night before he left, Robespierre is said to have predicted that the time was indeed coming when the Anguillettes would be mayors. It wasn't a particularly good prophecy since the mayor for the next few years was actually going to be de Fosseux, while l'Anguillette never got further than the *comité de surveillance,* but it contrasts rather markedly with Robespierre's own irony about 'a man well-known in Saint-Omer under the nickname of Bobo, who has long carried on an honourable trade in lettuces which has not brought him a fortune'.[48] That was at the time of the lightning-conductor case.

He was scarcely older than me when he said that, objected Mac. What matters is that, by the time he went into politics, he really believed that men were equal, when de Fosseux only thought that nobles were equal to nobles.

Proyart claimed that he borrowed ten louis (about £10) and a trunk from Mme Marchand, the editress of the *Affiches d'Artois,* who was a friend of Charlotte. He gives a full inventory of Maximilien's wardrobe, which shows that someone had a good memory – or imagination.[49]

Two contemporary comments on the successful deputies are worth a glance. Guffroy, who had sat with Robespierre on the bishop's court and was to join him in the Convention, in a satire

47. *Affiches d'Artois.* 48. Proyart, p. 77; Le Gallo, op. cit., p. 48.
49. pp. 79-81.

on prospective candidates, referred to one man who claimed, 'I have discussed the rights of the Third Estate against the nobility with such angelic sweetness that my enemies have been forced to *do me the justice of calling me the rabid lamb*'.[50] If this refers to Robespierre, which seems quite likely, it suggests that his peculiar style of oratory aroused the contemptuous mockery of some of his audience. A more striking example of this appeared in the *Affiches* in the form of a satirical article by an Arras notary which discussed the merits of the sixteen deputies as though they were the products of the racing stable. Robespierre received much more detailed treatment than any of the others: 'The *Enragé, double bidet à crains,* impetuous, intolerant of bit and stick, vicious, only dares to bite from behind, fears the whip. Its inclusion was a surprise but it is said to be destined to provide a comic turn after the brilliant performances of Mirabeau, Bergasse, Malouet etc. whose actions it has been trained to mimic in a ridiculous fashion.'[51] Once again there's this contempt for someone who hasn't enough courage or talent to do as much mischief as he would like.

What did he say about the other horses, asked the reverend.

I admit that he was rather patronising about all the *curés* and obsequious to the nobility; but he was only really offensive about Robespierre.

Well, he was certainly wrong about the talent, said the party member, so I don't see why we should take his word for it about the rest. Presumably any favourable comment would have disappeared after his death and if you allow people to be judged by what their enemies say about them, we're all going to be in trouble.

It's not the only evidence, Mac, said the man from the ministry. Don't forget the speeches and the pamphlets – it all fits. I've got quite a convincing picture of the public school revolutionary, obsessed with his own disinterestedness, convinced that he's born to be at the top – not because of birth or wealth it's true, but because he's got four quarterings of morality that entitle him to tell the poor what's good for them and consign to perdition anyone who disagrees with him.

I must confess to sharing some of Ted's doubts, said the rever-

---

50. Jacob, pp. 32-3.
51. Reprinted in Walter, p. 654. There is a manuscript version at the end of the copy of *A la nation artésienne* in the Bibliothèque Nationale.

end, but this is only the beginning of the story. We've a long way to go yet — and if we carry on at this speed it looks like taking us all winter.

I'm sorry about that, I said. You see, once he gets to Versailles we know a lot more about his public life but very little about everything else. So I thought you would like to look as carefully as possible at this early period before the man disappears behind the deputy. I'm not suggesting that he didn't develop after 1789, but a good deal of what we've been looking at is going to illuminate what came later.

It looks like being a long, hard winter, said the man from the ministry.

III The Tribune of the People

Why don't you just write a book, asked the man from the ministry, so that we can get the general picture and tell you what we think about it?

I confessed that I had indeed been tempted. But I haven't got anything to add to the authorities: no new documents, no unsuspected collection of Robespierriana or anything like that.

Perhaps there isn't any general picture, said the reverend. Or perhaps what I mean is that where each of us ends up depends on the turnings he chooses to take on the way.

You can choose what you like, objected the party member, but 'though you break the bloody glass you can't hold up the weather'. You can't alter what happened and that's where the meaning is.

Shall we see what did happen? After all, 1789 was an eventful year. From then onwards Robespierre was very much a public figure and what he said is part of French history. So before we start it might be helpful if you told me what you'd like me to tell you.

Just give us the main facts, said the man from the ministry and we'll make up our own minds.

You've told us quite a bit about Robespierre's personality, said the party member. What I want to know is why he mattered; what were the issues; which side was he on and what sort of difference did he make?

We do want to know that, put in the reverend, but I hope you'll give us more than that. If I was to talk about his soul you might object, so I'll put it another way. Presumably he was either a gangster of genius or a tragic hero or something equally out of the ordinary. I'm interested in the man. If you can't give us some idea of his inner life I shall feel that something is missing, perhaps what matters most.

Well, let's begin by considering the quality of the evidence. In 1967 the *Société des Etudes Robespierristes* completed their five-volume edition of his speeches.[1] This prints the different press

1. *Oeuvres de Maximilien Robespierre*, vols. VI–X, ed. M. Bouloiseau and A. Soboul, Paris, 1950-67. Unless otherwise indicated, all references to Robespierre's speeches are from this edition.

reports of each of his speeches and we are never likely to get much nearer to knowing what he actually said. Ten of the speeches he made in the Constituent Assembly, which sat from May 1789 to September 1791, have survived in printed versions. Four of them were published at his own expense and three each by the Assembly and the Jacobin Club. In these cases we know exactly, if not what he actually said, at least what he wanted on the record. All the rest survive only in press reports, some of them very short. It looks as though they cover all his speeches of any importance in the Assembly itself, but reporting of what happened in the early days of the Jacobin Club was much more sketchy. We have references to only three speeches by Robespierre in the Jacobins before the autumn of 1790 and there is obviously a good deal missing here. The press probably gives a reasonably accurate account of the general argument of his speeches, especially if we check one newspaper against another, but there are important differences and on at least one occasion he complained about the publication of a 'speech' that he had never made.[2] So we can't draw any safe conclusions either about the actual words attributed to him or about any omissions in the surviving record.

This is even more true of his correspondence.[3] What has been preserved is obviously no more than a tiny fragment and most of it concerns his public life. It gives us very little indication either of his private thoughts or of how he lived. Comments by his contemporaries, with one or two exceptions, do very little to fill the gap. Those written after his fall are generally too spiteful to be very convincing and the rest are mostly concerned with his political opinions or his character as a public figure.

We can get a pretty accurate impression of his political career and rather tentatively infer something of his beliefs from the policies he advocated and the way he defended them, but that's about as far as we can go. His private life – and whether he had much of a private life – is almost unknown. We do know that, when he first went to Versailles, he shared lodgings with the farmers from Artois and not with his fellow-lawyers. When the deputies moved to Paris in the autumn he went to live on his own in the *Marais,* a good way from the Assembly. With a salary

2. *Oeuvres,* vol. VII, pp. 593-4.
3. *Correspondance de Maximilien et d'Augustin Robespierre,* ed. G. Michon, 2v. Paris, 1926, 1941.

of almost a pound a day he would have been quite well off if he hadn't been supporting Charlotte and Augustin back in Arras. They wrote from time to time to ask for more help and as they still employed a maid in 1791 and Augustin made occasional visits to Paris, they probably cost him a good deal.[4] A man called Villiers, who claimed to have acted as Robespierre's secretary for seven months in 1790, said that he gave a quarter of his salary to a mistress, 'a woman of about 26 who worshipped him but whom he treated rather badly'.[5] Friendly and hostile historians have read quite a lot into that, just because there is so little other evidence. But it has now been shown that Villiers was probably never in Paris in 1790 and the whole story looks like something he invented to make his memoirs sound more interesting.[6] That should serve as a warning against starting with preconceived ideas, 'proving' them with a few scraps of doubtful evidence, or the absence of evidence to the contrary, and presenting the result as the verdict of history.

That may be impeccably academic, said the man from the ministry and it might be right to reject everything that can't be positively proved, if we were trying him for murder, but unless I'm mistaken, *your* verdict of history is always going to be 'not proven'. It may go down well in the senior common rooms but outside the sacred walls it looks more like a loss of nerve. I've been reading that biography of Gallo's that you mentioned. What he says about Robespierre being flawed from childhood by his ambivalent reactions to his absconding father may be carrying speculation too far but his character study of Robespierre is a good deal more convincing than anything you've given us so far.[7]

It makes him seem more real, if you like, and it may well be true. But it's a guess. A good deal of his evidence for the loneliness theme is negative evidence. It may be quite misleading. It's what he begins by assuming that makes his inferences from what *is* known seem convincing and anyone who starts with different preconceptions is likely to come up with different conclusions.

The reverend wondered how far anyone was bothered by an

4. *Correspondance*, vol. I, pp. 70-1, 73-4. H. Fleischmann, *Mémoires de Charlotte Robespierre*, p. 231.

5. P. Villiers, *Souvenirs d'un déporté*, Paris, 1802, p. 2.

6. R. Garmy, 'Aux origines de la légende anti-robespierriste: Pierre Villiers et Robespierre', in *Actes du Colloque Robespierre*, Paris, 1967, pp. 19-33.

7. M. Gallo, op. cit., especially pp. 89-97.

Oedipus complex before psychiatrists told him that he ought to be. I suppose Ted would argue that the fact that he didn't mention it only meant that he couldn't identify his symptoms and J.S. would call that negative evidence.

Look, I said rather impatiently, if you don't stick to what people thought they were and why they thought they did what they thought they were doing, you might as well give up history altogether. If you want to understand Robespierre's policies, you've got to put them in their political context. There were two ways of interpreting what was going on between 1789 and 1791 and though people couldn't keep them clearly separated when events were so complicated, they did understand the difference. On the one hand, they saw the Constituent Assembly, which is what the Estates General soon called itself, as the means by which the entire French nation provided itself with a new social contract. From this point of view the Assembly was sovereign – over the king and his Ministers and over any faction that might want to coerce it. What the Assembly voted was law and had to be obeyed by everyone. Its members enjoyed parliamentary immunity. It had the power to bind the future by drafting a constitution. The constitution and the Declaration of the Rights of Man determined the rules by which politics would henceforth be carried on. On the other hand, most of the deputies, at one time or another, believed that they were making a revolution, in the sense that they were involved in a violent conflict to overthrow the old order and create something new. The justification for their readiness to use force was their belief in the existence of imprescriptible human rights, by which the past was condemned and to which the future must conform. From this point of view the Declaration of the Rights of Man was not so much a legal charter as the formal recognition of the principles by which the Assembly itself might be judged. The Assembly was merely a means to a necessary end and if it deviated from its duty it could legitimately be coerced. Since the new order was morally superior to the old, the revolution was a crusade and those who resisted it were traitors, not merely to France but to humanity as a whole. Revolutionary tactics were merely a matter of expediency and though violence was to be avoided if possible it was legitimate if the unrighteous would otherwise prevail.

All the more radical deputies found themselves trapped between these two conflicting attitudes. There were times when they recognised the need for violence. Although they were not responsible for the nation-wide revolts of July 1789 they came to accept them as the necessary means by which the Court was defeated. When two unpopular royal officials were murdered in the streets of Paris, Barnave, in the Assembly, suggested that their blood was not particularly pure. By the end of 1789 most people thought that the revolution and its legitimate violence were behind them. The question then became how much further change was required to form an acceptable basis for a new constitutional regime. Lafayette, Mirabeau and the 'Triumvirate' (Duport, Barnave and Alexander de Lameth) led rival political groups. Each hoped to consolidate the revolution to its own political advantage and each became increasingly afraid of anarchy. Popular disorder continued in the provinces and the Assembly was reluctant to entrust the king with the means of effective repression since it suspected him of aspiring to overthrow the entire revolutionary order. Without his co-operation no constitutional monarchy could possibly work. Realising this, each of the groups tried to negotiate a compromise – which meant offering concessions. They went back on the democratic implications of the Declaration of the Rights of Man and the constitution that the Assembly was drafting became steadily more conservative. This alarmed a handful of deputies on the extreme Left, of whom Robespierre was one. (The political terminology of 'Left' and 'Right', by the way, originated at this time, from the places where the different groups sat in the Assembly.) The extreme Left came to believe that any settlement which did not betray the principles of 1789 would have to be imposed on the king and the aristocratic faction. For the time being they accepted the parliamentary rules, which meant endorsing a constitution that they did not like, but they lived in expectation of a violent counter-revolution. Their fears seemed to be justified in June 1791 when the flight of the royal family produced a second revolutionary situation. When the king had been recaptured the dispute over whether or not to keep him on the throne led to the emergence of a violent republican movement in Paris. This was bloodily suppressed by the National Guard – of which Lafayette was Commander-in-Chief – and he and the Triumvirate then resumed their hopeless policy of winning royal acceptance of an amended constitution, in an atmosphere poisoned by general disbelief in the king's sincerity and bitter memories of the blood shed by the National Guards.

Before we go any further, said Ted, your extreme Left seems to have been saying 'Heads I win, tails you lose'. Constitutional means were fair enough – provided they won. If they didn't they would resort to force.

Everyone was saying that, replied Mac, and what else do you expect them to say in a revolution? The king pretended to accept the revolution when he meant to overthrow it as soon as he could and the people who actually resorted to violence were the men who ordered the National Guard to fire on the crowd. They were the ones who did the killing. This isn't a matter of political bias, it's a question of intellectual honesty.

It might be as well to go back to the beginning, I said, to see where Robespierre stood. His first problem was to get a hearing – both literally and metaphorically. There were nearly 1,200 members in the Assembly and, at least to begin with, there were no proper rules of debate. Both in Versailles and when they moved to Paris, they met in enormous halls with very poor acoustics. It was difficult for anyone to be heard unless his colleagues thought him interesting enough to suspend their private conversations, and it took the personality – and the lungs – of a Mirabeau to silence opposition. Since this was the beginning of French parliamentary history no one had a political reputation to start with but a good few deputies were eminent in one way or another and likely to be heard with interest, if not always with approval. Robespierre was completely unknown. Some regional groups of deputies had a national reputation – the Bretons for extremism and the men from Dauphiné for moderation – because of the events of the previous year. Artois seems to have been regarded as one of the more radical areas but its complicated electoral conflicts were not well enough known for its deputies to excite much interest. So Robespierre had to make his own way and his problems may have been increased by stage-fright. Dumont, one of Mirabeau's secretaries, claimed in his Memoirs that Robespierre had confessed this to him and Fréron said much the same thing in a very hostile obituary notice.[8] Once again, the evidence is suspect. Fréron continued: 'He was always forced to stop by jeers and uproar. His oratory at that time was verbose in expression and incoherent in its ideas.' One has only

8. E. Dumont, *Souvenirs sur Mirabeau,* ed. J. Bénétruy, Paris, 1951, p. 144; *Papiers inédits trouvés chez Robespierre etc.,* 3v., Paris, 1828, vol. I, p. 155.

to glance at Robespierre's speeches to see that, whatever may be said of his wordiness, his arguments were as precise and well-developed as those of most of his colleagues. Eloquence has to be judged by contemporary standards, which in this case means what the papers said. This normally reflects their political bias: those who agreed with what he said praised the way he said it, and vice versa. They did seem to share the view that he went on too long. Even sympathetic papers accused him of exhausting the Assembly's patience while the *Ami du Roi* claimed in 1790 that he achieved the minor miracle of uniting all parties in a common yawn.[9]

Walter has shown that Dumont's description of how Robespierre startled the Assembly by a brilliant improvisation as early as 6 June is probably a gross exaggeration.[10] He seems to have made little impression during the summer, although the more radical newspapers were already calling attention to his name, even though they often didn't know how to spell it. On 25 August he was easily silenced by an interruption and there are signs that he was regarded as something of a joke. On 10 October he proposed that future laws should have the solemn preamble: 'Peoples, this is the law you must obey. Let it be inviolable and sacred to all.' When a rich Gascon accent was heard objecting 'We don't want any canticles' the whole Assembly burst out laughing.[11] The *Actes des Apôtres,* a satirical royalist paper, alleged that on one occasion he delighted his colleagues by his frequent references to *aristocrassique* plots.[12] The *Actes des Apôtres,* one of whose editors was a former teacher of his, singled him out for particular attention, but despite their efforts he seems, by the end of 1789, to have established himself as a serious – and very persistent – speaker, even if his opinions carried little weight with the majority.

During the critical months of the summer of 1789 we can trace the evolution of his ideas with reasonable accuracy. A long letter to Buissart, written about 18 May, gave his first impressions of the Estates General.[13] He took the hostility of most of the nobility for granted and was very suspicious of the clergy. His comments on some of the men who had been expected to emerge as leaders of the Third Estate – Mounier, Target, Mirabeau and Malouet – were

---

9. *Oeuvres,* vol. VI, p. 675.
10. Walter, pp. 78-9; Dumont, op. cit., pp. 63-4.
11. *Oeuvres,* vol. VI, p. 114.   12. Walter, p. 657n31.
13. *Correspondance,* vol. I, pp. 36-42, where it is wrongly dated 24 May.

all scathing, although he was later to revise his opinion of Mira-beau. He does not refer to the fact in his letter, but he may have made contact with Necker. If so, he was quickly disillusioned by his old hero.[14] These were the reactions of most of the more radical deputies, very suspicious of any talk of compromise with the Court, and need not imply any particular jealousy on Robes-pierre's part. His first speech, which he describes in the letter, was an attempt at a tactical compromise in order to exploit divisions within the clergy. It was ruled out of order on technical grounds, although Robespierre claimed that a good many deputies had told him they would have voted for it. This is interesting as an example of his sense of political tactics, which some of his biographers have tended to overlook, in their preoccupation with ideology. Robes-pierre told Buissart that he was favourably impressed by the Assembly as a whole, on the rather curious but very typical ground that 'there are over a hundred citizens in the Assembly capable of dying for their country'.

The crisis of July, when the king massed troops around Paris and was defeated by armed insurrection, led Robespierre to stop thinking of tactical compromises and to adopt the perspective of civil war, which implied that whatever was necessary for victory was legitimate. He was already convinced, as he explained to Buissart on 23 July, that the events of the past few days were of transcendental historical importance.[15] The enemy 'proposed nothing less than to slaughter half the Nation so that they could despoil and enslave the rest'. Unlike many of his colleagues, who had mixed feelings about the recent violence in Paris, Robespierre's enthusiasm was unqualified. The governor of the Bastille and the *prévôt des marchands*, or mayor, had been 'punished' – i.e. mur-dered by the crowd. In a speech on the 20th, opposing a motion that called for order in Paris, he had already said that 'it is the insurrection that the motion condemns which has saved the capital and the whole kingdom'.

Which was true, said the party member, at least from the revolutionary point of view.

He was right when he stressed to Buissart that the Parisian revolt had been a relatively orderly business. What's more ominous is that one newspaper quoted him as saying there had been 'not much

14. Proyart, p. 82.   15. *Correspondance*, vol. I, pp. 42-50.

blood spilt, a few heads struck off, no doubt, but guilty ones'. You pointed out a few minutes ago that Barnave had said much the same.

Robespierre maintained this civil war attitude for the next two or three months. He was in favour of opening letters taken from the Genevan ambassador and addressed to the comte d'Artois, who had fled the country. He took the dangerous line that violation of the secrecy of the mails, which would be inexcusable in a 'tyrant', was legitimate when done on behalf of the sovereign people. He approved of the illegal arrest of Besenval, who had commanded the royal forces brought up to intimidate Paris. Augustin, who was visiting Paris, may have been reflecting his brother's views when he wrote to Buissart on 5 September that 'the majority of the Assembly are the declared enemies of liberty'.[16] This meant that they favoured giving the king a suspensive veto over legislation. Maximilien who, like many other deputies, failed to get a hearing, printed at his own expense the speech that he had intended to make, attacking any form of veto. This was cogently and persuasively argued but would have had no hope of success. His colleague, Dubois-Crancé, still remembered it in 1792 when he condemned Robespierre's all-or-nothing attitude.[17] Robespierre's tactics over the veto certainly contrasted with his first speech in the Assembly. In September he took it for granted that the Assembly would have to face the opposition of the Ministers, if not of the king himself, for the indefinite future.

In that case, said the man from the ministry, wasn't it unrealistic to assume that a constitutional monarchy could be made to work?

There wasn't much alternative since he and almost everyone else took the existence of the monarchy for granted. I should have thought you would have approved of his statesmanship in not forcing issues but relying on the continuous pressure of events to brings things round to his own way of thinking.

When the bishop of Tréguier, in Brittany, tried to turn his diocese against the revolution – with a conspicuous lack of success – Robespierre sounded the alarm. 'The security of the State is in danger: a particularly atrocious conspiracy has been formed. The Nation is threatened once again . . .'[18] The lynching of a Parisian

16. *Correspondance,* vol. I, pp. 50-2.
17. Quoted in Jacob, op. cit., p. 83. 18. *Oeuvres,* vol. VI, p. 118.

baker led some of the more moderate deputies to propose the immediate drafting of a martial law bill. Robespierre objected to this on the improbable ground that 'all our ills, including riots, are the products of a plot against public liberty'.[19] According to one report, he demanded the creation of a special court to try enemies of the revolution, whose members were to be drawn from the Assembly itself, anticipating the charge that this would make justice political with, 'Don't talk to me about the constitution when everything combines to stifle it in its cradle'.[20]

Well? said the party member.

Well what?

Was he right? Was it true that the danger of violent counter-revolution was acute enough to justify extra-constitutional action?

Or was he just trying to divert attention from some of the messier activities of the sovereign people, put in the man from the ministry.

How do you expect me to answer that?

How do you expect us to judge his policies if you don't?

I'm not asking you to judge his policies but to understand them. You remember what I was saying about revolutionary periods and constitutional periods. He thought this was a revolutionary period and he advocated revolutionary rather than constitutional methods.

We understood all that, said the party member impatiently, but was it a reasonable view of the situation or was he panicking?

And did he create counter-revolutionary opposition by assuming that anyone who disagreed with him was a counter-revolutionary?

On the whole the press seems to have agreed with him.

Never mind the press. Was he right?

How do you two propose to set about finding out, enquired the reverend. I agree that we can't form an opinion of his statesmanship unless we answer your questions, but I feel rather sorry for J.S. Whatever he says one of you will accuse him of bias.

I don't think there is an answer, I replied. It's true that plenty of influential people, including a good many army officers, were looking for a chance to overthrow the revolution and string up its leaders. But they knew that, for the time being at least, if they started a civil war they would lose it. It's not true that the bishop of Tréguier was dangerous in 1789, though a religious civil war in

19. *Oeuvres*, vol. VI, p. 122.   20. *Oeuvres*, vol. VI, p. 124.

the west was going to endanger the revolution two or three years later. It's not true – so far as I know – that there was any political intrigue behind the lynching of the baker, but it is true that the Martial Law Act was to make possible the 'massacre' of July 1791. Robespierre probably took the will for the deed and the deed did follow; but a good deal happened in between, so you can argue either way.

We haven't got very far, said the reverend, but I don't think we're going to get much farther.

Look, I said, I don't want to dodge any difficulties but those two have got an over-simplified view of historical relationships. If Walter is right, it was about the time of these speeches that the press of the Right began to consider Robespierre worthy of attention – I suppose Ted would say, understandably so.

He would, said Ted.

But it was about the same time that he seems to have come to the conclusion that things weren't as bad as he had imagined. He still thought there were plenty of people prepared to use force to overthrow the revolution but he seems to have believed that the majority in the Assembly would be more than a match for them. So he reverted to constitutional tactics and playing by the rules. In other words, if he *had* been what Ted would call a rabble-rouser in the autumn, he stopped being one just about the time that the counter-revolutionary press began to say he was one.

I suggest we let that one lie, said the reverend, and see what happened next.

I don't want to suggest, I went on, that Robespierre changed his principles. He was, in fact, a good deal more consistent than most of the deputies of the Left. Like them, he couldn't always reconcile practice with political theory, but at least he didn't trade his convictions for his own advantage. So far as he was concerned – and I don't think he ever moved from this view – the revolution was about popular sovereignty. Political power was to be transferred from a king who was merely the mouthpiece of various hereditary vested interests to the representatives of the people as a whole. Since the interests of the majority could not differ from those of the nation at large, the introduction of political democracy meant the substitution of the general good for sectional privilege and *ipso facto* the moralising of politics. He went further than this in assuming that the wealthy in general and the old privileged orders

59

in particular were exposed to all kinds of temptations by their way of life and the defence of their sectional interests. Working people, on the other hand, lived more natural lives and could find their personal advantage only in the progress of society as a whole. All this was brought out very clearly in his published speech of December 1790 on the organisation of the National Guard.[21] 'It is the people who are good, patient, generous; our revolution bears witness to this, as is shown both by the crimes of its enemies and its own innumerable heroic deeds in the recent past, which come naturally to it. The people ask only for peace, justice and the right to live. The rich and powerful thirst after honours, wealth and sensual enjoyment. The interest and desire of the people is that of nature itself, of humanity; it is the general interest. The interest and desire of the rich and powerful is that of ambition, pride, greed and the wildest fantasies of passions that are fatal to the happiness of society as a whole. The abuses that have ravaged society were always their doing. These men have always been the scourge of the people. Who made our glorious revolution? Was it the rich? Was it the people? Only the people could will it and achieve it. For the same reason the people alone can maintain it.'

I can see what that man meant about canticles, said Ted. It's one thing to advocate democracy on the ground that all men are equally fallible and self-interested and it's something quite different to make a god of an idealised 'people' that only existed in Robespierre's imagination. He's really worshipping himself and if the real people didn't react as they ought to have done, he wouldn't say that he was wrong, he'd say they had been misled.

Nevertheless, if we take 'people' to mean the nation and not just the poor, this was the attitude of all the revolutionaries in the summer of 1789. It was the whole basis of the Declaration of the Rights of Man: 'The aim of every political association is the preservation of the natural and imprescriptible rights of man.' 'The principle of all sovereignty resides essentially in the nation.' 'The law is the expression of the general will. All citizens have the right to share in its formulation, either personally or through their representatives.' But the majority of the political leaders, after popular support had made their victory possible in 1789, soon came to believe that the revolution should be entrusted to those

21. *Oeuvres*, vol. VI, pp. 616-46.

who were educated enough to understand its principles and not so poor as to be likely to use political power in order to redistribute property.

I'd been waiting for that, said the party member. Now that the poor had made the revolution they were to be told to run away and play while their superiors cornered the power, the honour and all the rest of it.

I can sympathise with Mac's reaction, said Ted. But there's more to politics than fair play — whatever your friend Maximilien may have thought to the contrary. It's a question of what's practicable. How many people voted during the revolution?

The Assembly disfranchised those who didn't pay a — very low — amount in direct taxation. I say 'disfranchised' because anyone who paid *any* direct taxation had been able to vote in 1789. Between half and two-thirds of the adult male population could vote to choose electors but in practice only a small minority of the electorate bothered to vote.

And the voting was public?

That was more or less inevitable when there was so much illiteracy.

So democracy would have meant putting political power in the hands of labourers and tenant farmers, voting in public in the presence of their landlords. I doubt if Mac would have been very pleased with the result. I seem to remember that in 1848 universal suffrage produced an anti-democratic assembly and I don't see why things should have been any different fifty or sixty years earlier.

That's true, I agreed, but Mac still has a point — and it was Robespierre's point. It wasn't merely a matter of who voted. What he was afraid of was an attempt to fix things so that the abolition of formal privilege would merely substitute wealth for birth and an oligarchy for an aristocracy, leaving society as divided as ever, with the dice still loaded against the majority. There was a hint of this in the debates on the Declaration of the Rights of Man. Robespierre objected to the definition of taxation as 'a proportion taken from the wealth of each citizen', perhaps because it seemed to legitimise property. What he proposed was 'a part of the citizens' goods held in common to pay for public expenditure'.[22] At the time his main objective was probably to establish the Assembly's

22. *Oeuvres*, vol. VI, p. 65.

control over taxation, but there is at least a hint of the kind of social definition of property that he was to formulate in 1793.

Where he differed from most of his colleagues was shown in August 1790 when the Naval Committee submitted a draft penal code that provided barbarous punishments if ratings committed offences for which officers would merely be cashiered. When Robespierre objected he was told that 'officers are punished by the loss of their honour, which is what a Frenchman holds most dear'.[23] Since the Assembly facilitated the passage of merchant navy officers (commoners) into the royal navy in time of war, this incident is a good example of how many deputies of the moderate Left saw the revolution as a process by which those who would have been regarded as 'gentlemen' in England were to acquire the kind of status that had previously been reserved for nobles in France.[24]

Casuistry, said Ted. What they probably meant was that an officer risked spoiling his career while a seaman hadn't much to lose.

On logical grounds at least, Robespierre often had the better of the argument but he rarely got the better of the voting. He kept reminding the deputies of what they had promised in 1789 and preferred to forget. It may be true that the mass of the people didn't consist of latter-day Spartans, as Robespierre liked to think, but it was hard to argue that those who had made the revolution couldn't be trusted with any share in the constitution that emerged from it. The moderates didn't trust the Ministers any more than he did and if it came to the pinch they too were prepared to use force against a threat of counter-revolution. Since they were being denounced all the time by extremist journalists such as Marat and Desmoulins, they were in a very difficult position.

You were suggesting earlier on, said the reverend, that there were contradictions in Robespierre's position too.

He argued that the revolution had been (they all assumed that it was over) in the interests of the nation as a whole. Public opinion must therefore support the Assembly since the Third Estate had been elected by virtually universal suffrage and the Assembly had helped to make the revolution. The Assembly was sovereign – he argued, for tactical reasons, in September 1789 that its decisions

23. *Moniteur*, 19 August 1790.
24. See N. Hampson, 'The *comité de marine* of the Constituent Assembly', *The Historical Journal*, vol. II, no. 1 (1959), pp. 130-48.

could not be made subject to a referendum – but he believed that its sovereignty was conditional upon its remaining true to the principles embodied in the Declaration of the Rights of Man. If it violated these principles, as he claimed it did when it limited the franchise, then it forfeited its moral claim to obedience, but there was nothing anyone could do about it since any popular revolution against the Assembly would almost certainly lead to the restoration of the ancien régime.

There were also circumstances where the principles of 1789 didn't offer any clear guidance. The Assembly didn't know what to make of the situation in Avignon and the Comtat Venaissin, two Papal enclaves in France, which had revolutions of their own. Avignon asked to be incorporated in France but the Comtat did not. This brought up the question of self-determination versus treaty rights and Robespierre cut through the Gordian knot in a way that would have done credit to a nineteenth-century nationalist. He argued that no section of a people can be detached from the nation to which it belongs, and Avignon 'belonged' to France and not to Rome. No section has the right to detach itself from its parent nation. The Comtat must therefore be reunited with France since this was the 'real' will of its inhabitants, however vigorously they might protest the contrary. 'We must not judge hatred of tyranny by the number of those who condemn it but by the inner feelings of each man. That part of the population of the Comtat which does not support reunion must be regarded as oppressed. Every people wants to be free and despots would have been banished long ago if peoples had been able to make their views heard.'[25] Robespierre's speeches on Avignon are some of his least convincing efforts; his arguments would have implied conceding independence to Corsica which was scarcely an integral part of France, but he had nothing to say about giving up territory. Nevertheless, these opinions at least went down well in the Assembly and a speech on Avignon was the first of his that it ordered to be printed. The deputies perhaps didn't pay too much attention to his theorising; what they wanted was a respectable pretext to eliminate a safe haven for counter-revolutionary activity in the heart of France.

I wonder how far that was true of Robespierre as well, said the

25. *Oeuvres,* vol. VII, p. 257.

reverend. You've mentioned his practical sense and his inability to square practice with theory all the time. One could perhaps argue that he was simply rather better than the others at finding elaborate theoretical justifications for what he wanted to do anyway.

It's too early for us to talk about that, I said, but it's something I'd like to come back to later.

What Henry's hinting at, even if he's too polite to say so, said Ted, is what I said earlier on. Robespierre knew what was right and if the Assembly disagreed it forfeited its moral authority and whether or not one then tried to intimidate it or overthrow it was simply a matter of tactics.

What you're forgetting, said Mac, is that in private the majority agreed with him. They acted against their own principles – and a more or less democratically elected assembly hasn't the right to disfranchise those who elected it. I agree with J.S. that his arguments about Avignon look a bit sinister – but Ted can't object to them if they had majority support.

I'm inclined to suspect all this majority business. As I said before, I don't think he really cared. It was a matter of what coincided with the Divine Right of His Revolutionary Majesty.

He wouldn't be the first to see nothing quite conclusive in the art of temporal government, said the reverend. I don't think this talk about sovereignty is getting us anywhere at all. What did he *do*?

He went on suspecting plots everywhere. When the Genoese put in an optimistic claim for the recovery of Corsica, that was an English plot. When Spain requested French support in a colonial quarrel with England, under the terms of the Franco-Spanish alliance, that was a royalist plot to get France involved in a war. The Avignon business was a plot to provide a safe base for counter-revolutionaries. The Ministers were plotting to rig the municipal elections. Peasants who burned châteaux were the tools of secret agents who were trying to discredit the revolution. Sometimes he convinced the deputies but on other occasions his suspicions were a source of ridicule. 'M. de Robespierre, as usual, spoke of plots, conspiracies etc., etc.,' wrote Duquesnoy, a fellow-deputy, in January 1790. Two months later the *Mercure de France* said that he had 'once again enlarged on the plots and conspiracies of which he alone held the secret'. He repeated time and again that only the protection of Providence could have saved the revolution from so many enemies. It's not merely a matter of his credulity, but of his pessimism. At a time when most people wanted to believe that the revolution was over and the country was settling down satisfactorily, Robespierre was always warning of new dangers, secret enemies and future ordeals. When a major crisis did blow up, in the summer of 1791, he was naturally given the credit for having foreseen it.

Well, *we* ought to give him credit for having realised that things weren't as settled as most people thought, said Mac.

In spite of all this, he consistently defended the right of royalist deputies to parliamentary immunity and the right of newspapers to print whatever they liked – including pornography, since he didn't think this could be suppressed without opening the road to political censorship.[26] As a man who tried to base all his views on principle and to avoid *ad hoc* judgments, he sometimes surprised both supporters and opponents by his moderation, when the circumstances of a particular case provoked the passions of the deputies. He opposed a motion to silence for three months Mirabeau's aggressively royalist brother, for mocking the Assembly. He proposed the release of the comte de Toulouse-Lautrec, a deputy from the nobility who had been arrested by the municipality of Toulouse on a counter-revolutionary charge. He upheld the secrecy of the mails and defended the right of anyone who wished to leave the country. He laughed off as absurd the open opposition to the revolution of such superannuated bodies as the Estates of Cambrésis and the Parlement of Toulouse, when some of his colleagues wanted to make examples of them. On occasions his unexpected attitudes produced shouts of 'Go and sit on the Right'.

How far was his concern for freedom of the press and so on the reaction of a man in the minority who knew that, sooner or later, any suppression of unpopular opinion was liable to be turned against himself?

There may have been an element of tactics in it but his speeches suggest that there was genuine conviction as well. He was a target for especially vicious calumny himself but he never sought legal protection. He made a particularly interesting speech, arising out of a real case, on the question of whether one ought to offer sanctuary to a friend who was wanted on a counter-revolutionary

26. *Oeuvres,* vol. VII, p. 543.

charge. Barère's report, in his newspaper *Le Point du Jour*, suggests that this was one of the few occasions when Robespierre found it difficult to make up his mind. The Spartan side of him said that 'friendship cannot authorise us to share a friend's crimes against the nation. Humanity consists above all in loving one's country and benefiting the community, not in sacrificing the interest of society as a whole to that of one individual.' But if civic duty debarred a man from helping a friend to escape, 'honour, or rather an imperious feeling of pity and humanity, does not allow us to denounce him and hand him over to the courts'. The *Moniteur*, however, published a very different version according to which Robespierre specifically excluded from the right to asylum anyone suspected of political crimes against the nation.[27] This is a warning, by the way, against building any elaborate theories about his principles or policies on the basis of one or two quotations from his speeches.

As I said, he himself was subjected to the most vicious calumny and misrepresentation. The royalist press peddled the story that he was related to Damiens, the man who stabbed Louis XV. His enemies made a thorough job of destroying his reputation in his own province. Duquesnoy wrote in February 1790, 'Several of the Artois deputies assured me that last June M. Robespierre had such a hold over the minds of the inhabitants of the province that he could have had all the châteaux burned. (He has not got that authority now.) Far from using it in that way, he was always writing to urge calm, peace and moderation and preaching harmony.'[28] If these letters had survived we might have had a very different picture of him. This is confirmed by the *Adresse au Peuple belgique* (not Belgians, but inhabitants of northern France) that he wrote on behalf of some of his colleagues, towards the end of 1789.[29] In this pamphlet he carried moderation to extraordinary lengths. He began with a warning against trouble-makers: 'All those interested in the preservation of the old abuses of which you were the victims are doing all they can to excite your mistrust, to set you against each other and give you a fatal prejudice against the decrees of the people's representatives.' After describing at length all the benefits conferred by the Assembly – and

27. *Oeuvres*, vol. VI, pp. 514-16.   28. *Oeuvres*, vol. VI, p. 238.
29. Bib. Nat. Mp 2656.

suppressing all his own reservations – he endorsed its misleading claim to have *'entirely destroyed the feudal régime'*. He invited his readers to bless the Assembly and even tried to dispel their fears of the Martial Law Act (which he himself had passionately opposed) on the ground that it was directed only against the enemies of the people and he concluded his argument with an edifying 'Let us give thanks to Providence'. Despite all this, as soon as trouble broke out in northern France, early in 1790, the Finance Minister, Lambert, immediately accepted as genuine a forged letter attributed to Robespierre that was being hawked around in the province. When he invited Robespierre to undo the harm for which this letter was responsible, Maximilien can scarcely be blamed for giving him a rather cool reply.[30]

It was Beaumetz who seems to have done most to destroy his reputation in Arras. Robespierre, trying to get his own province a more favourable franchise, had argued in the Assembly that to apply the national standard and base the right to vote on the payment of direct taxation would be unfair since most taxation in Artois was indirect. That was in January 1790. Beaumetz waited until April, when local elections were almost due, before writing to tell his father in Arras that Robespierre had said the province was under-taxed. This libel was busily spread throughout Artois, to the alarm of Augustin and one of Maximilien's aunts who wrote to remind him that Beaumetz had tried to prevent his election in 1789 by accusing him of attacking religion.[31] When a *curé* used Beaumetz's letter as propaganda at an election meeting, Augustin tried to have the election annulled.[32] Maximilien was eventually induced to publish a refutation of Beaumetz in June, but by that time the libel had already served its purpose.[33] After carefully exposing his legitimate grievances against Beaumetz he suddenly took up a melodramatic tone: 'Nowadays, Monsieur, calumny is not enough to assuage the hatred of the people's enemies against its defenders; we must have outrages of a still more atrocious kind. We do not know if the audacity of the people I have described can go as far as such excesses, but we are resigned to whatever may happen and at least we shall take with us the knowledge that the

30. *Correspondance,* vol. I, p. 61.
31. *Correspondance,* vol. I, pp. 75-6.
32. Jacob, pp. 54-6.
33. *Lettre de M. de Robespierre à M. de Beaumetz,* Bib. Nat. Lb[39] 3482.

crimes of tyrants can only strengthen the liberty and welfare of peoples.'

It's a pity he spoiled his case by a spot of calumny of his own, said Ted. I agree that it wasn't an edifying business and I'm prepared to admit that he wouldn't have stooped to such behaviour himself. But if you go into politics you've got to be prepared for that sort of thing. I imagine a man like Danton would just have laughed it off. Perhaps his main trouble was that he was too thin-skinned.

At the end of his letter to Beaumetz he printed a sort of testimonial signed by several of his colleagues. Three of the four farmers signed, together with a lawyer and a merchant from Arras and two of the nobility, Charles de Lameth and de Croix. We don't know why anyone signed or refused but it's odd that none of the curés joined in, since Robespierre had once or twice spoken up in defence of the interests of parish priests. Perhaps they believed the propaganda about his being an enemy of religion. Incidentally, he wasn't the only member of the family to see things in a melo-dramatic light. Augustin, writing in June 1790, prophesied: 'You will seal the people's cause with your blood. They may even be misguided enough to strike you themselves, but I swear to avenge your death and to merit it as much as you.'[34] From his own point of view that was not a bad guess.

He may have exaggerated, said Mac, but one can see why he was worried about intrigues and foul play. You haven't told us much, though, about what he did in the Assembly.

He spent most of his time failing to defeat or modify legislation he didn't like. He opposed the Martial Law Bill and anything that seemed to divide the country into 'ins' and 'outs', such as the property qualifications for voting, which was then used to justify the exclusion of 'passive citizens' from the National Guard. He advocated full political rights for Protestants, Jews and actors; the Protestants and actors got them but the Jews had to wait. He was more concerned with political issues of this kind than with social reform. He did speak in favour of the retroactive banning of enclo-sure by seigneurs but he didn't make any other contribution to the important debates on manorial rights. He didn't oppose Le Chape-lier's law of 14 June 1791 which banned trade unions and em-

34. *Correspondance*, vol. I, pp. 82-3.

ployers' associations. Perhaps he didn't understand its importance – Marat denounced it on purely political grounds and none of the deputies of the Left opposed it. He was rather more active on religious matters, although mainly on points of detail. He made no major contribution to the debates on the Civil Constitution of the Clergy which provided France with a national Church and led to a breach with Rome. Robespierre intervened to propose pensions for elderly monks, to object (successfully) to the high salaries suggested for bishops and (unsuccessfully) to propose an increase in the pensions of retired *curés*. An otherwise unexciting speech on the Civil Constitution ended with the plea that the clergy should have the right to marry. This created an uproar in the Assembly and annoyed Mirabeau who accused Robespierre of losing a cause that he had hoped to win himself. It brought Robespierre at least two letters of thanks from parish priests – a whole flood of them, if one accepts the evidence of Villiers, his self-styled secretary.

He had rather more to say about the reform of the legal system, as might be expected. He was probably in agreement with most of the Assembly's work here and tended to concentrate on measures to prevent the courts being abused by political opponents. In May 1791 he and Duport – who was by now his political enemy – attacked the death penalty, which it was proposed to retain for the single crime of rebellion against the legislature. His subsequent admirers have tended to ignore the limited scope of the debate; Walter, on the opposite tack, suggested that he might have a *political* motive for not wanting to execute rebels and overlooked the fact that both Robespierre and Duport argued the case for abolition on general grounds, and argued it very well indeed, although without convincing the Assembly. Robespierre's opinion scandalised the abbé Maury and was mildly criticised by Marat. Of course everyone points to the paradox of Robespierre the abolitionist becoming Robespierre the terrorist, but there's really nothing strange about it. In 1791 he was drawing up the laws of civil society, which he always insisted were to embody all the eighteenth-century ideals of humanity. In 1794 he was fighting a civil war which he thought was the only way to bring this civil society into being. Whether he was right or wrong, there's no contradiction between what he thought appropriate then and his earlier attitude, when he said it was better to acquit a hundred guilty men than to punish one innocent, or insisted that while legal proof was necessary for any verdict of guilty, it wasn't sufficient and it should be disregarded if the jury had a moral conviction of a man's innocence.

Like many other deputies, he spoke with two voices on the question of the relationship between regenerated France and royalist Europe, which was to become of critical importance in 1792. He took a pacific foreign policy for granted and was quick to suspect the Government of wanting war for its own purposes. On the other hand, when it was a matter of incorporating Avignon into France, he snapped his fingers at the Pope and said that the Powers would only make such action by France a *casus belli* if they were already resolved on war. Always afraid of military rule, he looked forward to a time when the National Guard could take over the duties of the regular army. This splendid example would induce neighbouring peoples to revolt against their own armies and the taxation necessary for their upkeep.[35] He could be as unrealistic as anyone on some subjects and quite hard-headed on others.

What you've told us so far, said the reverend, suggests that his views were no more extreme than those of plenty of other people. Where did he stand politically and why should he have acquired a special reputation?

He never built up much support in the Assembly itself. He, Buzot and Pétion were the best-known members of a little radical group – what Mirabeau called the 'thirty voices'. There was never any party discipline in any of the revolutionary assemblies, although a kind of party line sometimes emerged when the Jacobins debated issues before they were discussed in the Assembly. One result of this was that speeches actually affected the way people voted. The radicals couldn't carry the Assembly on basic issues such as the franchise but they could sometimes modify policies in detail. All the same, Desmoulins was not far off the mark when he wrote about Robespierre in February 1791, 'I doubt if a single law that he has proposed has ever been carried.'[36] He was never elected to any of the committees that drafted the legislation by which the whole of French society was transformed. Deprived of a share of collective responsibility of this kind, he remained something of a *franc-tireur*. The Assembly changed its president – or Speaker – and secretaries every fortnight. Robespierre was once elected secre-

35. *Oeuvres*, vol. VI, pp. 632-3.　　36. Jacob, pp. 59-60.

tary but when he stood for president in June 1791 he was narrowly defeated by a virtually unknown colleague.

He was much more successful outside the Assembly. He was already being singled out by the press in the summer of 1789. Desmoulins doesn't seem to have paid any attention to him in his newspaper until the end of the year but he made up for lost time afterwards, praising him extravagantly and making as much as he could out of the fact that he and Robespierre had been at school together. *Mon cher Robespierre* was the great hero of the *Révolutions de France et de Brabant*. Robespierre, in turn, supplied Desmoulins with copies of his speeches and acted as a witness at his wedding in December 1790. If we can accept the evidence of Desmoulins' mother-in-law in 1794, that Robespierre was at one time considered a possible husband for her second daughter, this must imply that both politicians were *habitués* of the Duplessis household.[37] However close their relationship, Robespierre probably saw himself as the legislator and Desmoulins – despite his personal liking for the man they all called 'Camille' – as no more than a clever journalist.

The case of Marat was very different. There was virtually no personal contact between the two and Marat wrote in 1792 that Robespierre's first words to him had been to criticise his blood-thirstiness.[38] Robespierre never seems to have had any personal sympathy for the older man but this did not deter Marat from commending him as one of the few uncorrupted revolutionaries. Since the *Ami du Peuple* was a very influential paper and Marat was savagely critical of almost everyone else, to be saluted in his pages as 'the worthy Robespierre', 'the only deputy who seems to understand basic principles and perhaps the only true *patriote* sitting in the senate', was a passport to the favour of those who were coming to be known as sans-culottes.

We know very little about the early days of the Jacobin Club, which was to become Robespierre's main political fortress. He had been a member from the beginning and he was probably more at home in its smaller debating hall, where one did not have to shout, than in the Assembly. Originally confined to deputies, its membership was thrown open to the public before the end of 1789 but the

37. H. Fleischmann, *Robespierre et les femmes*, p. 104.
38. Jacob, p. 105.

high subscription confined it to those who were relatively wealthy.[39] In this congenial world Robespierre soon made his mark. He was elected president in March 1790 and in a stormy debate at the end of the year, when Mirabeau challenged him it was Robespierre who won the support of the great majority of the members.[40] Since the Jacobins maintained an intense correspondence with the many affiliated clubs in the provinces, Robespierre's leading rôle in the Paris club made him a national figure. In the Assembly he was something of an outsider but to the activists all over the country he must have seemed to be one of the leaders of the revolution.

He cultivated his provincial contacts very carefully.[41] The few fragments of his correspondence that have survived provide plenty of evidence for this. When the Assembly left Versailles for Paris, Robespierre kept in touch with the Versailles Jacobins and in the autumn of 1790 he was elected president of a new court in Versailles, although he later resigned the office when chosen as public prosecutor in the Paris criminal court. His defence of the municipality of Toulon at the end of 1789 was the beginning of an association that led to his being made an honorary citizen in 1791. He made contact with the Jacobin Club at Marseilles and after the death of Mirabeau in April 1791 the town council invited him to act as its spokesman in the Assembly. He also cultivated the Jacobin Club at Lille and he may have had many more connections with the provinces for which the evidence has not survived. He kept the provincial clubs supplied with copies of his publications and the Marseilles Jacobins were so impressed by his speech on the National Guard that they petitioned the Assembly in support of his conclusions and invited other clubs to do the same. This set off Versailles, which began circulating the speech in its turn. Besançon was so enthusiastic about the copy it received from Versailles that it ordered its reprinting. Clubs unable to obtain a copy wrote directly to Robespierre. By the spring of 1791 he was one of the best-known politicians in France. If his popularity in Paris was greatest amongst the sans-culottes and the passive citizens, his provincial supporters were probably wealthier and better educated.

39. See Thompson, pp. 114-17; Walter, pp. 130-4.
40. See Desmoulins' account in *Oeuvres*, vol. VI, pp. 613-14.
41. Walter, pp. 143-51.

His election as public prosecutor suggests that, in Paris too, he was not short of supporters amongst those with political influence. All this was achieved by constitutional means and Robespierre, unlike Danton and his rowdy following in the Cordelier Club, never had to resort to insurrectionary tactics to assert his importance.

You said there were no organised parties in the Assembly, said Ted, but there must have been groups of some sort with recognised leaders.

I've already mentioned Mirabeau, who had a personal brains trust but no proper parliamentary following, Lafayette, who was influential in army circles and amongst the liberal nobility, and the Triumvirate – Duport, Barnave and Lameth – who normally commanded a good deal of support in the Assembly. Lafayette was not much of a politician and although he retained the loyalty of many of the National Guards, he gradually lost support since he was the man responsible for the suppression of popular agitation. Mirabeau had taken a leading part in overthrowing royal absolutism in 1789 but he thought the revolution had gone too far in the opposite direction. Whether from conviction or for money, he made a secret agreement with the Court and was playing a double game, making extremist speeches on minor issues to preserve his popularity, while trying to strengthen the power of the Crown as far as he could and to build up a political machine that would win a majority for the royalists at the next elections. His equivocal behaviour aroused the suspicions of many revolutionaries, but Robespierre, although he frequently opposed his policies, seems to have believed in his sincerity until Mirabeau's death in April 1791. He joined in his funeral procession and delivered a kind of eulogy of him in the Assembly.

The death of Mirabeau encouraged the Triumvirs to try to contact the Court themselves.[42] There was nothing discreditable about this but it was a bad tactical mistake. Since the king refused to accept the revolution, no agreement was possible. The universal suspicion of the Court meant that the Triumvirs had to act secretly, which put them at the mercy of the king who could betray them at any time that suited him. In pursuit of their unattainable compromise they reversed their policies in the Assembly and retreated

42. A. Michon, *L'histoire du parti feuillant: Adrien Duport*, Paris, 1924, *passim*.

73

from the principles that they themselves had proclaimed in 1789. Although they managed to retain a good deal of parliamentary support they soon lost their popularity outside the Assembly. The British Embassy reported to the Foreign Office in April 1791, 'As for Barnave and the Lameths their consequence, as a party, is so much destroyed that they are wavering whether they should give themselves to the Republicans or the friends of a limited monarchy. The present constitution has no friends and cannot last.'[43] This defection of the former leaders of the Left made Robespierre and the small band of radicals the champions, not merely of the sans-culottes but of all those who had not abandoned their former convictions in the pursuit of social and political stability. The radicals picked up some support from the extreme Right, which shared their fear of a compromise between the king and the majority, and Robespierre won more parliamentary victories with their support than he had ever done against their opposition.

Ever since 1789 he had been more afraid of the false friends of the revolution than of its open enemies, for whose emotional identification with the ancien régime he showed some understanding. The new political situation seemed to justify his previous mistrust besides encouraging the alarmism to which his pessimism always inclined him. As early as February he was warning the Assembly against those who were trying to create a new privileged hierarchy. It was probably his fear of the Triumvirs that led him to propose on 7 April that no deputy should become a Minister or accept any other royal office for four years after the dissolution of the Assembly. The fact that this was voted shows that it was welcomed by the Right. In May he obtained a self-denying ordinance by which the deputies swore that they themselves would not be eligible for any future assembly.

Wasn't that going a bit far, asked Ted.

It certainly suggests that he was personally disinterested himself, put in Mac.

But it looks to me like the action of a man obsessed by personalities. After all, these were the only people in France with any political experience. If the only way in which he could prevent his rivals from dominating the next assembly was to deny the

43. *The Despatches of Earl Gower*, ed. O. Browning, Cambridge, 1885, pp. 79-80.

sovereign people the right to vote for them, he had an odd idea of democracy and a pretty pessimistic view of the extent of support for his own principles. If he feared a counter-revolution as much as he said he did, he was taking a dangerous gamble. His new friends on the Right must have been delighted.

They certainly approved and the Assembly ordered both his speeches on the subject to be printed. The *Révolutions de Paris,* which was a paper of the Left, called his motion 'absurd'. It was welcomed by the extremists on both sides, by Marat and Desmoulins and by the *Ami du Roi* which suddenly discovered unsuspected talent in Robespierre. 'His consistency and courage on an occasion like this give grounds for thinking that he is more concerned with principle than with self-interest; if he is a demagogue it is in good faith and all he needs is more intelligence and better judgment to be an excellent citizen and even a good legislator.'[44]

I wonder if it *was* a tactical move, said Henry rather doubtfully. After all he was an odd sort of man and this kind of theatrical gesture of disinterestedness, in the best classical tradition, might have appealed to him for its own sake.

One can't be sure. Of course he didn't mention any names when he denounced ambitious politicians. The press certainly thought that it was a tactical move and even if he didn't mean it that way he ought to have realised that it was bound to weaken the centre and strengthen the extremes. My own guess is that he meant what he said when he called the Triumvirs traitors – that he thought they really would sell out to the Court on any terms at all. But that's only a guess and I'm here to tell you what happened, not to speculate.

It's just as well we're here then, said Ted, or we'd end up with an almanach. He was risking the future of the revolution, either for a certificate of personal good conduct, or so that he could dish his rivals. I'd call that irresponsible.

Trust a civil servant to think that everything will go to pot if it's not left to the experts, said Mac rather rudely. We'll have to wait for the next assembly before we can make our minds up, but it looks to me as though he took the only chance of saving what they had all been fighting for in 1789.

44. *Oeuvres,* vol. vii, p. 419. For a good account of this important debate see Walter, pp. 102-10.

The completion of the constitution and the king's continuing resistance to it gave everyone the impression that some sort of a crisis was building up. On 10 June it was proposed to withdraw troops from all French towns and make their officers swear allegiance to the nation and the law as well as the king. Robespierre, in the most violent language, denounced that as inadequate. All his hatred of noble officers came out in a tirade against the *'incivisme* and the injustice, the persecutions, calumnies and intrigues of the officers'. Anyone who failed to see the need to renew the entire officer corps was a fool and anyone who saw the need but didn't campaign for it, a traitor. 'The State and liberty must be saved; if they are not saved by the deputies they will have to be saved by the nation.'[45] This threat of insurrection had won the approval of the Jacobins two days earlier, when they had ordered it to be printed, but it drew no support at all in the Assembly.[46] Robespierre had possibly been ill a week or two before and a letter of 12 June gave hints of nervous exhaustion. It may have been his own state of health as much as the crisis that produced this untypical outburst.

If Robespierre did believe that the country was moving towards a new revolutionary situation, his suspicions were confirmed on 21 June by the news that the royal family had escaped from Paris. If the king succeeded in reaching Bouillé's army on the frontier the result would probably be civil war. Marie Antoinette had no intention of accepting any compromise with renegade nobles like Lafayette and the Lameths. The Triumvirate, however, kept the door open by getting the Assembly to vote that the king had been 'abducted'. This at once raised the natural, if unjustified suspicion that they were involved in his flight.

A rather odd incident that day will help us to feel the atmosphere of tension and intrigue in which the politicians had to move. A woman called Deflandre passed on to the revolutionary journalist, Fréron, a letter that she claimed to have received through the intermediary of Madame de Rochechouart, one of the queen's friends, implicating Lafayette and the mayor of Paris, Bailly, in the flight. Fréron printed the letter in his *Orateur du Peuple* and took the woman to his Section. Desmoulins then persuaded the Section to send a deputation to invite Robespierre to denounce the two men in the Assembly. According to Desmoulins, Robespierre

45. *Oeuvres*, vol. VII, pp. 468-77.
46. See the letter from Pio to Desmoulins in Jacob, pp. 60-1.

and Buzot were preparing to do so when Pétion arrived and convinced them – although not Desmoulins – that the letter was a forgery.[47] The fact that Madame de Rochechouart was involved is enough to suggest that this was indeed a royalist intrigue.[48] Three weeks later the search of Fréron's flat revealed a document proposing that Robespierre should be made dictator. His enemies were to make a good deal of capital, in 1792, out of this charge that he aspired to dictatorship, for which there never seems to have been any serious evidence.

On the night of 21 June Robespierre told the Jacobins that what worried him was not the flight itself or the threat of foreign invasion, which he brushed off – 'if all Europe combines against us Europe will be defeated' – but the apparent unity of crypto-royalists and self-styled revolutionaries: 'The national assembly is betraying the interests of the nation.' After urging the Jacobins to refuse to fraternise with a deputation of Ministers, representatives of the local authorities and constitutional monarchists, which was on its way to the club – advice which they disregarded – he wound up with a testimonial to his own clear-sighted self-abnegation and, paraphrasing Rousseau's motto, *vitam impendere vero,* claimed to have sacrificed his life to truth and the nation.[49]

Ted thought this wasn't giving much of a lead.

True, said Henry, but it's difficult to know what he could have suggested. If he was right about Lafayette and the Triumvirate being in concert with the king, there wasn't much that he or the Jacobins could do about it.

Except intoxicate himself with the glories of martyrdom. It's this eternal 'I' that gets on my nerves. After all, he wasn't the only honest revolutionary, even by his own standards, but he didn't seem to care about anyone else provided he got his bespoke halo.

The arrest of the king, a few miles short of Bouillé's army, transformed the whole situation. The Triumvirate could now hope that the collapse of his prestige would put him in their pocket. Three deputies were sent to escort the royal family back to Paris and while Pétion showed off his revolutionary principles before the king's sister, Barnave took advantage of the opportunity to make

---

47. Hamel, vol. I, pp. 483-4; Walter, p. 175.
48. See below, p. 205.
49. *Oeuvres,* vol. VII, pp. 518-23.

contact with Marie Antoinette. The policy of the Triumvirs was henceforth to play down the whole business, get the king suspended until they could revise the constitution to make it acceptable to him and then restore him as their agent. They could reasonably count on a majority in the Assembly but they ran up against a new insurrectionary movement of the Parisian sansculottes, organised by the Cordeliers and other popular clubs.

This seems to have been a genuine popular movement but there may have been an attempt to manipulate it so as to replace Louis XVI by the duc d'Orléans. Although the immediate issue was constitutional, opinion tended to divide along social lines. As the sans-culottes began to assert themselves, the leaders of the Assembly, Lafayette and Bailly, sounded the alarm, stressed the danger of social subversion and prepared for violent repressive measures.

As the tension mounted Robespierre appeared infrequently and said very little. Matters finally came to a head when the Assembly began debating the king's fate on 13 July. On the following day he put forward his own proposals: the restoration of the king would either leave him with sufficient power to destroy the revolutionary settlement or hand him over to the tutelage of 'a handful of factious men who would serve him, betray him, flatter him and intimidate him in turn, in order to reign in his name'. He exposed the hypocrisy of exonerating the king while trying those responsible for his 'abduction' and proposed that the king's fate should be submitted to a referendum, while elections to the next assembly should be carried through as quickly as possible.

In other words, said Ted, he was still obsessed with the idea that the main danger came from the Triumvirs. A referendum would certainly take the decision out of their hands but it would set the whole country by the ears and as likely as not produce a genuinely royalist majority.

It wasn't really an answer to the dilemma he exposed in his speech, agreed Henry, but perhaps there wasn't any answer. I don't suppose he could have got a majority for a republic in the Assembly; it might have led to a civil war and, in any case, it wouldn't have solved the problem of who was actually going to govern.

He certainly dissociated himself from the insurrectionary republican movement that was building up in the streets. There is, admittedly, a printed version of a speech attributed to him which argued that Louis XVI deserved a death sentence and could not be restored – but it's probably a forgery.[50] His attitude seems to have been that the Triumvirate and their allies wanted trouble in order to suppress it by force, that they had the power to do so and that the best the Jacobins could hope was to protect themselves by remaining strictly within the law.

On 15 July the Cordeliers organised a petition against the restoration of the king.[51] When a deputation from the petitioners asked some of the radical deputies to present this to the Assembly, Robespierre, Pétion, Grégoire and Prieur told them that it was too late since a vote had already been taken. The deputies then changed their minds about the constitutional propriety of a petition, but Robespierre still opposed the idea – unsuccessfully – in the Jacobins that evening. Clubs were, in any case, not allowed to organise collective petitions, and when the Jacobin petition was read out on the 16th the majority of the members, including all but half a dozen of the deputies, walked out and set up a rival club at the Feuillants. During the night, when they heard that the Assembly had now taken its final vote, the Jacobins stopped the printing of their petition. On the following day members of the Cordeliers and other clubs organised yet another petition, on the Champ de Mars. It was while a Sunday afternoon crowd, including many women and children, were attending the signing of this petition, that the municipality profited from an incident earlier in the day when two men had been murdered, to proclaim martial law. National Guards advanced on the crowd, shooting and sabring as they went, and a good many people were killed and wounded.

The 'massacre' was the signal for a period of quite severe repression. Martial law remained in force for weeks, Marat, Fréron and Desmoulins had to abandon their papers, others implicated in the petitioning went into hiding and Danton left Paris. For once Robespierre had some reason to believe that his life was in danger. On the night of the 'massacre' he told the Jacobins that it was the fault of those who 'want to perpetuate themselves; they

---

50. *Oeuvres*, vol. VII, pp. 571-5.
51. For these very complicated moves see A. Mathiez, *Le Club des Cordeliers pendant le crise de Varennes et le massacre du Champ de Mars*, Paris, 1910 and F. Braesch, 'Les pétitions du Champ de Mars', *Revue Historique*, vols. CXLII, pp. 192-205, CXLIII, pp. 1-37 and 181-9, and CXLIV, p. 88.

want to reign; for the past two years you have seen these men sacrificing everything to their own ambition . . . As for me, I can't appear in the Assembly. They attribute to me all the atrocities that are committed or invented. Only a moment ago in the Champs-Elysées they published over my name a seditious speech of which I never spoke a word.' The Jacobins formally voted their loyalty to the constitution and submission to the Assembly. That night, instead of making his dangerous way to his distant lodgings in the *Marais*, Robespierre accepted the hospitality of an admirer, Duplay, who lived near the club.

It's odd, said Henry, that when there really was some danger he didn't talk about martyrdom.

Though he didn't forget to bring everything round to himself, added Ted.

It seems to me that he came out of this very well, said Mac. He saw that there just wasn't a revolutionary situation. He kept his nerve and he kept the Jacobins within the law. As an unexpected bonus he got rid of the more conservative members of the club.

I'm glad to know Mac's such a stickler for legality. I always suspected it.

You're just being clever. It was the Paris authorities, with their calculated showdown and the blood on their hands, who had appealed to force. If Robespierre thought they had forfeited any moral right to obedience can you disagree with him? But since Lafayette's bully-boys were bound to win, all he could do was to preserve a base for taking up the fight again later on.

You could be right, Mac, but perhaps your Maximilien was a man of resolutions rather than of resolution.

The walk-out from the Jacobins didn't look like a bonus at the time, I said. It nearly wrecked the club, especially when the Feuillants began winning over some of the provincial societies. Some of the faithful thought that the game was up and suggested merging with the Feuillants. Robespierre got that defeated. He held the club together, gradually built it up again and won over most of the provincial clubs. That's where his national reputation must have made all the difference.

The Assembly and the Paris authorities were now openly at odds with a good deal of revolutionary opinion. The Feuillants, in their eagerness to make the constitution acceptable to the king, went further than some of the deputies would have liked, but the majority of the Assembly were in favour of their policy of compromise. Robespierre took a leading part in opposing the Feuillants' attempt to revise the constitution in a royalist sense. He scored impressive debating victories over Barnave and Duport who were obliged, for tactical reasons that they could not admit in public, to speak against their own personal convictions. Nevertheless Robespierre was defeated on almost every vote: on the franchise, on courts martial in the army and on legislation concerning the colonies, where the Assembly, reversing a decision it had taken as recently as May, gave the racialist colonial assemblies what amounted to a veto on the application of French laws. One can see why Robespierre thought there was nothing legitimate about decisions which undid some of the work of the previous two years and were contrary to the inner convictions of most of the deputies. His problem was that what was written into the constitution could not be reversed by the next assembly. But whatever his reservations, he stuck to parliamentary tactics, accepted the constitution with all its imperfections and put his trust in the elections. When the session ended on 30 September the waiting crowd gave an ovation to him and Pétion as they came out arm in arm.

Shortly before this he had defined his position in an *Adresse au peuple français*.[52] In this pamphlet he asserted that the powers of the deputies were circumscribed by the imprescriptible rights of the people. They could only write into the constitution 'what is constitutional by the very nature of things and not what some people find it convenient to think so'. 'The [doctrine of the] absolute independence of the people's representatives is monstrous in both theory and practice.'

Here we go again; what I don't like isn't legal.

You can't over-simplify like that, said Mac. He was assuming a general consensus about certain principles and merely saying that the Assembly had no right to violate the principles it had been elected to implement.

It had been elected to do nothing of the kind. In point of fact it had been summoned to offer advice to Louis, by the Grace of God King of France and of Navarre.

I don't see any point in our getting bogged down again in an argument about abstractions which merely makes us all feel self-

52. British Museum F 849(1) and 856(1).

righteous, said Henry. In practical terms, Robespierre doesn't seem to have been saying more than that he reserved the right to work by constitutional means for the amendment of what didn't seem to him to be in the public interest. J.S. hasn't produced any evidence to suggest that he contemplated coercing the Assembly from outside. Just the opposite: he dissociated the Jacobins from anything of the kind. The fact that he was popular with people who did advocate that sort of thing – and that he didn't repudiate them – may have alarmed some people, but that's rather different. He does seem to have thought that he was the only man who knew what the right principles were, but I don't suppose he was alone in that.

It might help, I said, if we looked at what contemporaries thought. A German who was a member of the Jacobin Club and met Robespierre socially said that he 'sees only one side of the question he is treating and thinks himself the elect of heaven. He despises everything else. He behaves more like the leader of a religious sect than of a political party . . . He can be eloquent but most of the time he is boring, especially when he goes on too long, which is often the case.' Oelsner then criticised Robespierre's moralising, his passion for martyrdom and his belief that he alone stood for *vertu* and justice. He thought that he had the strength of will of a great man but that he lacked courage, political sense and knowledge of the world. In company he was contemptuous of others and Oelsner was surprised that Pétion, 'who is far superior to him, lets Robespierre speak to him so arrogantly'. 'I know no one so insufferable, so arrogant, so taciturn and so boring.' Very shrewdly, he said that Robespierre's sense of his own superiority prevented his seeing through flatterers. 'He will find it difficult to dominate the élite and if he carries his bloodthirsty projects through to the end he will finish in a bloody catastrophe.'[53]

Pétion may have been patient at the time but after he and Robespierre had quarrelled he described his former friend in much the same terms as Oelsner.[54] 'Robespierre is extremely touchy and suspicious; he sees plots, treason and precipices everywhere . . . Imperious in his opinions, listening only to himself, intolerant of opposition, never pardoning those who have wounded his amour-

---

53. Jacob, pp. 78-81.
54. *Discours de Jérôme Pétion sur l'accusation intentée contre Maximilien Robespierre*, Bib. Nat. Lb[41] 162.

propre, never admitting his own mistakes, denouncing irrespons-
ibly and taking offence at the slightest suspicion, always thinking
that people were concerned about him and were persecuting him,
boasting of his services and speaking of himself without restraint,
disregarding conventions in such a way as to harm the causes he
was defending, seeking the favour of the people above everything
else, courting the people and going out of his way to win its
applause . . .'

A pamphlet in the name of Merlin de Thionville, a fellow-
deputy, written after Robespierre's fall and violently hostile to him,
claimed that he was overshadowed by the superior talent of his
colleagues before 1791. 'The revolutionaries of the Constituent
Assembly dishonoured themselves, he recovered and thought that
he was responsible for their overthrow . . . He would never have
won the attention of the Assembly if he had not won that of the
public galleries and he would not have obtained that if he had not
posed as a prophet when the revisers of the constitution had justified his previous declamations.' 'It was events outside Robespierre's own schemes that explain the extraordinary fortune of this
very ordinary man.'[55] A manuscript biography which was perhaps
the first draft of this pamphlet makes a point that Ted suggested
some time ago: 'How many "traitors" did he create by accusing
blameless citizens of treason?'[56]

Dubois-Crancé, another colleague, published his impressions of
the leading members of the Constituent Assembly in 1792 and his
treatment of Robespierre was a good deal more sympathetic.[57]
Although conceding his pride and jealousy, Dubois-Crancé said
that he was 'always steadfast in the austerity of his principles; he
never deviated. He was the same at the end as he had been in the
beginning, which is a tribute one can pay to very few of his
colleagues . . . The *patriotes* themselves respected him but did not
like him . . . After the death of Mirabeau, the defection of the
patriote party, the treason of the Lameths, Robespierre showed
great strength of character and in spite of the extreme unpopularity
of his opinions he forced the respect of his enemies.' He went on

---

55. *Merlin de Thionville, représentant du peuple, à ses collègues*, Arch. Nat.
29 AP 78. Although bearing Merlin's name this pamphlet was perhaps written by
Roederer.
56. *Qu'était-ce donc que Robespierre?*, Arch. Nat. 29 AP 78.
57. Jacob, pp. 82-4.

to say that Robespierre's popularity with the public and the press made him disliked in the Assembly where his insistence on taking the limelight resulted in the defeat of motions that might otherwise have been carried. 'If the Assembly had been composed entirely of Robespierres, France would today be no more than a pile of ruins. But amongst so much intrigue, baseness, vice and corruption, in the battle of opposing interests and opinions, amongst the tumult, the calumny, the fear and assassination, Robespierre was a rock and an impregnable rock.'

Thinking about all these comments we have obviously got to disregard a certain amount of political bias, said Henry, but they do seem to agree that he owed his special position to the fact that he stuck to his principles when other people changed theirs; in other words, it was a triumph of character rather than ability.

I don't see anything particularly admirable in sticking to principles when circumstances change and all that they can produce is civil war. He certainly seems to have been pretty insufferable in private life.

We're not considering him as a possible Sunday School teacher, said Mac. You can't lead a revolution by just being a nice chap. What he wanted was what the rest said they wanted too. He meant it and they didn't – not when they found they could use the revolution to their own advantage. All right, he was too unpopular in the Assembly to be subjected to the same temptation, but that doesn't mean he would have succumbed to it. He wasn't just out for popularity and some of the things he said went down badly with his own side. What's perhaps more interesting is that contemporaries should have spotted that he didn't matter all that much. It was the conservative swing in the majority that split the revolutionaries and forced the sans-culottes to go it alone. They needed a spokesman and that's why Robespierre became important. That's what I've been saying from the beginning: we ought to be looking at the social conflicts if we're to understand why individuals mattered.

It depends what you think politics are about, said Ted. Leaders are supposed to provide leadership and what Robespierre wanted just wasn't on. He couldn't see beyond his precious principles. I still think they would have produced nothing but a civil war that wouldn't have done anyone any good.

You can't say that when he didn't suggest appealing to force.

He left that to the other side. In fact, what you're really saying is that a revolutionary regime mustn't carry out its programme if the opposition threatens to revolt.

I suppose, said the reverend slowly, that it's a matter of assessing possibilities. It may be heroic to defend lost causes but it may simply mean sacrificing others to one's own incorruptibility. On the other hand, who decides when they *are* lost? I'm inclined to agree with Mac that those who give up too soon are simply allowing the unscrupulous to prevent change. But are we assessing the political pros and cons or investigating Robespierre's actual motives? Perhaps he was actually heaven-bent on martyrdom for a cause that, at heart, he thought too good to succeed. Is there any room for political saints and who decides which ones are really devils?

You seem to be coming up with more questions than answers, I said, so perhaps we'd better wait and see what happened next.

IV The Defender of the Constitution

Before we look at Robespierre's career during the Legislative Assembly, I said, I'd like to go back for a moment to August 1791. You remember my telling you that on the night of the Champ de Mars business he was sheltered by Duplay, a keen Jacobin who lived near the Assembly and the Jacobin club. Sometime during the next month he accepted Duplay's invitation to move in permanently. Apart from a short spell with Charlotte when she came to Paris in the autumn of 1793, this was where he lived for the rest of his life.

In the words of La Réveillière-Lépeaux, a colleague of Robespierre's in the Constituent Assembly and the Convention, 'A rich cabinet-maker called Duplay, his wife, three or four daughters and his son of 15 or 16, all good people at heart, but narrow extremists, had become passionately involved in the revolution.'[1] Duplay, who had accommodation to spare, collected revolutionary politicians. At one time or another, Dom Gerle of the Constituent Assembly, Anthoine, the three Robespierres and Couthon lodged at his house. His nephew Simon, who lost a leg in the first serious battle of the revolution, at Valmy, was another resident. Duplay's daughter, Elisabeth, married Le Bas, a deputy of the Convention and member of the Committee of General Security. Duplay himself became a juror on the revolutionary tribunal during the Terror. Politically speaking, Robespierre must have found them impeccable.

Socially too, they represented the kind of values he found most congenial. Duplay had built up a prosperous business by his own efforts and at the time Robespierre came to live with him he owned three houses and had a useful income of 1,500 livres a year from investments. He found it impossible to get tenants for his houses in 1793 and when his debtors paid him off in depreciated paper currency he is said to have sold his own houses to pay off his own debts at their real value.[2] If the story is true it offers an excellent illustration of precisely what Robespierre meant by *vertu*. There

1. Jacob, p. 119.
2. Stéfan-Pol, *Autour de Robespierre: le Conventionnel Le Bas*, Paris, n.d. pp. 67-9.

may well have been a Rousseauesque honesty and simplicity about Duplay. Looking out of his study window over the cabinet-maker's yard, Robespierre perhaps saw himself as a kind of honorary sans-culotte. If he did, he would have been playing at sans-culotterie in the same way that Marie Antoinette had played at dairying, for there was all the difference in the world between the bourgeois comfort of the Duplays and the daily preoccupation with rationing and the cost of living of the Parisian poor during the Terror. The Duplays, like the heroine of Rousseau's *Nouvelle Héloïse,* believed in maintaining social distinctions. Elisabeth wrote indignantly to Lamartine that 'workmen who frequented the Jacobins were never admitted in the evenings into the intimate family circle. Democrat though he (Duplay) was, he always knew how to maintain the distinction which separates the head of the family from his servants. He loved the people but without flattering them. In his home he entertained only friends and relations.'[3] Even if the workmen were excluded, there was still a big difference between the Duplay's family circle, where in 1793–4 Buonarotti played the piano, Le Bas sang and Robespierre recited Racine or Corneille, and the revolutionary salons of Madame de Stael or Madame Roland.[4] Robespierre was leading the kind of life that sans-culottes might dream of, even if few of them could attain it, while his opponents, however similar their political views may have been, had not broken away from the social habits of the ancien régime.

Robespierre's position in this family must have been rather a curious one. At 53, Maurice Duplay was almost old enough to have been his father and Maximilien may have felt that, for the first time in his life, he belonged to a real family. Elisabeth claimed that he became engaged to her elder sister, Eléonore, though this was vigorously denied by Charlotte, a bitter enemy of both Madame Duplay and Eléonore.[5] At the same time he was something of a trophy and the pride of the whole family. La Réveillière-Lépeaux – not a particularly hostile witness – said that when he visited the Duplays at the time of the Legislative Assembly, after Robespierre *s'était impatronisé* in their house, the whole place had been transformed. 'Robespierre was worshipped there. The small study

3. Stéfan-Pol, pp. 58-9.   4.   Stéfan-Pol, p. 97.
5. Stéfan-Pol, p. 150; H. Fleischmann, *Mémoires de Charlotte Robespierre,* p. 229.

in particular was given over to his cult. His bust was enshrined there, with various ornaments, verses, emblems, etc. Even the drawing-room was adorned with small terra-cotta busts in red and grey and lined with portraits of the great man in pencil, in charcoal, sepia and water-colour. He himself, in a well-groomed and powdered wig and an immaculate dressing-gown, was stretched out in a big armchair in front of a table loaded with the finest fruit, fresh butter, milk and steaming coffee. The whole family, father, mother and children, tried to anticipate his every desire and fulfil it in a second.'[6] Fréron, in the vicious character-study written soon after Robespierre's death, said that he always had in front of him a pyramid of oranges which the Duplays dared not touch.[7] Charlotte admitted that the Duplays looked after him very well and she apparently complained in 1794 that they used their political influence to get him white bread and other scarce commodities.[8] She said that he was 'excessively appreciative of that sort of thing' and claimed that she and her aunts had provided similar attentions at Arras.[9] He probably found the Duplay household rather more lively.

Elisabeth Duplay left an account of his life in her family home, written long after the revolution. This has to be taken with caution, partly because she herself was so warm and ingenuous – even Charlotte liked her – and partly because of her proud loyalty to a husband who died with Robespierre. Even allowing for this, her leitmotif, *il était si bon,* carries conviction. She said that 'he defended us whenever our mother scolded us . . . When I had any worries I told him everything. He was never a severe judge; he was a friend, a friend who was good; he was so *vertueux.* He held my father and mother in veneration. We all loved him very dearly.'[10] She also said that he often reproached her with not having a strong enough faith in the existence of a Supreme Being and told her that this was man's only consolation on earth.[11]

What you've just been telling us, said Ted, is partly a matter of subjective impressions, with everyone running true to form. But

6. Jacob, p. 120.
7. *Papiers inédits trouvés chez Robespierre etc.,* vol. I, p. 157.
8. Despatys, *La Révolution, la Terreur et le Directoire, 1791-9, d'après les Mémoires de Gaillard,* Paris, 1909, p. 266.
9. H. Fleischmann, *Mémoires de Charlotte Robespierre,* p. 225.
10. Stéfan-Pol, p. 104.   11. Stéfan-Pol, p. 150.

there's also the question of fact: was the place a kind of Robespierre museum or was it not?

La Réveillière-Lépeaux is hardly likely to have invented that, though he may have exaggerated. Barbaroux, who was admittedly hostile to Robespierre, said much the same thing in his Memoirs.[12] I think we can assume that it was more or less true. One doesn't hear similar stories about anyone else.

It's rather revealing. One suspects that a lot of politicians feel like that, but they daren't do it because they're afraid of ridicule. The Duplays must have fed him plenty of flattery as well as oranges but it's odd that he didn't mind showing it off to anyone who called. Can you imagine the reactions of any of his political acquaintances who dropped in? He wasn't even a deputy at the time and he had never sat on a committee or exercised any real power. He must have been a queer sort of man to accept a cult that would shock his friends and provide ammunition for his enemies.

He was certainly an unusual man, agreed Henry, and I take Ted's point about his narcissism. At the same time I'm impressed by the way the Duplay evidence corroborates Charlotte's – I mean about his being so pleasant and easy to get on with at home.

So long as there weren't any rivals around, said Ted.

Perhaps. But he doesn't seem to have posed as the Great Man, aloof in his dignity.

Even Fréron, I said, admitted that Desmoulins could make him laugh till he cried, though he claimed that Robespierre's normal state was one of black melancholy.[13]

I've read about S.S. men who were model fathers, said Henry, but I'm not sure there's any parallel. It wasn't that he led one life in public and another at home. He seemed to combine both at the Duplays. I wonder if he needed to be always reassuring himself about being right in politics. That might explain why he was so touchy when anyone challenged him. We can't get away from the fact that, even when they sympathised with his policies, his political friends described him as a rather unpleasant man and his personal friends said just the opposite.

If I could take up Ted's point about his not liking rivals around, I said, his opponents maintained that the Duplays kept him to

12. *Mémoires de Barbaroux* (ed. Alfred-Chabaud), Paris, 1936, p. 144.
13. *Papiers inédits,* vol. I, p. 158.

themselves and their own circle. This is how Fréron put it: 'So long as he lived with Humbert he was accessible to his friends and to the *patriotes*. Once at the Duplays he was virtually invisible. They sequestered him from society, worshipped him, intoxicated him and destroyed him by inflating his pride.'[14] Taschereau, a former friend, trying to argue himself out of the gaol where Robespierre's fall had landed him, said that when he returned to Paris in the summer of 1793, after an absence of six months, Robespierre was a changed man surrounded by a voracious and bloodthirsty horde.[15]

How convenient for friend Taschereau, said Mac. Even if one believed it, it would suggest there had been nothing wrong with him in 1792 after he had had over a year of the Duplay treatment. And if we believe Fréron, it means that he must have been leading a perfectly normal social life until the summer of 1791, so you can't attribute his behaviour to his psychological make-up if it changed every time he changed his address. I don't think much of this sort of evidence.

We do know something about the people he met at the Duplays. Le Bas's son named them as the Lameths and Pétion in the early days (Robespierre had broken with the Lameths before he went to live with the Duplays so they would scarcely have been welcome); infrequently: Legendre, Merlin de Thionville and Fouché (all members of the Convention); frequently: Taschereau, Desmoulins, 'Piault' (probably Pio, a Jacobin); all the time: Le Bas, Saint-Just, David, Couthon and Buonarotti.[16]

That's second-hand information which he presumably got from his mother, said Henry. But she wasn't a bad source. Ted can scarcely call them a fan club and they were anything but nonentities.

There was a more specifically Duplay circle: his brother-in-law, Vaugeois, from Choisy-le-Roi, neighbours like the locksmith, Didier and the distiller, Gravier; another neighbour, Nicolas, and his lodger, Madame de Chalabre, a noblewoman living apart from her husband who adopted Robespierre early in 1792 and could possibly have been a royalist spy; Cietty, an Italian paper-maker and the

---

14. *Papiers inédits*, vol. I, p. 157.
15. *P. A. Taschereau-Fargues à Maximilien Robespierre aux Enfers*, Paris an III, p. 9n[1].
16. Stéfan-Pol, p. 84.

grocer, Lohier.[17] Most of them got jobs from the Government during the Terror and they did form a political clientèle that wouldn't argue with Robespierre. But that doesn't dispose of Henry's objection. Until the spring of 1794 at least, it does look as though he mixed with his political equals. After that everyone was getting so suspicious that most people kept to the company of those they thought they could trust. Some of the criticism of Robespierre probably came from the fact that men like Fréron, whom Robespierre suspected and didn't want to see, found it hard to get at him.

Leaving the Duplays for the time being, in October 1791 Robespierre went on a long visit to Artois.[18] He may have wanted to travel incognito, as Charlotte claimed, but Augustin told the Arras Jacobins all about his coming and tried to organise a public reception. On his way, he stopped at Bapaume, where he was given a noisy welcome by a battalion of Parisian National Guards who were passing through. Walter suggests that it was probably their presence which induced the local authorities to give him an official welcome. He got an enthusiastic reception in Arras and both Maximilien and Charlotte commented on the fact that even his opponents lit up their houses, 'a fact that I can only attribute to their respect for the will of the people'.[19]

Ted thought that was rather a tactful way of explaining that they didn't want their windows broken.

The town council, which had already refused him a civic reception on the ground that he was no longer a deputy, sent the police to have all the lamps extinguished as soon as Maximilien was in his home. Madame Marchand, of the *Affiches d'Artois,* complained that he should have prevented some of the officers of the Parisian National Guard who had moved on from Bapaume to Arras, from trying to bully her into changing the political bias of her paper.[20] There were obviously two schools of opinion in Arras.

Rather curiously, Maximilien didn't stay at his old home but took up his quarters at an inn. He was fêted by the Arras Jacobins. They included Guffroy, an old colleague from the bishop's court,

---

17. G. Lenotre, *Robespierre et la Mère de Dieu,* Paris, 1926, pp. 123-7.
18. For the best account see Walter, pp. 189-202. Thompson (p. 188) is mistaken in thinking that Pétion went with him.
19. Robespierre to Duplay; *Correspondance,* vol. I, p. 124.
20. Jacob, p. 93.

but it looks as though most of his old acquaintances, apart from the faithful Buissarts, had turned against him. He soon left Arras for the surrounding countryside. It is a pure guess that he went to stay with Le Bon, a priest who had written to congratulate him on his opposition to the compulsory celibacy of the clergy, and that the former friend, mentioned by Charlotte, who gave him an icy welcome, was Dubois de Fosseux. He spent a few days at Béthune and called at Lille before returning to Paris, getting an enthusiastic welcome from the Jacobins at both places. Although he was the hero of the revolutionary minority in this conservative region, there was not much to hold him in Arras and he can't have felt many regrets when he set off back for Paris.

While in the provinces he obviously kept in close touch with the political situation in Paris. In a private letter he accused the new Assembly of debating the religious problem in theoretical terms, instead of realising that any convert to the non-juring clergy who rejected the Revolutionary religious settlement was a recruit for the counter-revolution. When this letter was communicated to the press and published by Gorsas, Robespierre wrote to protest. He seems to have been particularly anxious not to irritate the new deputies by posing as an elder statesman. He wrote to Duplay, soon after his arrival in Arras, to say that he was hoping Pétion would be elected mayor of Paris.

Do you think he meant it? asked Ted.

Beyond any reasonable doubt. Although he might reasonably have hoped to be elected himself, he was delighted when Pétion easily defeated Lafayette. During the next six months he went out of his way to commend Pétion's qualities of heart and head, in the warmest possible language.[21] If you want to accuse him of anything, it would be that he allowed personal friendship to blind him to Pétion's weaknesses as a political leader.

Which is not the kind of charge people usually make, said Henry. I think this could be important. At least it means that when he breaks with former friends we shall have to look at the reasons very carefully and not just assume that he was jealous of other people's success.

His return to Paris on 28 November must have felt like a homecoming. After dining with Pétion – in spite of the mayor's luxuri-

21. *Oeuvres*, vol. VIII, pp. 69, 197, 224-7, 274.

ous quarters, Robespierre told Buissart *son âme est toujours simple et pure* – he went along to the Jacobins. Collot d'Herbois insisted that Robespierre replace him in the chair, to general applause. He wrote a cheerful letter to Buissart two days later: 'I think the present Assembly is full of resources; unlike everyone else, I find it much superior to the previous one.'[22] The political dog-fighting seemed to be going well: the Jacobins put him on a committee which was to draft an address warning the Assembly of the intrigues of the Paris *département,* which now included his old enemy, Beaumetz. The address was warmly praised by Brissot.[23]

What was he doing for money, asked Ted suddenly.

I don't know. I told you that he had been elected public prosecutor. That carried a handsome salary of 8,000 livres, but the court wasn't inaugurated until 15 February and I don't suppose he got any pay before then, although I may be wrong. Duplay was probably happy to put him up for nothing but the visit to Artois must have cost quite a lot and he was still, I imagine, looking after Augustin and Charlotte. Marat said that he had a private income of only 600 livres a year and that wouldn't go far.[24] He may have saved a good deal of his salary when he was a deputy. I can't think of any other source of income, but there's nothing to suggest that he was on anyone's secret payroll.

I wasn't making insinuations, said Ted placidly. I was only wondering.

When Robespierre returned to Paris he found important changes in the membership of both the Assembly and the Jacobin club. He himself had ensured that former deputies could not be re-elected. Some, like Pétion or Robespierre himself, had been elected to offices of various kinds and remained in Paris but many had gone back to their native provinces. Their places were taken by men who, for the most part, had built up a political reputation in the law courts or in local government; men like Vergniaud, Guadet and Gensonné from the Gironde, the Provençal Isnard or Couthon from Clermont-Ferrand, who seems to have been on good terms with Robespierre from the earliest days of the session.[25] These people might be described as the first professional politicians in

---

22. *Correspondance,* vol. I, pp. 130-1.
23. *Oeuvres,* vol. VIII, p. 29; Hamel, vol. II, p. 30.
24. Jacob, p. 102.
25. See Robespierre's letter of 16 October, *Correspondance,* vol. 1, p. 124.

French history. There was nothing discreditable about that. Augustin Robespierre was one of them, although an unsuccessful one, as he complained to his brother towards the end of the year. There were others – like the former Franciscan monk and womaniser, Chabot, who saw politics primarily as a means of making money. He was an extreme case; starting with virtually no resources of his own, he already had a bohemian outfit for the Jacobins and an elegant wardrobe for his social calls. Narbonne, who was War Minister in the spring of 1792, claimed that Chabot – who posed as a revolutionary extremist – was in his pay.[26] Chabot's motives may have been clear enough but those of others were more ambiguous. The ministerial practice of subsidising friendly journalists was something that all the revolutionaries decried when in opposition and practised when they got the chance. When Robespierre's Jacobin opponents were in office for a few months in the spring of 1792 the journalist, Robert, astonished them by asking for the Constantinople embassy, for which his main qualification seemed to be an attack on Robespierre in the *Révolutions de Paris*.[27] When he failed to get the embassy he switched to the other side.

The Jacobin club was invaded at this time by a good many people, some of them graduating from the less respectable Cordeliers, who saw the revolution as a means of compensating for past failures of various kinds. Many of them had come to Paris in their youth, looking for fame and fortune. Finding neither, they had been forced to earn a living as hack pamphleteers, writers of pornography – such as Louvet – or even as police informers, for which Brissot had offered his services.[28] During these years they became involved in relationships which survived into the revolution. Many of the Parisian journalists of 1792, such as Brissot, Desmoulins, Fréron, Carra, Gorsas, Robert and Louvet, came from this background. However respectable their present occupations and ambitions, some of them were open to political blackmail. When they quarrelled, their rivalry took on a particularly vicious character as they hinted at what they could reveal about each

26. De Bonald, *François Chabot*, Paris, 1908, p. 51; L. Jacob, *Fabre d'Eglantine, chef des fripons*, Paris, 1946, pp. 171, 173.

27. Mme Roland, *Mémoires*, ed. P. Faugère, Paris, 1864, vol. I, pp. 163-71.

28. R. Darnton, 'The High Enlightenment and the low life of literature in pre-revolutionary France', *Past and Present*, 1971; 'The Grub Street style of revolution: J-P. Brissot, police spy', *Journal of Modern History*, 1968.

other and occasionally, as they put it, 'lifted a corner of the veil'. Condorcet's *Chronique de Paris* said that Desmoulins was on sale to everyone but that no one was prepared to buy. Desmoulins replied with *J.-P. Brissot démasqué* and his claim that Brissot was a former police spy was joyfully taken up by the royalist press.[29] Even Marat, though he was in a different category, would have found it awkward to be reminded in print of the days when he had been in the service of the comte d'Artois, had worn a sword and tried to prove his noble ancestry.[30] The fact that he was the only radical journalist to attack Brissot at this time may not have been wholly unrelated to Brissot's having defrauded him of the royalties on the English edition of his *Chains of Slavery*.[31] Danton, who had been the leader of the Cordelier group, was said by the Minister, Molleville, to have been regularly bribed.[32] It was perhaps Danton's reputation that led Robespierre to dissuade the Jacobins from supporting his candidature for the Paris Commune when he had no inhibitions about campaigning for Anthoine and Buzot a few weeks later.[33]

When Robespierre returned to the Jacobins, political loyalties were beginning to polarise around the question of war. The close of the Constituent Assembly had seen a sharp increase in the number of *émigrés*. Robespierre himself had seen the inns full of them when he was in Artois. The *émigrés* planned to overthrow the revolution by a combination of invasion and civil war. They were in touch with dissident movements within France but thought that foreign support would be necessary for victory. They openly despised Louis XVI for his concessions to the revolution and they wanted to set up an aristocratic regime rather than to restore the power of the monarchy.

The king and queen were well aware of this and mistrusted the *émigrés*. Their Ministers were now mostly constitutional monarchists who were trying to make the constitution work. This implied peace, but Barnave, who was now the secret adviser of Marie Antoinette, hoped to enhance the prestige of the king by an ulti-

29. Hamel, vol. II, pp. 96-102.
30. G. Walter, *Marat*, Paris, 1933, pp. 50-1.
31. id., p. 154.
32. B. de Molleville, *Private memoirs relating to the last year of the reign of Louis XVI*, first edition (in English), London 1797, vol. II, pp. 162-3.
33. *Oeuvres*, vol. VIII, pp. 27, 70.

matum that would force the minor German princes in the Rhine-land to disperse the *émigrés* in their territory. A note to the Habs-burg Emperor, Leopold II, was to reassure him that France had no intention of invading Germany, and to enlist his co-operation.[34] The king and queen and their private advisers were pursuing a radically different policy and they were prepared to take any risks rather than accept the constitution. Rejecting the *émigrés*, they put all their trust in the Powers – Leopold was, after all, Marie Antoinette's brother – and in liberation by invading German armies. Leopold, however, was a cautious man, with enough troubles of his own. To Marie Antoinette's fury, he complied with the official request from the French Government rather than with the queen's covering note, urging him to make a *casus belli* of the business, and Austrian pressure led the German princes to comply with the French demands.

Not all the constitutional monarchists opposed war. Some of them, notably Narbonne, Dumouriez and Lafayette, saw it as a means of concentrating power in their own hands so that they could impose their terms on both the king and the Assembly. Nar-bonne, the illegitimate son of Louis XV and the lover of Madame de Stael, Necker's daughter, was Minister of War from December 1791 to March 1792. Dumouriez, an adventurer heavily in debt, held the Foreign Office from March until June. Lafayette, who had resigned as Commander-in-Chief of the National Guard, was given command of one of the three armies on the eastern frontier, in December.

In the Assembly itself one could distinguish, although not with any precision, between a majority of constitutional monarchists who, in the last resort, would reject a breach with the king, and a minority of more radical members whose prime objective was to suppress opposition to the revolution, although they hoped to do this without being forced to take action against the monarchy. Some of these radicals, led by Brissot, decided that a limited war against Austria would whip up popular support for the revolution and drive the king off the fence. Others felt that so dangerous a gamble might well lead to the destruction of the revolution by foreign arms. In March 1792 Louis XVI, who shared Brissot's

---

34. See A. Söderhjelm, *Marie Antoinette et Barnave: correspondance inédite,* Paris, 1934, *passim.*

impatience for war, though for rather different reasons, appointed three of Brissot's political friends as Ministers. The war party then called for national unity in support of the Government and the war effort, while their opponents clung to their old suspicions and insisted that Brissot and his allies were the conscious or unwitting tools of the Court. This division of the Left, which degenerated into a savage faction fight, was the beginning of a permanent breach that was to bedevil the whole future of the revolution. Which side one took at the time was as much a matter of accident and temperament as of political conviction, since all were more or less agreed on long-term objectives and the immediate issue was one of tactics. Although the two sides became sharply distinguished, one can't give them meaningful names. Most of the 'Girondins' or 'Brissotins' were neither from the Gironde nor had any close links with Brissot.[35] The other side, who became known as *Montagnards* when they sat on the highest seats on the Left of the Convention in the autumn of 1792, can scarcely be called 'Jacobins' when the club was the main battleground between the two sides.

There were many political factions, some of them working for ends that it would have been embarrassing to admit in public. Any specific policy was supported and opposed for such conflicting reasons that anyone could hope to discredit his particular opponents – whether or not he actually believed them to be traitors to the king or the revolution – merely by pointing to those who shared their views. Since the fate of the revolution was clearly going to turn on the outcome of the war – it was eventually declared in April – there were all the ingredients for an explosive mixture of passion, confusion and suspicion.

You're rather good at complications, said Ted. But I always thought historians were supposed to clarify issues instead of getting lost in the fog themselves.

You can do the clarifying if you want, I replied. My job is to describe the fog.

When Robespierre took the chair at the Jacobins on 28 November, opinion seemed to be setting in favour of an ultimatum to the German princes, although Dubois-Crancé, a Jacobin, had warned the Assembly on 31 October that the most dangerous enemies of

35. On this subject see M. J. Sydenham, *The Girondins*, London, 1961, *passim*.

the revolution were to be found within France. The Jacobins, on the 28th, were debating an address that the Assembly was considering sending to the king, inviting him to order the German princes to disperse the *émigrés* in their lands. Oelsner had written earlier in the year that Robespierre was lacking in the most elementary knowledge of foreign affairs.[36] He certainly misjudged Leopold's attitude, complaining that the Emperor was supporting the princes and arguing that any protest should be sent to Vienna. 'If the nation's representatives present such a request with dignity and the French Government accepts it, we have nothing more to fear from internal or foreign enemies. We must convince ourselves that liberty can only be maintained by courage and contempt for tyrants. The national Assembly and the executive must treat foreign enemies as a free people treats despots.'[37]

Ted was inclined to agree with Oelsner and he muttered something about ignorant ranting.

Don't forget that he'd only just got back from Artois and he was rather out of touch. He probably sat up when Albitte warned the Jacobins in the same session that, in the event of war, it would be impossible to trust the officers. On 5 December Billaud-Varenne, a Cordelier who had migrated to the Jacobins, said baldly that the executive could not be trusted with control of the army and that if war broke out, the king should be dethroned. Two days later Narbonne was made Minister of War and within a week he had given an army to Lafayette, whom Robespierre regarded as mainly responsible for the shooting in the Champ de Mars during the previous summer. Narbonne, who was looking for radical support for his war policy, made overtures to Brissot and Condorcet. This was enough for Robespierre, whose views quickly began to change. On 9 December he urged that, if war broke out, it should be fought as a defensive campaign on French soil, where it would be possible to organise popular resistance and to keep an eye on the generals. Two days later he said that war was the most dangerous of the possible policies.

The pressure for war now came entirely from the French side since Leopold had had the *émigrés* dispersed and informed the French Government of his pacific intentions. Brissot and Narbonne however abandoned the policy of a localised war against the Rhine-

36. Jacob, p. 80.   37. *Oeuvres*, vol. VIII, pp. 24-5.

land princes in favour of an attack on Austria itself, unless Leopold was prepared to make a somewhat humiliating repudiation of all the enemies of the revolution. On 16 December Brissot expounded his arguments in favour of war to the Jacobins and, if one accepts that eighteenth-century opinion regarded war as a legitimate extension of foreign policy, he made out quite a powerful case. He maintained that counter-revolutionaries within France rested all their hopes on foreign support. A patriotic war would arouse enthusiasm for the revolution and a vigorous assertion of French strength would force the domestic opponents of the revolution to come to terms with the inevitable. If the king accepted this policy he would become the prisoner of the revolution. If he tried to betray the revolution Brissot implied that he would be deposed.

Robespierre replied to Brissot at the next meeting of the Jacobins, on 18 December. As he saw it, this was the crisis of June and July 1791 all over again. The open opponents of the revolution were too discredited to be dangerous, unless they could shelter behind the constitutional monarchists. The real threat came therefore from men like Narbonne and Lafayette, who still enjoyed enough popularity to mislead. Since he believed them to be secret agents of the Court, war was 'in the hands of the executive, merely a means of overthrowing the constitution, merely the final stage of a deep plot to destroy liberty'. He challenged Brissot's optimistic assumption that invading French armies would be welcomed as liberators, referring to the devastation of the Palatinate by the French during the reign of Louis XIV and the national hatred that this had aroused in Germany. On the whole it was a moderate speech, apart from his demand for the execution of the leading counter-revolutionaries in France. He referred to Brissot as the *législateur patriote* but his conclusion : 'Woe betide those who . . . fail to sacrifice to the common good the spirit of party, their passions and even their prejudices!' sounded a warning note.[38]

Brissot replied on 30 December, probably went further than he intended and was made to withdraw the remark that his opponents were anarchists who were attacking the constitution. It was, in fact, Brissot who claimed to be hoping for *grandes trahisons* that would allow the king to be dethroned, whereas Robespierre took the cautious view that the constitution, with all its faults, was to be

38. *Oeuvres*, vol. VIII, pp. 47-64.

preferred to a crisis that might endanger the revolution itself. When Robespierre answered Brissot, on 2 January, he repeated some of his earlier arguments at unnecessary length, although in memorable language.[39] He remarked laconically that no one appreciated armed missionaries. He explained very acutely that the circumstances that had created the revolution in France – a rash aristocratic offensive against the monarchy that had so weakened the Establishment that the *patriotes* had been able to seize power for themselves – would prevent its imitation elsewhere since foreign nobles would have learned their lesson from the mistake of their French peers. He argued that if the Court visibly betrayed the nation, a general insurrection throughout France would be impossible to organise and any partial revolt could be suppressed as seditious. He exploited Brissot's weakness in having to pretend to confidence in a Government that he actually distrusted, and implied that Brissot had his eye on ministerial office for his friends. Robespierre's tone was sharper than before – as when he condemned Brissot's 'long and pompous dissertation on the American war' – but he did not cast any doubts on Brissot's patriotism.

Well? said Ted.

You mean, who was right?

It seems a fair question.

And the only possible answer is: neither and both. The effects of the war were quite unpredictable and your verdict depends on the time-scale you choose to adopt. Brissot was right in thinking that war would arouse patriotic enthusiasm and allow his group to overthrow the Government and assume office themselves. Robespierre was right in thinking that, whoever the Ministers happened to be, the Court would support France's enemies and that war would endanger the very survival of the revolution. Brissot was right to argue that the revolutionaries would win and that war would destroy the monarchy – and also put his friends in power. If you look as far ahead as 1799, Robespierre was right to think that a victorious war would leave the revolution at the mercy of a military adventurer. When he failed war brought back the Bourbons in 1814. Now you tell me who was right.

So you think the historian's job is merely to describe what happened?

39. *Oeuvres*, vol. VIII, pp. 74-92.

It's certainly not to ask unhistorical questions.

Unhistorical poppycock! What you're implying, J.S., although I don't think you realise it, is that we can never judge a politician by the consequences of his policies. Does that mean you think they're all alike?

You two seem to be as right and wrong as Brissot and Robespierre, said Henry pacifically. I'm pleased to see J.S. agreeing that man proposes but God disposes.

I never said anything of the kind.

Well, you certainly argued very plausibly that man didn't dispose. On the other hand, Ted wants it all cut and dried. It seems to me that we can only judge things in contemporary terms . . . Perhaps we can't *judge* them even then – it depends what we mean by judge. Brissot was taking a gamble and J.S. hasn't told us enough yet for us to know whether it was a reckless one. Robespierre was perhaps being too cautious. He wasn't content with his constitutional half-loaf and yet his policy meant accepting the stalemate. It's certainly interesting to see his reluctance to force a crisis; it rather confirms his attitude in the previous June. But I don't see how he proposed to make any progress.

We haven't reached that yet, I said. He did have a policy for suppressing the counter-revolution at home.

And when he told the Jacobins all about it, said Henry, I expect they gave him a round of applause and voted to have his speech printed at their expense.

As a matter of fact, they did.

And where did that get them or him? You've already said that the radicals were in a minority in the Assembly so he couldn't do anything by constitutional means and I thought that was the whole point of the policy.

You're as bad as J.S. said Ted. Brissot may have been too reckless and Robespierre may have been too cautious and if we want to know which, all we can do is see what happened next – even if it was completely different from what either of them expected!

If you stick to personalities all the time, said Mac, you can play ring-a-ring-a-roses till you're dizzy. It looks clear enough to me: Brissot stood for interests that wanted to stabilise the revolution, provided it gave them political power, whereas Robespierre and his lot realised this meant capitulating to the Court.

I don't think it's clear at all, I objected. They would both have preferred a democratic republic to the status quo, but they didn't know how to get it. They didn't disagree about strategy – at least, not then; only about tactics.

And even if Mac was right, said Ted, politics isn't about what one wants; it's about what's practicable. Let's give Henry's idea a chance. Tell us about the contemporary terms.

Robespierre repeated much the same arguments, at considerable length, on 11 January.[40] He seemed to think that he was taking rather a negative line so he said that, instead of looking for foreign enemies, the Assembly should have over ridden the king's veto on a penal law against the *émigrés* in the previous December.

In the first place, they hadn't done, said Ted. And in the second they couldn't do – unless they violated the constitution. That doesn't look very constructive to me.

He ended his speech on an extraordinarily melodramatic note, pretending to call up all kinds of people to the defence of France, only to find that they had been shot by Lafayette, dismissed from the army for sedition, and so on. It reads rather artificially now, but according to Desmoulins it had half the club in tears.[41] A week later he insinuated that Brissot had published a letter favourable to Lafayette in his *Patriote français*. This was little short of dishonest since Brissot's paper, like several others, had merely copied the letter from the *Moniteur* and in any case it didn't imply any approval of Lafayette.[42]

If I remember rightly, said Ted, he had taken it rather badly when Beaumetz did something like that to him in 1791.

Brissot seemed disinclined to challenge Robespierre in the Jacobins. He didn't reply to Robespierre's major speeches. On 20 January he made a very conciliatory statement and both parties accepted an invitation to demonstrate their respect for each other with a fraternal embrace. After that Brissot seems to have taken little part in the meetings of the club. He and his supporters may have realised that Robespierre would exhaust the patience of the Jacobins if they left him alone and that even if the club supported his policies it could not influence events. On the 25th Robespierre repeated his old arguments. The Jacobins had his speech printed, but what was more important was that, earlier in the day, the three

40. *Oeuvres*, vol. VIII, pp. 95-114.   41. *Oeuvres*, vol. VIII, p. 115.
42. Walter, p. 253.

leading orators from the Gironde, Vergniaud, Guadet and Gensonné, had persuaded the Assembly to send an ultimatum to Leopold. On the following day Robespierre demanded yet another discussion on the war but he was overruled by the president, amongst some disorder. He was back again on 10 February when he made a speech on the means of saving the nation. It's worth looking at this rather more closely since it shows the emergence of ideas that he was to develop over the next two years.[43]

He began by assuring his audience that everything he intended to propose was strictly constitutional. This was immediately followed by a flat rejection of the lessons of the previous 1,500 years : 'With the exception of a handful of the ancients who tried to base the welfare of society on ethics and the qualities of the heart, history shows us only political charlatans who plunged their peoples into the depths of vice and misfortune because they spurned probity and common sense.'

As he saw it, the revolutionaries had a double problem in front of them : to suppress counter-revolution and to liberate *l'esprit public* from the shackles that had so far prevented it from developing its true potential. He then accused successive Ministers of doing all they could to provoke war and at the same time doing nothing to strengthen French defences. This was followed by a catalogue of his own unsuccessful attempts to remedy the situation during the Constituent Assembly : 'Je proposai . . . Je proposai . . . Je demandais . . . Je demandais . . .' He then went on to advocate specific measures to strengthen, not so much the national defences as the forces that could be relied on to defend the revolution : preventing the dispersal of the French Guards who had gone over to the revolutionary side in 1789; authorising the Paris Sections to meet whenever they wished; stimulating revolutionary enthusiasm by a rally in Paris of National Guards from the provinces and getting Pétion to preside; support for the friends of the revolution in the provinces, coupled with mistrust of the Ministers – even if they should be drawn from the Jacobin club itself. 'Heaven preserve us from that at the moment. If it were to happen I should not have any more confidence in the patriotism of the Court and I should have much less in the *vertu* of the men who were chosen.' The next section of his speech dealt with the need for government to be

43. *Oeuvres*, vol. VIII, pp. 157-84.

carried on under the eye of the people: local government should be public and a palace ought to be built where the Assembly could deliberate before at least 10,000 spectators. 'I should like it to be made a rule that not a week should go by without helping or avenging some *patriote* who had been persecuted by tyranny; either an individual or a whole country.' Measures should be taken to help indigent revolutionaries and to fight financial speculation which was forcing up the cost of living. The military and penal codes should be humanised to protect ordinary people from the abuse of authority. Peasant support should be cultivated by the more vigorous enforcement of the laws that had abolished or curtailed manorial rights. Revolutionary enthusiasm should be stimulated by public fêtes and suitable plays. He then proposed an address to the French people that would explain why the revolution had hitherto failed to come up to their expectations and describe 'the charms of equality and the happiness of free men' that could be theirs if they responded to the challenge of their sublime mission. 'Let them see for once a body, entrusted with wide powers, speaking, thinking and acting like the people themselves. Try the effect on men's hearts of *vertu*, freedom, reason, and you will see its limitless scope. You will see the French people appear again in all its majesty, pacific but imposing, generous and indulgent, but ready to hurl its thunderbolts at the signal of the law, at the first cry from assaulted liberty.' Working himself up to a passionate peroration, he asked, 'Is it in vain that heaven has favoured us with prodigies it reserved for this century and denied to other peoples?' 'To what worthier end could one devote one's life? It is not enough to find death at the hands of tyrants; one must have deserved it . . . If the first champions of liberty must be its martyrs they must carry tyranny itself to their tombs. The death of a great man must awaken the sleeping peoples and its price must be the welfare of the world.'

All right, said Mac, I can see what you are getting at. But if you disregard the self-advertisement it's a pretty shrewd assessment of what revolutionary policy ought to be. I like his emphasis on the need to earn popular support by making sure that the revolution actually did something concrete for the majority of the people. There's not much doubt about where his heart was and it's not surprising if the sans-culottes thought he was their man.

I like Mac's cavalier dismissal of anything in the speech that he finds indefensible, said Ted. I was just wondering how long it would have taken to build that palace with the seats for 10,000 spectators. They would have needed a public address system if they were going to hear well enough to know which of their legislators to intimidate.

Your trouble, said Mac, is that you don't think people can be improved.

Not by governments anyway.

Even if that's true, and we won't argue about it now, if you don't assume that they can, you divorce politics from ethics. In other words, anything goes. Since you don't believe in anything yourself, you assume that no one else does – and that justifies you for being as bad as you assume them to be. If you take people as they are, as I suppose you'd put it, you make them worse.

You'll be doing Henry out of a job if you go on like this, said Ted. I thought you were supposed to be some sort of a materialist. The only trouble with your theories is that, in practice, improving people always means forcing them to pretend they've adopted standards that they haven't.

What most interests me, said Henry, is the ending. Of course he's said it all before – even before 1789 – and I suppose he must have been living with it all the time. It's not that he despairs of the Promised Land, but it almost sounds as though he doesn't want to get there himself.

Romanticism, said Ted.

Not in the usual sense, anyway. He's not attracted by the idea of the gallant fight against impossible odds and the heroic but inevitable defeat. He thinks they can get there. Where society is concerned he's much less of a pessimist than Rousseau – and more of an Enlightenment man since he thinks the path to Heaven is paved with good legislation. But he won't be satisfied unless he has to die just before they arrive. If it were only an oratorical trick he wouldn't repeat it so insistently. It must correspond to something deep inside him.

You mean Gallo's father-fixation, death-wish and that sort of thing, I said.

Those are only formulae. It could be seen, I suppose, as a perverted form of religion . . . seeing himself as a new Christ. I expect it won him some disciples – particularly amongst simple people.

Especially women.

I wonder what his colleagues made of it. After all, he wasn't a passive resistance man and if he went on talking about his own martyrdom while he was busy smiting the unrighteous it's not surprising if some people thought he was a hypocrite.

While he was busy exposing his soul to the Jacobins, I went on, Brissot and company were getting what they wanted, sometimes by rather devious means. Brissot's paper presented his personal reconciliation with Robespierre as meaning that Maximilien had stopped opposing the war. On 22 February Billaud-Varenne discovered that the Jacobin correspondence committee, where Brissotin influence was very strong, was telling the affiliated societies in the provinces that the *société mère* was in favour of war. When the committee was accused of putting across its own view without informing the society as a whole, there was another bitter row on the 26th. Louvet challenged Robespierre, the two sides seem to have been more or less equally matched and the meeting ended in uproar.

Things evolved rapidly in March. Leopold died and was succeeded by his son, who was much more ready to go to war. The French Government broke up when Narbonne forced the resignation of Molleville and was then dismissed himself.[44] Brissot, in revenge for the dismissal of Narbonne, had the Foreign Minister, Delessart, impeached. On 23 March the king appointed three of Brissot's political friends, Roland, Clavière and Servan, to be Ministers. This brought a new battle between Robespierre and Brissot, almost tore the Jacobins apart and split the revolutionaries for good. For Brissot, the new Ministry was the vindication of his war policy. It was now the duty of all patriots to support the Government and unite in the patriotic cause. War was declared – by France – on 20 April. The Brissotins appealed for discipline in the army and confidence in its leaders. Robespierre, as he had announced in advance, took the view that the Court was merely buying time. He thought Lafayette was a royalist agent and the new Ministers the more or less innocent victims of a confidence trick. Without attacking them, he continued his campaign against Lafayette and defended troops who mutinied against their officers. Each side convinced itself – or at least tried to convince everyone else – that the other was actively supporting the Court and counter-revolution.

44. For the divisions within the Government, see Molleville, op. cit.

On 23 March Robespierre had tried to persuade the Jacobins to express their opposition to war in a circular to the provincial clubs.

After accusing his opponents of doing exactly the same thing.

Not at all. They tried to slip it through without the knowledge of the club as a whole. He didn't. In his proposed address he included a reference to the danger of exhausting 'the patience of heaven which has insisted on saving us in spite of ourselves'.[45] Guadet interrupted to accuse him of superstition. Robespierre, instead of saying that he had merely been using a figure of speech, launched into a passionate defence of his deist faith: 'Alone with my soul, how could I have supported labours beyond human endurance without elevating my soul? . . . This divine sentiment more than compensated me for the advantages open to those who were prepared to betray the people.' The Jacobins don't seem to have been very impressed and the session again degenerated into anarchy. A royalist paper claimed that they almost came to blows and broke up with some members calling Robespierre an *aristo-crate*. A few days later he withdrew his proposed circular.

On 10 April Robespierre resigned his post as public prosecutor. As recently as 15 February he had told the Jacobins, in a rather self-righteous way, how he meant to discharge his duties as prose-cutor but, in fact, he doesn't seem to have taken much interest in the court. The presiding judge – admittedly after Robespierre's death – said that he had been very negligent and a frequent absentee. He resigned before he actually presented any cases.[46]

I remember some years ago, said Henry, when I was at Versailles I saw an exhibition about Marie Antoinette. It was rather a good one. In the last show-case there was the letter in which Robes-spierre accepted the job of prosecutor and I assumed that he must have had something to do with her trial.

You were probably meant to. It just shows that some people are still fighting the good fight. As I said, he never prosecuted anyone and in any case Marie Antoinette was tried by an entirely different court. Robespierre was probably mistaken in accepting the job in the first place. It may have seemed a sensible thing to do when it looked as though the revolution was over and the deputies of the Constituent Assembly had excluded themselves from a political career in the future, but things looked very different now. He had

45. *Oeuvres*, vol. VIII, pp. 229-37. 46. *Papiers trouvés*, vol, III, p. 277.

told the Jacobins on 15 February that he wouldn't hesitate to resign if he found that his new office was taking up more time than he could spare from politics.

He didn't give it much of a chance, said Ted.

Of course he may have felt that it was a good moment to show his own disinterestedness when Brissot's people had just accepted ministerial office. If he did, he probably miscalculated. When his place was taken by a moderate he was accused of having let the enemy in, and quite a few people suggested that he had been paid by the Court to do so. Brissot and Condorcet's papers both implied as much. When Robespierre started a paper of his own, the *Défenseur de la Constitution*, in May, the *Révolutions de Paris* speculated about whether the Court had put up the money as a reward for services rendered. The paper, which had been quite sympathetic towards him in the past, pretended to disbelieve a story that the deal had been concluded at a secret meeting between Robespierre and Marie Antoinette, but it made sure that its readers heard all about it. It seems quite likely that the two hostile articles it published were written by Robert and Sylvain Maréchal in the hope of getting jobs from the new Ministers. Perhaps it's not surprising that he should have felt his own tactics were on a different moral plane from those of his opponents. With Gorsas's paper now hostile too, he could only count on Marat, Hébert's *Père Duchesne* and the *Tribune du Peuple* that Desmoulins was editing in collaboration with Fréron, and Hébert didn't share his suspicion of the Girondin Ministers.[47] It was perhaps the barrage of press criticism that led even the sensible Oelsner to ask himself whether Robespierre, Marat and the Cordelier Club were not working for the counter-revolution.[48]

At the Jacobins things went from bad to worse. On 23 April Robespierre promised that the following Friday (the 27th) he would unmask the traitors. It was an ambiguous speech and he probably only meant that he was going to reveal one particular intrigue which was part of a more general plot.[49] Walter suggests that all he actually intended to do was to complain of the manoeuvres of Lafayette's supporters in the Jacobin club in Strasbourg but his melodramatic language implied something much

47. P. d'Estrée, *Le Père Duchesne*, Paris, n.d., p. 88.
48. Jacob, pp. 114-15. 49. *Oeuvres*, vol. VIII, pp. 295-6.

more sensational : 'a plan of civil war presented to the Assembly by one of its members.'[50] Whatever his intentions, he provoked the panic – or fury – of his opponents. On the 25th Brissot accused him of dividing the *patriotes*, although what Brissot said can scarcely have been audible above the uproar. On the same day Madame Roland, who had held him in particular esteem the previous year, finally broke with him.[51] On the 26th, ignoring a letter from Pétion calling for a truce, he demanded the right to reply to Brissot. When Louvet, who was in the chair, gave the floor to Guadet, he accused Robespierre of shaking his fist at him and one of Robespierre's supporters shouted that Louvet would not escape from the Jacobins alive.[52] Guadet, to the accompaniment of howls from Robespierre's supporters in the public galleries – Robespierre himself had to appeal for silence so that he could hear the charges against him – accused Maximilien of putting his own pride before the public interest and demanded that he ostracise himself. On the 27th everyone was waiting for the denunciation. Robespierre made a promising start : 'Whatever people say, I have not come here to take up your time by talking about one or two individuals or about myself. It is the public cause that is the object of all this dispute.'[53] After complaining of being attacked in the press when he had merely intended to reveal an intrigue without mentioning any names, saving *des vérités importantes* for another occasion, he replied briefly to Guadet and Brissot. Brissot had rather rashly asked what Robespierre had done to earn the right to criticise others and this gave him the pretext for a long and detailed justification of his career, going back to the years before the revolution. He then offered his opponents a truce if they would join him in attacking the Court and its agents and support the friends of the revolution. If he had originally intended to reveal any plot he either changed his mind or forgot all about it. As the *Thermomètre du Jour* told its readers, 'Everyone was waiting impatiently for the disclosure of the plot and M. Robespierre provided no *proof*. Instead he gave us the story of his life, his apologies and his conjectures.'[54]

This is something worth remembering the next time he invites

---

50. Walter, p. 288.
51. J. Roberts, *French Revolution Documents*, Oxford, 1966, pp. 455-6.
52. *Correspondance*, vol. I, pp. 147-8; Walter, p. 286.
53. *Oeuvres*, vol. VIII, pp. 304-18.　　　54. *Oeuvres*, vol. VIII, p. 321.

us to believe in his plots, said Ted. He uses the plot gambit rather too often. It may have gone down well enough each time with his fan club in the public galleries but the Jacobins must surely have seen through it.

You may be right. They seem to have had enough. On 2 May he was shouted down when he opposed a motion that any future denunciations should be made to a committee, which would only bring them to the floor of the meeting if it thought them substantiated. Of course, you have to remember that he hadn't really got any other means of publicity. His paper was a dull affair which devoted a good deal of its space to printing his speeches and I doubt if it had much of a circulation. Roland, the Minister of the Interior, was using official channels to circulate one of Brissot's speeches and apparently subsidising the *Sentinelle*, a wall-news-paper that Louvet had just started. Most of the press was hostile to Robespierre and not too particular about its methods. The *Patriote français* ran a particularly vicious series of innuendoes suggesting that Robespierre was in the pay of the Court.[55] He must have felt that almost everyone was against him and he lashed out wildly in every direction. On 10 May he objected to a motion to exclude from the Jacobins those who couldn't produce proof that they had paid their taxes, on the ground that it was designed to keep out those too poor to be liable – as though they could have afforded the subscription. When this produced the usual pandemonium he shouted, 'The more you isolate me, the more you cut off all my human contacts, the more justification I find in my conscience and the justice of my cause!'[56] When it had been a matter of trying to prevent the outbreak of war, he had had plenty of supporters. It was his negative attitude in May, even though he didn't attack the Ministers themselves, that seems to have lost him a good deal of support.

Perhaps, said Mac, but it takes two sides to make an uproar. He must have had some following apart from the people in the galleries or the club would have shut him up.

He could be quite vicious himself. In the Jacobins and in his paper he accused the Brissotins of being the puppets of Narbonne and Lafayette, said they betrayed the secrets of the Jacobins to the Court and implied that Brissot and Condorcet had been responsible

55. *Oeuvres*, vol. VIII, pp. 339-40.   56. *Oeuvres*, vol. VIII, p. 349.

for the bloodshed on the Champ de Mars.[57] When the Assembly voted to form an armed camp at Paris of National Guards summoned up from the provinces – these were the men who were going to lead the attack on the royal palace on 10 August – Robespierre suspected another plot. Deserted by his usual supporters, he denounced the Bill and threatened the Assembly: 'The Assembly itself is subject to the general will and when it openly thwarts it the Assembly can no longer exist.' The *Patriote français* naturally didn't miss this further 'proof' that Robespierre had unmasked himself as an agent of the Court.[58]

The Jacobins had been reduced to a state of virtual paralysis when the king unwisely took advantage of a hectoring letter written for Roland by his wife, to remind the Ministers of where power really lay. On 12 June he dismissed the three Girondins and Dumouriez, who had been working with them, followed a day or two later. Robespierre seems to have seen this as a possible hint of a coming coup d'état. On the 13th he praised the Ministers and called on all *patriotes* to rally round the Assembly that he had been threatening only a few days before. It obviously cost him an effort to call off the polemic against Brissot, but after Chabot, in the chair, steered him away from a nasty reference to people who had got the Ministers to distribute their speeches for them, he went on, 'I declare that if the people I have been describing will unite with the *patriotes* and with me in particular . . . I will bury in oblivion the most horrible system of defamation that was ever invented.'[59] It was perhaps not much of an overture but it helped to calm things down at the club.

The situation was now too serious for quarrelling. On 18 June Lafayette denounced the Jacobins as a whole, in a letter to the Assembly. Ever mindful of the events of the previous summer, which he regarded as the result of royalist provocation, Robespierre warned against *insurrections partielles* that would provide a pretext for repression. Disregarding his advice, the more impatient revolutionaries organised an armed demonstration on 20 June. This produced an invasion of the Tuileries but failed to bully any concessions out of the king. It was followed, as Robespierre had expected, by a swing of opinion in favour of the humiliated

---

57. *Oeuvres*, vol. VIII, p. 358, vol. IV; *Défenseur de la Constitution*, pp. 12, 83-94.
58. *Oeuvres*, vol. VIII, p. 368. 59. *Oeuvres*, vol. VIII, p. 374.

monarch. Somehow or other he resisted the temptation to say 'I told you so'. On the 28th Lafayette, who had left his army without permission, appeared in person before the Assembly, where he still had the support of a majority of the deputies. He probably intended to lead the National Guards in a march on the Jacobins, but the Court, which feared him more than it did the extremists, helped to frustrate his plans. Failing to get effective support, after a few days he returned to his army. Robespierre had at last realised that Lafayette was not a royal agent but was hoping to make himself an independent arbiter between the Court and the Assembly. Since he could not be discredited as a royalist and he enjoyed a good deal of support in both the army and the Parisian National Guard, there was a real possibility of his succeeding in a coup d'état. This at least was Robespierre's opinion and he became almost hysterical in his denunciations. He accused Lafayette of allowing the baker, François, to be murdered in the autumn of 1789, as a pretext for the Martial Law Act; he said the general had arranged the murder of the two men on the Champ de Mars, in July 1791, which had led to the proclamation of martial law; he implied that Lafayette was quite capable of having the king murdered so that he could seize power for himself.[60] Both his speeches and his newspaper articles took on a wild exaggeration that was not like his usual style. He put the Champ de Mars casualties at 1,500 and repeated atrocity stories of 'the children of Brabant slaughtered in their mothers' wombs and carried all bloody at the end of Austrian bayonets'.[61]

He wasn't very good in crises, was he, asked Ted. You suggested last week that he more or less cracked up just before the king's flight, in 1791, and this sort of ranting was enough to drive any reasonable man over to Lafayette's side. When he lost his nerve he could bring himself to believe anything about anybody.

He was convinced that a major crisis was coming, I said, and he couldn't see any way forward. He thought Lafayette was preparing to march on Paris, where the royal family was entrenching itself in the Tuileries to hold out until it was liberated by the Allies. Prussia had joined in the war and a Prussian army was approaching the frontier. The Assembly was the prisoner of its

60. *Oeuvres*, vol. VIII, p. 399.   61. *Oeuvres*, vol. IV, p. 225.

constitutional principles and would take no decisive action, either to arouse the country or to dethrone the king by more or less constitutional means. The majority of the deputies refused to condemn Lafayette and they would not take any revolutionary action even though their inaction looked like destroying the revolution itself. For a long time Robespierre went on hoping that they would change their minds. He probably felt that the constitution had broken down so palpably that insurrection was legitimate, but he thought it desperately dangerous. A partial revolt would provide Lafayette with exactly the pretext he needed. It was impossible to assess in advance how much support there would be for an insurrection and its failure would mean the final defeat of all his hopes. Even a successful insurrection might merely hand over a republic to his enemies – his old fear of 1791. He found it very hard to see any possible way out. When he drafted a petition to the Assembly on behalf of the *fédérés* – the National Guards from the provinces who were now beginning to arrive in Paris – it merely called for the punishment of Lafayette and his supporters in the army and local government; it was apparently the spokesman himself who added a demand for the suspension of the king.[62]

Billaud-Varenne, who had probably helped to turn him against the war in December, once more supplied him with a programme. On 15 July Billaud called for the deportation of all the Bourbons, the purge of army, lawcourts and administration and the election of a Convention, or new constituent assembly. A fortnight later, Robespierre told the Jacobins that 'the state must be saved, by whatever means'.[63] 'The only thing that is unconstitutional is what makes for its ruin.' He could still see no solution to the problem of the monarchy. To suspend the king would probably work in his favour, as it had done the previous year. To dethrone him would mean combining legislative and executive powers in a single assembly, which he considered 'the most intolerable of all despotisms'. Leaving that problem on one side, he demanded the election, at the earliest possible date, of a Convention that should be chosen by universal suffrage. The constitution would have to be revised so as to reduce both the prerogative of the executive and the independence of the legislature. 'The source of all our troubles is the absolute independence which the deputies created for them-

62. *Oeuvres*, vol. IV, pp. 287-94.   63. *Oeuvres*, vol. VIII, pp. 408-20.

selves in their relationship with the nation.' To counteract this the electors should meet at frequent intervals, with the right to recall their deputies. Local government and the courts should be purged. Finally, he fell back on his old panacea : the self-exclusion of those elected in 1789 and 1791 from the new Convention. It was not, perhaps, a very convincing programme. It offered no solution to the problem of the monarchy, or to the more urgent problem of keeping the Allies out of Paris until the end of the campaigning season. Neither he nor his audience knew how his solutions could be imposed on either the king or the Assembly. But if a new revolution should happen, it would provide the revolutionaries with some sort of a policy and the idea of convening a new constituent body probably appealed to a good many people, although not to the Girondins.

By the middle of July the Girondins presumably thought that the king had been sufficiently intimidated to accept their tutelage. Vergniaud, Guadet and Gensonné tried to open negotiations with the Court. Louis, although too much of a gentleman to publish their letter, was still staking everything on the Allied armies and he failed to respond. According to Mathiez, the Girondins were not discouraged and Guadet had a secret meeting with the queen.[64] Despite warnings in the Jacobins against trying to use the growing agitation in Paris merely as a means of recovering office, Brissot and Condorcet, on 26 July, proposed that the king should be urged to recall the Girondin Ministers. The public galleries greeted this with shouts of 'The villains! Barnave again!'[65] In the Assembly Brissot called for the maintenance of the constitution, excluding both the dethronement of the king and the election of a new assembly. It was perhaps Robespierre's call for new elections and a self-denying ordinance, on the 29th, that ended the precarious truce between him and Brissot. Just as the Feuillants had walked out of the Jacobins in 1791, Brissot and his supporters in turn left them for a new club, the *Reunion*.[66] It was here that, on the 30th, Brissot and Isnard undertook to have Robespierre impeached for treason. This was promptly denounced to the Jacobins

---

64. A. Mathiez, *La Révolution française*, Paris, 1946 ed. vol. I, p. 211.

65. Buchez and Roux, *Histoire parlementaire de la Révolution française*, Paris, 1834–8, vol. XVI, p. 142.

66. See A. Mathiez, 'Un club révolutionnaire inconnu : le club de la Réunion' in *Girondins et Montagnards*, Paris, 1930.

on the following day. If the Girondins turned their fury on Robespierre when they had disregarded Billaud's similar proposals, it seems reasonable to suppose that what they particularly resented was his suggestion that deputies should not be eligible for re-election. On 8 August the Assembly's vote, by a majority of 424 to 206, to take no action against Lafayette, showed the parliamentary weakness of the Girondins and the bankruptcy of their policies. If the radicals were not to be out-manoeuvred by their opponents or suppressed by the Prussians there was no alternative now to a trial of strength between Paris and the Tuileries.

This was not a prospect much relished by the Jacobins, who seem to have had little confidence in the success of an insurrection. Robespierre wrote in his paper about 5 August, 'Every moment increases the danger and reduces our resources.'[67] Marat, if one can believe Barbaroux, was pestering him to procure his escape to Marseilles, rather improbably disguised as a jockey, as late as the evening of 9 August.[68] Danton left for Arcis-sur-Aube on the 5th and although he played an active part in the insurrection after his return on the 9th, his original intention may well have been to keep out of the way when the crisis erupted. The *fédérés* and the Parisian Sections were planning an insurrection, but although each group had its own central committee, it proved difficult to organise a concerted revolt. There seem to have been one or two attempts before 10 August, which came to nothing. The Tuileries were well-protected by Swiss Guards and royalist volunteers and the allegiance of some of the battalions of National Guards was uncertain. When the insurrection had succeeded, of course, everyone exaggerated his own rôle and belittled that of everyone else. Subsequent historians have tended to perpetuate the old quarrels. It all seems rather unnecessary. The leaders were all understandably cautious about setting off a revolt that was quite likely to fail. They were more or less active on the 10th of August itself, but none of them actually risked getting shot, while they would all have been liable to be hanged if the coup had failed.

The central committee of the *fédérés* met once or twice at the Duplays' and Robespierre was presumably in close touch with them and perhaps with the Paris Sections as well, although he kept in the background. Barbaroux, a Marsellais already in Paris, who acted

---

67. *Oeuvres*, vol. IV, p. 336.   68. *Mémoires de Barbaroux*, p. 142.

as one of the leaders of the Marseilles *fédérés,* maintained – although only after he had quarrelled with Robespierre – that early in August, Fréron and Panis hinted to him that Robespierre should be made dictator and that Maximilien himself said that the popular movement would lose its impetus unless 'some very popular man declared himself its leader'.[69] There is room for plenty of misunderstanding about what Robespierre meant by *chef,* if he actually used the expression, and of course 'dictator' was employed in the classical sense of a man entrusted with sovereign powers for a limited period. If Robespierre did play with the idea, which is far from certain, he did very little about it.

On 10 August he and the other Jacobin leaders were saved when the Tuileries were stormed, after a bloody battle, by a popular insurrection that Robespierre welcomed and had perhaps helped to inspire, but had probably done little to organise.

I suppose you've got to give us this sort of ball-by-ball commentary, said Mac. We want to get the facts straight, but we do lose the wood while looking at the trees. It's easy to miss the drift of a man's policy while you're following all its twists and turns. You didn't like it some time ago when I said that Robespierre stood for some sort of people's revolution while the Girondins wanted the status quo plus themselves in office. But that's the way it worked out. His most loyal support in the Jacobins came from the poorer people in the public galleries. It was the gentlemen who slandered him, and the people who did the fighting on the 10th of August probably hero-worshipped him. I'm less interested in temperaments than in policies. That's what matters. He may have gone through a bad patch in May and June, beat his breast and suspected anyone who disagreed with him, but that doesn't matter. He'd managed to keep in touch with the sans-culottes all the time and if he was their man, if that's where his support lay, he'd have to give them the sort of things they wanted. They were right to back him since he was more responsive to their real needs than most of the other people and – at least for as long as he was being challenged on his Right – he would have to back them. All the rest is embroidery.

Scale does alter perspective, said Henry. The more the detail, the more petty the men seem to be. I don't think there's anything the

69. *Mémoires de Barbaroux,* pp. 143-6.

historian can do about that. If one man opposes another on grounds of principle, he's likely to attack specific policies for particular reasons – which often seem related to his own self-interest. Whether you say that the principles are a rationalisation of the self-interest or the self-interest is an accidental by-product of the principles may depend on how closely you happen to be looking at the evidence. I think Mac's right too when he says that what really matters is not the initial disagreement, but where the two sides end up, which may not be where they intended but where their support comes from. All the same, power matters and when power is in the hands of individuals, personalities matter. I don't think J.S. could have spared us all those rather squalid wrangles. Robespierre's reactions under pressure lifted a corner of the veil, as he would have put it. He wasn't just some sort of faceless 'friend of the people', certainly not an ordinary demagogue. He was a man with a mission all right, and as we've seen before, it was primarily a moral mission. There's another thing too : I think it was necessary to know just how deep that quarrel with Brissot was. What I'd like to ask J.S. is whether he thinks they believed the things they said about each other.

That's a question that gets harder and harder to answer as Robespierre's career develops. Up to now most of the personal abuse had come from Brissot and I don't see how he could have believed that Robespierre was an agent of the Court. I imagine that Robespierre himself felt – to put it into present-day jargon – that Brissot and company were 'objectively' counter-revolutionary, the unconscious agents of the Court rather than its accomplices. That didn't make them any the less dangerous – and of course it would be easy to transfer them from one category to the other if they didn't mend their ways when Robespierre told them to. But he did praise them when they turned on Lafayette at the end of June. Buzot, who had been on friendly terms with him in the Constituent Assembly, said that Robespierre told him some time in the spring, that he didn't think Brissot was corrupt but that his war policy had convinced him that he was no *patriote*.[70]

What about his absurd charges against Lafayette?

That's a different case. One can't tell, of course, but my own impression is that he did believe them. Accusing Lafayette of plot-

70. *Mémoires inédits de Pétion et Mémoires de Buzot et de Barbaroux* (ed. Dauban), Paris, 1866, p. 17n[1].

117

ting to murder the king didn't serve any tactical purpose and it would have been easier to go on denouncing him as a royalist agent. I think he may have been prepared to believe that no sort of villainy was beyond counter-revolutionaries but he was rather more level-headed when he was dealing with those who were basically on the side of the angels.

Which is all very well, said Mac, so long as it's clear which the sides were, which I suppose it was, up to 10 August, with the democrats lined up against the aristocrats and the oligarchs.

It's not very well at all, said Ted. A man who can convince himself that any of his opponents are monsters is a political menace and it won't take him long to put them all in the same category. The best you can do for him is to assume that he didn't believe a word of that silly stuff about Lafayette but just hoped that some of the mud would stick.

From his own point of view, said Henry, the outcome of the battle must have convinced him that Providence was still on the side of the revolution. He couldn't see any alternative to an insurrection and yet he thought it was quite likely to fail. J.S. suggested that it was actually touch and go.

When it was over, Barbaroux thought that the king would have won if he had stayed behind to defend the Tuileries instead of escaping to the Assembly.[71]

The victory doesn't seem to have been due to anyone's master plan; it must have reinforced his belief that Providence was protecting the people and it was up to those who aspired to be political leaders to draw the appropriate conclusions.

If we leave Providence to look after itself and come down to earth for a minute, said Ted, I think you're both wrong. Robespierre had slipped back a long way in the past year. In the autumn of 1791 he had a national reputation, both as a deputy and as the unchallenged leader of the Jacobins. So far as the Parisian sansculottes were concerned, he and Pétion were the only men who mattered; Marat was only a journalist and Danton's sphere of action was limited to the Cordeliers. Robespierre moved out of the limelight when he stopped being a deputy. It was the Girondins whose speeches would be read in the provinces. I don't suppose

71. *Mémoires de Barbaroux*, p. 149.

many people subscribed to newspapers that told them much about what went on in the Jacobins.

There were the affiliated clubs, I said.

Which would take their cue from the circulars sent out by a correspondence committee that you said the Girondins controlled. In any case he was interrupted a good deal in the Jacobins and sometimes shouted down. His opposition, not merely to the war, but also to the Ministers who were trying to win it, must have struck a lot of people as petty-minded and unpatriotic. He didn't campaign for an insurrection and whatever he may have done to encourage it in secret meetings wouldn't be widely known, especially outside Paris. Danton seemed to deserve at least as much credit for the eventual victory. His endless self-praise and suspicion of everyone else had begun to bore his old supporters in the Jacobins. For the political activists he was now only one possible leader amongst others and for the country at large he was last year's hero. The trouble is that we know he was going to come to the top in the end. If we didn't, I think we'd consider him a spent force.

I thought we were going to have a discussion, I said, and you're all talking to yourselves. We seem to get farther apart the more we go on. I'm not even sure that you disagree but you're all talking about different things.

Courage, said Henry. We're just your bowl of many-coloured glass. It's up to you to provide the white radiance of a definitive historical verdict, though I must admit you don't seem to be making much headway in that direction.

V The Revolutionary

I'd like to go back to 10 August 1792 for a moment, I said. After weeks of crisis the Paris Sections had presented the Legislative Assembly with an ultimatum: if it didn't dethrone the king by midnight on the 9th they would take action themselves. The first move of their central insurrectionary committee was to replace the Commune with its own nominees. In the next day or two each of the 48 Sections sent representatives to the Hôtel de Ville to form a new Insurrectionary Commune. The mayor, Pétion, found himself in an impossible situation. He was responsible for the maintenance of order and personally sympathetic towards the Girondin leaders who had hoped to use the *threat* of an insurrection in order to recover office. He therefore tried to postpone the rising and when he failed, arranged to be locked up and kept out of the way on the night of the 9th–10th.[1] Although the first objective of the insurrection was to storm the Tuileries, it was acting in defiance of the Assembly and, at least by implication, rejecting its claim to represent the nation. The success of the revolt therefore left a discredited Assembly face to face with a Commune which claimed a mandate not merely from Paris but from revolutionary France as a whole and could quote the participation in the fighting of the *fédérés* from the provinces as evidence in its support.

This was not how the Girondins saw the situation. After 10 August the constitutional monarchists who had formed something like two-thirds of the deputies, went into hiding. What was left of the Assembly could be relied on to support Brissot and his friends. It immediately voted the election of a Convention, to be chosen by universal suffrage, but until this could meet it insisted that it was the only representative of the national will. It restored to office the three Girondin Ministers, reinforced by Danton at the Ministry of Justice. This naturally gave the men who had carried through the insurrection the impression that they had pulled the Girondins' chestnuts out of the fire for them. In this way the overthrow of the monarchy did nothing to appease the quarrels that

1. See *Oeuvres*, vol. v, pp. 98-107, 141-3 for Robespierre's own account.

had been tearing the Jacobins apart all through the spring. The old rivalry appeared in a new form as a struggle for power between the Assembly and the Insurrectionary Commune.[2]

The issue was one of power rather than of policies. The rump of the Assembly was as radical as any Jacobin could wish. In three weeks it ordered the deportation of priests who refused to accept the revolutionary religious settlement, virtually abolished the surviving manorial dues without compensation and ordered the sale of *émigré* lands in small lots. Guadet persuaded his colleagues to decree the demolition of the frontier town of Longwy, when it should be recaptured, because of its failure to offer serious resistance to the Prussians. Where the monarchy was concerned, however, the Girondins were rather more tentative. They suspended the king, leaving it to the Convention to decide whether or not to dethrone him and voted that a tutor should be chosen for his son. But Robespierre himself had always insisted that what mattered was not the form of government but the kind of society that was created within the framework of monarchy or republic. His speech to the Jacobins on the night of 10 August, calling for the election of a Convention, the impeachment of Lafayette, the retention of their arms by the insurgents and the despatch of emissaries by the Commune to explain the new revolution to the country at large, contained nothing that the Girondins could not have accepted.[3]

It was their determination to discipline what they saw as the rival power of the Commune that created the first conflict, soon to be intensified when the Commune demanded the creation of a special court for the summary trial of all those responsible for what it regarded as the Court's challenge to the revolution. Robespierre now played a new part as one of the leaders of the Commune, to which he was elected by his Section. He declined any position that might take him out of the political arena. Danton, who was busy finding jobs for his friends, offered him a place in the Ministry of Justice. On 15 August he was elected to preside over the new court and he refused this too, on the ground that he would be judging men who had been his political opponents.

He can't have it both ways, said Ted. If you accept his argu-

---

2. See F. Braesch, *La Commune du 10 août,* Paris, 1911 *passim.*
3. *Oeuvres,* vol. VIII, p. 427.

ment that revolutionary situations suspend the normal constitutional rules, then this either was one or it wasn't. If it was, he should have accepted. If it wasn't, the Commune had no right to consider itself more than the city council of the biggest town in France. He was obviously angling for bigger fish.

There's nothing necessarily wrong about that, replied Henry. A man doesn't have to accept anything he's offered. If he did see himself as having more to offer as a politician he could hardly say so without laying himself open to the charge of careerism. I think we've got to accept that a politician can't always reveal everything that's in his mind – or anyone else for that matter.

In the last issue of his *Défenseur de la Constitution* – it obviously couldn't survive under that title – published in the second half of August, he showed how much importance he attached to the events of the 10th. 'Thus has begun the finest revolution that has ever honoured humanity, indeed the only one with an object worthy of man: to found political societies at last on the immortal principles of equality, justice and reason. Frenchmen, remember that the destinies of the universe are in your hands.'[4] He drew from this a rather sinister conclusion, that since the stakes were so high, mercy towards 'tyrants' was a crime against humanity. For the moment, at least, he seemed to think of tyrants only as foreign rulers and he showed himself quite well-disposed towards the Assembly, although critical of its manipulation by Girondin politicians.

The trouble started when he appeared as spokesman for the Commune which 'petitioned' the Assembly in language much too forceful for its taste. On 12 August he appealed against a provocative attempt to subordinate the Commune to a newly-elected Department of Paris. 'When the people have saved the nation, when you have ordered your replacement by a national Convention, what else is there for you to do but to satisfy the people's wishes? Are you afraid to rely on the wisdom of the people who are keeping guard over a nation that only they can save?'[5] Three days later, protesting against the Assembly's attempt to circumscribe the jurisdiction of the new court, he warned it that 'the people are resting but not asleep. They want the guilty punished and rightly so. You ought not to give them laws that contradict

4. *Oeuvres*, vol. IV, p. 358.   5. *Oeuvres*, vol. VIII, p. 430.

their unanimous will.'[6] It was not only Girondins who objected to this sort of language. Future Montagnards such as Choudieu, Thuriot and Basire joined in the growing protests which led to the decision – soon reversed – to order the replacement of the Commune by new elections.

One result of this rivalry was to paralyse public authority in Paris at a time of acute national danger. The war, which everyone had regarded as an instrument of domestic politics, took on a new shape when a Prussian army crossed the frontier, quickly over-ran the two fortified towns of Longwy and Verdun and prepared to march on Paris. In a manifesto published at the end of July, its commander-in-chief, Brunswick, had threatened the population of the capital with dire penalties if any harm came to the royal family. As the Prussian advance brought matters to a crisis at the end of August, Parisian opinion was inflamed both by the military danger – deliberately dramatised by the authorities in order to stimulate recruiting – and by its unsatisfied urge to avenge the hundreds who had fallen in the attack on the Tuileries. The story spread that counter-revolutionaries would profit from the absence of the able-bodied at the front to open the prisons and seize Paris. One or two Sections began to call for the preventive massacre of both political and common-law prisoners. On 2 September the massacres began and they went on for several days, resulting in the murder of over a thousand men and women. None of the authorities in Paris made any determined effort to stop them – which would have meant mobilising the National Guard and risking another Champ de Mars. The question of how far the massacres were spontaneous and how far they were encouraged, if not actually organised, by one or two politicians, is probably beyond a precise answer, but we ought to have a careful look at the evidence for Robespierre's possible involvement.

It is generally agreed that the Commune as a whole did not plan the slaughter in the prisons, although its *comité de surveillance* may well have been concerned in them. This committee had been reorganised on 30 August by Panis, a friend of Robespirre's. Panis co-opted Marat on to the committee and Marat had been advocating the murder of counter-revolutionaries in his paper, although there was nothing new about that and his articles had had no effect in

6. *Oeuvres*, vol. VIII, p. 437.

the past. Robespierre had a certain amount of respect for Marat's integrity but he had already explained that he found his blood-thirstiness repellent. Robespierre's own reply to the charge that he was involved in the massacres was quite explicit: 'I had stopped attending the *conseil général* of the Commune before they started ... I only heard what was going on in the prisons from rumour, no doubt later than most of the citizens.'[7]   Unfortunately this is not true and since Robespierre had a good memory it isn't likely that he simply forgot what had happened.

He spent most of 1 September at the Commune, where Pétion accused him of saying that 'the land of liberty must be purged of the conspirators who infect it'. According to Pétion – who was admittedly an opponent by this time – one of those present wanted to denounce Robespierre for his violence and Pétion stopped him.[8] At the evening session Robespierre certainly read out a proclamation to Paris that he had been invited to draft. This was a general defence of the Commune's activities since the 10th and an attack on individual Girondins who were involved in a plot to 'divide the state, to sacrifice the people of Paris and perhaps to hand us over to the sword of the enemy'. In his final sentence he asserted that the people were 'in chains as soon as they slumber, despised as soon as they are no longer feared, defeated if they pardon their enemies before they have completely tamed them'.[9] This may have been no more than irresponsible, but on 2 September Robespierre and Billaud-Varenne appeared at the Commune to denounce 'a plot in favour of the Duke of Brunswick, whom a powerful party wants to put on the throne of France'.[10] That is the version of the Commune's minutes. Louvet – a member of the Commune himself and a bitter enemy of Robespierre – said that Brissot was denounced by name. On the following day Brissot's flat was searched by commissioners whose original orders had been to arrest him. Once in gaol his fate would have been more or less certain. Robespierre's reply to these specific charges against him is quite unconvincing. 'People have dared to insinuate . . . that I wanted to compromise the safety of several deputies by denounc-

7. *Oeuvres*, vol. IX, p. 90.
8. *Observations de Jérôme Pétion sur la lettre de Maximilien Robespierre*, Paris, 1792, p. 9.
9. *Oeuvres*, vol. VIII, pp. 449-57.
10. *Oeuvres*, vol. VIII, p. 458.

ing them to the *conseil général* during the execution of the conspirators –

That's rather delicately put, interrupted Ted.

' – I have already replied to this infamous charge by recalling that I stopped going to the Commune before these events happened.' He then admitted having denounced 'the persecution of the Commune by the two or three people in question' but put on a show of indignation to ask, 'What is this appalling doctrine that to denounce a man is the same thing as to kill him?'[11] That might have been valid if the first part of his statement had been true, but to get people arrested on 2 September was to connive at their murder.

Well, for once J.S. actually seems to have made up his mind, said Ted, so I think we can take his word for it; and a singularly nasty business it was.

Not so fast, put in Mac.

Now look here, you may think you're impatient for the last red fight to begin, but Henry and J.S. and I know you yourself wouldn't hurt a fly, even if it had a swastika on its back. This was an utterly damnable and indefensible business.

I'm not defending it. But you've got to use your imagination. I remember your telling us once how, at the end of the war, your unit handed over to the Russians a bunch of displaced persons who said they were political refugees. When you told Henry about it at the time he thought you'd done the right thing.

Henry said nothing.

That was a mistake – and we didn't know what they could expect, whereas Robespierre did.

And you weren't in a revolutionary situation and you had absolutely nothing to fear from them. Robespierre probably thought – wrongly if you like – that Brissot was out to wreck the revolution.

That's what he said to Pétion in a private conversation, I said.[12]

He couldn't prove his case and there wasn't much point in denouncing him to an Assembly that was controlled by Brissot's friends.

So he thought it was all right to have him hacked to pieces.

---

11. *Oeuvres*, vol. IX, p. 98.
12. *Discours de Jérôme Pétion sur l'accusation intentée contre Maximilien Robespierre*, Paris, 1792, Bib. Nat. Lb[41] 162, pp. 15-16.

It was only a month or so since Brissot had boasted that he would have Robespierre impeached before the High Court on a charge of treason. I'm not defending either of them but I'd like to know why it's always Robespierre who is singled out for special treatment. Why didn't Louvet denounce Billaud-Varenne? If Robespierre really felt that the revolution was the beginning of the millennium you can understand his thinking it his duty not to take any chances, especially with a Prussian army actually marching on Paris. If you can't, it's because you've forgotten how you once felt yourself.

I've said that I was wrong.

But you don't think it makes you a villain and I don't either. It's the situation that controls people and not vice versa.

They didn't all behave like Robespierre, I said. When the Commune tried to arrest Roland, Danton got the warrant withdrawn. He took Robespierre along with him too.

Well, that's something in Maximilien's favour. In any case, Danton wanted to strike a bargain with the Girondins. As Minister of Justice he hadn't done much to stop the massacres either.

Even if I accept all your special pleading, said Ted, it's clear enough how his mind was working: the revolution is something of transcendental importance. Therefore all means are legitimate to destroy its enemies. *He* knew who they were, although they had succeeded in pulling the wool over the eyes of a good many loyal revolutionaries. Therefore anyone he suspected should be put to death, whatever the Assembly or the Jacobins might think about him.

That's too logical to make political sense, said Henry, intervening for the first time. You have to know what he suspected them of doing, on what grounds, how dangerous he thought they were, what were the prospects of dealing with them by legal or constitutional means and so on. Since both sides were ready to have their opponents executed on suspicion, the difference between them is a matter of political judgment rather than competitive moral rectitude.

All I can say is that some people can't make up their minds about anything. Even J.S. knows where he stands on this one.

Thank you, I said, so let's move on to the next business, which concerns the elections to the Convention. Robespierre's name was put forward in two constituencies. In the Pas-de-Calais, which included Arras, he was the first to be elected, on a secret ballot, but he polled only 412 votes out of 721.[13] Carnot, who came next, got 677 out of 753 and the following seven deputies each polled more than Robespierre, so he obviously still had a good many enemies. Augustin, who had had a meteoric career in local government, especially since 10 August, and now held the most important post in the Department, did not stand. This suggests that he was very confident of being elected in Paris.

Robespierre managed the elections in Paris with quite remarkable efficiency. He first persuaded his own Section to recommend that voting should be public and that the 'electors' who would actually choose the deputies should meet in the Jacobins, so that their business could be transacted in public too. He took his Section's petition to the Commune – of which he was, of course, himself a member – and the Commune ordered public voting throughout Paris. The Sections chose 990 electors who first met at the Evêché. The Jacobins rejected one request for the use of their premises but reversed their decision as soon as they received an invitation from Robespierre and Collot. Robespierre's next move was to persuade the electors to exclude anyone who had been a member of a monarchist club or signed the protest against the occupation of the Tuileries on 20 June. That got rid of about 200 who would have been likely to vote the wrong way. The actual selection of deputies began on 5 September. The method adopted – which seems to have been common practice in revolutionary France – was to elect one deputy at a time, holding repeated ballots until someone got an absolute majority. This was a slow process but it allowed the Jacobins to concentrate maximum support on each of their candidates in turn. Robespierre's name was the first to be considered and he was elected by a rather undistinguished margin of 64% – which did not prevent an admirer telling the Jacobins that he had 'collected all the votes'.[14] The reason for his rather poor showing was that 136 votes were cast for Pétion, as against his own 338.[15] This defeat of Pétion was an expensive concession to Robespierre's amour-propre. The mayor, who thought he should have been chosen first, took the business badly and on 6 September announced his withdrawal in Paris since he had been returned for the Eure-et-Loir. When he later complained of the slight he had

13. Arch. Nat. C. 180.   14. *Oeuvres*, vol. VIII, p. 461.
15. Arch. Nat. C. 180.

received in Paris, Robespierre rather naïvely replied that the electoral assembly was going to vote for him unanimously on the following day, which suggests that not much was left to chance.[16] On 6 September Danton was elected with a 91% poll and Collot with one of 97%. Next day an elector complained that although the assembly had voted to express its regret to Pétion that Paris had not chosen him before Eure-et-Loir, this had been left out of the minutes. There was some argument as to whether the motion had actually been carried and the matter was dropped. Perhaps Pétion was wise to opt for his bird in the hand.

On the 8th there was a hint of trouble when 230 votes for the Girondin, Kersaint, prevented the election of Desmoulins on the first ballot. Robespierre then carried a motion that an hour at least should be devoted every day to a discussion of the merits of the various candidates.[17] This disposed of Kersaint, whose vote promptly fell to 36. Support seemed to be building up for the British scientist, Priestley, who had been offered French nationality in August. On the 8th he polled more than the combined votes for Kersaint and Marat. Next day Robespierre, to use his own words, 'proposed some general observations on the rules that might guide the electors in the exercise of their functions'.[18] According to the admittedly hostile Gorsas, these 'general observations' consisted of telling the electors that the need was not for exceptional talent, especially foreign talent, but for men whose defiance of the monarchy had driven them to live in cellars, or even for butchers.[19] Curiously enough, Marat's vote shot up from 25 to 420 and on the following day the butcher, Legendre, polled 561. He was the only candidate to have his profession recorded in the minutes. By this time Priestley had sized up the situation and withdrawn, Tallien, who had been one of the Commune's secretaries and was running strongly, was second in the poll that elected Legendre. It seemed to be his turn but when his case was discussed he made the extraordinary mistake of introducing himself by saying, 'I am not Brissot. I am not Robespierre either.' That finished him. His vote dwindled from one ballot to another and after eleven tries, in five of which he came second, he admitted defeat and accepted election for the Seine-et-Oise.

---

16. *Oeuvres*, vol. V, p. 147. 17. *Oeuvres*, vol. VIII, pp. 461-2.
18. *Oeuvres*, vol. VIII, p. 462n[2] 19. *Oeuvres*, vol. IX, p. 81n.[12]

Augustin's name first appeared on the 15th, when he received a respectable 86 votes. His subsequent progress was rather erratic and it took him six ballots before he was finally elected. Pétion quoted his case as proof of the fact that the elections were controlled by his brother. Maximilien replied unconvincingly that Augustin was 'known to the *patriotes* of Paris and to the Jacobins, who had witnessed his civic spirit' – it would not have been easy to show how, when or where – but admitted that 'he was more vigorously attacked than any other candidate', which seems something of a *non sequitur*.[20] Since the voting was so carefully organised, the fact that Hébert never secured more than six votes in any ballot is an interesting pointer to his standing at the time.

Despite one or two minor difficulties, Robespierre and the Jacobins could be well satisfied with their work. Of the 24 Paris deputies, 16 came from the Commune, and there would have been 17 if Tallien had not been punished for his stupidity. Eleven of them lived in a single Section, the *Théâtre français*, the home of Danton's political machine.[21] This is perhaps a warning against regarding the elections as all Robespierre's own work. Danton got his friends and followers chosen, and Danton, Marat and Chabot secured the election of the duc d'Orléans (who now called himself Egalité), despite Robespierre's opposition.[22] None the less, it had generally been Maximilien who supplied the helpful words of advice and controlled the voting. The fact that he was merely a member of the Commune when Danton was a Minister with prestige, patronage and money behind him, suggests that Robespierre must have had more of a hold over Parisian opinion than Ted believed.

Rigging the elections like that should have opened one or two eyes. One can almost admire it as a virtuoso performance, but it doesn't go down very well with all that disinterested stuff about excluding all previous deputies from the new assembly.

That didn't go unnoticed at the time, I said. Méhée, an assistant secretary of the Commune, asked his readers in a pamphlet how Robespierre could have forgotten his own principles. 'Let him be only one elector like the others and not spoil by his intrigues all

---

20. *Oeuvres*, vol. IX, p. 146; *Observations de Jérôme Pétion*, p. 23.
21. J. Guilaine, *Billaud-Varenne*, Paris, 1969, p. 96.
22. L. Madelin, *Danton*, Paris, 1914, p. 182; A. Mathiez, *Danton et la paix*, Paris, n.d., p. 76.

that he has done for the people.' Robespierre tried to get Méhée sacked for this, but he was defended by another secretary. In the circumstances it wouldn't be surprising if that was Tallien.[23]

The election of so many members of the Commune, including those most plausibly accused of responsibility for the massacres, to a Convention to which the Girondins had been returned *en bloc*, ensured that the battle between Paris and the Girondins would go on without interruption. On 15 September, before the Convention actually met, Marat told his readers that it was full of traitors and would need supervision by Paris.[24] Brissot's paper asserted a week later that two systems were in conflict, one tending towards 'the destruction of all extant institutions and general levelling' and the other towards the provisional maintenance of the status quo and a policy of gradual reform.[25] When the new assembly met, the majority of the deputies kept aloof from both factions. The Girondins, more a loose agglomeration of coteries than a coherent party, could rely on the support of perhaps a couple of hundred deputies. Their Montagnard opponents were almost confined to the 24 deputies from Paris to begin with, although they gradually attracted wider support. The Girondins controlled the executive – Danton resigned his Ministry when he was elected to the Convention – and dominated all the Assembly's committees except that of General Security. They could well have afforded to disregard their opponents but preferred to use their parliamentary strength to try to destroy them.

You can understand that they might feel safer that way, said Ted.

They were endlessly raking up the September massacres – which they themselves hadn't condemned at the time – and presenting Paris as the home of anarchy. They demanded a provincial guard for their protection and on 25 September they accused Marat, Danton and Robespierre of aspiring to dictatorship, with the obvious intention of getting them expelled from the Convention.

Robespierre, when he defended himself, was unable to resist the temptation to tell the tale of his revolutionary life to a new

23. *Oeuvres*, vol. VIII, p. 467.
24. J. Jaurès, *Histoire socialiste de la Révolution française*, Paris n.d., vol. III, p. 130.
25. Buchez and Roux, *Histoire parlementaire*, vol. XVIII, p. 64.

audience.[26] He appealed to the new deputies to judge the situation
for themselves and not accept on trust the partisan views of those
who were trying to split the Convention. His account of his own
services to the revolution irritated the deputies and he was interrupted a good deal, but the evidence against him was too flimsy
for the Girondins to get any action taken. Robespierre himself
seems to have hoped at first that the old quarrels could be forgotten,
or at least that his implacable opponents could be isolated. Towards
the end of September he began a new paper, *Lettres à ses commet-
tants,* which included regular parliamentary reports. These were at
first so detailed that by mid-November he had not got beyond
the September debates – he was not very good as an editor. His
early reports were surprisingly moderate: he treated Roland with
some respect and thought Buzot the unconscious tool of the Girondins.[27] It was not the fault of Robespierre or the Montagnards if
their opponents insisted on treating every issue in party terms.

Robespierre summed up his own views towards the end of
October in a speech to the Jacobins that amounted to a general
survey of the revolution. As he saw it, revolutionary history was
repeating itself, with the Girondins, like the Feuillants before
them, abandoning their former principles for the pursuit of
power.[28] 'Take away the word "republic" and I see no change.' The
Girondins were 'more criminal in their tactics than all the factions
that had preceded them' and no different in their aims. They
would not shrink from restoring the monarchy if it suited them
and they were turning themselves into champions of social con-
servatism. 'They are the gentlemen, the right people of the
republic; we are the sans-culottes, the riff-raff.'

That's interesting, said Ted. He might pose as the people's
friend but he didn't like being put with the sans-culottes. He
saw himself as the public school headmaster of a slum school,
devoted to his pupils and all that – so long as they remembered
that they were his and that they were only pupils.

The Girondins controlled both central and local government.
They had a permanent majority in the Assembly and most of the
press – encouraged by substantial subsidies from Roland – was on
their side. All that the Jacobins could do, in Robespierre's opinion,

26. *Oeuvres*, vol. ix, pp. 14-26.   27. *Oeuvres*, vol. v, pp. 26-8.
28. *Oeuvres*, vol. ix, pp. 43-62.

131

was to soldier on and avoid any provocative gestures. He hoped in time to persuade the majority in the Convention that it was being manipulated by the Girondins for their own purposes. This was a good speech; sensible, well argued and much more free from rhetorical extravagance than most of his earlier efforts. Whether or not his experience on the Commune had taught him the effectiveness of plain and simple speech, his style had become much sharper and more cogent.

On 29 October Roland delivered another lament over the situation in Paris, quoting a letter which denounced 'those who incite to murder . . . They don't want to hear of anyone but Robespierre and pretend that he alone can save the nation.' Guadet, who was in the chair, tried to prevent Maximilien from replying to this underhand attack, but Robespierre managed to get a hearing and defied his enemies to come out into the open. Louvet, who had been carrying around a *Robespierride* in his pocket for the past month or so, took up the challenge and read a long denunciation of Robespierre's career ever since his first breach with the Girondins. Maximilien was given a week to prepare his reply which proved to be one of his most skilful performances.[29] His denial that he had influenced the elections in Paris or had any connection with the September massacres may not have been true but it probably sounded quite plausible to those not very well acquainted with the facts. On the broad question of how the revolutionaries should regard the events of August and September he was unanswerable. Showing how the Girondins' niggling search for party advantage was turning them against the revolution as a whole, he proclaimed defiantly, 'All these things were illegal, as illegal as the revolution, as the destruction of the throne and the Bastille, as illegal as liberty itself.' He asked his colleagues to consider events 'not as justices of the peace but as statesmen and legislators to the world'. He expressed his regrets for the massacres but refused to condemn them and accused his opponents of forgetting all about the victims on the revolutionary side and reserving all their sympathies for those killed in the prisons. 'Do you want to dishonour in the eyes of Europe the revolution that produced the republic, and to put arms into the hands of all the enemies of freedom? This is indeed a truly admirable love of humanity that perpetuates the misery

29. *Oeuvres*, vol. IX, pp. 79-101.

and servitude of people and hides a savage desire to bathe in *patriote* blood.'

He may be getting more eloquent, said Ted, but he seems to me to be getting a lot harder as well. He was always a bit of a fanatic but he used to get his satisfaction out of posing as a sacrificial lamb. Now he's as skilful as any of them when it comes to denying inconvenient facts and it's a short step from considering things as statesmen to justifying *raison d'état*.

He had had quite a lot to put up with, said Henry and you can't expect a man to be in the thick of revolutionary politics for three years without contracting some of the less attractive attributes of the politician. In the past you've accused him of just the opposite, of never having his feet on the ground.

Robespierre's conclusion was moderate enough, I said. He had every right to denounce Roland's unscrupulous tactics but all he said was, 'Nature did not shape you either for great deeds or great crimes . . . Out of regard for you I will not go any further . . . But next time take a more careful look at the instruments people put into your hands.' He didn't sing his own praises and he didn't attack his opponents. 'The only revenge I ask is concord and the triumph of liberty.' The speech went down quite well with the Assembly which refused Louvet a second innings and the Girondins had to abandon, for the time being, their attempt to unseat their opponents.

I don't want to seem a niggler myself, said Ted, but what other card could he play? He hadn't a hope of turning the majority against the Girondins. The injured-innocence line may have been good political tactics but I doubt if the leopard had changed his spots since August and September.

He was taking stock, I went on, and realising that he had outgrown some of his earlier ambitions. In the course of one of his replies to pamphlets by Pétion, in his newspaper, he said that he didn't believe any longer in the great men of history.[30] 'Our revolution has made me feel the full force of the axiom that history is fiction and I am convinced that chance and intrigue have produced more heroes than genius and *vertu* . . . I have come to suspect that the real heroes are not those who triumph but those who suffer, not those who shine on the world's stage or the horizon of

30. *Oeuvres,* vol. v, p. 156.

posterity but those whose very names are buried in the tombs where tyranny flung them.'

That's the most impressive thing he's said so far. In a way, of course, it's a continuation of his old idea of martyrdom, but there's a new depth to it. He's thinking of ends as ends and he's got past the adolescent idea of relying on posterity to avenge him on the present. I like that notion of history as fiction – as though he were a character that we were inventing.

That won't do for me, Henry, objected Ted. He can be a fictional character if he likes but I'm not. I'm real enough and I insist on my right to judge him as though he were too.

It's only our obscurity that prevents us from being fictional too, said Henry. No one will bother to re-create us in his own image.

We're dealing with History, not fiction, I said firmly. Let's get back to the facts. He seems to have been ill sometime during the autumn. There's no medical evidence about these recurrent illnesses. His doctor, Souberbielle, who left a few notes about him, doesn't talk about his illnesses and one has to infer them from his absence from debates. This particular attack was probably the one that affected his domestic arrangements. When Augustin was elected to the Convention he brought Charlotte to Paris with him. She stayed at first with the Duplays but she seems to have been jealous of Mme Duplay's hold over her brother. According to her own account she managed to persuade him that a man of his distinction ought to have an establishment of his own. They took lodgings together and when he fell ill Charlotte looked after him. When Mme Duplay got to know of it she accused Charlotte of neglecting him and eventually persuaded Maximilien to return to her house. Charlotte, who was perhaps more loyal to her brother in her memoirs than she had been at the time, explained his decision as further proof of his obliging nature, but she doesn't conceal that she took it badly. If one can believe her, this is not surprising, since Mme Duplay turned away her servant, who was taking some sweetmeats to Maximilien, with the remark that she didn't want him poisoned.[31] Both women may have tried to conceal their dislike of each other from Maximilien but Charlotte became something of a problem for both brothers. Incidentally, Robespierre himself, in one of his replies to Pétion, claimed that

31. H. Fleischmann, *Mémoires de Charlotte Robespierre*, pp. 226-9.

although he might be touchy about public matters, those who knew him best found him easy-going and good-natured in private life.[32] All the evidence suggests that this was true.

The Convention, which had so far achieved virtually nothing, now began to discuss what to do with the king, whose position was further compromised by the discovery, on 20 November, of some of his secret correspondence with the *émigrés* and with members of the earlier Assemblies. The Girondins, although they were more divided on this than on most issues, managed to give the impression that they were defending Louis XVI. The majority of the Assembly was reluctant to put him to death but could scarcely keep him in prison untried or try him without getting enmeshed in legal contradictions about his constitutional inviolability and the Assembly's lack of competence as a court. The young deputy, Saint-Just, in his first major speech on 13 November, cut the Gordian knot by declaring that the king should not be judged at all in the legal sense but condemned out of hand as a public enemy. Robespierre, just as he had followed Billaud's lead on the war and on what to do after the overthrow of the monarchy, now took his cue from Saint-Just. When he spoke on 3 December even his style seemed modelled on that of his younger colleague. 'There is no case to plead here. Louis is no defendant; you are no judges; you are and can only be Statesmen.'[33] His argument was similar to the one he had used against Louvet. 'If Louis can be tried Louis can be acquitted; he may be innocent. Indeed, he is presumed to be innocent until he is convicted. But if Louis is acquitted, if Louis can be presumed innocent, what becomes of the revolution?' 'People appeal to the constitution in his favour . . . The constitution prohibited everything that you have done. Even if he could only be dethroned you had no right to do that until you had tried him. You had no right to keep him in prison and he is entitled to his release and to damages. The constitution condemns you : go and beg for pardon at his feet.' He was probably right when he said that the hesitation of the Assembly had encouraged the revival of open royalism in Paris. When he came to discuss the nature of the king's punishment he was on more difficult ground since he was still an opponent of the death penalty in the criminal courts. He asserted that the only justification for capital punishment – the

32. *Oeuvres*, vol. v, p. 110.   33. *Oeuvres*, vol. IX, pp. 121-30.

protection of individuals and of society – never applied in the case of the common criminal but did demand the execution of the king. 'Neither exile nor prison can make his existence of no consequence to the public well-being . . . Louis must die because the nation must live.' It was a powerful speech but it did not overcome the scruples of the deputies who decided that the king had to be tried.

Robespierre then devoted all his energies to securing Louis's execution. He warned the Jacobins that the Girondins were hoping to provoke a riot in Paris in order to discredit the capital and the campaign of some of the Sections for the death penalty. When the Girondins proposed consulting the electorate about the penalty, Robespierre argued that simple people could easily be misled and implicitly conceded that the elections had only gone well in September because the Right had been frightened away from the polls.[34]

When the Girondins pointed out that Robespierre had advocated a plebiscite on the fate of the king, after his flight in 1791, his reply really amounted to saying that at that time the Assembly was more favourable to the king than public opinion at large whereas now the situation was probably reversed. Brissot, as he pointed out, was equally illogical in having advocated war in order to dispose of the monarchy and now warning against the king's execution in case it added to France's foreign enemies.[35] On 28 December he tried hard to overcome the reluctance of his colleagues to shed the king's blood. 'I felt my own republican *vertu* faltering in the presence of guilt humbled by the sovereign power [of the nation]. Hatred of tyrants and love of humanity have a common origin in the heart of the just man who loves his country. But, fellow-citizens, the final proof of their devotion that the people's representatives owe to the nation is to sacrifice these immediate promptings of natural sensibility to the safety of a great people and of oppressed humanity. Citizens, the sensibility that sacrifices innocence to crime is a cruel sensibility; clemency that makes concessions to tyrants is barbarous.'[36]

I wish I could feel that he meant it, said Mac. I take his argument and I think I accept his conclusions, only I wish he'd put

34. *Oeuvres*, vol. IX, p. 189. 35. *Oeuvres*, vol. V, pp. 200-4.
36. *Oeuvres*, vol. IX, p. 184.

more emphasis on the love of humanity and less on the hatred of tyrants.

For once I agree with Mac, said Ted. One can't help suspecting that he saw the king's head as a football he wanted to put through the Girondin goal. Of course the arguments are all very noble, but J.S. has only shown him on his best behaviour, trying to convert the Assembly.

He was rather more aggressive in the Jacobins, I admitted. On 12 December for instance, he said that he despaired so much of public liberty that he invited Roland to assassinate him.[37] If you compare that with the way he had treated Roland in the Assembly on 5 November you can't help thinking that he adjusted his feelings and his language to his audience and wondering when he meant what he said. At all events he got his way. The Convention found Louis guilty, voted for the death penalty and refused to consult the electorate about the verdict. There was probably a good deal of bribery in one direction and intimidation in the other and at least Robespierre wasn't involved in either of those.

He took the verdict as a sign that the Girondins had lost their majority and became positively euphoric. You can see his attitude changing. On 12 December he had been very pessimistic at the Jacobins. On the 28th he objected to people talking about the majority and the minority, 'There is no permanent majority because it does not belong to any party. It re-forms every time there is a free debate.' About the same time he told his readers that the period of the king's trial was the most dangerous crisis of the whole revolution.[38] He attacked Roland in the Convention on 6 January, accusing him of playing the game of England and Prussia. Roland resigned on the 23rd and three weeks later the Montagnards got their candidate, Pache, elected mayor of Paris. On 15 February Robespierre told the Jacobins 'The majority of the Convention is pure. I affirm its good intentions. On vital issues the big principles will always carry the day there.'[39] He wrote in his paper, 'Pitt is tottering in England (Robespierre had taken no part in the debates which led to the declaration of war on England and Holland on 1 February) and the hypocritical intriguers who serve him are unmasked in France . . . Already the majority of the Conven-

37. *Oeuvres*, vol. IX, p. 157.   38. *Oeuvres*, vol. V, p. 227.
39. *Oeuvres*, vol. IX, p. 267.

tion, freed from the meshes of the intrigues in which a criminal faction had entangled it, has raised itself to the stature of its mission and shown itself worthy of the despots' anger and of the esteem of the nations.'[40] It was perhaps the first time since 1789 that he had sounded so confident.

Towards the end of February this brief period of optimism was interrupted by an unwelcome intrusion that took all the deputies by surprise. War expenditure and ineffective tax collection had produced severe inflation. The flight of many wealthy Parisians, who were still draining specie out of the country, was probably responsible for a good deal of unemployment in the luxury trades, while the uncertainty of the political situation discouraged capital investment of all kinds. In the almost total absence of precise information we can only guess but it seems very likely that while the Jacobins proclaimed the virtues of the sans-culotte his standard of living was falling quite sharply. A well-informed observer wrote early in May, 'This class has suffered a good deal since the revolution; it is the class that has taken the Bastille, carried through 10 August etc. It has packed the public galleries at every kind of assembly, passed resolutions, joined in all the discussions and – achieved nothing. The woman who owned a watch, ear-rings, rings, jewels, has taken them to the pawnshop and they have been sold. What is the position of these people today? They have nothing left; they have parted with all their precious furniture which gave them an idea of property, of owning something.'[41] As people of this kind whose impoverishment might well be directly proportionate to their political militancy, if not actually a product of it, became more desperate, radical leaders, collectively known as *Enragés*, emerged to channel their discontent into political action. On 12 February petitioners to the Assembly, demanding price controls on corn, made disparaging remarks about deputies 'who sup well every night'. Ten days later, when the Jacobins refused the use of their premises to women who wanted to discuss food supplies, they had the unfamiliar experience of being collectively barracked from their public galleries. On the 25th crowds invaded some of the grocers' shops, selling off soap, candles and sugar at what they considered to be fair prices.

40. *Oeuvres*, vol. v, p. 305.
41. A. Schmidt, *Tableaux de la Révolution française*, Leipzig, 1867, vol. I, p. 190.

There was nothing very surprising or very dangerous about this sort of activity which had been common enough, in times of scarcity, before the revolution. But in the over-heated atmosphere politicians of all sides attributed the disturbance to the machinations of their opponents. At the Jacobins, on the night when the grocers' shops had been raided, Robespierre, like Marat and Collot, attributed the whole affair to political intrigue. One 'proof' of this was the fact that some of the rioters had denounced 'not the intriguers and the counter-revolutionary side of the Convention . . . but the Montagnards, the Paris deputies and the Jacobins, whom they described as hoarders.'[42] 'I don't say that the people are guilty . . . but when they rise in revolt, should they not have a worthy objective? Should they be concerned with paltry merchandise? . . . The people must rise, not to collect sugar but to lay low the brigands.'

When you think of all that white bread, jam and fruit at the Duplays', said Ted, this was pretty cool.

It certainly suggests that he was out of touch, agreed Mac. But you can see how it must have looked from his point of view. He'd been warning the Jacobins for months that their enemies would try to discredit them by creating trouble in Paris and it looked as though this was it. He may have been mistaken but he was sincere, both in his sympathy for the sans-culottes and in thinking that this was a political intrigue – and everyone else seems to have thought so too.

You'd better be careful or you'll end up on the wrong side of the barricades. The whole thing showed that he was living in a fantasy world and that all his talk about equality was abstract and unreal. He knew better than the sans-culottes, not merely what was good for them, but what they really wanted. He wouldn't have thought much of your saying that he was no worse than the others since he always considered himself to be someone special. I'll grant you his sincerity up to a point, though it could be rather flexible when he was in a corner, but you've shifted your ground a good deal. I thought we were supposed to be dealing with the realities of social conflict rather than the *états d'âme* of individuals.

I think Ted is perhaps drawing too many conclusions from an

42. *Oeuvres*, vol. IX, pp. 274-6.

isolated case, said Henry. You could argue that Robespierre was right in a way, at least as regards the short run. The educated Montagnards knew enough about economics to realise that you couldn't just charm away inflation by selling a few groceries at cut prices. They genuinely meant their policies to benefit ordinary people and they hadn't had much of a chance to apply them so far. Of course you can understand the frustration of the sans-culottes but there was no answer to their problems.

I still think 'paltry merchandise' could only have been said by a man who had never been short of things like that himself.

There was going to be more trouble of this kind, I said, but this particular incident blew over – which probably strengthened Robespierre's conviction that it had been a put-up job. He soon recovered his optimism and his conviction that the best course for the Jacobins was to follow a moderate policy that would allow them gradually to win a majority in the Convention. On 27 February he opposed a proposal by Desfieux that the Jacobins should campaign for the unseating of deputies who had voted for a plebiscite on the fate of the king.[43] A week later he again disagreed with Desfieux, who wanted to create a revolutionary tribunal: 'The national Assembly is the best assembly that we have had so far; it contains enough *patriotes* to ensure the public good . . . The time has arrived when the intriguers, exposed in the eyes of the public, have lost most of their influence.'[44] All that was needed was a sustained publicity campaign and no talk of revolutionary action. The first French defeats in Belgium left him unperturbed, since he always assumed that success in the war was the direct consequence of pursuing the right domestic policies. He told his colleagues in the Assembly that things had been much worse in the previous summer. 'I have no doubts about the courage of our troops. No one dares to doubt the invincibility of a French army, properly led against the tyrants . . . I have confidence in Dumouriez [the commander-in-chief on the Belgian front]. Three months ago he wanted to invade Holland. If he had done so, not merely would we have escaped our present misfortunes, but there would have been a revolution in England.'[45] When the Convention voted to create a revolutionary tribunal on 10 March, Robespierre was not enthusi-

43. *Oeuvres*, vol. IX, pp. 278-9.   44. *Oeuvres*, vol. IX, p. 296.
45. *Ouevres*, vol. IX, p. 308.

astic and feared that it might become the political instrument of a faction. 'It is important to define carefully what you mean by conspirators; otherwise the best citizens may be the victims of a court intended to protect them against counter-revolutionaries.'[46].

That sounds more like self-preservation than moderation, said Ted.

You may be wrong there. On the night before, a handful of extremists, supported by the Cordeliers and one or two Sections, had tried to carry out some sort of a coup d'etat in Paris. The whole business is very obscure and the intention of some of the leaders at least could have been to provide Dumouriez with a pretext for marching on Paris to maintain order. The intended insurrection was vigorously opposed both by the Commune and by Collot, Billaud-Varenne, Jeanbon Saint-André and Dufourny at the Jacobins. Robespierre gave them his support on the 13th, despite barracking from the public galleries. One can almost use his various estimates of the casualties in the Champ de Mars 'massacre' as a thermometer indicating his own revolutionary temperature: in July they had been 1,500 and in the crisis of the following spring they were to go up to 2,000; this time they were down to 500. He was beginning to take a rather more gloomy view of the situation but still opposed to any talk of violence. 'I was confident enough to tell you that the Convention would always be the bulwark of liberty. I have not come here to deny that but to tell you that the Convention has been led astray and cruelly abused and that its mistakes could lead the nation to its ruin. We must rally all the good citizens.'[47] He still maintained that minor riots would only serve the purposes of the Girondins, who were trying to incite them. Despite *grands murmures,* he affirmed, 'We are not asking for the destruction of freedom's enemies; we are asking that they convert themselves and that they live.' On the 22nd he defeated another motion of Desfieux's, who again wanted to agitate for the expulsion of the *appellants* from the Convention. Marat, who had also been recommending a moderate policy, was beginning to change his ground and to despair of constitutional action. On 27 March he proposed that the Sections should ask the Assembly, as they had done before 10 August, whether it was capable of saving the nation. Robespierre defeated this too: 'The Sections have nothing to ask the

46. *Oeuvres,* vol. IX, p. 314. 47. *Oeuvres,* vol. IX, p. 322.

Convention. Has it not got the same interest as the Sections in saving itself?'[48]

It was during this relatively sunny period that Mme Jullien, the mother of one of the deputies, invited the Robespierres to dinner and her description of the family has the merit of not having been revised in the light of subsequent events. 'He [Robespierre] is as fit to be a party leader as to catch the moon in his teeth. He is abstracted, like a thinker, dry as a man who spends all his time in his study, but as gentle as a lamb and as melancholy as Young. I can see that he has not our tender sensibility, but I like to think that he wants the good of the human race – more from motives of justice than from love. You have only got to see him face to face to judge that nature only gives such gentle features to a noble soul. The younger Robespierre is more lively, more open, an excellent *patriote,* but a mediocre intelligence and so touchy as to bring discredit on the Montagnards.'[49]

That fits in with what everyone else said about him in his private life, said Henry. It's interesting to find someone who was more or less neutral – and a woman – finding him quite pleasant to look at, when his opponents kept repeating after his death that he looked like a cross between a cat and a tiger.

When Danton's wife died during his absence on mission in Belgium, Robespierre wrote to him so warmly as to suggest that Mme Jullien may have underestimated his emotional depth. Calling himself a 'tender and devoted friend', he went on, 'Je t'aime jusqu'à la mort. Dans ce moment je suis toi-même.'[50]

About the end of March everything began to go wrong. It became clear that the insurrection in the Vendée, touched off by the attempt to impose conscription there, was no flash in the pan, but a major civil war. After the successes of the previous autumn, when Belgium and the Rhineland had been occupied, the French armies were now retreating on all fronts and the Allies had a whole campaigning season in front of them, in which to finish off the revolutionaries. Dumouriez was badly beaten at Neerwinden on 18 March and retreated to the French frontier. There he began

48. *Oeuvres,* vol. IX, pp. 342-3.
49. E. Lockroy, *Journal d'une bourgeoise pendant la Révolution,* Paris, 1881, pp. 345-6.
50. *Correspondance,* vol. I, p. 160.

to denounce the Jacobins in terms similar to those that Lafayette had used a year before, negotiated an armistice with the Austrians and prepared to march on Paris. In the capital itself the Jacobins could no longer count on the support of the sans-culottes, exasperated by rising prices and increasingly responsive to new militants who saw the Convention as an obstacle to their ambitions.

Faced with these new dangers, the Assembly provided itself with the machinery that was eventually to bring victory – at a price. The revolutionary tribunal, originally intended only for high-ranking conspirators, was set up on 10 March. On the 21st the Convention voted to create *comités révolutionnaires* in each commune and in each Section of the major towns. These were originally intended to keep an eye on foreigners but from the start, in Paris at least, they were inclined to arrest any kind of suspect. A formidable repressive power was thus put in the hands of the small minorities who controlled the various Sections and the Sections themselves became battle-grounds between rival factions. A situation was soon to develop in which those with local influence could silence personal or political enemies by having them locked up on the vaguest of charges. Since all sides loudly protested that everything they did was for the benefit of the revolution, it became almost impossible for anyone – then or now – to penetrate the fog of confusion and suspicion. Towards the end of April a special levy of 12,000 men was ordered in Paris, to fight in the unpopular civil war in the Vendée. This was accompanied by a new tax on the wealthy to equip the troops and pay for their dependants. Who was drafted and who was taxed might well depend on which faction had secured control of a particular Section. Everyone had a new incentive to attend the nightly meetings; more people than usual did, and there were pitched battles in many of the Sections. The least important of the emergency measures at the time was the creation on 9 April of a Committee of Public Safety, originally of nine members, meeting in secret. This was eventually to become a kind of War Cabinet but its influence in the spring of 1793 was very limited.

The new crisis revived the conflict between Montagnards and Girondins. The despatch to the provinces of over 90 deputies – mainly Montagnards – to accelerate recruiting, enabled the Girondins to recover their majority. As tension rose in Paris, fear of disorder may well have helped to reinforce this. Both sides prepared for a fight to a finish. There were apparently talks between Danton and some of the Girondin leaders in March, when Danton urged a truce, only to be rebuffed by Guadet: 'War, and may one side perish!'[51] Each faction – with more or less conviction – accused the other of being in league with Dumouriez and, since one of his aides-de-camp was Egalité's son, the future Louis-Philippe, of plotting a royalist restoration.

Robespierre's first reaction was relatively moderate. His appeal on 29 March for a general insurrection to destroy the enemies of the revolution was not intended as more than a call for emergency measures supervised by the Convention.[52] On 1 April he argued that 'the most fatal measure of all would be to violate the representative body of the nation'.[53] But while trying to wean the Jacobins from any thought of violence, he urged the Convention to arrest the Girondins as accomplices of Dumouriez.[54] By the 3rd he had become pessimistic about the prospects of parliamentary action and he now told the Jacobins that it was necessary to raise an army of sans-culottes in Paris.[55] Gorsas – an opponent – perhaps went too far when he claimed in his paper that Robespierre had said, 'The blood of the villains must be shed' and urged the Sections 'to force us to arrest the disloyal deputies'. The same remark was attributed to Augustin two days later.[56] The Jacobin Club did approve a circular to this effect, signed by Marat, who was in the chair. The *Halle aux Blé* Section took the Jacobins' advice and circularised the other Sections with a petition to the effect that the *majority* of the Assembly was corrupt and that guilty deputies should be arrested. When Pétion denounced this to the Assembly on the 10th, Robespierre became almost hysterical. 'A powerful faction is conspiring with Europe's tyrants to give us a king.' 'This suits all those with ambitions, the *aristocrates bourgeois,* who are horrified by equality and have been made to feel apprehensive about their property.' 'The republic only suits the people, men of all conditions with pure and lofty souls, philosophers, friends of humanity, sans-culottes.' He gave his own version of the history of the revolution, in which the Girondins appeared as the successors of the Feuillants. He accused the Ministers of deliberately sabotaging the invasion of Holland, Dumouriez of getting himself defeated on purpose and

51. ˉMadelin, *Danton*, p. 225.
52. *Oeuvres*, vol. IX, pp. 344-50.
53. *Oeuvres*, vol. IX, pp. 354-5.
54. *Oeuvres*, vol. IX, p. 367.
55. *Oeuvres*, vol. IX, p. 358.
56. Aulard, Jacobins.

the War Minister, Beurnonville, of wrecking the country's defences. He concluded by calling for the trial of Orléans (whom he no longer called *Egalité*) and his agents, and indicated that he would like to see Vergniaud, Guadet and Gensonné and, according to one report, Marie Antoinette, tried as well.[57]

Was he suggesting that Marie Antoinette was involved in a plot to put Orléans on the throne, asked Ted. It doesn't sound very likely.

He seems to have lost all control over himself as he had done in the previous July. He must have known that wild talk of this kind would merely stiffen the resistance of the Assembly. The Montagnards had a shock on the 12th when the Girondins won a vote to send Marat before the revolutionary tribunal for signing the Jacobin circular. This was a tactical mistake on their part, both because it provided a precedent for purging the Assembly and because Marat was triumphantly acquitted, but its immediate result seems to have been to check the Montagnard offensive. Robespierre urged the Jacobins to appeal to the Sections for calm. The Montagnard plan of getting the electorate to recall some of the deputies misfired. When Pache presented a petition to this effect from 33 of the Sections, on the 15th, the Girondins immediately adopted the idea and extended it to the country as a whole, seeing it as an unexpected opportunity to renew their own mandates and get rid of their opponents. Robespierre quickly reversed his own policy, told the Jacobins on the 17th that the idea of convening the *assemblées primaires* was a Girondin plot and urged them – not altogether to their liking – to have confidence in the Committee of Public Safety and the new War Minister, Bouchotte.[58] This left them without any positive policy and Le Bas wrote a gloomy letter to his father on the 21st saying that the Girondins had been on top for the past twelve days because so many deputies were absent on mission. When they returned he hoped for a revival of 'the majority that overthrew the tyrant.'[59]

If we can accept your interpretation of what all this meant, said Ted, it's an interesting departure from his usual policy of wait and see. I think this is the first time we've seen him actually trying to force a crisis and he soon had enough.

---

57. *Oeuvres*, vol. IX, pp. 376-413.   58. *Oeuvres*, vol. IX, pp. 443-6.
59. Stéfan-Pol, *Autour de Robespierre*, p. 52.

Garat, the Minister of the Interior, claimed in his memoirs, in one of those long verbatim accounts that are obviously made up afterwards, that Robespierre said to him, sometime before 10 March, 'I am weary of the revolution. I am ill. The country was never in such danger and I doubt whether it will come through.'[60] It seems very unlikely that he said anything of the kind in February or March but he may well have done so in May. On 2 May he apologised to a correspondent for delay in answering his letter, because he had been ill.[61] On the 10th the Convention moved into more spacious premises where the acoustics were even worse. Robespierre, who had already complained that his voice was not strong enough for the old building, probably found the new one an additional strain. He does not seem to have spoken in the Assembly between 5 May and 27 May or in the Jacobins between the 13th and the 24th. When he did speak it was to warn against unconstitutional action. On 8 May he presented a radical programme to the Assembly, for the arrest of suspects, the payment of men on National Guard duty and the acceleration of arms production. When he repeated this to the Jacobins in the evening, with the addition of payment for attendance at the meetings of the Sections, he used more violent language: 'There are only two parties in France: the people and its enemies. We must exterminate these miserable villains who are eternally conspiring against the rights of man.' But he insisted that he was not preaching class war. 'Don't distinguish people by their wealth and station but by their character. The sans-culottes have never pretended to equality of wealth but to equal rights and equal happiness.' He went on to make it clear that what he wanted was no more than the voting of exceptional powers to deal with counter-revolutionaries. 'You may think that you ought to revolt and put on an insurrectionary air. Not at all; we must exterminate all our enemies with the law in our hands.' Once again he said that the Convention was strong enough to deal with any factions.[62] On the 13th he urged the Jacobins not to contemplate extreme measures until they had exhausted all those that would not compromise the Society. 'Even then such measures should not be proposed in a Society which must remain cautious and political.'[63] This could possibly indicate that

60. Garat, *Mémoires*, Paris, 1862, p. 95.
61. *Correspondance*, vol. I, pp. 167-78.   62. *Oeuvres*, vol. IX, pp. 480-94.
63. *Oeuvres*, vol. IX, p. 517.

he was aware that other measures were being prepared elsewhere. Robespierre was probably haunted by his memories of the Champ de Mars crisis of 1791 but his audience found all his talk of caution and legality somewhat uninspiring. He had to appeal to the Jacobins to stop attacking the Montagnards and in the public galleries any talk of caution was dismissed as *du Robespierre*.[64]

In Paris itself a moderate offensive was making some headway in the Sections. This was probably why Guadet proposed, on 18 May, that the Commune should be replaced by the presidents of the Sections and the *suppléants* or reserve deputies convened at Bourges in case of any insurrection against the Assembly. In order to defeat this dangerous motion, which might well have been the signal for civil war, Barère persuaded the Convention to set up a committee of twelve to investigate the activities of the Commune. The Twelve, according to the Montagnard, Levasseur, included three actual royalists as well as some of the more militant Girondins.[65] They took the offensive with a vigour that threatened to destroy the hold of the radicals over Paris, which was probably a good deal more precarious than is generally realised. They arrested Hébert and Varlet on the 24th and Dobsen, the president of the *Cité* Section two days later. For some time now there had been meetings at the *Evêché* to plan an insurrection. As May drew to an end it was becoming clear that things could not go on like this much longer and both sides were preparing to strike.

Robespierre's attitude is not at all clear. On the 26th he made what sounded like a call to insurrection at the Jacobins. 'When all the laws are violated, when despotism is at its height, when good faith and decency are trampled underfoot, the people must rise. That moment has now come.' This sounded clear enough, but, as usual, he qualified his remarks in a way that could either have been intended for self-protection or could equally well imply that he had been wrapping up moderate intentions in violent language in order to make them more palatable to his audience. He invited the people *à se mettre dans la Convention contre tous les députés corrompus*. 'I declare I will put myself in a state of insurrection against the president and all the members sitting in the Convention.'[66] If his words have not been badly distorted in the surviving

64. Schmidt, op. cit., vol. I, p. 244.
65. R. Levasseur, *Mémoires*, Paris, 1829, vol. I, p. 217.
66. *Oeuvres*, vol. IX, p. 527.

press reports his audience must have wondered whether he intended them to organise an insurrection or merely to ensure that Montagnard deputies were able to get a hearing in the Assembly. Three days later, when the crisis was breaking and crowds had already begun to threaten the Assembly, he was equally ambiguous. 'If the people do not rise in their entirety, liberty is destroyed.' This was as much a warning against an *insurrection partielle* as a call to arms. He urged the Commune, not to revolt, but to 'resist oppression and demand justice for the persecution of *patriotes*'. His conclusion was scarcely a war-cry: 'I am incapable of prescribing to the people the means of its salvation. That is beyond me, exhausted as I am by four years of revolution and the oppressive spectacle of the victory of all that is most corrupt and vile. It is not for me to indicate measures, consumed as I am by a slow fever and even more by the fever of patriotism. I have spoken and I have no other duty to perform.'[67]

It looks fairly clear to me, said Ted. He knew that an insurrection was being prepared and he was in favour of it provided that it won, but he thought there was a good chance that it wouldn't. In that case he wanted to safeguard both himself and the Jacobins. Not a very heroic attitude perhaps, but quite a sensible one that had proved its worth in the past.

You may be right, but I think there's more to it than that. It depended on who was going to run the insurrection. It's quite likely that the people behind it were working quite independently of the Jacobins and that the Club was very much in the dark about what their intentions were. Everything connected with the *journées* of 31 May and 2 June is quite extraordinarily complicated and obscure and the subject has never been investigated in depth.[68] There were too many groups involved and competing with each other. There seem to have been two plans for the 31st, one of them perhaps organised by extremists who were suspect to both the Jacobins and the Commune. Some of the men on the Commune and the Girondin, Dulaure, said afterwards that these extremists were, in fact, counter-revolutionaries.[69] Desfieux, who had been urging

67. *Oeuvres*, vol. IX, pp. 537-8.
68. See D. Guérin, *La lutte des classes sous la première république*, Paris, 1946, vol. I, chap. II.
69. J.-A. Dulaure, *Esquisse historique des principaux événements de la Révolution française*, Paris, 1823, vol. II, pp. 390-1.

extreme measures all through the spring and had been opposed by Robespierre, was one of the leaders and it was certainly odd that so many of them should have been foreign. One or two of the Sections declared for the Girondins, who seem to have thought, at one time, that the insurrectionary movement as a whole was on their side. At one point there was almost a pitched battle between the three radical Sections of the faubourg Saint-Antoine and the conservative *Butte des Moulins.* It rather looks as though the Jacobins and the Commune had been planning some sort of *insurrection morale* and that they were anticipated by a rival group in the *Evêché.* They then managed to fuse with this latter group and to dominate it but the result was so much restraint that they failed to intimidate the Convention. On 31 May the Assembly refused to do more than to abolish the Committee of Twelve. The Commune, which had apparently tried to prevent a march on the Convention on the 31st, then took the lead in organising another one on 2 June. This time the deputies were browbeaten into ordering the house arrest – but not the *accusation* – of the leading Girondins, the Committee of Twelve and two of the Ministers, Clavière and Lebrun.

Perhaps it might be as well if we stuck to Robespierre, said Henry.

That doesn't help very much. We don't know what he did – if he did anything – or what he thought about the situation when it was changing almost from hour to hour. When it was all over, of course, like everyone else he had to pretend that it was a glorious victory, but that doesn't prove anything. Tissot, a contemporary historian who had a relative in the Convention, said that Robespierre and Danton had been hesitant and that the leaders were Marat, Billaud and Chabot.[70] Robespierre's only intervention during the crisis itself was to propose – unsuccessfully – the *accusation* of the Twelve and the 'accomplices of Dumouriez' on the 31st. He said nothing on either of the next two days. A recent historian, Guérin, suggests that Dobsen, who was added to the committee at the *Evêché,* was an agent of his who was put on the committee to restrain it, but he doesn't produce any evidence for this.[71] Sénart, an employee of the Committee of General Security, whose 'revela-

70. R. F. Tissot, *Histoire de la Révolution française,* Paris, 1839, vol. IV, p. 298.

71. D. Guérin, op. cit., vol. I, p. 120.

tions', implausible as they often are, suggest that he did have access to a good many secret files, asserted that the insurrectionary com-mitttee favoured Danton and that it was pushed aside by Dufourny and Robespierre.[72] None of this tells us very much.

There is one piece of hard evidence, a personal memorandum found in Robespierre's papers.[73] 'We need a single will (*Il faut une volonté une*). It has to be either republican or royalist. To make it republican we need republican Ministers, republican news-papers, republican deputies, a republican government. The foreign war is a mortal disease so long as the body politic suffers from revolutionary sickness and the division of wills. The danger in the interior comes from the bourgeois. To overcome the bourgeois we must win the support of the people. Everything was arranged to put the people under the yoke of the bourgeois. They have triumphed at Marseilles, Bordeaux, Lyons and they would have triumphed in Paris but for the present insurrection. The present insurrection must go on until the measures needed to save the Republic have been taken. The people must ally themselves with the Convention and the Convention must serve the people. The insurrection must spread according to the same plan, the sans-culottes must be paid and kept in the towns [instead of being sent to the front]. We must find arms for them, stir up their anger, enlighten them. We must whip up republican enthusiasm by every possible means. If the deputies [i.e. the Girondins] are merely unseated the Republic is lost; they will continue to mislead the provinces and their *suppléants* will be no better . . . Foreign policy: alliance with the small Powers; but impossible so long as we have no national will.' Sainte-Claire Deville, in his history of the Commune, dates this memorandum to 16–19 May, which would prove that Robespierre had approved of the insurrection in advance.[74] But this dating is clearly wrong since the Montagnards at that time were under the impression that things were going well at Lyons and did not hear about the moderate coup there until 1 June. Almost certainly the memorandum was written between 1 June and the arrest of the Girondin leaders on the following day.

72. Sénart, *Révélations puisées dans les cartons des Comités de Salut Public et de Sûreté Générale*, Paris, 1824, p. 88.

73. Arch. Nat. F⁷ 4436; reproduced in Courtois's reports on Robespierre's papers (p. 181) and in *Papiers trouvés chez Robespierre etc.*, vol. II, pp. 15-16.

74. P. Sainte-Claire Deville, *La Commune de l'an II*, Paris, 1946, p. 44.

In other words, said Henry, it tells us very little that we didn't know already.

It does show that he had serious reasons for wanting his opponents locked up and not merely unseated and it shows his way of looking at the insurrection, not so much as a political purge but as the starting-point for the creation of a unified republican will, based on popular support. I think that meant a good deal to him.

The emphasis on will rather than measures *is* revealing, said Henry. I don't think a Danton would have written something like that. That's where he differs from most of the others – in looking all the time for a kind of philosophical meaning. At the same time he was no mere theorist; he had as sharp an eye as any of them for the tactical side.

Judging from his performance to date he was a tactician of the Plaza-Toro school, said Ted. He certainly led his regiment from behind when there was any fighting.

This is the 10th of August all over again, said Mac. All you can see is an individual. What matters is the defeat of a group that events had pushed into a reactionary position and the victory of the forces that wanted to carry the revolution forward in an egalitarian direction. Ted's right in saying this wasn't Robespierre's doing. At the same time he saw the way things were going. He was on the side of the future, if you like and that's what makes him important, or at least interesting.

Don't be too impressed by that business about the bourgeois and the people. What he seems to be offering is all circuses and no bread. He thinks it's up to him to show them what they ought to do and how they ought to think. As Henry said, it's all will and no policy.

We'll see about that. The sans-culottes had certainly more to expect from the Montagnards than from the Girondins and, as I said before, the leaders have got to go where their support comes from.

So long as there's free competition, said Ted. But I fancy we've seen the end of that. If he gets his *volonté* and his republican this, that and the other I reckon the sans-culottes are going to get their marching orders.

They certainly thought they'd been robbed after 2 June, I went on. They didn't get the social measures they wanted and, in the short run at least, the main result was the political advantage of the Montagnards. Robespierre must have realised that nothing had been finally settled: there were still as many Girondins as Montagnards in the Assembly, where the neutral majority never forgave the forcible purge. On 6 June Barère, in the name of the Committee of Public Safety, produced a report on the insurrection that almost suggested it had been a calamity. This got a bad reception from the Montagnards in general. Robespierre advised the deputies against trying to put the clock back. A tug of war developed over the future of the insurrectionary committee. The Sections and the clubs wanted to preserve it and the Commune wanted it disbanded as a rival body.[75] They solved that problem by incorporating it into the revolutionary bureaucracy as the Committee of Public Safety of the Department of Paris, but the incident may have suggested to Robespierre that there were more obstacles to the creation of a single revolutionary will than the obstruction of the Girondins. As news poured in of military reverses and a new civil war provoked by those Girondins who had broken house arrest to raise their provinces against Paris, Robespierre made an almost defeatist speech to the Jacobins on 12 June. 'If we were united, if we were agreed on principles, every *patriote* would have an energy and a confidence that he doesn't have now. So far as I am concerned, I declare my own insufficiency. I have no longer the vigour it needs to fight the intrigues of the aristocracy. Worn out by four years of arduous and fruitless toil, I feel that my physical and moral faculties are far from the level needed for a great revolution and I declare that I shall resign.'[76] Only two days later he bounced back into the ring full of fight and self-confidence: 'We have two dangers to watch: defeatism and over-confidence, excessive mistrust and *modérantisme* which is even more dangerous. We have already destroyed religious fanaticism, the reign of the people is approaching; this is the time to be ambitious.' When the power of the people had put men of integrity in control of the Convention, 'the people must not listen to those who preach universal suspicion'. The main object of this speech seems to have been to appeal for unity in the face of new threats of another purge. He maintained that, if the Montagnards and the people remained united, 'liberty and reason will triumph and within six months, perhaps, all the tyrants will have been destroyed'.[77]

75. H. Calvet, *Un instrument de la Terreur à Paris: le Comité de Salut Public ou de surveillance du Département de Paris*, Paris, 1941, p. 44.
76. *Oeuvres*, vol. IX, p. 553.   77. *Oeuvres*, vol. IX, pp. 558-61.

From this time onwards his energy revived and he addressed himself to practical problems. He denounced unscrupulous journalists who misrepresented the Montagnards. This produced a grovelling letter from the parliamentary correspondent of the *Moniteur*: 'Only two years ago people thought that a newspaper should give equal weight to the arguments on both sides . . . but you must have noticed that the *Moniteur* gave much more space to Montagnard speeches than to the others.'[78] It would be interesting to know what Robespierre thought of this. He knew that it was not even true and it probably did little to enhance his opinion of the press. When the Government was advocating conciliation in the hope of disarming the provinces Robespierre put the emphasis on exploiting the victory of 2 June to the full and making sure of the final defeat of the Girondins. He became fond of invoking *la glaive de la loi* which contrasted with his earlier abhorrence of the death penalty.

To be fair to him, said Henry, you've got to adopt what he called the perspective of the statesman rather than the justice of the peace. The question was, which would save more lives in the long run, clemency or severity.

He did try to limit repression to those he considered actively dangerous. When the Declaration of Rights of the new constitution was voted on 23 June, Billaud-Varenne called for an *appel nominal* to identify its opponents and Robespierre got this defeated. But there was a new ruthlessness all the same. He persuaded the Assembly to deny a hearing to the sisters of Léonard Bourdon in case they appealed against the death sentence imposed on the nine 'assassins' of their brother. He had been beaten up at Orleans but he survived his 'assassination' for another fourteen years. At the same time, Robespierre disapproved of the growing trend towards the indiscriminate denunciation of all men in office. 'I notice', he said to the Jacobins on 10 July, 'that this denunciation of the Ministers in general also included a specific denunciation of Danton. Do they want to make us suspect him too? It is true that anyone in office is still a target for calumny by the mere fact of his office. One sacrifices one's whole life to liberty in vain since the evilly-disposed can destroy in a quarter of an hour the confidence you have merited in so many ways and deprive you of the fruit of your labours.'[79]

78. *Correspondance*, vol. I, p. 175.   79. *Oeuvres*, vol. IX, p. 619.

For 'you' read 'me', said Ted. It all adds up, I suppose. Union of the revolutionaries; confidence in their leaders; protection for those who have been misled, in the hope that they will come round; death for all opponents, in the name of the nation or the revolution or whatever you like to call it. It's one will all right, but I'm glad I wasn't around at the time.

One of the things that was always in his mind, I said, was the continuous slaughter at the front. If a controlled Terror could shorten the war he would probably have argued that it saved lives in the end. Part of the trouble was that he saw everything in political terms. If you read the reports sent to the Minister of the Interior by his observers, you get an extraordinary impression of the gulf between Robespierre's 'people' and the real ones.[80] It wasn't that they disagreed; they lived in separate worlds and whenever any issue impinged on both worlds it looked quite different, according to one's point of view. The outside world of rising prices, food shortages and unpaid allowances to soldiers' wives intruded into the political world just as the Assembly completed the constitution that Robespierre saw as the bond that would unite all true *patriotes*.

When the Commune congratulated the Assembly on the completion of the new Declaration of the Rights of Man, on 23 June, the *Enragé* priest, Jacques Roux, requested permission to read an address on behalf of the Cordeliers and the Gravilliers Section.[81] Robespierre, who seems to have known what was coming, got him denied a hearing, but Roux managed to present his petition two days later.[82] It was a ferocious indictment of the Assembly for its failure to improve the standard of living of the poor. All the Montagnards, especially the more radical, such as Billaud-Varenne and Léonard Bourdon, were outraged. Robespierre denounced Roux's 'perfidious intention' and on 28 June implied that he was in league with France's foreign enemies. From that time onwards the Jacobins hunted him down. They hounded him from the Cordeliers and, with some difficulty, got him disowned by his Section. In the autumn he was illegally arrested and he eventually

80. See Schmidt, op. cit., *passim*.
81. On Roux, see W. Markov, *Die Freiheiten des Presters Roux*, Berlin, 1967.
82. See A. Mathiez, *La vie chère et le mouvement social sous la Terreur*, Paris, 1927, chaps. v-vii.

committed suicide in gaol. His allies, Varlet and Leclerc, were similarly persecuted.

Which would seem, Mac, said Ted, the answer to your argument that the Montagnards were forced to follow where the people led.

It wasn't quite so simple, I said –

Nothing ever is with you, interrupted Ted.

– Roux wasn't merely asking for a square deal for the sans-culottes. He had built up a political machine of his own in the clubs, some of the Sections and the Cordeliers and he was threatening the Convention with a rival power. I think it may have been this that infuriated Robespierre. It looked like a repetition of 25 February. It was the second time that, when things seemed to be going reasonably well, the unity of the revolutionaries was disrupted by a political faction that was all the more dangerous because it enjoyed a good deal of sympathy from the very people the Montagnards claimed to represent. And Roux didn't ask, he demanded.

If Ted expects me to jump in scattering approval here and anathemas there, he'll be disappointed, said Mac. I'd have to know a great deal more – perhaps more than anyone can ever know – to sort this out. It's both a question of motive and a question of practicability. The first priority was to win the war – without that there was no hope for any of them. If Roux really was challenging the Convention, he might have endangered the war effort by pushing the deputies into radical policies that the country wouldn't accept. Besides, as Ted has already pointed out, you can't abolish the limitations of a pre-industrial economy by an Act of Parliament. Given the decline of the luxury trades and wartime inflation, I'm not sure what any government could have done – in the towns. It was different on the land; one could redistribute property there, though it wouldn't have been easy to make any permanent change. But in the short run you could only hold down food prices in the towns by coercing the peasants – and they were, after all, the majority. From a Marxist point of view the bourgeoisie were the progressive force and the sans-culottes with all their medieval ideology were trying to put the clock back. That doesn't mean that I think Robespierre was right. He doesn't seem to have known or cared much about economics and he may well have resented the fact that Roux was breaking down a nice little fantasy world where he was the father of the people who knew what was best for them and patted them on the head when they told him how much they loved him. There may well be something in that, but then again Robespierre was only behaving like the other Montagnards so one can't make this a personal thing. I'm not sure that you can see this as class conflict at all. The sans-culottes weren't a class, they were more like a consumer movement.

So far as Robespierre was concerned, I said, he does seem to have thought that Roux really was a counter-revolutionary, though that may only mean that he could always persuade himself that what he wanted to believe was true. The whole situation became much more dangerous when Charlotte Corday murdered Marat on 13 July. He had been very popular with the sans-culottes and he had kept them more or less behind the Montagnard line. After his death Roux and Hébert – who was both an official of the Commune and the editor of the *Père Duchesne* – competed for Marat's following and each of them had political ambitions of his own. Robespierre, by the way, made an odd speech to the Jacobins after Marat's death.[83] He said that his only reason for speaking was that *he* was now destined for the honours of the assassin's dagger and that it was merely a matter of luck that Marat had been the first to go. He objected to Marat's body being put in the Pantheon, which provoked a nasty retort from Bentabole about jealousy. He was against giving Marat a public funeral, on the ground that it was more important to avenge him than to honour him. In fact, Marat did get his *fête funèbre,* when, according to Collot, Robespierre made a long speech without mentioning him once.

It looks as though Bentabole had a point, said Ted.

If he had, it concerned Robespierre's special relationship towards Marat. He had paid moving tributes to Lepeletier and Lazowski earlier in the year.[84] Perhaps he envied Marat his martyrdom, or perhaps he just couldn't bring himself to say things he didn't believe about a man he had never liked.

Marat had the last laugh, said Ted. Robespierre had objected to his violence in the past but he seems to have become a convert.

I think it was a general trend, I said. Before 31 May the war had been fought between armies – even if they were French peasant

83. *Oeuvres*, vol. IX, pp. 623-5.
84. *Oeuvres*, vol. IX, pp. 248-53; 472-5.

armies in the Vendée – and at least you knew who your enemies were. Now there was a civil war in which each side thought it was defending the republic against traitors. Without noticing it they seem to have got into the habit of thinking that the only thing to do with a defeated enemy was to execute him. Robespierre was certainly using expressions now that would have shocked him a year earlier and they weren't mere threats. But on the other hand he did respect the integrity of the Montagnards and even their right to disagree with him.

Since the purge of the Girondins he had been a very loyal supporter of the Committee of Public Safety. On 14 June he invited the Jacobins to stop sniping at it and to judge it by its record as a whole. More strikingly, on 8 July he opposed Chabot, who wanted to keep the three members closest to Robespierre himself – Couthon, Saint-Just and Jeanbon Saint-André – and to change the rest, saying that Chabot was too much of a perfectionist.[85] Unless he was playing a very devious game indeed, we can only assume that he had no part in the campaign against the Committee which, on 10 July, renewed the membership of the three named by Chabot and some of the others, but eliminated Danton and Delacroix. Gasparin, who had only been put on the Committee on the 10th, resigned on the 26th, ostensibly on grounds of health. Robespierre attended a meeting that day and was officially added to the Committee on the 27th, on the proposal of Jeanbon. The later story, attributed to Barère, that Couthon advised putting him in the Committee because he opposed everything with which he was not personally involved, seems to be completely untrue.[86] There was nothing surprising about his election. What was curious was that he should have joined the Committee in this apparently accidental way and not in the major re-shuffle that displaced Danton. Robespierre may not have wanted to seem to be challenging Danton or he may have changed his mind after an earlier refusal. He himself said that he joined reluctantly. Whatever his motives, he was now part of what was coming to be the government and it was the first time, since the beginning of the revolution, that he had held any executive office.

85. *Oeuvres*, vol. IX, pp. 561-2; 612-14.
86. *Mémoires sur Carnot par son fils*, Paris, 1861, vol. I, p. 336.

VI The Statesman

I've been thinking, I said, about something you mentioned a week or two ago: that the degree of concentration we brought to history influenced the kind of conclusions we drew from it. Alfred Cobban made the same point in an essay on Robespierre's ideas. 'At the closest level of inspection politics often seems to become a mere network of intrigue.'[1] We shall have to look very closely at his period on the Committee of Public Safety and you are certainly going to get plenty of intrigue, so before we start I'd like to try to draw together some of his views about the nature and significance of the revolution and what he thought about the new France that he was helping to create. On the whole he had a remarkably coherent view of things and it was probably this that made him the spokesman, not merely of the Committee but of the Montagnards as a whole, both for his contemporaries and for posterity.

He was convinced that he was living through one of the great climacterics of human history. 'The two opposing spirits that I have shown contending for domination over nature [*vertu* and vice] are fighting it out in this great epoch of human history, to determine for ever the destinies of the world. France is the theatre of this terrible combat.'[2] Time and again he insisted that the revolution was more than a mere change of government. 'The French Revolution is the first to be based on the theory of the rights of man and the principles of justice. Other revolutions called only for ambition; ours demands *vertu*.'[3] The first revolution of 1789 had been no more than a beginning since the popular forces involved had been manipulated by the petty ambitions of a social élite in revolt against the ancien régime. The real revolution did not assume its true characteristics until 1792.[4] It then became, in words of his that I have already quoted to you, 'the finest revolution that has ever honoured humanity, indeed the only one with an object worthy of man: to found political societies at last on

1. A. Cobban, *Aspects of the French Revolution*, London, 1968, p. 155.
2. 5 February 1794. *Oeuvres*, vol. X, p. 356.
3. 26 July 1794. *Oeuvres*, vol. X, p. 544.
4. August 1792. *Oeuvres*, vol. IV, p. 352.

158

the immortal principles of equality, justice and reason.'[5] 'Until our own day, the art of government was the art of deceiving and corrupting men; [henceforth] it must be that of enlightening them and making them better.'[6] The significance of the revolution was therefore universal: 'What we have to do is to establish the felicity of perhaps the entire human race.'[7] It was the glory of France to have shown the way. France was 'above all the peoples that have been called free by the enslaved nations [of the past]'.[8] 'The French people seems to have out-distanced the rest of the human race by two thousand years.'[9] This thought obviously moved Robespierre very deeply. He went on, 'O my country! If it had been my fate to be born in a distant foreign land I should have addressed continual prayers to heaven for your prosperity . . . I am French, I am one of your representatives . . . O sublime people, receive the sacrifice of my entire being!'[10]

It may be moving, said Ted, but there is a nationalist edge to it that I don't like.

You have to distinguish between two kinds of nationalism, replied Henry; the xenophobic variety that claims rights it denies to others and a forward-looking nationalism that bases its pride on the claim to have shown others the way. That was his kind. It *is* moving, to anyone except a cynic.

I don't feel cynical about him but he's really a preacher proclaiming the City of God. That's why he appeals to you, Henry.

If men don't aim at the City of God they live like animals. That's why he appeals to me. But J.S. is all agog to tell us about the content of this new order of his.

He defined it most fully on 5 February 1794 in a speech on the principles of political morality that should guide the domestic policy of the Convention.[11] We want an order of things in which all the base and cruel passions are locked up, where every beneficent and generous passion is awakened by the law; where ambition shall be the desire to win glory and serve the nation; where distinctions arise from equality itself; where the citizen obeys the magistrate, the magistrate the people and the people justice; where the nation

5.   *Oeuvres*, vol. IV, p. 358.   6.   7 May 1794. *Oeuvres*, vol. X, p. 445.
7.   15 April 1793. *Oeuvres*, vol. IX, p. 436.   8.   id., p. 439.
9.   7 May 1794. *Oeuvres*, vol. X, p. 445.   10.   ibid.   11.   id., pp. 350-67.

assures the welfare of every individual and every individual is proud to share in the prosperity and glory of the nation; where every soul is developed by the continual communication of republican sentiments and the need to earn the esteem of a great people . . .

'In our country we want to substitute morality for egoism, probity for honour [he meant the eighteenth-century aristocratic conception of a code of personal honour], principles for conventions, duties for social obligations, the empire of reason for the tyranny of fashion, contempt of vice for contempt of misfortune, pride for insolence, greatness of soul for vanity, love of glory for love of money, good people for the right society, merit for intrigue, genius for wit, truth for show, the charms of true happiness for the satiety of lust, the greatness of man for the pettiness of the great, a magnanimous, powerful and happy people for an agreeable, frivolous and miserable one; in other words, all the virtues and miracles of the Republic for all the ridiculous vices of monarchy.'

Might I, without being accused of cynicism, be allowed to suggest that this was rather a tall order, enquired Ted.

I disregarded this. His vision of the new society and of the Republic was essentially moral, as it had been ever since 1789. 'In the system of the French Revolution, whatever is immoral is bad politics, what corrupts is counter-revolutionary.'[12] He had already said much the same thing in the previous autumn. 'The very spirit of the Republic is *vertu,* in other words love of one's country, that magnanimous devotion that sinks all private interests in the general interest. The enemies of the Republic are the cowardly egoists, the ambitious and the corrupt. You have driven out the kings, but have you driven out those vices that their fatal domination bred within you?'[13]

There *is* something attractive in his sense of new possibilities, said Mac, and if you get behind the pulpit style that hasn't worn very well, you can see that he was trying to substitute genuine values for the specifically aristocratic values of the old order. To that extent he's talking sense and he's less woolly than he sounds. But all the same I'm inclined to agree with Ted that when he got on to this tack he was more of a preacher than a politician and he

12. *Oeuvres*, vol. x, p. 354.   13. September 1792. *Oeuvres*, vol. v, p. 17.

doesn't seem able to distinguish between public and private morality.

He was trying to prove that one couldn't, I said. But in practice he didn't follow his own advice. He didn't mind working with men whom he suspected of corruption, so long as they were going in the right direction. He was no prude and, unlike Charlotte, he doesn't seem to have objected to Augustin's liaisons.[14] When the Bordeaux Jacobins proposed to expel all bankrupts from their club, Maximilien opposed this and he himself distinguished between public and private morality.[15] Of course he thought that the two were related: the man who would do anything for money was likely to end up on the side of the counter-revolution since that was where the money was. But what concerned him was not private morality in the narrow sense, but putting the community first. As he saw it, petty ambition had been the main cause of the backsliding of people like the Girondins whose main concern seemed to be to win political power for themselves. 'All our quarrels are merely the struggle between private interests and the general interest, between cupidity and ambition on the one hand and justice and humanity on the other.'[16] There was some truth in this and he himself had certainly not looked for office.

Mac's quite right. He *was* conscious of the way in which what purported to be moral values were often merely expressions of social prejudice. He contrasted the universal condemnation of the sneak thief with people's tendency to admire political careerists. 'The human mind is so inconsistent that crime seems to lose its repulsiveness in proportion to the show that surrounds it and to the extent of the damage it does to men.'[17]

Through tattered clothes small vices do appear, said Henry to himself; robes and furred gowns hide all.

All right, said Ted, but what exactly did he propose to do? Even if you assume that his regenerated society would work, what about the old reprobates who would make up the first generation of his Brave New World?

Give me time, I said, and I will try to tell you. I've already explained that, ever since 1789, he had distinguished between revolutionary periods, when the new order was fighting to defeat

14. H. Fleischmann, *Charlotte Robespierre et ses Mémoires*, pp. 51-4.
15. *Oeuvres*, vol. x, pp. 530-1.
16. June 1792. *Oeuvres*, vol. IV, p. 110.   17. id., pp. 112-13.

the old, and revolutionised societies which could enjoy the fruits of victory in peace. He enlarged on this on Christmas Day 1793.[18] 'The theory of revolutionary government is as new as the revolution that has brought it into being. It is not to be sought in the books of political theorists, who did not foresee anything like this revolution . . . The aim of constitutional government is to preserve the Republic; that of revolutionary government is to create it. The Revolution is the war of liberty against its enemies; the Constitution is the regime of liberty victorious and peaceful. Revolutionary government calls for extraordinary activity precisely because it is at war . . . Constitutional government is mainly concerned with civil liberty and revolutionary government with public liberty. In a constitutional regime it is almost enough to protect the individual against the abuse of public power; in a revolutionary regime public authority has to defend itself against all the factions that attack it.' It was therefore misguided, if not actually indicative of counter-revolutionary intentions, to suggest that revolutionary government should observe the rules that a constitutional regime must obey. It had, however, rules of its own. Its activities, however violent, must never be arbitrary, but always subject to the public interest. 'It must approximate to the ordinary general principles in every case where these can be rigorously applied without endangering public liberty . . . It must be as terrible to the wicked as it is favourable to the good.'

Where counter-revolutionaries were concerned, the main problem was their identification. Once detected, the same arguments applied that Robespierre had used against the king: as public enemies they had no rights and the only problem was to find the most effective means of destroying them. 'The Declaration of Rights offers no safeguard to conspirators who have tried to destroy it.'[19] Revolutionary justice must therefore be political in the sense that its justification lay not in the observance of certain rules but in punishing the right people. 'The advantages or disadvantages [of revolutionary laws] depend entirely on the spirit which dictated them and the spirit in which they are applied.'[20] In such circumstances, the 'suspicions of enlightened patriotism' might offer a better guide than formal rules of evidence, since the public

18. *Oeuvres*, vol. x, pp. 273-82.
19. 5 August 1793. *Oeuvres*, vol. x, p. 51.
20. March 1793. *Oeuvres*, vol. v, p. 332.

interest was more concerned with the suppression of counter-revolution than with guaranteeing the protection of the innocent if this should allow dangerous enemies of the Revolution to escape.[21]

I don't know if that frightened the counter-revolutionaries, said Ted, but it certainly frightens me. I prefer what he said in 1789 about 'the fatal tendency to convict on presumption alone'.

I pointed out that Robespierre wasn't alone in thinking along these lines. Some of the Girondins had said the same thing when they thought that they were in control. You can see where all this was leading if you look at the letters of Payan, the *agent national* of Paris in the summer of 1794, and a former juror of the revolutionary tribunal, who seems to have been close to Robespierre. Referring to Orléans' execution, he wrote, 'Even if he had been innocent he had to be condemned if his death could be useful.'[22] In a letter of advice to a member of the revolutionary court at Orange, he said, 'People are always telling judges to take care to save the innocent; I tell them, in the name of the nation, to beware of saving the guilty.'[23]

This is quite intolerable, said Henry. If you're fathering on Robespierre the sins of everyone connected with him, I don't know what you expect to prove.

I agree that he would not have accepted – at least in public – the execution of the innocent *pour encourager les autres,* if only because he managed to convince himself that all his opponents were guilty. But I think he might well have accepted Payan's second point. He never faced up to the argument that the safeguards of the law were needed to sort out the sheep from the goats. But he did have a point when he said that the revolutionaries had been responsible for the slaughter of thousands at the front because of their clemency towards incompetent or counter-revolutionary generals – even if he himself protected some of those who mismanaged the war in the Vendée. 'For whom do they show their indulgence? Is it for the 200,000 heroes, the élite of the nation, harvested by the swords of the enemies of liberty and the daggers of royalist and federalist assassins? Oh, no, these were only

21. 9 December 1793. *Oeuvres,* vol. X, pp. 245-6.
22. *Papiers trouvés chez Robespierre etc.,* vol. II, p. 348.
23. id., vol. II, p. 371; also in Courtois's *Rapport,* p. 396.

plebeians, *patriotes;* to be entitled to their solicitude you must be at least the widow of a general who has betrayed the nation a score of times.'[24]

This is what Robespierre meant by the Terror: the summary execution of the enemies of the revolution. The severity of the punishment was proportionate to the danger. That meant some indulgence towards the rank and file but no mercy for the leaders.

And despite Henry's shilly-shallying, said Ted, you can only justify this sort of political justice by saying that the end justifies the means.

Some ends do justify some means, replied Henry. If you accept his viewpoint of the revolution as a state of war it all looks rather different. You don't blame Wellington for the French casualties at Waterloo and nobody would think the worse of him if a few civilians got included by mistake. What Robespierre was trying to do was much more worthwhile than winning a battle and I don't see why he should be judged by an entirely different standard.

What he was trying to do was to realise some impossible dream. The only thing that was real about it was the casualty list.

You'll never get anywhere with him, said Mac to Henry. You know the story: you can't change human nature; nothing ever changes except imperceptibly; the Russian revolution didn't happen.

I thought it just as well to steer Mac away from the Russian revolution. Buonarroti, I said firmly, maintained afterwards that when Robespierre fell he was on the point of succeeding in the complete redemption of humanity.[25]

Which doesn't say much for Buonarroti. What does Henry make of that? Do you really think it makes any perceptible difference to us now, whether he won or lost?

I don't know how much difference it would have made, said Henry slowly; perhaps more than you think. He would probably have stood no nonsense from Bonaparte and that might have saved a million lives or more. There have only been one or two revolutions on this scale and one can't say what might have been possible. We're all the prisoners of the society we live in. That decides

24. 5 February 1794. *Oeuvres,* vol. x, p. 358.

25. Quoted, apparently with approval, by A. Mathiez in *Etudes sur Robespierre,* Paris, 1958, p. 260.

what looks possible and what doesn't. If this were 1793 we should all feel very differently and there's no reason to assume that our own times have any privileged access to the truth.

He couldn't have escaped from the fact that there was no economic basis for a non-capitalist society, said Mac.

Look, I explained patiently, these aren't historical questions. You can't speculate like this because there isn't any evidence. You've got to stick to the facts.

Shall we get rid of J.S., asked Mac. He's more trouble than he's worth. He knows quite a bit but he doesn't understand anything and he gets in the way.

He's doing his best, said Henry.

He does provide some sort of continuity, added Ted. If we got rid of him I think we might go round and round.

As you have been doing for the last five minutes. If I could bring you back to the point, a short while ago Ted was asking what Robespierre proposed to do about the transitional stage – how to create a new society when most of the people involved to begin with had been corrupted by the old one. Robespierre was very much aware of the problem: 'We are raising the temple of liberty with hands still scarred by the fetters of servitude. What was our previous education if not a continual lesson in egoism and stupid vanity?'[26] 'A people that passes suddenly from slavery to liberty finds itself in a very critical situation when its customs and habits are in conflict with its new government.'[27] He thought that the conflict would be intensified as a direct consequence of the revolution since the ambitious, disappointed in their search for Court patronage, would try to use the revolution itself as a career and create a republic organised for the benefit of the rich and the civil servants.[28] When these hopes were disappointed, those who had embraced the revolution as a career would fall away and go over to the opposition.[29] It would therefore be reckless to assume that 'a few victories of *patriotisme* would mean the end of all our dangers'.[30] The strengthening of opposition posed a dual problem. In moral terms, the difficulty was that 'to form our political

26. 10 May 1793. *Oeuvres*, vol. IX, p. 497.
27. June 1792. *Oeuvres*, vol. IV, p. 115.
28. September 1792. *Oeuvres*, vol. V, p. 17.
29. 5 February 1794. *Oeuvres*, vol. X, pp. 356-9.
30. id., p. 359.

institutions we should need the habits of mind which they themselves will one day create for us'.[31] The political problem was to
create a government powerful enough to force everyone to conform to the national interest, without its being in a position to
usurp political power for itself.[32] He thought that the answer to
the moral problem lay in the fact that the mass of the population
had escaped the multiple corruptions of the ancien régime. 'The
interest of the weak is justice . . . The people know neither flabbi-
ness nor ambition, the two most fertile sources of our ills and our
vices. They are nearer to nature and less depraved.'[33]

If he means that the interest of the majority is the interest
of the majority, said Ted, I think we could accept that. If he
means any more it suggests that he went around with his eyes
shut.

And that he didn't read people like Restif de la Bretonne, I
added.

And that you're a pair of incorrigible bourgeois, said Mac. You
know perfectly well that he didn't mean that every poor man was
a Parsifal. Basically he was right: the interests of the sans-culottes
and the peasants were the collective interest. They might conflict
but they were related to the national interest, whereas the people
he suspected were thinking in terms of personal ambition or sectional advantage. His ideas about the transitional stage have got
something in common with those of Marx.

I wondered how long it was going to take you to see that, said
Ted. Well, what was Robespierre's answer to the problem of a
dictatorship *of* the proletariat that wouldn't dictate *to* them?

All power to the Convention! The deputies were the product of
universal suffrage and the Committee of Public Safety was responsible to them. Its powers had to be renewed every month. By 1794
it had become a War Cabinet with unprecedented powers over the
economic as well as the political life of the nation, but it had to get
the approval of the Assembly for any legislation and it could be
changed at any time.

You haven't told us anything about 1794 yet, said Ted, but
from what I know already I shouldn't have liked to be the man to
move a vote of censure. It's like everything else; it meant one
thing in Robespierre's mind and something quite different in

31. September 1793. *Oeuvres*, vol. v, p. 20.
32. id., p. 18.   33. June 1792. *Oeuvres*, vol. iv, p. 115.

practice. But perhaps we'd better leave 1794 for the time being. You've told us about the revolution and transitional stage, what about the New Jerusalem itself?

He naturally drew on the theoretical writings of the Enlightenment for some of his ideas. In his speech of 5 February 1794 you can almost hear him arguing with Montesquieu to convince himself that, during the actual revolution, it would be possible to use despotic powers against the enemy without the state itself becoming despotic. His main inspiration probably came from Rousseau. On 10 May he began a speech on the constitution with a deliberate paraphrase of the *Social Contract*: 'Man is born for happiness and freedom and everywhere he is enslaved and unhappy.'[34] This probably went down well with his contemporaries. He was the man who showed them the political theory behind the Revolution and their day-to-day decisions. It was Robespierre more than anyone else who convinced them that they were actually implementing the ideas of the Enlightenment that had made France the tutor to Europe. At the same time it would be quite wrong to regard him as an abstract thinker who had strayed into politics.[35] He was one of the most experienced of the revolutionary politicians and he saw every situation in political terms – although he was very skilful in finding a theoretical justification for whatever seemed tactically expedient. He never hesitated to reject the arguments of the *philosophes* when they proved inconvenient. He was never entirely convinced by Rousseau's thesis that the general will was morally superior to the subjective individual conscience. He was more old-fashioned than Rousseau in the sense that he still conceived of individual liberty in Montesquieu's terms, as freedom from the state. In June 1792 he argued that obedience was due to the law only when it had the support of the majority. He later rejected this view, with its danger of majority tyranny, and said that respect for the law 'depends on opinion, which is essentially free and independent. The legislator is certainly not infallible, even if the people itself is legislator.'[36] It was on these grounds that he justified the absolute freedom of the press, so that individuals could arrive at their own conclusions, by which governments could be judged. In

34. *Oeuvres*, vol. x, p. 495.
35. For the opposite view see J. L. Talmon, *The Origins of Totalitarian Democracy*, London, 1952.
36. *Oeuvres*, vol. iv, p. 144.

the debates on the constitution in the spring of 1793 he at first accepted a qualification to this, applicable only in time of revolution, but he seems to have seen the illogicality of putting into a declaration of rights what referred only to a revolutionary situation that was *ipso facto* illegal and assumed the violation of the rights of man. When he presented to the Assembly a revised version of the draft that he had first submitted to the Jacobins, the freedom of the press appeared without any qualifications.[37] There was perhaps too much classical Stoicism in this thinking for him to renounce the idea of the individual as being ultimately sovereign.[38]

Robespierre had always respected the original Declaration of Rights of 1789 and even after the abolition of the monarchy he maintained that the 1791 Constitution was basically sound and needed only a few modifications. His suggested amendment to the Declaration consisted mainly of a new definition of property, the right to education and the obligation of free nations to help each other and to support wars of liberation. His ideas had evolved since 1789 but they remained basically liberal, in the sense that he saw the state as the servant of its individual citizens. 'In every free state the first objective of the law is the defence of public and individual liberty against the abuse of authority by those who govern. All institutions are bad if they are not founded on the assumption that the people are good and their magistrates corruptible.'[39]

The problem of both revolutionary and constitutional governments was 'to give the government enough power to ensure that its citizens always respect the rights of other citizens and to arrange things so that their rights can never be violated by the government itself'.[40] The difference lay in the fact that, once the revolutionary period was over, the emphasis shifted from the defence of the revolutionary government to the protection of the individual and from the maximum centralisation to the maximum devolution of power. He called upon the Convention to 'shun the former mania of governments to want to govern too much'.[41]

37. April 1793. *Oeuvres*, vol. IX, pp. 462, 465.
38. On Montagnard Stoicism, see the comments of R. Andrews in *Gilbert Romme et son temps*, Paris, 1966, pp. 189-200.
39. 20 April 1793. *Oeuvres*, vol. IX, p. 469.
40. ibid.   41. 10 May 1793. *Oeuvres*, vol. IX, pp. 501-10.

He rejected Montesquieu's doctrine of the separation of the powers within the central government, on the ground that British experience showed that they would always combine to assert the interests of government against those of the governed. His objection was directed against the British rather than against Montesquieu since his own proposals were very much in line with the principles of the *Spirit of the Laws*: the fragmentation of executive power and extreme decentralisation with local authorities responsible for all local taxation and expenditure. He favoured the maximum possible publicity at all levels and considered voting in public a safeguard against intrigue, seeming unaware of the extent to which it would put tenants at the mercy of their landlords. He insisted that the electorate should have the right to recall deputies at any time but found himself in difficulties over the question of parliamentary immunity. He always maintained that deputies should not be liable to prosecution for opinions expressed in the Assembly but at first proposed that they should be obliged to seek a vote of confidence from the electorate at the end of the session. A negative vote would disqualify them from future public office. After the overthrow of the Girondins he changed his mind about this, on the ground that it might expose the ex-deputy to political intrigue in his constituency. Robespierre then advocated complete parliamentary immunity for opinions, although not for breaches of the law.[42] At the same time, while transferring as much power as possible away from the central government, he insisted on representative, as distinct from direct, democracy. This too seemed to constitute a withdrawal from the more radical position he had taken up in April, when he appeared to concede the right of the electors in a constituency to meet at will.[43] His growing caution was perhaps due to his awareness of the deep division of republican opinion after the purge of 2 June and to his realising that an excessive reduction in the controlling power of the central government could lead to anarchy.

This is all very well as far as it goes, said Ted –

– and it goes rather a long way, put in Henry. After all, they did vote a constitution along these lines.

They soon suspended it for the duration of the war, I said.

42. 15 June 1793. *Oeuvres*, vol. IX, pp. 565-6.
43. *Oeuvres*, vol. IX, pp. 467, 557.

Naturally. Even Ted would scarcely expect them to go over to a peacetime government in the mess they were in during the summer of 1793. What we have to ask ourselves is whether the new constitution was merely a propaganda exercise or whether Robespierre hoped that a speedy end to the war would allow them to give it a trial. What J.S. has been saying suggests that he did.

That's what I was going to say if you hadn't interrupted, said Ted. It's not a matter of intention, it's a question of whether the thing was practicable. When it came to the point, would he have accepted the right of the electorate to disagree with him or would he have said that disagreement showed they were still the dupes of the counter-revolutionaries? It's always easy enough to claim that one is a democrat in principle but that the time isn't quite ripe – and to prolong the transitional stage for ever. There was quite an impressive Soviet constitution in 1936, I seem to remember, but it didn't stop the people in power from saying that the class war was still getting fiercer, a whole generation after their revolution.

I wish you and Mac wouldn't keep bringing in Russia, I said, and I wish you wouldn't keep asking hypothetical questions. No one know what Robespierre *would* have done in 1795.

And what we think tells us more about us than about him, said Henry. Ted's entitled to his own opinion but he can't expect *me* to condemn Robespierre for what *he* thinks Robespierre might have done.

I'm beginning to sympathise with J.S., said Mac, when he wanted to stick to the facts. You said Robespierre introduced a new definition of property into his Declaration of Rights. Where did he stand on social issues?

He said that property was a social institution and not an absolute right. He defined it as 'the right of each citizen to enjoy that part of his goods which is guaranteed to him by law'. 'Like all other rights, it is limited by the obligation to respect the rights of others.'[44]

That can mean as much or as little as one likes, said Mac.

He was thinking essentially in moral terms. 'Ask that trader in human flesh what property is and he will tell you, pointing to the long coffin that he calls a ship, where he has boxed in and chained up men who seem alive, "That is my property; I bought them at

44. 21 April 1793. *Oeuvres*, vol. IX, p. 455 and 24 April 1793, vol. IX, p. 465.

so much a head." Ask the gentleman who owns land and vassals, or who thinks the universe turned upside down since they have been taken away from him, and he will give you much the same definition of property.'[45] Property could not relate to people. Robespierre also went beyond the economic liberals in denying the right to the absolute ownership of things. What came first was society's obligation 'to provide for the subsistence of all its members, either by procuring them work or ensuring the means of subsistence to those unable to work.'[46] It was on these grounds that he had disagreed with Saint-Just in the debates on the control of the grain trade towards the end of 1792, when his younger colleague took up the orthodox liberal position. Robespierre maintained on the contrary that 'whatever is necessary for the conservation of human life is property that is common to society as a whole. It is only the surplus that is private property and can be left to the activities of the merchants. Any mercantile speculation that I engage in at the expense of my fellow-men is not trade but banditry and fratricide.'[47]

You couldn't expect him to go much further than that, at the time, said Mac.

Forwards or backwards, enquired Ted innocently. There's nothing socialist about this. It's a return to the old idea that lordship implied responsibility and the government was responsible for seeing that no one starved. Both the idea and the means of implementing it were traditional. It must all have seemed reassuringly familiar to the sans-culottes.

Robespierre dismissed all talk of a *loi agraire* – the redistribution of land on an equal basis – as 'a spectre invented by rascals to frighten imbeciles'.[48] Not merely that; he would have liked to limit restraints on trade to food grains alone. He claimed that sugar and coffee 'only serve to satisfy artificial needs'. But he regretfully recognised that habit had led to their being regarded as necessities.[49] It was not merely that he thought economic equality impossible; from his point of view it was irrelevant. 'As for me, I think it even less necessary to private happiness than to the public

45.   24 April 1793. *Oeuvres*, vol. IX, p. 460.
46.   21 April 1793. *Oeuvres*, vol. IX, p. 456.
47.   2 December 1792. *Oeuvres*, vol. IX, pp. 112-13.
48.   24 April 1793. *Oeuvres*, vol. IX, p. 459.
49.   27 July 1793. *Oeuvres*, vol. X, p. 9.

171

good; it is much more a question of making poverty honourable than of proscribing wealth.'[50]

He did advocate progressive taxation – which Brissot's *Patriote français* denounced as 'an absurd tax, destructive of equality and the ruin of industry'.[51] But he attacked the proposal for a forced loan to be imposed on the wealthy, both as inquisitorial (he wanted self-assessment) and because he thought that liability for taxation had been extended to those of only moderate means. The original proposal had included all unearned income above 1,200 livres for bachelors, with an allowance of 1,000 for a wife and 600 for each child. This was quite severe, but it applied only to unearned incomes, not to wages and salaries and it was not a tax but a loan; receipts could be exchanged at once for the confiscated property of the Church and the *émigrés*. In view of all the circumstances, Robespierre's objection seems a little exaggerated.[52]

Historians determined to re-create Robespierre in their own image have argued that he became increasingly inclined towards economic levelling in 1794. The evidence for this rests on the *ventôse* decrees of February and early March. These measures, introduced by Saint-Just, provided for the examination of the hundreds of thousands of suspects in the gaols of revolutionary France. Six *commissions populaires* were to liberate the innocent, detain for deportation after the war those who were regarded as passive opponents of the Revolution and send suspected counter-revolutionaries before the revolutionary tribunal. The property of the men in the last two categories was to be confiscated and used for the benefit of the poor. Saint-Just certainly presented this as a new kind of social policy. 'The force of circumstances is perhaps leading us to new conclusions. Wealth is in the hands of many enemies of the Revolution. Their needs make working people dependent on their enemies . . . The Revolution leads us to recognise the principle that the man who has shown himself to be the enemy of his country cannot hold property within it.'[53] Since there were so many suspects, the majority of whom probably came from the wealthier sections of the population, and the two commissions that

---

50. 24 April 1793. *Oeuvres*, vol. IX, p. 459.
51. id., p. 462. Cobban (op. cit., p. 166) is mistaken in saying that Robespierre thought it better not to mention the proposal in his newspaper.
52. 21 June 1793. *Oeuvres*, vol. IX, p. 586; *Moniteur*, 9 June 1793.
53. *Moniteur*, 8 *ventôse* (26 February 1794).

were actually set up were reluctant to acquit any of them, the implementation of the decrees would certainly have resulted in a substantial transfer of property. This does not mean that they were regarded by their author as class legislation. Wealth as such was not proscribed and it was never made clear how far Saint-Just envisaged the transfer of property to the poor and how far he intended it to be sold to the highest bidders and the proceeds devoted to poor relief. What is more to the point, so far as we are concerned, is that Robespierre never referred to the measures at all. Mathiez claimed that his speech of 17 *pluviôse* (5 February 1794) – which Mathiez dated the 18th – 'contained in embryo all the social policy that was to follow' but his argument is wholly un-convincing.[54] Robespierre's speech was entirely concerned with moral and political issues and offered no hint of any social innova-tions. Saint-Just may have attached great importance to them and believed that they were being delayed by his colleagues on the Committee of Public Safety but Robespierre himself seems to have said nothing about social policy after he joined the Committee. He may well have accepted Saint-Just's argument that since wealth implied power it could not be left in the hands of the counter-revolutionary and corrupt, but this is mere speculation and if he was hoping to wind up the Terror he would not have been attracted by the prospect of a new social upheaval on an immense scale. The positive evidence suggests that he was thinking along different lines. When welfare state legislation was voted in May 1794 it was introduced by Barère, not by Robespierre. From Maxi-milien's point of view, republican government was concerned with more important things than the standard of living. It did owe a decent livelihood to all, since the desperately poor were unable to elevate themselves above merely economic preoccupations. But a tolerable degree of poverty offered protection against the vices of affluence and the true *patriote* had better things to think about than acquiring wealth.

Which means, said Mac, that even if we judge him – as we must – in contemporary terms of what thoughts were thinkable and what action was possible, he doesn't come out very well. He never seems to have had any idea of what poverty really meant. It was all abstract to him, as seen from his study at the Duplays'. More

54. *Girondins et Montagnards,* Paris, 1930, p. 119.

than that, there was a sort of economic puritanism about him: privation was a good thing since it made for purity. It's true that he didn't go in for luxurious living himself but that was more a matter of taste than renunciation and there was all the difference in the world between the kind of simplicity he enjoyed and the kind of squalor that most people had to endure. I'm not blaming him for not doing much for the sans-culottes since I don't see what he could have done, but for not being interested.

There's something in that, agreed Henry. But few of the Montagnards knew what poverty really felt like. They'd grown up with it as an unchangeable background. And although it seems a harsh thing to say, in the context of the appalling conditions of the time, Robespierre was right. To argue that the primary aim of government is to provide more and more consumer goods is both degrading and self-defeating since the more people have the more they think they need. The necessary minimum is being extended all the time. Robespierre thought sugar and coffee were luxuries that people were coming to regard as necessities. Now it's cars. If we all get cars it will be something else. Unless you can break out of the system you go round and round like a hamster in a cage. He did see that government must satisfy essential needs – which is more than most of his contemporaries did. Looking back from the twentieth century we're bound to think that he put the bottom level too low. One may disagree about that but his basic attitude was right.

This was a favourite topic of theirs on which they always exchanged the same arguments without coming to any conclusions, so I hastily changed the subject. Robespierre saw the future, I went on, as a period when people would have acquired different attitudes, when *vertu* would come naturally to them, so to speak. One of the main agents that he relied on to produce this change was education. This was a subject that the Constituent Assembly had neglected. Robespierre himself does not seem to have been fully aware of its importance until 1793, when it became one of his main preoccupations. He included the right to education in the draft declaration of the rights of man that he submitted to the Assembly in April. In June he tried unsuccessfully to get this obligation written into the Montagnard constitution.[55] A fortnight

55. 18 June 1793. *Oeuvres*, vol. IX, p. 581.

later he persuaded the Assembly to set up an Education Committee, of which he soon afterwards became a member.[56] When he joined the Committee of Public Safety he was originally in charge of education and in the autumn of 1793 he was put on another committee to revise previous educational legislation.[57]

In the Assembly itself the Girondins and many of the other deputies thought of education primarily in terms of making knowledge available to the most intelligent children, regardless of parental income. Robespierre and some of the Montagnards saw it as a process of character-formation that must be universal if it was to be effective.

That sounds familiar, said Ted.

Yes and no. You'll see that it was more than an argument about comprehensive schools. As always, Robespierre started from certain fixed principles but varied his policy to suit the tactical considerations of the moment. He first took up the subject of education in an article in his newspaper in January 1793.[58] Appropriately enough, it opened with a paraphrase of the first sentence of Rousseau's *Emile*. 'Man is good when he comes from the hands of nature [Rousseau had said "the hands of God"] . . . if he is corrupted this aberration must therefore be imputed to bad social institutions.' He specifically linked the educational system to the problem of getting the new social attitudes of regenerated republican man to strike root. 'I am apprehensive lest intrigue should once again take hold of future generations so as to perpetuate the rule of humanity's vices and wretchedness.' Because he believed that any educational system must reflect the values of the society in which it originated, he urged that the first need was to provide France with republican laws. Since, at this time, the Montagnards were still in a minority in the Convention, Robespierre stressed the need for an educational system that would be independent of the government. 'Public authority must leave it to public opinion to improve both laws and government.' 'It follows that the education of the citizens must not be entirely dependent of those who govern.' Fighting a rearguard action against the activities of Roland's propaganda agency, the *Bureau de Formation de l'Esprit*

56. 3 July 1793. *Oeuvres*, vol. IX, p. 607n[2].
57. *Mémoires sur Carnot par son fils*, Paris, 1861, vol. I, p. 342; *Oeuvres*, vol. X, p. 167n[1].
58. *Oeuvres*, vol. V, pp. 207-11.

Public, he rejected the Spartan concept, as he saw it, of a politic-ally-oriented educational system, not as wrong in itself, but as inappropriate at a time when the central government was controlled by men whom he suspected. The prospect tempted him, as he revealed to his readers; 'I could dazzle you with descriptions of *fêtes nationales* and perhaps produce a momentary illusion by showing you the shadow of Spartan institutions that bear no rela-tionship to our present situation.' He was scornful of the educa-tional plans of the Girondins: 'no moral or philosophical basis; well-paid posts put at the disposal of the dominant party; new means of deceiving public opinion and handing it over to the present government.' He advocated waiting until the political situation should change before introducing a new educational system.

I'm acquiring some respect for his political shrewdness, said Ted. When he had both feet on the ground he was quite ingenious at reconciling his tactics and his principles – but then he would get on his hobby-horse and lose himself in some dream of a quite impos-sible future. He would have made a very formidable leader of the opposition – if only he'd stayed there.

When he made his second major speech on education, in July 1793, the political situation had completely changed and the Montagnards were now in control of the Assembly. To be accurate, it wasn't his own speech. Félix Lepeletier asked for permission to read a memoir on a national educational system written by his brother, who had been murdered at the time of the king's trial. The Convention merely ordered the memoir to be printed but Robespierre, as spokesman of the Education Committee, insisted on reading it out on 13 July and again on the 29th.[59] We can't assume that he approved of every detail of the plan but his persis-tence in bringing it forward must mean that he endorsed its general principles. Lepeletier's memoir began by emphasising the importance of education: 'The Convention must leave three monu-ments to history: the constitution, a code of civil laws and public education.' The objective of education was nothing less than 'to effect an entire regeneration and, so to speak, to create a new people'. In his conclusion he said that the effect of his plan would be to create 'a renewed race, strong, laborious, disciplined, cut off

59. *Oeuvres,* vol. IX, p. 621; vol. X, pp. 10-42.

by an impenetrable barrier from polluting contact with the prejudices of our own enfeebled species'. With more frankness than
Robespierre might have shown, he went on to say that 'the revolutions of the past three years have done everything for the other
classes of citizens and practically nothing as yet for what is perhaps
the neediest of all, for the proletarian citizens whose only property
is their labour'.

That certainly doesn't sound like Robespierre's language, said
Mac. This man's got a much firmer grip of the situation.

Don't unfurl your red flag just yet. He went on, 'This is the
revolution of the poor . . . but a gentle and peaceful revolution
which neither frightens property nor offends against justice.' He
distinguished sharply between *instruction* which meant what we
call education in the narrower sense, especially higher education, and
éducation which was essentially a matter of character-formation.
His Bill was concerned only with the latter. He saw that if all
children were to be given the same republican conditioning it was
necessary that 'the raw material should never leave the mould' and
the children should be under 'surveillance from day to day and for
every moment'. That meant removing them from the corrupting
influence of their families as early as possible, which, unfortunately,
was not before they were five. From five to twelve (eleven in the
case of girls) all children were to be brought up in co-educational
state boarding schools. They were to wear the same uniform and
to be subjected to a process of physical toughening that would fit
them for any future occupation. 'They will sleep rough, their food
will be healthy but frugal, their clothing convenient but coarse.'

Apart from the clothing, said Mac, it sounds very much like my
alma mater, though they didn't tear us away from the corrupting
influence of our families quite so early.

Lepeletier and Dr Arnold had more in common than one might
think, I said, though Lepeletier wasn't trying to equip a minority
for leadership. His unfortunates were not to get any meat and
they were to learn a manual trade. He obviously shared the old
idea that the unemployed were people who either didn't want to
work or didn't know how to do the work that was available. In his
own way he was as far as Robespierre from understanding the real
problems of an over-populated country with a pre-industrial
economy. But he did see that relieving the poor of the cost of
feeding and clothing their children for half of the time before they

177

could contribute to their own keep, was going to make an enormous difference to the parents, whatever the children thought about the arrangements.

How did he propose to finance it, asked Ted.

By a special tax on incomes. He didn't suggest making this progressive but the poor would pay less in taxation than the cost of feeding their children and the rich would pay much more. That was why he called it the revolution of the poor.

Well, Mac, said Ted, however painful your own memories, I don't see how you can object to such a splendid scheme of comprehensive education.

I wish you wouldn't keep on seeing everything in twentieth-century terms, I said. It was nothing of the sort. It was more like a period of compulsory military service. What you mean by education wasn't intended to start before twelve and Lepeletier had in mind a kind of 'twelve plus' examination that would select the brightest 2% of the population for secondary education in conventional schools. Half of this 2% would then go on to higher education. Both secondary and higher education would be free. So the scheme would have provided for a state-supported educational élite and of course there would have been nothing to prevent the wealthy from sending their children to private schools at twelve or providing them with tutors. The system was intended to give the children a common outlook but it was based on the recognition that the great majority would have to take up manual occupations. In practice, selection for higher education on a basis of either merit or money would not have been very different from what happened under the ancien régime.

I suppose the whole business was compulsory, said Ted.

Lepeletier insisted that it should be, but the Committee climbed down and allowed parents to opt out at the price of losing their civil rights and paying a double education tax while their children were of school age.

If they'd tried to enforce it, said Ted, the Vendée would have been a picnic compared to the trouble they would have stirred up.

Most of the deputies seem to have agreed with you. When they discussed education on 13 August Robespierre failed to get priority given to Lepeletier's scheme and that was the last that was heard of it.

It does look as though it corresponded to his own point of view,

said Henry, and I don't think I understand him. I take your point
that what he said in January about the need for the educational
system to be independent of the state was only a tactical argument.
But you have been suggesting that he had two policies, one
intended to concentrate power in the government while the fate
of the revolution was still in the balance and a liberal policy for
the period after the victory of the revolution. This educational
scheme was obviously intended as long-term policy and all its
emphasis on control and supervision suggests that he didn't really
believe that people would ever fit naturally into his new republic
and so the process of conditioning would have to go on indefinitely. Even the poor, who were supposed to be uncorrupted, had
to be subjected to the process to make them fit for what was supposed to fit them.

One shouldn't say 'I told you so', said Ted. But since I did I
will. It's always the same. The transitional period goes on for ever
and what it means is that everyone else is manipulated by the
people who have managed to fight their way to the top.

Back to 1793, I said. It wasn't so much a political conditioning
as a moral one, to make them tough and hard-working and so on.
That still doesn't answer Henry's point. Robespierre, like Lepeletier, was probably attracted by the social side of the Bill, a sort of
family allowance in kind. But that isn't a proper answer either. In
terms of pure logic I think there is a contradiction here, but there
nearly always is in politics. Could we say that he saw the scheme
as a means of reinforcing values that he expected to emerge from
the new society itself.

We could, but I don't think it means anything, said Ted. Still,
it's probably the best you can do. If you start from totally false
premises about human nature you're bound to tie yourself in
knots.

Ignoring this, I went on. Lepeletier had expressly excluded
denominational religious teaching from the general moral training
in his schools and I'd like to tell you something about where Robespierre stood on religion. Ever since his Arras days he had felt
himself to be in emotional communion with some superhuman
force which gave him courage to persevere in his political battles
and consoled him when he seemed to be defeated – and he talked
far more about dying for the cause than about any final victory.
He showed how important this religious feeling was to him when

he denounced Guadet for scoffing at the idea of Providence, and he was still quite heated when he remembered the incident two years later.[60] What is much less clear is what he understood by God. He seems never to have thought in terms of an abstract First Cause, but to have conceived of his Supreme Being in much warmer and more personal terms. In fact, his conception of the relationship between Man and God was not very different from that of the Christians. 'God accepts all kinds of prayers. God welcomes the vows, not merely of the most wretched, but of the most guilty of men.'[61] He attacked the death penalty on the ground that irrevocable punishments should be reserved for him whose eternal eye sees into the depths of men's hearts.[62] At the same time, he appeared utterly indifferent to Christianity and with the single exception of a reference to the son of Mary – which did not imply his belief in the divinity of Christ – he never used specifically Christian terminology.[63] He had a good deal of sympathy for parish priests as preachers of ethics – at least in the early days of the revolution – but only on condition that they kept out of politics. He was perhaps more suspicious of *curés rouges* – whether or not they abjured their calling – than most of his fellow-Montagnards.

His fullest exposition of his religious ideas was given in his newspaper.[64] 'My God is he who created all men for equality and for happiness, who protects the oppressed and exterminates tyrants; my worship is that of justice and humanity. I dislike priestly power as much as anyone. It is one of humanity's fetters, but an invisible fetter of the spirit which reason alone can break.' He thought that 'superstition' was dying and that soon nothing would be left but 'those impressive dogmas that lend their support to ethics and that sublime and moving doctrine of virtue and equality that the son of Mary once taught to his citizens'. 'If tyrants tore up the declaration of the rights of humanity, we should find it again in the religious code that priestly despotism offered for our worship.'

In other words, said Ted, God was a Montagnard.

I agreed that, although the language was very different, Robes-

60. See above, p. 107.
61. 9 May 1791. *Oeuvres*, vol. VII, p. 313.
62. 30 May 1791. *Oeuvres*, vol. VII, p. 436.
63. December 1792. *Oeuvres*, vol. V, p. 117.
64. *Oeuvres*, vol. V, pp. 116-20.

pierre's conception of God had something in common with Hébert's *sans-culotte Jésus*.

He would not be the first man to re-create God in the image of his highest aspirations, said Henry. There's something extraordinarily modern about all this, even if much of the inspiration did come from Rousseau. If you think of what religion meant to most people at that time, he is much nearer to present-day Christianity – whatever he thought about dogma – than all the de Maistres and Bonalds.

Where he did belong to his time, I said, was in his belief in divine intervention in human affairs. In this context he generally referred to God as Providence. From his pessimistic viewpoint, the survival of the revolution through so many perils and betrayals was only explicable as the work of Providence. He said this over and over again from 1790 onwards. In July 1794 he personalised it to the extent of claiming that Providence had saved him from assassination. Besides protecting him, Providence would offer a final consolation in the event of failure: death was 'a safe and precious asylum that Providence has reserved for *vertu*'.[65]

I'm getting lost, complained Mac. Providence was both going to save the revolution and to console Robespierre when *he* failed to save it. Like most religious visionaries, he seems to have believed whatever he needed to comfort him at any particular time.

He may have been inconsistent, I said. The point I'm trying to make is that it was a real faith and not an intellectual abstraction. In particular, he believed in some sort of after-life in which the virtuous would be rewarded. In his last speech – which he called his 'testament' – he said, 'Death is the beginning of immortality.'[66]

Religion was not merely a question of personal belief, it was a political issue. In the autumn of 1793 radical revolutionaries tried to get Christianity outlawed and its churches closed. In its place they wanted to substitute what they called the worship of Reason. In theoretical terms this was perhaps not very different from Robespierre's view of things, although he probably felt that 'reason' smacked too much of a Voltairean First Cause. He may have believed that the partisans of 'Reason' were, in fact, atheists, or

65. 14 July 1793. *Oeuvres*, vol. IX, p. 623.
66. 26 July 1794. *Oeuvres*, vol. X, p. 575.

he may merely have pretended to do so in the hope of discrediting them. I'll show you later on that he had good grounds for thinking that some at least of the men who had launched the attack on Christianity intended it as a political manoeuvre and he suspected their real motives of being counter-revolutionary. When he decided to challenge them, in the name of religious freedom, he took his stand on political grounds. 'The Convention is not a writer of books or the author of a metaphysical system; it is a popular political body charged with enforcing respect, not merely for the rights but also for the character of the French people.'[67] He had used a similar argument in his newspaper a year earlier. 'To attack this cult directly is to attack public morality. One can conceive of a society of philosophers basing its ethics on other grounds, but those who are foreign to such profound meditation have been taught to identify the motives for *vertu* with the principles of religion.'[68]

We are getting pretty close to the opium of the masses, said Mac.

Not really. It is true that he saw religion partly as consolation, for which the poor had more need than the rich, but he identified it far too closely with the revolution and with egalitarianism for it to imply any sort of political quietism. When he told the Jacobins that to attack Catholicism was to stir up widespread opposition to the Revolution in France and to discredit it in foreign eyes, he was on firm ground. But, being Robespierre, he could never be content with a purely pragmatic argument without looking for a philosophical basis to it. He claimed to be speaking 'not as an individual or a speculative philosopher, but as a representative of the people' when he said that atheism was *aristocratique* since the rich needed no prospect of compensation in another world for their experiences in this one.[69] This led him to move away from his purely political justification of religious toleration and to assert dogmatically that belief in Providence was 'engraved in every pure and feeling heart'. Logically, this implied that the atheist could not attain to the moral qualities expected of a citizen of the new republic and would have justified the persecution of disbelief on purely religious

67. 21 November 1793. *Oeuvres*, vol. x, p. 196.
68. December 1793. *Oeuvres*, vol. v, p. 117.
69. 21 November 1793. *Oeuvres*, vol. x, p. 196.

grounds. This was a step that Robespierre never took. 'Any philosopher, any individual, can adopt whatever religion he chooses.
Anyone who would make this a crime is mad.' There was more
to this than a mere attempt to appease the anti-clericals. When
young Jullien, an agent of the Committee of Public Safety, in an
excess of Rousseauist zeal, proposed to expel atheists from the
Republic, Robespierre told the Jacobins, 'There are some truths
that have to be presented with caution . . . I believe we should
leave this truth in the writings of Rousseau and not put it into
practice.'[70] On the same day he denounced criticism of Lequinio's
atheism as political intrigue: 'Is the Convention trying to penetrate the thoughts of every individual and meddle with his private
opinions? No, its intention goes no further than what concerns the
salvation of free France. What does it matter to us what so-and-so
said or what he wrote?'[71] As usual, he was prepared to sacrifice
logical consistency to political common sense.

The final exposition of his religious policy is to be found in his
speech of 7 May 1794 which persuaded the Assembly to declare
its faith in a Supreme Being and to order a series of public festivals
in honour of the new religion.[72] He began by contrasting technolo-
gical progress with moral stagnation. 'Everything has changed in
the physical world; everything must change in the world of
morality and politics.' Obviously very moved, he appealed to his
audience to raise themselves to the new ethical heights that the
Revolution had brought within their reach. 'The only basis for
civil society is morality. All the combinations that make war against
us rest on crime.' This provided him with a text for the castigation
of the vices of the British in particular and led him to the conclusion that 'immorality is the basis of despotism as *vertu* is the
essence of the Republic'. He then drew a number of political conclusions, claiming to show that all the opposition to the revolution
since 1789 had been due to a single conspiracy of the egotistical
and the corrupt, which took in Orléans, the Girondins and
Danton.

He used this argument to say that the path to salvation through
the labyrinth of intrigue was to disregard everything except 'the
welfare of the nation and the interests of humanity'. These rested

70. 15 May 1794. *Oeuvres*, vol. x, p. 467.
71. *Oeuvres*, vol. x, p. 468. 72. *Oeuvres*, vol. x, pp. 442-65.

on a religious basis. Then came a qualification: 'I do not need to point out that there is no question of attacking any particular philosophical opinion or of denying that a philosopher, whatever his opinions, may have been *vertueux*, even in spite of his opinions, by reason of his fortunate disposition or superior intellect. It is a matter of considering atheism as a national phenomenon tied up with a system of conspiracy against the Republic.' 'You will be on your guard against breaking the sacred link between men and the author of their being. It is enough for this belief to have once dominated a people for it to be dangerous to destroy it. Since the recognition of duties and the bases of morality are necessarily linked to this idea, to efface it is to demoralise the people . . . Anyone who can replace the divinity in the system of social life seems to me a prodigious genius; anyone who tries to banish him from men's minds without putting anything in his place seems to me a prodigy of either stupidity or perversity.'

That's fair enough, said Ted. He saw that one could divorce the social utility of religion from any dogmatic basis. But Voltaire had said it all before.

Robespierre didn't think so. He went on to discuss the ideological origins of the Revolution in the Enlightenment and handled the Encyclopaedists pretty roughly, as time-serving materialists who 'were proud in their writings and servile in ante-chambers'. He had turned against them ever since he had been attacked by Condorcet. He said that the *philosophes* had persecuted Rousseau, the only one of them who had been 'worthy to be the tutor of the human race'. Condorcet brought him back to the revolution with a bitter contrast between the *civisme* of the ignorant artisan and the backsliding of the Condorcets and Guadets. Reassuring his audience that the worship of the Supreme Being would not lead to a revival of Catholicism, he denounced dogmatic religion as itself a kind of atheism in which priests had treated God as the *maires du palais* had treated Clovis, in order to rule in his name. He then moved on to propose his religious festivals. The idea had been in the air for some time and Danton had put it forward in the previous year. It probably went back to Rousseau's *Letter to d'Alembert* of 1758, the object being to create something along the lines of the games and festivals of ancient Greece.

It's a strange mixture, said Henry, and the polemics get all mixed up with the religion. What I find difficult to understand is the combination of real moral insight – and he's quite unfanatical whenever he talks about religion – with the black-and-white picture of all his opponents as atheists, cowards and corrupt careerists. At least he didn't refer to them as Antichrist. It must have made some sense to him. But how could a man like Danton be relegated so suddenly from a comrade in arms to a villain? Perhaps he was simply trying to discredit his opponents by inventing unpleasant names for them. But if he could lie on that scale in the middle of a sermon on morality, nothing would make much sense. If we disregard that side for the time being, there's a certain grandeur about the rest of it. He wasn't asking anyone to admire him, but urging them to make themselves worthy of admiration. I don't pay any attention to the pathetic pagan trappings which don't matter. In essence it was a Christian programme as I understand Christianity – much more so than what was being preached in most of the pulpits of the time.

He's made one convert at least, said Ted, though, like Robespierre's priests, I think you're creating a saviour in your own image.

I agree that he wasn't, in fact, preaching the opium of the masses, said Mac. In other words, it wasn't a real religion. It was a faith so carefully constructed to fit the revolution that no one but Robespierre could take it as real. One can't see this sort of religion comforting anyone very much. He probably did deceive himself but for almost everyone else religion must have meant the Church and if you were for it you were against the revolution. The closing of the churches was a political fact and if Robespierre couldn't see what the practical consequences of a religious revival were bound to be, he wasn't really much of a politician.

We'd better leave the political consequences till we look at that period, I said. Perhaps that's as far as we can go for the time being. But there's one other subject I'd like to raise: what he thought about the relationship between revolutionary France and the rest of the world. This was a matter of both war and foreign policy and Robespierre was no authority on either. He knew nothing of strategy and possibly resented the professional expertise of men like the army engineers, Carnot and Prieur de la Côte d'Or, his colleagues on the Committee of Public Safety. Unlike Saint-Just he never saw any fighting. Disregarding strategy and logistics, he always insisted that victory or defeat would depend on the way in which the government implemented the basic tenets of the revolution in its domestic policy.[73] His own view of the war fluctuated a good deal with the changing political situation. He had made it clear in 1792 that he was not opposed to war as such, but to risking the fate of the revolution when the government and the army were in suspect hands. His warnings against military dictatorship, which his admirers have sometimes presented as prophesying the advent of Bonaparte, were made in May and June 1792 and actually referred to Lafayette.[74] In July 1792 he wrote that 'when a powerful nation wages a war of liberty it rises in its entirety and marches under leaders it has chosen for itself'.[75] Later, when he himself was a member of the government, he resisted popular pressure for a *levée en masse,* insisting that the real need was to exterminate traitors and to repress the counter-revolution at home.[76]

When the victories of the autumn of 1792 seemed to have confirmed the optimistic predictions of the Girondins, Robespierre's over-confidence led him to echo their ideological crusading. In November he dismissed a warning from the Foreign Minister that a general offensive could be expected in the spring. 'The destruction of the Prussian army, whose fate was in our hands, and the punishment of Louis XVI would have been enough to strike down that impotent league and paralyse all the despots.'[77] Forgetting his remarks about no one liking armed missionaries, he wrote that all France had to do was to help her neighbours to throw off the yoke of despotism and establish free peoples between herself and the tyrants.[78] He did warn against antagonising the feelings of the liberated peoples, especially over religion, but he had no doubt that French troops would be welcomed, at least as far as the Rhine.[79] In February 1793 he was confident that the imminent conquest of Holland would bring revolution in England. 'A thousand victories bear witness to the truth that with a French army it is impossible for a general not to win, unless he deliberately refuses to do so.[80] La Harpe admittedly wrote from gaol in May 1794 that Robespierre had risked his popularity by opposing Brissot's plans

---

73. See, for example, *Oeuvres,* vol. v, pp. 303, 354.
74. *Oeuvres,* vol. iv, pp. 98, 142.   75. *Oeuvres,* vol. iv, p. 225.
76. 29 March 1793. *Oeuvres,* vol. ix, pp. 346-8; 12 and 14 August 1793. *Oeuvres,* vol. x, pp. 66-8.
77. *Oeuvres,* vol. vi, pp. 47-8.   78. *Oeuvres,* vol. vi, p. 60.
79. *Oeuvres,* vol. vi, p. 303.   80. ibid.

to make war on England and Spain and had also criticised the invasion of Holland, but his only evidence for this was probably a speech that Robespierre made long after the war had begun.[81] The four concluding articles of his version of the rights of man included a commitment to support national liberation movements elsewhere. His presentation of these clauses included the casual admission that 'they may have the drawback of irrevocably antagonising the kings'.[82] In March 1793 he urged the Convention not to be alarmed by the initial defeats in Belgium since France was 'a great nation destined to punish all the tyrants of the world'.[83] He had already told his readers that 'today one Frenchman is more than a match for ten Prussians'.[84] Neerwinden and the failures of the summer of 1793 put an end to such jingoistic nonsense and Robespierre never spoke in this tone again.

Sobered perhaps by experience and by sharing in the responsibilities of government, he became increasingly cautious. Towards the end of 1793 he insisted that 'Frenchmen are not smitten with the mania of wanting to make any nation free and happy against its will'.[85] Except for the first six months of the Convention, he was always out of step with public opinion. He had opposed going to war when there was a good deal of belligerency in *patriote* circles. When the Committee of Public Safety at last provided France with the officers, men and material that she needed for victory, Robespierre became increasingly disenchanted. He savaged the harmless eccentric, Cloots, for advocating the policy of European revolution that he himself had seemed to favour a year before. His colleagues on the Committee accused him of indifference to the victories that Barère was at last able to trumpet forth to the cheering deputies. In his last speech he said with prophetic sadness, 'What does it matter if our armies drive before them the armed satellites of kings if we are falling back before the vices that destroy public liberty? What is the use of defeating kings if we ourselves are overcome by the vices that bring tyranny with them?'[86]

At least he learned, said Henry, and it's only human to get carried away by victory. I shouldn't like you to look too carefully at some of the things I wrote home during the war.

81. Jacob, op. cit., p. 138.   82. 24 April 1793. *Oeuvres,* vol. IX, p. 463.
83. 8 March 1793. *Oeuvres,* vol. IX, p. 303.
84. *Oeuvres,* vol. V, p. 293.
85. *Oeuvres,* vol. X, p. 230.   86. *Oeuvres,* vol. X, p. 572.

Where foreign policy was concerned, Robespierre tended on the whole to see the situation in national rather than ideological terms. He was consistent in his attempts to maintain good relations with the neutrals, especially with the United States, Turkey and Switzerland. This was the main point of his major speech of 17 November 1793 and in the previous spring he had already objected to the spreading of republican propaganda in Turkey and deprecated taking violent action to avenge an insult to the French ambassador in Rome.[87] The United States and Switzerland as republics, even of an inferior species, might be considered natural friends of revolutionary France, but to call Turkey, Montesquieu's old *bête noire* and the epitome of despotism for every French intellectual, a 'useful and faithful ally' suggested that the days of revolutionary crusading were over. In the course of his speech on 17 November Robespierre advanced the absurd argument that the British Government, unable to declare war on France because of the resistance of the Opposition and of public opinion, got Brissot to declare war on England and Spain so that France could be defeated. This is presumably what misled La Harpe into thinking that Robespierre had opposed the extension of the war at the time.[88]

The man who could say that could say anything, said Ted; he can't possibly have believed it.

I haven't got the key to his conscience, I said. It's impossible to know how far he had managed to convince himself that it was true. I think he probably did feel that the Girondins had got in the way of the revolution so often, with their war policy, their opposition to the attack on the Tuileries, their campaign against Paris, the attempt of some of them to save the king and their vendetta against the Montagnards, that they must have been doing it on purpose. It's also true, I think, that once he had decided someone was an enemy of the revolution, no accusation was too black or too implausible for him to use. It was the same with Pitt, whom he accused of being behind every counter-revolutionary plot in France. His attitude to England had always been somewhat ambivalent. In the early years of the revolution he praised its civil institutions but condemned the corruption of its government. He was probably irritated by the Anglomania of some of the more moderate revolutionaries – his domestic enemies – and by 1791 he

---

87. *Oeuvres*, vol. v, pp. 299, 334. 88. *Oeuvres*, vol. x, pp. 171-2.

had convinced himself that France had left England far behind. As late as May 1793 he could still assess the British constitution in reasonably objective terms.[89] After that a new note came in. As he came to believe that the main threat to the revolution came not from open royalists but from secret agents he became less discriminating in his denunciation of those he suspected of being their paymasters across the Channel. This was partly for tactical reasons. In the early days of 1794 he was hoping to use Anglophobia as a means of diverting the Jacobins from their internecine quarrels. But there was more to it than that. He had seen more clearly than most that the society of the ancien régime had rested on an aristocratic conception of honour that was incompatible with a republican ideology of *vertu*.[90] Under the pressure of the war, however, he began to endow *vertu* with some of the martial characteristics of honour, applied not to an exclusive social order but to the privileged nation. In the process, he became a nationalist of a new kind. In October 1793 he professed to be horrified by a deputy who said that France was at war with the British Government, not with the British people.[91] In January he said bluntly, 'I don't like the English; that word calls to mind an insolent people.'[92]

By the end of 1793 he seems to have been seeing the war as more of a national than an ideological conflict. This implied the possibility of making peace with some of France's enemies in order to concentrate on the others. He could not fail to be aware of the intimate relationship between the war and the domestic policies of the revolution. Since the summer of 1793 the advocates of more extreme policies had also been calling for an intensification of the war effort. How far Robespierre considered a total or partial pacification to be desirable, assuming it to be possible, would depend on his general view of the possibility of a return to constitutional government. In theory, revolutionary government was only a temporary expedient. When and how to move from the revolutionary to the constitutional phase were the main problems dividing the Montagnards and the transition was likely to prove both difficult and dangerous.

89. *Oeuvres*, vol. v, p. 268; vol. vi, pp. 86-95, 239, 308; vol. vii, p. 29; vol. viii, p. 177; vol. ix, p. 499.
90. See N. Hampson, 'The French Revolution and the nationalisation of honour' in *War and Society*, ed. M. R. D. Foot, London, 1973.
91. *Oeuvres*, vol. x, p. 144.
92. *Oeuvres*, pp. 348-9.

You can't just move on to the next stage like that, said Ted. We want a summing up.

I invited him to sum up.

Well, I think, and I've got the impression that Mac agrees with me, that there's not much meat in all this. His ideas on foreign policy don't go beyond some commonplace remarks about not offending the neutrals and a few windy nationalist platitudes. His religious festivals sound like the election of a Rose Queen. They would have bored everyone stiff once the novelty wore off. His educational policy – if it was his – never amounted to more than a day dream –

And his social policy, put in Mac, would strike any present-day conservative government as rather unambitious.

He may have been a skilful politician – I'm inclined to think that he was – but I can't understand why historians have made such a fuss about him. He didn't really have anything you could call a policy.

It wasn't only historians, I said. You've got to explain why he seemed to matter so much to his contemporaries.

Quite right, said Henry, and it's not difficult. He may not have worked out much of a long-term policy – and winning the war at home and at the front must have been a full-time job for the Committee of Public Safety – but he had a vision, which is more important. It's not easy to see that, in an age of technical expertise and moral confusion, but you won't inspire posterity by the dexterity of your Double-taxation Bills. The men who matter are the ones who stand for something. Events aren't significant in themselves – there were more executions in France between 1944 and 1945 than in 1793–4 but few people knew or cared – it's what they seem to stand for. It was because Robespierre personified the aspirations of the revolution and made them articulate that you can't escape him. He mattered then and he matters now. The Terror lasted only a year or two and most people lived through it. Even if it did preserve the conquests of the revolution, how much difference does that make now? What it meant to foreigners at the time and what it's meant to everyone else since then, depends on what it symbolised. For most of the Montagnards it was a job to be done. Robespierre was one of the few who saw further than that and his definition of its meaning gave it a new sort of reality. There's nothing you can do about that. However convincingly you

expose the limitations of his policies you won't make any difference. Posterity has made him a giant and it was quite right. I think
he glimpsed that himself; he was less concerned with what he
achieved than with what he stood for and so he outlived the men
who killed him. Either you can see this sort of thing or you can't,
but whether you can or not doesn't make any difference to his
stature. That's safe enough.

No one said anything so I went on. By the summer of 1794 all
his long-term problems as a statesman were becoming inseparable
from his short-term preoccupations as a politician. We can't begin
to understand them without understanding the political situation as
a whole. Since this was extremely complicated I should like you to
read about it for yourselves before we look at Robespierre's activities and I've brought you this article to give you an idea of the
background.

I can guess what's coming, said Ted, looking distastefully at the
xerox I had given him. It was too good to last. Just when it
seemed that you were knocking things into some sort of shape
you're going to break up the pattern again and lose us all in a
mass of detail.

Don't blame me, I said. That's the way it was.

VII Montagnard Politics

The *journées* of 31 May and 2 June left the Convention and Paris as a whole uncertain about what exactly had happened and divided as to future policy. When Bourdon de l'Oise said that everyone knew that the Convention had been forced into saving the Republic, he summed up the dilemma of the deputies. Very few had wanted the purge but the Montagnards had henceforth to include 31 May in the sacred calendar of the Revolution, as the glorious sequel to 14 July and 10 August. The majority of the deputies feared and distrusted the Montagnards but they had no desire to see the Republic overthrown by its domestic or foreign enemies. For the next fourteen months they were to be the reluctant accomplices of the minority. The Convention as a whole and the municipal authorities in Paris feared that the extremist forces unleashed during the crisis might have acquired a taste for direct action in support of radical social and economic policies that would turn the rest of the country against the capital. Conservative, if not actually royalist opinion remained strong in Paris and the minority of revolutionary militants had some reason to fear the kind of violent reaction that occurred in other French towns.

For the time being, the Commune and the Montagnards in the Assembly preached moderation. When the extremist, Leclerc, seemed to be justifying further bloodshed he was denounced by Hébert, the deputy *procureur*, who also rejected a proposal to purge nobles and priests from the municipal administration. The strength of conservative feeling was shown by the fact that Raffet, the candidate of one of the wealthier west-end Sections, polled more votes than Hanriot, the hero or villain of 2 June, in the first ballot for the election of a commander-in-chief for the Parisian National Guard. It took a good deal of pressure and gerrymandering to secure Hanriot's eventual victory. Two Sections even sent representatives to negotiate with those Girondins who had raised an armed revolt in Normandy, and though they were eventually induced to change their policy the Commune thought it wiser not to take any punitive action against them.[1]

1. See A. Soboul, *Les sans-culottes parisiens en l'an II*, Paris, 1958, pp. 21-91.

The coup d'état of 2 June was disowned by most of provincial France where attempts were made to raise local forces for a march on Paris. The Committee of Public Safety, under the leadership of Danton, replied with a policy of appeasement. Danton tried to negotiate a settlement in Languedoc and his attempts to buy off opposition in Normandy were later supplemented by the conciliatory mission of his colleague on the Committee, Lindet, who succeeded in restoring order with a minimum of repression.[2] The Committee's report on the arrested Girondins, entrusted to Saint-Just, was deferred for as long as possible. Although read to the Convention on 8 July it was not actually voted until the 28th. Despite the understandable proscription of those who had tried to organise armed revolt, its general tenor was moderate and perhaps closer to the views of the Committee as a whole than to those of its author. An ultra-democratic constitution was hastily drafted and its approval on 24 June was intended to refute the accusation that the Montagnards aspired to dictatorship, and perhaps to hold out the prospect of an amnesty. Any successful policy of moderation implied peace and Danton did what he could to open negotiations with England and Prussia, possibly offering to release Marie Antoinette.[3] In view of the need to stimulate revolutionary patriotism by inflammatory propaganda, even the search for peace had to be kept secret and those responsible laid themselves open to subsequent charges of treason and royalism when the policy failed.

Conciliation did win back the loyalty of much of France. Its failures, however, were more spectacular. Lyons, the second city, drifted into open revolt and was besieged by a republican army. The insurrectionary movement that already controlled Marseilles spread to the great naval base of Toulon where almost half of the French fleet was lying. In August both Marseilles and Toulon opened negotiations with the British fleet that had just arrived off the Provencal coast. The Powers, with everything to gain from what promised to be a successful campaigning season, were not interested in peace and indifferent to the fate of Marie Antoinette. More or less aware that nothing positive was being achieved, the Assembly became restless. Its changing moods were reflected in the

2. For Danton's attitude to Normandy, see Michelet, *Histoire de la Révolution française*, Book XI, chap. iii, and G. Bouchard, *Prieur de la Côte d'Or*, Paris, 1946, p. 180.
3. A. Mathiez, *Danton et la paix*, Paris, 1928, pp. 138-72.

tug-of-war over the direction of the War Office. The Minister, the radical Bouchotte, who was turning his great military bureaucracy into a sans-culotte bastion, was challenged by the partisans of Beauharnais, a noble, who enjoyed the support of the Committee of Public Safety. Bouchotte offered his resignation and the Convention twice voted to replace him, only to rescind its motion each time.[4] The Committee of Public Safety itself came under increasing fire, not merely from extremists like Marat but also from men who were, or were to become, the allies of Danton, such as Legendre, Chabot and Bourdon. When Danton's friend, Desmoulins, led the final attack that resulted in the committee's being changed on 10 July, there was some reason to suspect that Danton himself was ready to retire. Prieur de la Côte d'Or, in his *Révélations sur le Comité de Salut Public,* claimed that one of Danton's agents whom he met in Normandy, told him as much at the time.[5] If, on the other hand, Danton hoped that a partial re-shuffle would strengthen his control over the committee, he was disappointed. He and Delacroix were replaced by Thuriot and Prieur de la Marne while the rest of the committee was unchanged. Of its nine members only Thuriot had any close links with Danton. A fortnight later Gasparin, a sick man, gave up his place, which was taken by Robespierre.

The new committee was soon to show that it had the will to govern but for the time being it could only survive by swimming with the flooding time of extremism. The capitulation of Condé, Mainz and Valenciennes, defeats in the Vendée, the murder of Marat and the counter-revolution at Toulon, all within a month, produced growing popular pressure for exceptional measures against foreign enemies and domestic traitors. Marat had provided the Montagnards with a political lightning-conductor. Politically ineffective, his verbal violence had diverted his sans-culotte readers from taking action on their own. His murder on 13 July led to an immediate struggle for his inheritance between the Enragés, Roux and Leclerc, and Hébert. The Montagnards were virtually unanimous in their determination to be rid of Roux, who threatened Convention, Jacobins and Commune with direct action from the streets. In July they recaptured the Cordelier Club, which had

---

4. General Herlaut, *Le colonel Bouchotte*, Paris, 1946, vol. II, chap. vii.
5. Bouchard, op. cit., p. 438.

briefly taken Roux's side, and after a rather more difficult struggle they succeeded, in August, in destroying his hold over the Gravilliers Section. By September he was in gaol and the Enragé leadership had been discredited.[6]

The disappearance of Roux, but not of the popular discontent that had given him his strength, led to a polarisation of forces within the Montagnards that was to last until the following spring. The Committee of Public Safety increasingly saw itself as a national government whose main concern was the defeat of domestic and foreign enemies. It was ready to take exceptional powers for this purpose but opposed to the introduction of economic controls and determined to preserve its own authority. It tried to buy itself a respite from popular pressure by intensified repression. Saint-Just's report outlawing nine of the Girondin leaders was voted on the day that the Committee admitted the fall of Mainz, and the capitulation of Valenciennes was greeted by the decision to try Marie Antoinette. As the bad news continued and intensified, such measures proved inadequate to hold the Committee's control over the rising wrath of Paris.

Within the Montagnard minority, the men centred round Danton began to constitute a more distinct group. This consisted of people who, for one reason or another, hoped to stabilise the revolution and to resist popular pressure for more violent policies. Its main spokesmen at this time, Danton himself, Delacroix, Desmoulins, Thuriot and Legendre, were not so much moderates by temperament as men who were satisfied with the position and wealth that they had won through the revolution. Most of them were old Cordeliers – the name Desmoulins chose for the newspaper he launched in December – and their past record had been as violent as anyone's. Their language still was, for they could only hope to retain their political influence by concealing their real aims behind a smokescreen of verbal extremism. Their immediate policy was the consolidation of the power of the Committee of Public Safety, presumably on the ground that only a very powerful government could restrain the trend towards anarchy and violence. In the coming months, however, they attracted the support of men

6. A. Mathiez, *La vie chère et le mouvement social sous la Révolution*, Paris, 1927, pp. 200-365; R. B. Rose, *The Enragés: Socialists of the French Revolution?*, Melbourne, 1965, *passim*.

such as Bourdon and Philippeaux who had quarrelled violently with the more radical agents of the Committee and saw Danton and his friends as an alternative government.

In opposition, both to the government and to the 'Dantonists' there emerged a new Cordelier group of the dissatisfied, who hoped to harness popular radicalism to the furtherance of their own ambitions. These men were well entrenched in the centres of revolutionary power. Hébert (who was defeated by Danton's protégé, Paré, in the election for a new Minister of the Interior), besides his position on the Paris Commune, won over much of Marat's following for his racy and oath-ridden newspaper, the *Père Duchesne*. At the War Office Bouchotte allowed a great deal of political influence to pass into the hands of his Secretary-General, Vincent, a violent man of twenty-six. With Roux out of the way, Hébert and Vincent were able to establish some control over the Cordeliers and Hébert was an influential member of the Jacobins as well.

The political situation was complicated and confused. Without any party organisation, individuals aligned themselves with different groups over different issues, as their ideals, interests, hopes and fears dictated. Group interests and rivalries created other divisions. The Assembly was inclined to resent the growing power of the Committee of Public Safety. The Commune, which claimed to speak with the voice of Paris, suspected any independent action by the Sections. The Sections themselves were often political battle-grounds, with control over the general assembly, the *comité révolutionnaire* and the local *société populaire* disputed between rival groups. Revolutionary ideology forced all to pretend to the single-minded pursuit of a common cause. Since party was equated with faction and current policy held to be unchangeable orthodoxy, all manoeuvres had to be veiled in double-talk. There must have been times when this proved almost as impenetrable to contemporaries as it does to historians. In cases where the hidden motive was the pursuit of private gain, public language could mean the exact opposite of what it purported to say and the uninitiated must often have been startled by sudden shifts of allegiance such as Chabot's eulogy of Danton on 23 August.

Tension rose towards the end of August and the parallel with the weeks before 31 May must have struck many who hoped or feared a similar dénouement. Defeat, invasion and treason at

196

Toulon, where the fleet was handed over to the British intact, suggested that the government, despite the addition to the Committee of Public Safety of two military engineers, Carnot and Prieur de la Côte d'Or, was incapable of winning the war. A contemporary historian suggested that the *levée en masse,* voted on 23 August, packed the meetings of the Sections with those hoping to avoid being conscripted.[7] The restlessness of the Sections communicated itself to the Jacobins, where a gap opened between the members and the sans-culottes in the galleries. The leading members of the club hoped to avoid a crisis but there were others who believed they could turn it to their own advantage. The situation was complicated by the fact that the men who had come up from the provinces to celebrate the acceptance of the new constitution at the fête of 10 August seem to have been made honorary members and their presence strengthened the radical wing. On 28 August the Jacobins voted to enlist the support of the Sections for a mass petition urging the Convention to extend conscription to the 25–35 age groups, to purge the army staffs and to expel all foreigners. On 2 September Hébert induced them to petition again, with the Sections and *sociétés populaires,* to demand the immediate trial of the Girondins.

The crisis broke two days later when the Commune was besieged by men demanding an increase in wages, men who were denounced as counter-revolutionaries by Robespierre but defended by some of his fellow-Jacobins. Hébert and Chaumette diverted the demonstrators into invading the Convention on 5 September. Robespierre, Barère and Jeanbon Saint-André appealed in vain for a free hand for the Committee of Public Safety. The demonstrators and their supporters in the Assembly insisted on an immediate vote for the creation of a sans-culotte revolutionary army that should prise food supplies from reluctant farmers and suppress all opposition in the provinces.[8] In a vehement but ambiguous intervention, Danton, on the pretext that the Sections were falling under the control of the wealthy and suspect, secured the payment of 40 sous per session to the poorer members – and the restriction of meetings to two per week. The *journée* taught the Committee of Public Safety the

7. G. Vasselin, *Mémorial révolutionnaire de la Convention,* Paris, 1797, vol. II, p. 224.

8. On the revolutionary army, see R. Cobb, *Les armées révolutionnaires,* Paris, 1961, 1963, 2v.

limits of its power and during the following weeks it had to accept other radical measures. Chief among these was the implementation of the decision of principle, voted in August, that suspects were to be arrested. Suspects were now defined in terms so vague as to open the door to every kind of political manipulation and their arrest was entrusted to the *comités révolutionnaires* of the Sections, which were first to be purged by the Commune. Controls were voted over wages and the prices of all necessities, although no attempt was made to enforce wage controls in private industry in Paris until the following July. Billaud-Varenne, who had taken a leading part in the noisy debates of the 5th, was elected to the Committee of Public Safety, together with Collot d'Herbois. Danton was also elected but declined.

The events of September had a lasting influence on the balance of political forces and the nature of revolutionary government. The Committee of Public Safety failed to get Hanriot chosen as commander-in-chief of the new revolutionary army. Ronsin, who obtained the post, was the Cordelier candidate.[9] The law of suspects henceforth made it easy for those with political influence to secure the indefinite imprisonment of their opponents. This made everyone insecure and drove them to cover themselves by violent protestations of revolutionary zeal and to pack the *comités révolutionnaires* with their own supporters. When the control of *certificats de civisme* (whose possession was necessary for every kind of public employment and whose refusal made a man automatically a suspect) was transferred from the general assemblies of the Sections to their *comités révolutionnaires,* Fabre d'Eglantine observed that 'the Assembly has placed in the hands of the Commune a murderous weapon that adds incalculable force to its powers'.[10] The quarrels between the small fry led both sides to turn for protection to influential politicians who thus became involved in conflicts that they might have preferred to avoid. On 14 September the Committee of General Security, widely suspected of trafficking in the release of suspects, was purged, Chabot and Basire losing their seats.

Having bought off the threat from the streets at the cost of a good many concessions, the Committee of Public Safety was able

9. General Herlaut, *Le général rouge Ronsin,* Paris, 1956, pp. 161-3.
10. Archives Nationales F⁷ 4434.

to develop its strength within the Convention during the course of the autumn. It fought off an attack from disgruntled deputies, recalled from their missions and sometimes censured, on 25 September. On 10 October the government of France was declared revolutionary for the duration of the war. This meant that the new constitution was indefinitely suspended and the Committee was to continue to exercise most of the powers of a government, although it did not control finance or police. The decree of 4 December provided revolutionary government with a constitution of its own which placed local authorities and representatives on mission firmly under the control of the Committees of Public Safety and General Security. On the same day the former Committee vetoed the attempt of the *procureur* of the Commune, Chaumette, to establish control over the *comités révolutionnaires*.

The Committee's success was made possible by the visible proof that it was winning the war. Victories over the British at Hondschoote and the Austrians at Wattignies, in September and October, and the recapture of Lyons were followed at the end of the year by the expulsion of the British forces from Toulon and the annihilation of the Vendean army that had crossed the Loire in an unsuccessful attempt to seize a Channel port. These achievements allowed the Committee of Public Safety to survive, but events in the Vendée and at Lyons gave rise to new political problems. The whole Vendean campaign was bedevilled by the bitter antagonism of rival generals and of the deputies on mission who championed them.[11] The Committee, after some hesitation, opted for the 'revolutionaries', Rossignol and Ronsin, against their opponents, Biron, a nobleman, Danton's protégé Westermann and d'Eglantine's brother. Rossignol was denounced as incompetent by Bourdon who, on being recalled to Paris, carried on a noisy vendetta against Rossignol's chief, Bouchotte. Philippeaux, another deputy in the Vendée, adopted a similar attitude a little later in the year. The two therefore gave their support to Danton, while Rossignol and Ronsin were the heroes of the Cordeliers. After the fall of Lyons, Robespierre's associate, Couthon, was replaced in the captured city by Collot, with orders to intensify repression. Collot, supported by his fellow-deputy, Fouché, and by Ronsin with a

11. See Herlaut, *Le général rouge Ronsin*, Part II, and A. de Lestapis, *La 'conspiration de Batz'*, Paris, 1969, pp. 123-59.

detachment of the revolutionary army, acted with extreme ferocity, mowing down his victims with grape-shot in a number of mass executions. Other deputies elsewhere behaved with equal brutality, but the other members of the Committee who were sent on temporary missions, Saint-Just, Jeanbon, Prieur de la Marne and even Billaud, did not. Collot's savagery and his association with Ronsin made it difficult for the Committee to repudiate policies of which it probably disapproved, a fact that was to have important political consequences.

It is difficult to know whether the Committee as a whole tried to save Marie Antoinette and the Girondins from a trial by the revolutionary tribunal that would admit of only one verdict. There was so much intrigue surrounding each trial, with bribery cutting across political conviction and all parties pretending to the ferocity that revolutionary *bienséance* demanded, that it is impossible to know when any of them were sincere.[12] The fact that the trials were delayed so long, in the face of constant popular pressure, must indicate a good deal of hidden resistance. When the trial of the Girondins was finally decided on 3 October, Robespierre defeated a motion by Billaud for an *appel nominal* that would have identified their supporters for future vengeance. He went on to prevent Amar, of the Committee of General Security, from naming over 70 sympathisers who had signed secret protests against the purge of 2 June, and this action was to save their lives. It was perhaps in revenge for this that, on the same day, Billaud induced the Assembly to vote for the immediate trial of Marie Antoinette.

Typical of the deviousness that had invaded Montagnard political rivalries was the case of Lavaux. Lavaux complained to the Jacobins on 5 October that their official newspaper, the *Journal de la Montagne,* of which he was the editor, was being intercepted in the post by the Paris authorities. Levasseur disingenuously suggested that Lavaux had perhaps been criticising the Minister of War and the editor conceded that he had indeed accused Bouchotte of favouritism. Sijas, of the War Office, then revealed that the real complaint against Lavaux was that he had been spreading false

---

12. For the charges against Hébert, see below, pp. 205-6. Chabot, one of the main prosecution witnesses against the Girondins, was accused of having tried to save some of them for a price.

accusations of theft against Bouchotte's deputy, Vincent. Three days later Lavaux was arrested by the Luxembourg Section, quite illegally, since he did not belong to it. Vincent, however, did. The Jacobins shouted down Vincent's attempt to defend himself and Lavaux was soon released. A month later, however, Hébert attacked the *Journal de la Montagne* because of an article on religion, d'Eglantine accused Lavaux of antagonising the Swiss and the unfortunate editor found himself dismissed and his place offered to one of Hébert's protégés.

When the Committee of Public Safety might have hoped that it was moving into calmer waters the Parisian militants were once more stirred into action, this time in the unexpected cause of religion.[13] The Convention itself was unsympathetic towards priests and Catholicism. The introduction of a new calendar in October had abolished Christian chronology, saints' days and Sundays. Legislation provided for the confiscation from churches of anything that might serve the national economy or the war effort: sacred vessels, bells and bell-ropes. Acts of iconoclasm, when reported, met with a general welcome. One or two deputies, notably Fouché at Nevers and Moulins, before he joined Collot at Lyons, had moved further towards the proscription of Christianity itself. Despite all this, the irruption into the Assembly on 7 November of Gobel, the archbishop of Paris, who had come to resign his see, the Assembly's participation three days later in a *Fête de la Raison* at Notre Dame which, on the motion of the former Franciscan monk, Chabot, was transformed into a Temple of Reason, the closing of all Parisian churches and the noisy carnival of deputations mocking Catholicism on the floor of the Convention, all this represented something new. Politicians of different persuasions were quick to associate themselves with what seemed to be a popular movement; Chaumette in particular was later to pay for his encouragement of the new trend, but he does not seem to have been behind the events of 7 November, however he may have welcomed them. The men who had bullied Gobel into resignation were Cloots, an eccentric Prussian baron, and those responsible for the creation of a new central committee of the Parisian *sociétés populaires*. The latter consisted of Proli, an

13. See J. McManners, *The French Revolution and the Church*, London, 1969, pp. 86-98, and R. Cobb, op. cit., pp. 634-94.

Austrian who was thought to be the bastard son of the former Chancellor, Kaunitz, with Desfieux, Dubuisson and Pereira, a trio of political adventurers who were also members of the Jacobin correspondence committee. Cloots may well have been a harmless crank but Proli had previously been employed as an Austrian agent and Desfieux had received money from the king's civil list.[14] A sudden access of anti-religious enthusiasm on the part of such citizens must have struck the authorities as somewhat odd, especially after Fabre had secretly denounced the four as foreign agents.[15]

It could have been merely a coincidence that several different crises all came to a head in mid-November. The same men tended to appear in one confrontation after another, but this was perhaps to be expected in view of the polarisation of Montagnard politics. None the less, the two governing committees must have wondered whether they were not being challenged by obscure coalitions whose ultimate objectives were not necessarily identified with the welfare of the Republic.

On 9 November the Convention voted that one of its members, Osselin, should be tried on a charge of protecting a returned émigrée, without being given a hearing in the Assembly. On the following day Philippeaux advocated an investigation into the wealth of all the deputies. Basire and Thuriot secured the defeat of this inconvenient proposal. Chabot then demanded that in future no deputy should be sent for trial without a chance to clear himself in the Assembly and Thuriot, attacking the extremists, denounced the existence of what he called a system of terror in the Assembly itself. After a long debate in which Julien de Toulouse supported the other three deputies, Chabot's motion was carried. At the next meeting of the Jacobins, on the 11th, Dufourny attacked Chabot and Basire with the prophetic argument that if the Montagnards once relaxed their grip they would be exterminated by the enemies they had spared. Thuriot, he argued, was misled and less dangerous than the other two. Hébert, on the other hand, concentrated his fire on Thuriot, persuading the

14. A. Mathiez, 'Le Comité de Salut Public et le complot de l'étranger', *Ann. hist. Rév. fr.*, 1926, p. 308. On Dubuisson, see general Herlaut, *Deux témoins de la Terreur*, Paris, 1958, Book I; on Desfieux, J-A. Dulaure, *Supplément aux crimes des anciens comités de gouvernment*, Paris, an III, p. 129, and Arch. Nat. W389.
15. See below, p. 211.

Jacobins to expel him, whereas Chabot and Basire were merely to be the subject of an investigation. Philippeaux opened the important debate in the Convention on the 11th by attacking Ronsin and Rossignol. Proceedings were interrupted by the arrival of the mayor of Saint Denis (an ex-priest) who had come to deliver six cart-loads of church spoils. A spokesman for the Committee of General Security then explained the charges against Osselin, and Barère, of the Committee of Public Safety, profited from this to secure the repeal of Chabot's motion of the 10th. Next day the *Indulgents* appeared to be in full retreat. Basire thanked his Jacobin colleagues for having saved him from his own mistakes. Chabot, following suit, insinuated that the real counter-revolutionaries were those who wished to introduce the new constitution – a reference to Hébert and his ministerial ambitions. Thuriot tried to ingratiate himself at the expense of others by calling for the immediate trial of the 73 Girondin supporters who had been saved by Robespierre. On the same evening he appealed to the Jacobins against his exclusion but Hébert persuaded them to stand by their previous decision. When the Jacobins met again on the 16th it was Chabot's turn. Dufourny made a savage attack on his marriage to Léopoldine Frey, the sister of two Austrians who claimed to be political refugees from the Habsburgs. When Chabot had announced his marriage to the Jacobins in October, despite the objections of Dufourny, he had persuaded them to be represented at the wedding. Now they turned against him and ordered an investigation into his career. Chabot had probably prepared himself for this threat. On the morning of the 14th he had woken up Robespierre to denounce to him a vast foreign plot to corrupt and defame the leading members of the Convention with the intention of bringing about its dissolution.[16] This denunciation was to add a new dimension of hatred and suspicion to the Montagnard feuds and to play a major part in their self-destruction.

It is impossible to understand the political history of the Terror in terms of politics alone. Alongside the world of politics proper there existed another world of corruption in which many of the leaders were equally involved. The alliances, secrets, opponents to

16. Mathiez, in *Un Procès de corruption sous la Terreur: l'affaire de la Compagnie des Indes*, Paris, 1920, p. 37, is incorrect in saying that Chabot's denunciation followed the decision of the Jacobins to investigate him.

be conciliated or blackmailed into silence, created a political underworld whose alignments often differed from those of public debate. If the latter were devious, the former are almost impenetrable. New evidence is still being discovered and much that was said was never put on paper. The vicissitudes of revolutionary government meant that, at one time or another, many of those with an interest in destroying evidence had access to the archives and a great deal has probably disappeared. Enough information is available, however, even if it often falls short of legal proof, to demonstrate the importance of this underworld, although its full extent and political implications remain somewhat conjectural.

Danton has been shown to have made a good deal of money in ways that his 'explanations' failed to explain.[17] A letter from Mirabeau, in March 1791, casually referred to his having been paid 30,000 livres.[18] The royalist Minister, Moleville, claimed that Danton was bribed to avert the insurrection of 10 August, as was Delacroix.[19] He was commonly thought to have lined his pockets, and those of his secretaries, Fabre and Desmoulins, while Minister of Justice in August 1792. Contemporaries accused him and Delacroix of having plundered Belgium when on mission there in the spring of 1793.[20] The evidence of Sénart, an employee of the Committee of General Security, that Danton and Delacroix were responsible for the forging of assignats in Belgium and Germany is less convincing, for Sénart's 'revelations' inspire little confidence but it is curious that general Miaczynski, after his condemnation by the revolutionary tribunal, should have accused Delacroix (though not Danton) of the same thing.[21]

It has also been shown that some of the Parisian extremists, Chaumette at the Commune, Lulier, Momoro, La Chevardière and Raisson of the Department, together with the Minister of the Interior, Garat, and Santerre, protected the duc du Châtelet, a

---

17. G. Lefebvre, 'Sur Danton', *Ann. hist. Rév fr.,* 1932, pp. 385-424, 484-500; G. Pioro, 'Sur la fortune de Danton', id., 1955, pp. 324-41.

18. *Correspondance entre Mirabeau et le comte de la Marck* (ed. Bacourt), Paris, 1851, vol. III, p. 82.

19. *Private memoirs relative to the last year of Louis XVI,* London, 1797, vol. II, p. 162; A. de Lestapis, 'Un grand corrupteur, le duc du Châtelet', *Ann. hist. Rév. fr.,* 1953, p. 107 n[7].

20. A. Mathiez, *Autour de Danton,* Paris, 1926, pp. 165-73.

21. Sénart, *Révélations puisées dans les cartons des Comités de Salut Public et de Sûreté Générale,* Paris, 1824, p. 96.

returned émigré.[22] Santerre was also accused by Moleville of taking bribes before 10 August. Du Châtelet was not a hunted man who might have inspired pity in political opponents. He had already made his way to England and it is reasonable to suppose that his decision to return was politically motivated. It also seems likely enough that he was not the only beneficiary of false certificates of non-emigration. Although the evidence about du Châtelet was communicated to Chabot and Basire, and later to Voulland, the Committee of General Security took no action against any of the politicians involved. When some of them were later tried on other charges it was similarly ignored, except in the case of Lulier – who was the only 'Dantonist' not to receive a death sentence! It is perhaps worth noting that, of the men involved, Lulier seems to have been associated with the baron de Batz and that du Châtelet paid an unexplained visit to Boulogne, which seems to have been one of Batz's fiefs.

The evidence against Hébert is less conclusive and mostly concerns his alleged involvement in attempts to secure the escape of Marie Antoinette. Since Bouchotte was supplying the army with thousands of copies of his Père Duchesne, Hébert was presumably not short of money. The abbé Edgeworth, who accompanied Louis XVI to his execution, told the dead king's brother that a Mrs Atkins went over from England and bribed Hébert to let her see the queen, to whom she passed a note.[23] More seriously, the comte de Rochechouart repeated the account printed in a letter to the Moniteur in 1795 that Hébert had accepted from his mother a bribe of a million livres to save the queen.[24] This story was also repeated by Mallet du Pan, who knew the duchesse de Rochechouart.[25] Chabot, in his denunciation, claimed that the duchess herself had told him that she had induced Hébert to request Marie Antoinette's transfer from the Conciergerie to her former prison of the Temple, for which the Commune was responsible.[26] Such evidence might be dismissed if Hébert had not, in fact, made this

22. A. de Lestapis, art. cit., Ann. hist. Rév. fr., 1953, pp. 104-26, 316-39, 1955, pp. 5-26. See also Arch. Nat., W413.
23. P. D'Estrée, Le Père Duchesne, Paris, n.d., p. 319.
24. Rochechouart, Mémoires, Paris, 1892, p. 2.
25. Mémoires et Correspondance, Paris, 1851, p. 497.
26. Pièces trouvées dans les papiers de Robespierre et complices, Paris, an. III, p. 14.

rather curious proposal to the Jacobins on 27 September and admitted his contact with the duchess, although he claimed to have witnesses to his having driven out the *vieille pécadille* who had been sent to corrupt him.[27] The duchess was certainly a royalist and probably worked with Batz, so Hébert's explanation could well be true – although it would not explain his motion in the Jacobins. Chabot's further charge that Delaunay had often told him that Hébert was corrupt is hearsay at best and both men were thoroughly untrustworthy.

The evidence for Chabot's own corruption is much stronger. The Minister of War, Narbonne, claimed to have paid both Chabot and Basire during the Legislative Assembly.[28] Theodore Lameth said that he was one of the men used by Danton in his attempt to save the king.[29] On 18 August 1793 an unkind colleague said at the Jacobins that Basire *blanchirait un nègre* and a few days later Chabot complained that he himself was *partout moqué et hué*. The old Committee of General Security to which both belonged was changed because of the general belief in its venality. Julien and Alquier had secured the release of Louis XV's mistress, Madame Dubarry. Their successors on the committee promptly re-arrested her, and their agent, the Englishman Greive, requested a confrontation with Basire, Alquier and Julien to expose what he called their infamous conduct, a request that Fouquier-Tinville seems to have thought it prudent to disregard.[30] During the summer of 1793 Julien, seconded by Thuriot, who was then on the Committee of Public Safety, tried to protect the abbé d'Espagnac who was accused, not merely of profiteering from war transport, but also of using his organisation to provide a safe retreat for counter-revolutionaries.[31] D'Espagnac's career as a speculator had begun before the revolution when he and Clavière – the future Girondin Minister – had served as agents of Calonne in opposition to Calonne's rival, Breteuil, who employed Mirabeau and Batz. D'Espagnac had done the contracting for Dumouriez's army and

27. *J. R. Hébert, auteur du Père Duchesne à Camille Desmoulins et Compagnie*, Paris, an II, Bib. Nat. Lb[41] 3615, p. 8.

28. L. Jacob, *Fabre d'Eglantine, chef des fripons*, Paris, 1946, p. 173.

29. A. Mathiez, *Girondins et Montagnards*, Paris, 1930, p. 273.

30. Arch. Nat. W16, quoted in P. M. Laski, *The Trial and Execution of Madame du Barry*, London, 1969, p. 137.

31. By Hassenfratz at the Jacobins on 4 November. Mathiez said that d'Espagnac was also defended by Chabot and Delacroix (art. cit., p. 314).

been protected by him against the attacks of Pache and Cambon. He had been opposed by Ronsin and supported by Danton's friend, Westermann. Throughout the revolution, there seemed to be a secret link between financial speculation and political loyalties.[32] Chabot, Lulier and Delaunay joined in complicated manoeuvres in the summer of 1793 to threaten foreign bankers with the sequestration of their assets, in order to hold them to ransom.[33] Chabot was thought to have obtained 200,000 livres from the English banker, Boyd, in this way and to have hit on the ingenious idea of pretending to receive the money as Léopoldine's dowry, to explain his sudden affluence. Chabot himself said that he denounced to the Committee of Public Safety an attempt by an unknown *émissaire de Pitt* to bribe him with 200,000 livres to propose the freezing of the assets of all bankers. When Delaunay got this voted by the Assembly, Chabot acted as the Committee's agent in getting the decision reversed, but disregarded its advice to reveal the attempt to bribe him.[34]

If one can accept the unsupported testimony of Chabot – admittedly a big 'if' – the new Committee of General Security was scarcely better than the old. He claimed that David (said to be the lover of Delaunay's mistress) and La Vicomterie had connections with Batz and that Voulland and other members of *les comités* took bribes.[35] Chabot was an accomplished liar who was fighting for his life and any accusations of his require supporting evidence. In the case of Amar at least, this seems to exist. It was Amar who was in charge of his interrogation and Chabot complained repeatedly that Amar only noted what suited him. On 17 February he wrote to Robespierre from his cell, 'When I reproached Amar with his complicity with Delaunay to frighten the East India Company, *for it was Amar who was entrusted with this first part of the plot, perhaps unwittingly* [underlined in the text] Jagot wanted to resign' (from the interrogation).[36] Chabot had no incentive to invent this story if a simple question from Robespierre to Jagot

---

32. De Lestapis, op. cit., pp. 115-21.
33. Baron de Batz, *Les conspirations et la fin de Jean, baron de Batz*, Paris, 1911. pp. 156-62; A. Mathiez, art. cit., p. 307.
34. *François Chabot à ses concitoyens*, a memoir that Chabot apparently sent to Robespierre, Arch. Nat. F⁷ 4637.
35. *Pièces trouvées*, p. 3; Arch. Nat. F⁷ 4637.
36. *Pièces trouvées*, p. 56.

could disprove it. He repeated the same charge in a memoir which he hoped would vindicate his own innocence. Amar had, in fact, been charged with examining the accounts of the East India Company in July 1793 and had declared them to be in order. This could have been due to the negligence of the man he employed, Groune, who was arrested on 3 May 1794 – and released within a week of the death of Robespierre.[37] In 1795, however, when the directors of the East India Company had nothing much to fear, they claimed that they had been held to ransom by speculators, naming Fabre, Julien and Delaunay, and also Danton and Amar.[38]

Chabot cast his accusations so widely that it is worth drawing attention to the fact that, apart from Hérault, who was already suspected by his colleagues, and a passing remark that 'even' Billaud had a financial interest in the corn trade, he made no accusations against the members of the Committee of Public Safety.[39]

When Chabot denounced his plot to Robespierre on the morning of 14 November, Robespierre advised him to inform the Committee of General Security, recommending him, according to Chabot, to *ménager les patriotes*.[40] Chabot said that Robespierre told him the Committee of General Security would give him a safe-conduct (since he claimed to have appeared to participate in the plot in order to expose it) and that if they refused, the Committee of Public Safety would do so.[41] Chabot therefore made an oral report to the Committee of General Security which, at their request, he submitted in writing on the 15th. On the following day Basire did the same.[42] Basire had not very much to say and his evidence was entirely concerned with corruption. Delaunay and Julien had told him of a plan, concerted with Danton, to blackmail joint stock companies and bankers. Some time after 25 Septem-

37. A. Mathiez, *Un procès de corruption sous la Terreur*, pp. 30, 370.
38. Id., pp. 379-80.   39. *Pièces trouvées*, p. 11.
40. This was what he originally wrote, though he altered it to *recommandé la prudence. François Chabot à ses concitoyens*, Arch. Nat. F⁷ 4637.
41. This was presumably true since Chabot in his 'testament' (Arch. Nat. W342) says that the memoir which refers to the safe-conduct had been deposited with Robespierre. Mathiez, in his *Procès de corruption sous la Terreur* (p. 109), fails to make this clear.
42. Both statements are reprinted in Mathiez's *Procès de corruption*, pp. 77-108.

ber, Delaunay said that Danton and Thuriot had left the others. In the transcript prepared for the trial of Chabot and Basire the reference to Danton has been edited out, which perhaps shows that, at that time, there was no intention of involving Danton in the trial. Basire also referred to a dinner chez Batz, at which he, Chabot, Julien, Delaunay and Benoît had been present.

Chabot's own accusation was more detailed and more sensational. He described the attempt to blackmail the bankers, which he claimed he had foiled. Delaunay then initiated him into a new intrigue, to persuade the Convention to vote the liquidation of the East India Company. 'We will share with Julien, Thuriot, Basire and you . . . Danton, Lacroix (i.e. Delacroix) and Fabre . . . are speculating in a different way.' It was intended to blackmail the Company into securing its liquidation on relatively easy terms. This scheme was upset by Fabre, who had the decree amended so as to leave no loopholes for the Company, on 8 October. Chabot was therefore given 100,000 livres, which he handed over to the committee as evidence, to bribe Fabre. He claimed to have had too much respect for Fabre to attempt anything of the kind, but when the decree was eventually published on 27 October it did not incorporate Fabre's amendments. On the day before Osselin's arrest – i.e. on 8 November – the conspirators (presumably Delaunay and Batz's agent, Benoît) tried to frighten Chabot into leaving the country by revealing their real intentions: to destroy the Convention by inducing it to vote for successive purges, which would eventually include Chabot himself. After loftily defying them, he went to the Jacobins on the 10th with the intention of revealing all, but took fright when he and Basire were denounced and Thuriot expelled. He therefore made his disclosure to Robespierre [although not for another four days]. In a kind of postscript Chabot claimed that, earlier in the year, Benoît had offered to put him and Fabre, as agents of Batz, in control of the national finances, by ousting Cambon. Chabot insisted that the plot involved both corruption and diffamation, in order to discredit those Montagnards who could not be bought. David and Hébert's wife were involved in the second of these activities. The omission of Hébert himself was perhaps a concession to Robespierre's alleged advice to *ménager les patriotes,* since Chabot clearly implied his guilt and had no inhibitions about enlarging on this in his private letters to

Robespierre.[43] The entire plot, according to Chabot, was directed by Batz on behalf of Pitt. When the Committee of General Security failed to act on Chabot's invitation to set a trap for the conspirators (apparently Hébert and Batz) who were to be caught red-handed after accepting an invitation to his house, he threatened to expose the plot to the Convention, to which Jagot replied brusquely, *Nous saurions te répondre.* He was arrested on the following morning, before he could expose the plotters.

It is difficult to know what to make of this rambling story. There is independent evidence for the intrigue against the bankers, even if Chabot scarcely emerges as the Galahad he pretended to be. The forged decree for the liquidation of the East India Company can still be seen.[44] Chabot's diffamation plot seems to be a much more tenuous affair and perhaps represents no more than a desperate attempt on his part to silence Hébert. How far the Batz plot, assuming it to have existed, was a serious attempt at counter-revolution and how far it was merely a financial manoeuvre by the baron whose interests in fire and life insurance companies were threatened by the legislation of the summer, is not clear. Batz *was* a royalist as well as an expert in fraud. He had made a swashbuckling attempt to rescue Louis XVI on his way to execution and had tried to organise the rescue of the queen.[45] A very detailed contemporary denunciation of Batz presented him as the accredited agent of Louis XVI's brothers and of the Prince of Wales and asserted that Batz, in August 1793, had claimed to dispose of Danton, Chabot and Basire.[46] Even if the Batz plot was all that Chabot claimed, this would not necessarily imply that all his business associates shared his ulterior aims – to use Chabot's favourite expression, they could have been involved *à leur insu* – but this would not have protected them from political blackmail.

Any attempt to reconstruct what actually happened must be highly speculative, but the following interpretation perhaps contains some elements of truth. Danton and his followers broke away from Batz in August. Acting on his own or in concert with them, Fabre began to threaten the baron's financial interests. Batz and his

43. See *Pièces trouvées, passim.*
44. Arch. Nat. W342.
45. In his biography of his ancestor, the baron de Batz presents a good deal of evidence for Batz's counter-revolutionary activities.
46. Reproduced in Bonnemain, *Les chemises rouges,* Paris, an IV, pp. 178-85.

associates, Delaunay and Benoît, then turned for political support to Chabot and Basire and perhaps to Julien, who were all three members of the Committee of General Security. It was about this time that Fabre denounced a foreign plot of his own.[47] Some time after 12 October, at a joint meeting of men from the Committee of Public Safety and that of General Security, he posed 25 insidious questions, each beginning, 'How does it happen that . . .' Fabre accused Proli, Desfieux, Dubuisson and Pereira of being foreign agents who were leading Chabot by the nose and had arranged his marriage for their own purposes. They were also said to be putting pressure on Hérault to betray the secrets of the Committee of Public Safety to them. This denunciation of Fabre's may have had no connection with the East India Company affair since Fabre, unlike Chabot, kept his activities secret and could therefore not use them to suggest that he could be a dangerous enemy. Shortly before the publication of the forged decree for the liquidation of the Company on 27 October, Delaunay succeeded in buying Fabre's collaboration. This was probably done without the knowledge of Chabot who still maintained, in the 'testament' written just before his unsuccessful attempt at suicide, that Fabre was innocent.[48] Once the Batz-Delaunay team had bought more effective political protection – for Fabre was the friend of Danton and trusted by Robespierre – Chabot became expendable. Perhaps they knew that he had pocketed the 100,000 livres they had given him to buy Fabre. Delaunay therefore invented a wild story of successive purges that were to decimate the Assembly in the hope of frightening Chabot out of the country, offering at the same time to transfer any of his assets to a foreign bank of his choice. In a letter to the Convention, Chabot said that he did not hear about the wider aspects of the plot until 29–30 October, which would fit this interpretation.[49] When Chabot and Basire were denounced at the Jacobins on 11 November, both Dufourny and Hébert distinguished between them and Thuriot. Hébert's onslaught on Thuriot *could* be explained by Thuriot's having abandoned Batz while the attack on Chabot and Basire by the 'Dantonist' Dufourny *could* have been based on the assumption that they were still working

47. *Pièces trouvées*, pp. 75-81; A Mathiez, *La conspiration de l'étranger*, Paris, 1918, pp. 1-39.

48. Arch. Nat. W342.   49. ibid.

for the baron. At all events, persecuted by Dufourny and abandoned by Delaunay, Chabot may have felt that his only hope of safety was to cut his losses, surrender all or part of his share in the spoils of the East India Company and reveal the fraud, at the same time using the opportunity to destroy Hébert, whether or not he actually believed that the *Père Duchesne* was in league with Batz and whether or not he was right.

Contemporaries had, of course, realised that if revolutionaries were for sale the most likely buyers would be the Powers at war with France. In February 1793 the American Ambassador, Gouverneur Morris, wrote to Washington that venality had reached such a pitch that if there were no traitors it could only be because the enemy was lacking in common sense.[50] Common sense was a quality that the British liked to regard as peculiarly their own and the British Government seems to have had, if not a monopoly, at least the lion's share in subversion. There is some evidence to suggest that, even if the agents of Pitt were not under every revolutionary bed, as the more credulous were inclined to suppose, they did exist and were not without influence. As early as 1789 the French Ambassador in London warned his Government that a couple of singularly obscure men in Paris, Danton and Paré (at that time Danton's clerk) were suspected of being British agents.[51]

On 1 August 1793, Barère read to the Convention a letter which he said had been found on an Englishman who had been arrested. This appeared to have come from the headquarters of the Duke of York's army in Belgium. Although mainly concerned with military intelligence and sabotage it also referred to speculation against the assignat, the hoarding of essential materials to create local shortages and even mentioned assassination. It implied that British agents were active in Caen, Rouen, Grenoble, Nantes, Thouars, Bordeaux, Tours, Blois and Orleans. This 'evidence', even down to the incrimination of general Lamorlière, corresponded suspiciously to what the committees wanted to believe or, at least, to have believed. On the other hand, if they had forged the letter, they could have made it much more deadly. It made no mention of *political* action by the British agents, most of whom seem to have been Englishmen. The inclusion of an agent called

50. A. de Lestapis, *Ann. hist. Rév. fr.*, 1955, p. 6.
51. Mathiez, *La conspiration de l'étranger*, p. 129.

B–t–z was perhaps yet another tribute to the activity of the ubiquitous baron.

On 9 November the British Minister at Genoa, Drake, informed the Secretary of State for foreign affairs of the arrival in Paris on 17 October of a man called Baldwyn who had had a meeting with Hérault, Deforgues and Hébert. Hérault and Deforgues were in charge of foreign affairs, but the inclusion of Hébert looks rather odd. He could, of course, have been the man who introduced Baldwyn to the other two since 'Baldwyn is represented to be a furious daring Jacobin'. Drake wrote again on 19 January to say that Baldwyn had been arrested but had been released by the Commune *sans l'aveu du Comité de Salut Public et malgré Robespierre*. This is perhaps a good deal less sensational than it looks, if the protectors of the 'Jacobin' Baldywn were, in fact, his dupes.[52]

The case of Madame Dubarry may well conceal further British intervention. The whole business of her jewels being stolen by thieves who tried to dispose of them in England seems somewhat far-fetched. The thieves were caught and Madame Dubarry was entertained, when she came to claim her property, by her old friend Forth – who had been employed as a British agent in France during the War of American Independence. The French Embassy in London had suggested to the Foreign Ministry in July 1789 that if Forth was in Paris this might explain the disorders in the capital.[53] When she was in London, Madame Dubarry met Pitt. She was known to be a generous woman, but even so it seems rather extravagant of her to have lent the cardinal de la Rochefoucauld 200,000 livres. The Committee of General Security certainly thought her activities important enough to justify having her

52. Historical Manuscripts Commission: *The manuscripts of J. B. Fortescue*, London, 1894, vol. II, pp. 456 and 510. Baldwyn had been the English tutor of Orléans, Artois and Provence. An anonymous letter of 23 March 1794, which implied that he was still in gaol, accused him of being a British agent and said that his supporters were intriguing with the Committee of General Security and the police to have him liberated (Arch. Nat. F7 4584). He was eventually released soon after the fall of Robespierre. Mathiez, who describes him as a *furieux jacobin* (*La conspiration de l'étranger*, p. 155) seems to have misunderstood Drake's reference to him.

53. At Madame Dubarry's trial, Fouquier-Tinville described Forth as 'the wiliest spy that the British Government has sent to France' (Arch. Nat. F7 4774⁸³). On Forth, see also the article by A. Goodwin, in *War and Society*, ed. M. R. D. Foot. London, 1973.

followed by two agents, one in England and one in France.[54] At the trial of the 'Dantonists' the newspaper, *le Batave,* reported that Chabot was accused of having protected her.[55]

When the royalist émigré, d'André, sent a man to Paris in October 1793 with a message from the British Government about the possibility of opening peace negotiations, he was provided with letters of introduction to Chabot and Julien, whose British contacts were perhaps not wholly diplomatic.[56]

The most sensational evidence of British intervention is a letter dated Whitehall Friday 13 (presumably September, or possibly December 1793). This was addressed to the banker, Perregaux, though it has been placed with Danton's papers.[57] Written on paper whose watermark shows Britannia in a circle surmounted by a crown, it has an authentic look about it. The letter authorises payments to several agents whose names are indicated by initials — for once, there seems to be no sign of Batz — especially for 'the essential services they have rendered us *en soufflant le feu* [In French in the text] and carrying the Jac . ı . to a paroxysm of fury.' The recipient's last letter to England had been brought by one Staley. Mathiez assumed this to refer to the Stanley who was denounced as a British agent on 18 December, but a man with the less common name of Staley had been employed as a king's messenger by the British Embassy in Paris in 1792.[58] This letter would clearly seem to confirm the suspicions of those Montagnards who considered that some of the more extreme revolutionaries were in fact working for the British Government and, *pace* Chabot, not at all *à leur insu.* Perregaux's papers were examined by a committee under Cambon towards the end of 1793, when the banker was cleared of all charges. Mathiez inferred from this that Perregaux had already passed on the letter to its real addressee, Danton, but

54. P. M. Laski, *The Trial and Execution of Madame Du Barry,* London, 1969, *passim.*

55. A. Mathiez, *Un procès de corruption sous la Terreur,* p. 329. On d'André, see W. H. Fryer, *Republic or Restoration in France?,* and Harvey Mitchell, *The underground war against revolutionary France,* both published in London in 1965.

56. M. Reinhard, 'La guerre et la paix à la fin de 1793', *Ann. Hist. Rév. fr.,* 1953, p. 98.

57. Arch. Nat. AF II 49. Perregaux seems to have been Proli's banker. Arch. Nat. F⁷ 4774⁸³.

58. A. Mathiez, *La conspiration de l'étranger,* p. 134: O. Browning, *The despatches of Lord Gower,* Cambridge, 1885, p. 175.

this certainly cannot be taken for granted. The letter could have been used to blackmail Perregaux and eventually planted amongst Danton's papers. Danton could have acquired it in half a dozen ways, legitimate or otherwise. The surprising thing is that *anyone* kept a document so incriminating and it is presumably the lone survivor of many more. It would seem to be fairly conclusive evidence against Perregaux and unnamed members of the Jacobin Club, but one cannot safely infer anything more.

All such evidence has to be handled with great circumspection. Normal diplomatic soundings could easily be represented as treasonable communication with the enemy, especially if they involved offers to save the king's life or to surrender the queen. Secret agents who posed as revolutionaries may have been genuinely accepted as such. When every allowance has been made though, there is enough evidence here to show that the governing committees were not behaving with paranoid suspicion, even if they were sometimes wrong, when they believed corruption to be widespread and sometimes associated with treason to France and to the revolution.

On 18 November Amar, on behalf of the Committee of General Security, reported Chabot's denunciation of a foreign plot. If one can believe the press reports, he did not tell the Convention anything about the fraud concerning the East India Company. The committees ordered the arrest of accusers and accused but only succeeded in catching Chabot, Basire and Delaunay. Julien was also arrested but escaped in very suspicious circumstances.[59] The immediate sequel to this sensation was a political offensive against extremism, by Danton's friends, which succeeded in controlling the Convention and, at least partially, the Jacobins, for the whole of the next month. Chabot had told Danton's relative, Courtois, of his denunciation. Danton had been at home on leave since mid-October and Courtois was probably responsible for his return to

59. A. de Lestapis, op. cit., pp. 20-3. Although Delaunay was still at liberty his arrest had been ordered by the Committee of General Security on 6 November for unspecified offences which linked him with Ozenne, Bichard, Rouen and the vicomte de Maulde (Arch. Nat. F7 4667). Brichard was to be executed in February 1794 on charges of financial speculation and transferring money to *émigrés* (Arch. Nat. W324). In 1790 he had helped to float a loan for the Prince of Wales and the Dukes of York and Clarence. He had acted as Baldwyn's notary in 1792 (Arch. Nat. F7 4584).

Paris about 21 November. Danton apparently told Garat, the former Minister of the Interior, that his policy was to make contact with the Right in the Assembly, to launch a press campaign in favour of clemency, to build up the authority of the Committee of Public Safety, win over Robespierre and Barère and eliminate its more radical members: Collot, Saint-Just and Billaud. His long-term objectives were peace, the revision of the constitution and a return to economic liberalism.[60] This was, of course, a perfectly legitimate policy – even by the standards of those who equate opposition to Robespierre with counter-revolution.

For a time the policies of Danton and Robespierre seemed to coincide. It was Robespierre who opened the attack on the dechristianisers at the Jacobins on 21 November, when he obtained the expulsion of Proli, Desfieux, Dubuisson and Pereira. Five days later Danton adopted a similar attitude. Chaumette was soon silenced. By the 28th he too was advocating religious liberty and after the defeat of his attempt to assert his control over the *comités révolutionnaires* he seems to have accepted the leadership of the Committee of Public Safety. The organisation of revolutionary government, by the decree of 4 December, which greatly strengthened the powers of the two main Committees, was presumably welcomed by the 'Dantonists'. They were hoping to use their parliamentary strength to infiltrate or capture the Committee of Public Safety and the main losers from the new law were the extremists whose power lay for the most part in the semi-autonomous bodies thrown up by the Revolution, which it was now intended to discipline. The day after this law was voted Desmoulins launched his new journal, the *Vieux Cordelier,* whose opening number presented Danton's enemies as foreign agents.[61] On the 7th Thuriot, whose appeal against the Terror a month earlier had been turned against him, found the Assembly in a much more sympathetic mood when he proposed the creation of a committee to liberate good revolutionaries who had been arrested in error. Robespierre was to win a vote for the creation of such a committee, on the 20th.

It must have been about this time that Fabre, invited by Amar to join him in the investigation of Chabot's plot (in which both of

---

60. Garat, *Mémoires,* Paris, 1862, pp. 317-20.
61. See the edition by H. Calvet, Paris, 1936.

them had possibly been involved at one stage or another!) prepared a highly ingenious summary of Chabot's revelations.[62] Understandably enough, he passed over the East India Company affair as lightly as he could, putting all the emphasis on the political side of the plot, which he expanded to take in dechristianisation and the alienation of neutral Powers. Chabot had not referred to either but Fabre knew that they were subjects on which Robespierre held strong views. He incriminated the Commune as a whole, particularly Chaumette – who had not been mentioned by Chabot – and sprinkled well-judged flattery of Robespierre throughout his survey. Fabre the dramatist did a very competent job. He was, however, a worried man. However competently he and Amar managed the interrogation of Chabot and Delaunay it would be difficult to conceal Fabre's complicity in the forgery of the decree for the liquidation of the East India Company. Before this emerged he had not merely to silence his Cordelier enemies but to secure enough influence in the Committee of Public Safety to be sure that it would cover him. Fabre's understandable impatience may well have spoiled the whole *Indulgent* strategy.

On 12 December the *Indulgents* mounted an attack on the Committee of Public Safety itself and induced the Assembly to vote for its renewal – a piece of news so scandalous that the *Moniteur* prudently concealed it from its readers. This success was possibly achieved by surprise tactics. On the following day the Committee rallied its supporters and got the decision reversed. The two letters that Chabot wrote to Danton on 10 and 14 December were addressed to him as a member of the Committee of Public Safety, which presumably means that Chabot was a party to the plan and had taken the will for the deed.[63] Undeterred by this setback, Desmoulins, in his third number, made a fierce onslaught on the Terror as a whole, attacking not merely the relatively safe targets of Vincent, Bouchotte and Cloots, but also Collot and the Committee of Public Safety. On the 17th Fabre induced the Convention, by-passing its committees, to order the arrest of Vincent. When another member extended this to include Ronsin and Maillard, who controlled a small police organisation that might prove inconvenient, he was supported by Bourdon and the motion was carried.

<hr/>

62. Arch. Nat. AF II 49; reprinted by Mathiez in *Un procès du corruption*, pp. 145-67.
63. Arch. Nat. F7 4434.

These arrests were to constitute the high water mark of the *Indulgent* campaign. On the 19th the investigations of Amar and Jagot began to cast suspicion on Fabre. He was excluded from their investigation on the 26th and his guilt was revealed by the examination of Delaunay's papers on 4 January.

By this time the situation had been transformed by the return of Collot from Lyons on 21 December. Collot had sent Ronsin on before him and Ronsin had been arrested almost as soon as he reached Paris. Collot realised that his only hope of avoiding a similar fate was to take the offensive. He opened his campaign in the Jacobins, where the 'Dantonists' were relatively weak. At once Hébert, who had been strangely subdued for the past month, came to his support with an attack on Bourdon, Philippeaux, Desmoulins and especially Fabre, 'the mainspring of all these plots'. Rather surprisingly, Hébert included Danton with Robespierre as the two men in whom he claimed to have complete confidence. The Jacobins swung round and expressed their support for Vincent and Ronsin. Collot's intervention was decisive because it forced the Committee of Public Safety to abandon its benevolent neutrality towards the *Indulgents,* which would henceforth have split the Committee itself. Its divisions were revealed in the debate of 26 December; Robespierre's proposal to appoint a committee to investigate those arrested on political charges was attacked by Billaud and Barère – who always liked to be on the winning side – and the decision to set up the committee was reversed.

The *Indulgent* campaign continued for a little longer. Philippeaux, in a pamphlet published on the 26th, attacked the 'faction' [i.e. the 'Hébertists'] and its agents in the War Office, the Commune and the revolutionary army. *Le Vieux Cordelier* No. 5, which appeared on 5 January, accused Hébert of plundering War Office funds, revealed his contact with Madame de Rochechouart and accused him of trying to destroy Chabot and Basire when they exposed him. Two days later Philippeaux presented the Assembly with an accusation of Ronsin and Rossignol under 26 heads. By this time Robespierre had had enough and he called for a truce. At the meeting of the Jacobins on 8 January he denounced Fabre, who was arrested on the 12th. From this time onwards the battle that had been raging in the Jacobins subsided. Desmoulins brought out a very mild sixth number of his paper at the end of the month and then ceased publication. Some time after 18 March he referred in an unpublished note to the fact that, during the previous two months, *il n'a pas été permis d'écrire*.[64] Holding important hostages from each side, Vincent and Ronsin of the Cordeliers, and Danton's friend, Fabre, the Committee of Public Safety was able to impose silence on both – for a time. Sooner or later it would have to release or try the accused men, when the quarrel was likely to revive in a more acute form.

This perhaps explains why the Committee of General Security was so slow in its investigation of Chabot's plot, though Amar had perhaps his own reasons for proceeding with caution. Obvious suspects were not arrested for a considerable time and were then kept in gaol for long periods without interrogation. The directors of the East India Company, who were not arrested until 17 March, were never interrogated at all. The historian is handicapped by the selective destruction of much of the evidence; the 133 pages of Chabot's interrogation, for example, have not been seen since 1795. Inadequate press coverage of the debates and of Chabot's trial makes it dangerous to assume that what was not recorded in the press was not made public. Even the limited evidence that has survived suggests that more was involved than mere procrastination. On 1 March his colleagues presented Amar with an ultimatum, ordering him to prepare his report at once. When he had announced Chabot's arrest on 18 November, Amar had spoken of a counter-revolutionary foreign plot. His eventual report, which he did not present until 16 March, was concerned exclusively with corruption. It was attacked on these grounds by Billaud and Robespierre – an unusual example of public disagreement between the two Committees – and referred to the Committee of Public Safety for amendment. Three days later the *acte d'accusation* did briefly mention the intention of the conspirators to *diffamer et avilir* the Assembly (the aspect of the 'plot' that allegedly involved Hébert) but it still put all the emphasis on the East India Company fraud. By this time Hébert himself was in gaol. Wide and improbable as the charges against him were to be, they do not seem to have included those made by Chabot.

De Lestapis has suggested in his very illuminating *Conspiration de Batz*, that Hébert's arrest was due to an attempt by d'Espagnac to exploit the evidence that both he and Chabot had discovered, in

---

64. *Le Vieux Cordelier*, ed. Calvet, p. 285.

order to destroy both Hébert and his old rival, Batz. This seems to rest on an assumption of Hébert's guilt which de Lestapis admits elsewhere that he cannot substantiate. There are more obvious reasons for the downfall of the *Père Duchesne*. Vincent and Ronsin were released on 1 February, perhaps as the result of increasing popular pressure and threatening noises from the Cordeliers who had veiled the Declaration of the Rights of Man on the previous day as an expression of public mourning. As early as mid-January Amar had told Momoro of the Cordeliers that the Committee of General Security had no evidence against Vincent and there may well have been disagreement between the two Committees.[65] Vincent and Ronsin were not the kind of men to leave well alone and under their prompting the Cordeliers began threatening another 31 May to purge the Convention of their enemies. Momoro, who was one of the most active members of the club, denounced *les hommes usés* – which could refer either to Danton or to the government – while Hébert more cautiously attacked the advocates of clemency. According to the contemporary historian, Tissot, Saint-Just summoned Hébert, Vincent and Ronsin to the Committee of Public Safety on 20 February. Vincent declined the offer of a post away from Paris but the three agreed to moderate their policies.[66] When Ronsin, in spite of this, called for an insurrection, on 2 March, he was opposed by Hébert. Two days later, however, when the Cordeliers exploded again and the cry of insurrection was taken up by the deputy, Carrier, Hébert was unable to resist the reproaches of his fellow-members and the appeals to speak out in his rôle as the Père Duchesne. He accused Amar of protecting Chabot and Basire and went on to make an open attack on the Committee of Public Safety. There followed a brief period of negotiation between Jacobins and Cordeliers, with Collot trying to isolate the Cordelier leaders and the latter implying that the price of reconciliation was the destruction of their political enemies. Unable to discipline the Cordeliers and perhaps alarmed by signs of growing restlessness in Paris, the Committees eventually resorted to force. On the night of 13–14 March Vincent, Ronsin, Hébert and Momoro were arrested.

65. A. Soboul, op. cit., p. 350.
66. P-F. Tissot, *Histoire de la Révolution française*, Paris, 1839, vol. v, pp. 105-6.

What matters, in the case of the great political trials of 1794, is the decision to act against a particular group and the choice of the victims. Since an acquittal in any of these trials would have overthrown the government, heavy pressure was exerted on the normally accommodating jury and charges and evidence were selected with less regard for truth, or even verisimilitude, than for the discredit they would throw on those whose conviction was a political necessity. In the case of the Cordeliers, what was significant was that the Committees included Proli and his quartet, together with Cloots, but instructed Fouquier-Tinville to disregard all the evidence that over-enthusiastic witnesses offered against Hanriot and Pache.[67] Although the formalities of a trial were observed, including the testimony of dozens of witnesses, those responsible allowed as little publicity as possible. When Dufourny asked for detailed reporting, at the Jacobins, he was silenced by Robespierre and Couthon. The *Moniteur,* which had covered the trial of the Girondins in great detail, undertook to do as much for Hébert, but its next mention of proceedings was a mere list of those who had been executed. Fouquier constructed a melodramatic and largely imaginary plot involving a coup d'état by the revolutionary army, the creation of an artificial food shortage and rich meals with suspect bankers – anything that was likely to discredit the former popular leaders in the eyes of the sans-culottes. The whole business was perhaps best summed up in the disillusioned comment of a contemporary, 'Hébert, who had committed so many real crimes, died for imaginary ones.'[68]

By the time the 'Hébertists' were executed, Fabre, Chabot and Basire had already been committed for trial, together with Hérault who was suspected – probably wrongly – of betraying the secrets of the Committee of Public Safety to foreign Powers. The committees seem to have been determined to dispose of the *Pourris* but ready to leave Danton and Desmoulins alone if they did not intervene. They may well have been divided on this. Collot attacked an unnamed second faction at the meeting of the Jacobins on 19 March. Next day Bourdon rashly persuaded the Convention to

67. In 1795 the former archivist of the revolutionary tribunal said that its president had excluded witnesses ready to testify against Pache, Bouchotte, Audoin and Hanriot and that written denunciations of these men had been removed from the files (Arch. Nat. F^7 4773).

68. Riouffe, *Mémoires d'un détenu,* Paris, an III, p. 75.

order the arrest of Héron, the chief police agent of the Committee of General Security. Couthon immediately replied that the Hébertist plot was not the only one and Moïse Bayle of the Committee of General Security, together with Robespierre, got the decision reversed. Robespierre, however, criticised Tallien, at the Jacobins on the following day, for suggesting that the blow against the Left must be balanced by similiar action against the Right. Barère, on 22 March, told the Convention that the Committees would destroy those guilty of both corruption and diffamation, but his appeal 'May the exposure and punishment of this conspiracy serve to unite us all!' could be interpreted as an olive branch extended towards Danton.

If there were negotiations with Danton, as seems likely, they broke down. Perhaps he thought that the government was bluffing or relied on the majority in the Assembly coming to his support. His attitude gave the Committees little choice. If Danton intended to defend his friends in the Assembly, in spite of the evidence for their corruption, the Committees ran a serious risk of defeat. It was presumably to avoid the choice between such a danger and the acceptance of an amnesty on terms that Danton would dictate, that the Committees took the desperate step of including him in the 'plot'. On the night of 30–31 March he was arrested, together with Desmoulins, Delacroix and Philippeaux. Why Bourdon escaped is not at all clear. The elimination of Danton was a nerve-racking affair for the governing committees. Legendre attempted to defend him in the Assembly but was silenced by Robespierre. The trial began on 2 April before the ingenious Fouquier had had time to prepare any sort of a case. The only witness called was Cambon, who incriminated Chabot but seems to have exonerated Danton and Desmoulins. Danton, who indignantly denied having had any contact with Chabot, spoke for most of the time and won the sympathy of the audience. A hand-picked jury of only seven – there had been twice as many for Hébert – was subjected to exceptional pressure and eventually shown a letter said to have been sent to Danton from England.[69] Perhaps the argument that counted most was the one attributed to the juror, Souberbielle, who was also Robespierre's doctor. 'Which of the two, Robespierre or Danton, is

69. Fouquier's notes suggest the presence of thirteen jurors although only seven are known to have officiated (Arch. Nat. W173).

the more useful to the Republic? Well then, Danton must be guillotined.'[70] It was perhaps not quite so simple, but the acquittal of Danton would have brought down the government and some of its members at least could have expected short shrift from *Indulgents* who had been ferocious enough in their time. By 5 April it was all over. The only accused to escape execution was Lulier, charged during the course of the trial as an accomplice of Chabot (who had, in fact, denounced him). Lulier was the only man to be accused of collaboration with Batz, 'an out-and-out counter-revolutionary from the earliest days of the Revolution'. Both Hérault and d'Espagnac died with Danton.

A desperate attempt by Desmoulins's wife, Lucile, to organise a demonstration in his support provided the pretext for the grisly epilogue of 10–13 April when an *amalgame* of quite extraordinary virtuosity disposed of the wives of Hébert and Desmoulins, Chaumette, the archbishop of Paris and one or two remnants of the revolutionary army, all accused of participation in the same plot.

The government had now destroyed the leaders of each of the groups that had challenged it. No action had been taken against Batz's organisation although many if not most of his agents were in gaol. This was supposed to be the end of conspiracies and show trials. But, as the Committees knew well enough, important members of each faction were still at large: Thuriot, Bourdon and Dufourny on the one hand and Pache, Hanriot and Bouchotte on the other. Many more were angered by the death of men they still considered innocent and were alarmed for their own safety. The Montagnards had always been a minority in the Convention. Henceforth the minority itself was divided, suspicious and revengeful and the authority of the Committees depended increasingly upon fear.

70. L. Madelin, *Danton*, Paris, 1914, p. 310.

VIII The Politician

I'm glad you think that makes everything clear, said Ted.

I never said anything of the kind. Anyone who thinks it's clear hasn't even begun to understand what the problems are. All I said was that you couldn't follow what Robespierre was trying to do unless you had some idea of the political background.

I'm not sure how much the man who wrote that article knows, but there seems to be quite a lot that he doesn't. Why did you choose that particular interpretation?

It's not so much an interpretation as a convenient summary of the evidence.

Poppycock, said Mac. It's typical bourgeois history: all cool, detached and mildly ironical on the surface, pretending to be objective and actually shot through with subjective judgments. Why doesn't he admit that he's trying to sell his own particular wares, instead of posing as the Voice of History?

Mac's quite right, said Henry; except that your man probably doesn't realise he's doing it. Anyone else's account would present the same problems. I can see J.S's predicament: it would be diffi-cult for us to try to follow Robespierre through this rabbit warren without some sort of guide. At the same time, by choosing any particular guide, we lose our innocence, so to speak.

All the more so since we're probably not aware how far we have been conditioned by that man's insinuations, agreed Ted.

If you're so worried about your innocence, there's nothing to stop you reading all the other accounts of the period. If you'd care to come back in six months' time . . .

Can't you see that doesn't solve our problem, said Ted; or yours too, for that matter. None of us can start without taking other people's word for it that the things they choose to mention are what mattered and we can't have any views about what they all leave out.

We've come back to where we started, said Henry. What worries me is not our disagreement but our agreement. What we all take for granted is what's most likely to reflect the purely arbitrary assumptions of our own society.

If you won't accept the fact that there are laws of historical change, said Mac, you're bound to end up in this messy subject-ivism. Now –

Perhaps it would be as well if J.S. got on with his tale, said Ted.

I'd taken you up to the point where Robespierre joined the Committee of Public Safety in July 1793. By that time it had acquired an identity of its own and the most important positions were already taken. Robespierre soon gave up education and became a kind of Minister without Portfolio. Prieur de la Côte d'Or described his position in terms that sound plausible enough.[1] He says that Robespierre's first uneasiness in his new situation 'was followed by his complete abstention from the business dealt with in the specialist bureaux, especially those of Lindet, Carnot and Prieur de la Côte d'Or. He was delighted by their success; the military victories provided him with a sort of halo. In the meetings of the Committee as a whole he was accommodating and never opposed any useful plan. His colleagues, as a matter of fact, had a certain deference for Robespierre's views on political matters because of his influence over public opinion. All were working for the same ends and so Robespierre willingly acted as the defender of the Committee in the Convention and its protector in the Jacobins and elsewhere.'

Baudot, his colleague in the Convention, agreed that Robespierre's importance was in public relations rather than administration.[2] 'Robespierre's authority was very peculiar. It depended on a mistaken public opinion, revolutionary fanaticism and the magic of terror. As such, it could vanish in an instant. His power was therefore entirely abstract (*toute idéale*).' He had, in fact, less influence in the heart of revolutionary government than anywhere else.

If you're right about his power depending on persuasion, said Henry, his speeches will presumably show what he wanted others to think and not necessarily what he thought himself. We shall have to remember that.

There are other difficulties in the way of discovering what his policies were. The principle of Cabinet solidarity operated within

1. Quoted in G. Bouchard, *Prieur de la Côte d'Or*, Paris, 1946, p. 443.
2. M. A. Baudot, *Notes sur la Convention Nationale*, Paris, 1893, p. 3.

225

the Committee of Public Safety whose members defended in public decisions that they may have opposed within the Committee itself. Decisions were signed by any members who happened to be present and one can't draw any conclusions from the presence or absence of a signature. Admittedly, where the original minute is in the hand of one of the members it seems very likely that he approved of the policy, especially when he was the only man to sign. There aren't very many of these in Robespierre's case, as one would expect since he had no departmental responsibility. Although the register of attendance is unreliable it looks as though he was a conscientious member who was rarely absent unless he was ill. If one looks at the minutes he drafted himself, his main concern seems to have been with individuals. In the autumn of 1793 he was busy sacking generals whom he thought unreliable and in 1794 he transferred his attention to the personnel of the Paris Sections and the agents of revolutionary government. His most important contribution to the work of the Committee was delivering policy speeches to the Convention. These, as I tried to show you, reflect his own convictions, as well as the Committee's policy, but there were at least three occasions when his colleagues apparently suppressed political speeches that he had intended to make.

As Prieur suggested, it took him some time to identify himself with the Committee and to begin with he appeared to regard himself as an observer from the Jacobins. On 7 August he told his fellow-members of the club, 'The Committee of Public Safety believed we would take this news (about arson in military depots) with sang-froid.'[3] On the 11th he seemed to have doubts about remaining in the government at all. 'Called to the Committee of Public Safety against my will, I have seen there things that I should never have dared to suspect. I have seen, on the one hand, patriotic members trying in vain to promote the welfare of their country and, on the other, traitors plotting against the interests of the people in the heart of the Committee itself . . . If what I foresee comes to pass, I declare that I shall separate myself from the Committee and that no power on earth can stop me telling the whole truth to the Convention.'[4] The reference to traitors could have been aimed at Barère, who had oscillated for a long time between Girondins and Montagnards, or at Thuriot who was soon

3. *Oeuvres*, vol. x, p. 57.   4. *Oeuvres*, vol. x, p. 65.

to be accused of corruption. One can only guess. It has been suggested that Robespierre's apparent absence from the meetings of 14–17 August indicated his disapproval of the election of Carnot and Prieur de la Côte d'Or on the 14th. This is unlikely since both had, in fact, been attending meetings of the Committee for some days before they were formally elected members.

The threat from the Enragés and the danger of the Revolution being swept into policies of anarchic violence probably strengthened Robespierre's feelings of solidarity with his new colleagues. On 29 August he opposed a motion by Billaud-Varenne for the election of yet another committee, to supervise the Ministers. During the crisis of 4–5 September Robespierre defended Barère in the Jacobin Club and urged Jacobins and deputies to leave policy-making to the Committee. This time Billaud defeated him, persuading the Convention, on its own authority, to order the arrest of all suspects. The election to the Committee of Billaud and Collot put an end to Billaud's sniping and the next attack came from a different quarter. On 25 September a number of disgruntled deputies criticised it on various counts, implying that its policies were too radical. Robespierre threw the whole weight of his personal prestige behind the defence of colleagues 'whom I honour and esteem (and I am not known for being prodigal of such sentiments)'.[5] This critical debate left him the main spokesman of the Committee in the Assembly and reminded his colleagues of the value of his support.

During his first months on the Committee his main concerns were to preserve France from counter-revolution and the Montagnards from what he considered their unfounded suspicions of each other. He believed that the main obstacles to military victory and internal stability were disloyal generals, journalists and administrators. For once, we have a private 'catechism' which offers a faithful indication of his real feelings.[6] 'What is the objective? The implementation of the constitution in the interests of the people. Who will be our enemies? The vicious and the rich. What instruments will they use? Calumny and hypocrisy. What factors may favour the use of such means? The ignorance of the sans-culottes. The

---

5. Oeuvres, vol. x, p. 116.
6. Arch. Nat. F⁷ 4436; reprinted in Courtois, Rapport, p. 180, and Papiers inédits, vol. II, pp. 13-15.

people must therefore be enlightened. What are the obstacles to this? Mercenary writers who mislead them every day with their impudent impostures. What conclusions should be drawn from that? 1. That these writers must be proscribed as the nation's most dangerous enemies. [When he published this document, Courtois altered *ces écrivains* to read *les écrivains*.] 2. That we must spread sound writings in profusion. What are the other obstacles to liberty? The foreign war and the civil war. How can we end the foreign war? By putting republican generals at the head of our armies and punishing those who have betrayed us. How can we end the civil war? By punishing traitors and conspirators, especially deputies and guilty administrators, by sending *patriote* troops under *patriote* leaders to subdue the *aristocrates* of Lyons, Marseilles, Toulon, the Vendée, the Jura and all the other areas that have raised the flag of royalism and rebellion and by making a terrible example of all the villains who have outraged liberty and shed the blood of *patriotes*.' His summing up of the above includes an additional point: *subsistances et lois populaires*. In the margin of his manuscript he wrote, 'What is the other obstacle to the enlightenment of the people? Destitution. When will the people be enlightened? When they have bread and when the rich and the government stop subsidising treacherous writers and speakers who deceive it; when their self-interest is identified with that of the people. When will their self-interest be identified with that of the people? Never.'

Robespierre crossed out his various marginal points with vertical strokes, presumably as he incorporated them in a speech. The word 'never' is obliterated in a different way and perhaps reflected no more than a passing fit of pessimism. The 'catechism' as a whole probably served as the basis for the speech he made in the Assembly on 12 August which takes up all these points with the significant exception of *subsistances et lois populaires*.[7]

He's still asking for heads, said Ted and the stuff about journalists doesn't exactly tally with what he used to say about the freedom of the press before his side won. Still, I suppose Roland would have agreed with him about the need to use state funds to pay for one's propaganda.

There you go, said Mac, always fussing about the means and

7. *Oeuvres*, vol. x, pp. 66-7.

not about the ends. If his policies were right and Roland's were wrong, that's all we need to worry about. But were they right? He's obviously more interested in repression than in social policy. It comes in as an after-thought and gets left out of his speech. He's still ranting on about the vicious rich and the virtuous poor with all his old patronising paternalism. He's quite sure that he knows best and what they have to do is to take what they're given and be thankful.

I think you're possibly missing the point, said Henry. There are really two lines of thought here. He sets off by trying to work out how to get rid of the obstacles to constitutional government and the fact that he defines the goal as the implementation of the constitution is very important if we remember how he differentiated between revolutionary and constitutional government. Then he has some after-thoughts – almost daydreams – about the long-term prospects of creating a new kind of society.

He may have deceived himself into thinking that he wanted to get back to normal methods of government, said Ted, but there was always someone who had to be executed first – and there always would be.

Don't jump to conclusions until you've heard the evidence, I said. For the next few months he stuck to this programme. There are six *arrêtés* in his own hand dismissing generals during the period from August to November and only three after that. He supported Couthon in getting the journalist, Carra, sent before the revolutionary tribunal and he repeatedly called for the punishment of the local officials in rebel areas. He even proposed setting up a dozen revolutionary tribunals.[8] He may have been personally responsible for the decision to send Collot to replace Couthon at Lyons, after the city fell, with instructions to pursue a policy of more vigorous repression. Prieur said that 'Couthon had gone soft on the spot and wept like a woman' and that Collot was reluctant to replace him and only agreed under pressure from Robespierre.[9] Collot himself confirmed that he went at Robespierre's invitation.[10] This decision and Collot's interpretation of his instructions to intensify repression were to have disastrous consequences for Robespierre personally and for revolutionary government as a

---

8. *Oeuvres*, vol. X, p. 75.   9. Bouchard, op. cit., p. 446.
10. Courtois, *Rapport*, p. 282.

whole in later months. As always, Robespierre took the attitude that clemency towards disloyal men in high office was a form of sentimental self-indulgence that would have to be paid for in blood. In view of the desperate situation at the time, a repressive policy was inevitable and the Committee of Public Safety was agreed on this. Where Robespierre possibly differed from some of his colleagues was in the importance he attached to the evidence – if it *was* genuine evidence – that the British Government and the allied Powers in general were trying to stir up trouble in France. On two occasions – on 29 July and 7 August – he told the Jacobins that there were foreign agents amongst their own members.[11] He thought that the activities of these agents were mainly directed towards dividing the Montagnards from each other and this was one of the main reasons for his suspicion of the Enragés and the more militant Cordeliers.

On 5 August Vincent, of the Cordeliers and the War Office, attacked Danton. Robespierre used this as a pretext for another assault on Roux and Leclerc, not on account of their social policies but because he thought they were trying to discredit proved revolutionaries. 'He cited the example of Danton, who was being slandered – Danton, against whom no one had the right to make the slightest reproach.'[12]

I'll remember that, said Ted.

He was also worried in case the Enragés caused trouble during the celebrations on 10 August when representatives from the provinces were to attend a great fête in honour of the acceptance of the constitution.

So they were playing that game already, said Mac. The self-styled people's friend couldn't very well accuse the Enragés of making too much fuss about the poor so he called them foreign agents and trouble-makers – and he had the nerve to complain about wicked journalists misleading the gullible sans-culottes!

You may be right, I said. I'm certainly not suggesting that Roux and Leclerc actually were foreign agents. But I think Robespierre genuinely believed they were. He wasn't just inventing any old story to discredit them.

All right. He wasn't a rogue but he lived in such a fantasy world of plots and conspiracies that he was a political menace.

11. *Oeuvres*, vol. X, pp. 43, 55.   12. *Oeuvres*, vol. X, p. 52.

That's what some of his colleagues on the Committee claimed – afterwards. Of course, people had been saying much the same thing about him since 1789. According to Prieur, 'He used to complain all the time about conspiracies and treasonable plots that he saw everywhere.'[13] That doesn't necessarily mean that he was always wrong. What's important is the kind of men he suspected. For a long time he seems to have taken for granted the loyalty of all the leading Montagnards, the Cordeliers and the Paris Commune.

But you quoted him only a few minutes ago, said Ted, to the effect that there were traitors in the Committee of Public Safety and foreign agents in the Jacobin Club.

We'll deal with the Jacobins in a minute. He must have changed his mind about his colleagues, unless he had merely been referring to Thuriot. Even Prieur conceded that 'for a long time he was the protector of the leading members of the municipality of Paris as well as the friend of Danton'.[14] That's important and he couldn't have been their protector if others hadn't been attacking them. The men he suspected were minor men – some of them Jacobins – whose revolutionary credentials consisted mainly of the passion with which they denounced everyone else. It's certainly true that Robespierre defended the integrity of his fellow-deputies even when he disagreed strongly with the policies they advocated. When he said, on 25 September, 'I pledge myself never to divide the revolutionaries' he meant it. He defended Merlin de Thionville when he was attacked by the extremist ex-noble, Maribon-Montaut. He protected Barère. On 9 September he intervened in support of men as different as Hanriot, the violent Commander-in-Chief of the Parisian National Guard, and Bourdon de l'Oise. Even though Bourdon was attacking the Committee's Commander-in-Chief in the Vendée, Robespierre's own protégé, Rossignol, Robespierre prevented Bourdon's expulsion from the Jacobins. In the following month Julien de Toulouse – as shady a character as any in the Con-vention – was very roughly handled in the Club for a long report in which he seemed to be whitewashing the local authorities involved in the revolt of many of the provinces. This was a sub-ject on which Robespierre held very strong views and Julien, who had recently been expelled from the Committee of General Security

13. Bouchard, op. cit., p. 443.   14. ibid.

and was already suspected of corruption, was certainly no paragon of *vertu*. Nevertheless, when a Jacobin demanded his arrest Robespierre replied, 'What is all this talk of the guillotine? Citizens – not everyone can understand this yet – people are trying to destroy the Revolution by excesses . . . When I condemned a mistake I was far from calling for the proscription of the man who had committed it. I merely wanted to point out that, for the moment, he had left the right road. Let us not try to inflate the ranks of the guilty. Let us execute the tyrant's widow and the leaders of conspiracy, but after these necessary examples let us avoid bloodshed. I shall be accused of *modérantisme* but remember that we must always act in accordance with what is useful to the Revolution.'[15]

That's fair enough as far as it goes, said Ted, but you'll notice that there was always someone to be executed first.

Robespierre couldn't have saved Marie Antoinette and the Girondin leaders. There is virtually no evidence that he took any part in their destruction. Baudot, admittedly, said that he insisted on the execution of the Girondins, but he quotes no evidence and there is none to be found in Robespierre's speeches.[16] What does seem clear is the procrastination of the governing committees in the face of repeated pressure from the Jacobins, the Parisian Sections and *sociétés populaires*, extremists like Hébert and Desfieux and men like Julien who were trying to mend their own reputations at the expense of someone else. The public prosecutor, Fouquier-Tinville, kept complaining that the Committees were not giving him any material for his *acte d'accusation*. Whether Robespierre and the Committee of Public Safety actually hoped to avert trials whose verdicts were a foregone conclusion, one can't say, but that is certainly a possibility. When the Convention did take the decisive step against the leading Girondins, on 3 October, Robespierre risked his own popularity to save the 73 deputies who had signed secret protests against the purge of 2 June. They were arrested, but Robespierre defeated a motion to read out the charges against them, which would almost certainly have led to their execution. He intervened again in the coming months to keep them safely in gaol and out of Fouquier-Tinville's hands. They were well aware of this but their gratitude at the time didn't prevent their joining in the attack on Robespierre's reputation after his

15. *Oeuvres*, vol. x, pp. 151-2.   16. Baudot, op. cit., p. 228.

death. He crossed swords with Billaud-Varenne once again to prevent an *appel nominal* on the motion to try the Girondin leaders, which would have exposed their sympathisers and divided the Convention. This was the most that he could hope to achieve and no one else seems to have had the courage to support him. That he was taking a chance is clear from the fact that there were shouts of disapproval from the public galleries when he said again, 'The Convention must not inflate the ranks of the guilty . . . Many are only misled.'[17]

For a good deal of the time, said Henry, we've been speculating and groping around trying to make bricks with very little straw. For once, J.S. has come up with some firm evidence. And it all points one way.

We haven't finished yet, replied Ted.

What seems clear, I went on, is that by the end of October or early November Robespierre was convinced that the Revolution had almost succeeded. He never shrank from bloodshed when he thought that a revolutionary situation could only be resolved by force but his goal was always a return to humane constitutional government. As he identified himself more and more with the Committee of Public Safety, as the military situation turned in favour of the revolutionary armies and the collapse of the so-called federalist revolt, the fall of Lyons and Marseilles, the siege of Toulon and progress in the Vendée meant that the end of the civil war was in sight, he felt increasingly that if only the Montagnards remained united, peace and normal government could soon be restored. On 9 November he suggested that the purges in the army were coming to an end. 'At last we have expelled the traitors from the armies of the Republic.' His foreign policy speech on the 17th was more than an appeal to the neutral Powers. It proclaimed the beginning of a new phase.[18] France was 'emerging from the chaos into which the treason of a criminal Court and the reign of the factions had plunged the government . . . The French Republic exists.' 'Your enemies are well aware that henceforth you can only be destroyed by your own efforts . . . They want to divide you. Stay united.' 'Force can overturn a throne; only prudence can found a Republic. We must continually uncover the traps of our enemies. We must be both revolutionary and statesmanlike, terrible towards

17. *Oeuvres*, vol. x, p. 135.   18. *Oeuvres*, vol. x, pp. 167-88.

the wicked and charitable to the suffering. We must shun both the cruelty of *modérantisme* and the systematic exaggeration of false *patriotes*. You must be worthy of those you represent. The people hate excess. They want to be neither deceived nor protected; they want to be defended by men who respect them.'

If he really thought that the Revolution was coming to an end, said Mac, without either *subsistances* or *lois populaires*, that confirms my impression that his social programme was only window-dressing.

You really are an incurable romantic, replied Ted. The main grievance of the sans-culottes, when they weren't just complaining about life, was wartime inflation and the decline of the luxury trades. Whatever the rabble-rousers might say, the best thing that could happen to ordinary working people was the end of the war.

If Robespierre insisted so much on the need to preserve the unity of the Montagnards, I continued, this was not merely because the Jacobins were becoming increasingly quarrelsome as the improvement in the military situation made it safe for them to disagree. He also had in mind Fabre's denunciation of a foreign plot to members of the two Committees, about 12 October. Despite Fabre's suspicious affluence, Robespierre, who could be dangerously credulous, seems to have held a high opinion of him at this time.[19] Fabre's repeated attacks in the Convention on Delaunay's band of speculators probably impressed him, all the more so since he himself knew nothing about finance. On two consecutive days, 8 and 9 October, he supported motions of Fabre's. The denunciation also reinforced his own suspicions. It implied that the source of Montagnard divisions lay in the intrigues of Proli, Desfieux, Dubuisson and Pereira, who had links with foreign bankers. Julien de Toulouse was said to be collaborating with them and Chabot to be their unsuspecting tool.

Amongst Robespierre's papers were discovered the fragmentary notes of an undelivered speech which incorporated some of Fabre's charges.[20] If, as seems likely, part of the original document has disappeared, Robespierre's draft may well have gone on to reproduce other charges. Robespierre, unlike Fabre, denounced Roux,

19. On Fabre's reputation see J. A. Dulaure, *Supplément aux crimes des anciens comités du gouvernement*, Paris, an III, p. 116.
20. Printed in *Pièces trouvées dans les papiers de Robespierre et complices*, Paris, an III, pp. 90-9.

Leclerc and Varlet and the women's club, the *Républicaines Révolutionnaires*. He then repeated Fabre's accusations against Proli and Dubuisson. An entry in his private diary, which can be dated to around 10 October, also contained a reference to the 'conspiracy of Proli, Leclerc etc.'.[21] Robespierre's draft speech contains a reference to the death of the Girondins, who were executed on 31 October. He described the *Républicaines Révolutionnaires* as *sylphes anglaises,* which probably suggested to him the description of Proli as a *sylphe* invisible, in a speech on 21 November. In view of the fragmentary nature of the surviving draft one cannot draw any conclusions from the absence of any reference to Chabot's denunciation of 14 November and it could have been written at any time during the first three weeks of November. Its logical sequel would have been a demand for the arrest of the men denounced and one can only wonder whether friends of theirs were responsible for its suppression. Their most likely protectors in the Committee of Public Safety were both away on mission. Collot, who had associations with Desfieux, was in Lyons and Hérault, who shared the same house as Proli and had interceded for him when he had been arrested, was in Alsace.[22] Even so, the Committee may have felt that to denounce the quartet might stir up a hornets' nest. Whatever the reasons for Robespierre's silence, Fabre's denunciation seems to have impressed at least one of his colleagues. Saint-Just, who had heard Fabre, wrote angrily about Hérault's corruption, on 5 November, whereas Couthon, who had not, had written to Saint-Just on 20 October, *Embrasse Hérault et nos autres bons amis pour moi.*[23] How far the other members of Fabre's audience believed him, it is impossible to say.

Whether or not he was prevented from expressing his opinions in public, Robespierre's draft presumably indicates what he thought about Proli and the others in November. It was just at this time that they began to draw attention to themselves as advanced revolutionaries. They were involved in an attempt to create a central committee of the Parisian popular societies, which would have become a dangerous centre of extremism. When this committee announced its intention of carrying out household searches

21. A. Mathiez, *Etudes sur Robespierre,* Paris, 1958, p. 225.
22. For Hérault's intervention see Arch. Nat. F⁷ 4774⁸³.
23. *Papiers trouvés,* vol. II, p. 258; Courtois, *Rapport,* pp. 225-7.

the veto of the Committee of Public Safety, on 1 November, was written by Robespierre.[24] When the dechristianisation campaign was launched in Paris a few days later, Pereira, Desfieux and the eccentric German baron, Cloots, were amongst those responsible. They were, admittedly, joined by men from the Commune and the Cordeliers, notably Chaumette, Momoro and Hébert, and by some deputies such as Thuriot. At the time, Robespierre probably regarded the latter as their dupes. Dechristianisation, with its vulgar *mascarades,* offended both his deepest convictions and his respect for the dignity of the Revolution. As a member of the government he was well placed to appreciate the damage it would do in the provinces and the extent to which it played into the hands of enemy propagandists. He was quite capable of making allowances for the mistaken enthusiasm of genuine revolutionaries but he concluded that if men whom he already suspected of being foreign agents helped to organise something so obviously detrimental to the consolidation of the Revolution, their motives were unlikely to be primarily theological. The fact that they could enlist so much unthinking support from naïve enthusiasts merely emphasised the need to eliminate them before they could do more harm.

It was about this time – on 14 November – that Chabot brought him news of another plot.[25] Chabot made specific – and very plausible – charges of corruption against Delaunay, Julien, Thuriot, the baron de Batz and his agent, Benoît. He was much vaguer about the second aspect of the conspiracy, the alleged plot to discredit the Convention, about which he produced no convincing evidence. Between them, Chabot and Basire incriminated Hébert, Danton, David (of the Committee of General Security), the deputy Panis and Dufourny and Lulier from the Department of Paris. Robespierre's initial reaction, according to Chabot, was to advise him to *ménager les patriotes* and to ask if Proli was not implicated too. He had not been until then but Chabot did his best to make good the deficiency. Chabot was to say later that Robespierre had also advised Hébert to *ménager les patriotes.*[26]

Once again, the sequel to a denunciation was an undelivered

24. A. Aulard. *Recueil des actes du Comité de Salut Public,* Paris, 1889-1911, vol. VIII, pp. 159-60.

25. See above, pp. 208-12.

26. In an undated letter to the Committee of General Security, Arch. Nat. F⁷ 4637.

speech by Robespierre.[27] The editors of Robespierre's speeches place this in early March 1794 but this is unlikely. The draft includes another denunciation of Roux, whom Robespierre disregarded after his suicide early in 1794; it follows Chabot very faithfully and contains no reference to any later events. Its most likely date is therefore the second half of November or early December. The first part of this draft is similar to the previous one. After a break in the manuscript, Robespierre continued, 'At the head of this plot was the baron de Batz.' He went on to paraphrase Chabot as credulously as he had previously followed Fabre, repeating Chabot's tale of the double plot to *diffamer et corrompre* the Convention. His conclusion showed Robespierre – most untypically – unable to make up his mind whether Chabot had really pretended to involve himself in order to expose the counter-revolutionaries or whether he had merely turned state's evidence when he had become frightened. His failure to identify himself as the man who received Chabot's denunciation suggests that the speech was intended for the Convention and not for the two Committees who would have been familiar with the facts.

As in the case of Fabre, Chabot was confirming Robespierre's basic conviction that the main aim of the counter-revolution, after the failure of its military operations, was to induce the Montagnards to destroy each other in an orgy of mutual recrimination and mud-slinging. 'In spite of the hopes of Vienna and London, *cette grande affaire ne sera point le procès de la représentation nationale.*' This corresponds to an entry in his diary on 6 November, 'Save the honour of the Convention and the Mountain; distinguish between the main agents of corruption and those led astray through weakness.'[28] An anonymous pamphlet, published in the autumn of 1794, claimed that Robespierre was reluctant to agree to the arrest of Chabot, Basire and Delaunay and that 'Barère extorted it from him in spite of his fright'.[29] All the evidence suggests that Robespierre, whatever his views about *vertu*, was in fact prepared to overlook the private vices of the Montagnards and to protect their public reputations, so long as he was convinced of their revolutionary principles. At the same time, their vulnerability

27. *Papiers inédits,* vol. II, pp. 51-69; reprinted in *Oeuvres,* vol. X, pp. 397-407.
28. Mathiez, op. cit., p. 232.
29. *La tête à la queue,* Bib. Nat. Lb[41] 1351, p. 8n[1].

to blackmail and bribery made it all the more urgent to identify and exterminate the handful of men whom he believed to be intent on sabotaging the revolution for the benefit of the foreign enemy.

We can only speculate as to why the speech was never made. The Committees do not seem to have taken Batz seriously until the spring of 1794. If Amar really had been involved in the early stages of the East India Company scandal and Chabot knew, as he claimed to do, that other members of the Committee of General Security took bribes, there were perhaps good reasons for not putting anyone on trial. Robespierre himself may have realised that it would be difficult to *ménager les patriotes* if Delaunay and his associates chose to wash their dirty linen in public. So far as he was concerned, the *patriotes* did not include Proli and consorts. After a violent attack on 21 November – in striking contrast to his previous policy of defending Jacobins against each other – he had them expelled from the club. His assertion that Hébert had helped to reveal their plotting gave Hébert a *certificat de civisme* of sorts. On the following day Hébert and Chaumette were interrogated by the governing committees. What took place is not known, except that Chaumette claimed that they were defended by Robespierre and cleared by the Committee of General Security. It was about this time that Hébert suddenly dropped his press campaign against Chabot and this may not have been merely coincidental. On 28 November Robespierre read to the Jacobins a couple of forged letters addressed to Brissot and himself – which he attributed, without any evidence, to Proli – and warned the members of the club against their tendency to become the unintentional agents of the trouble-makers. His official attitude, and probably his private conviction as well, towards the end of November, was that the only serious danger to the Revolution came from a handful of foreign agents. Consciously or not, these were being helped by radical politicians, ambitious for power, who were trying to discredit some of the Montagnard leaders and to draw up new proscription lists just when the Revolution should have been giving way to a period of stability. Although he probably did not suspect the Cordelier group of anything worse than irresponsible careerism they were certainly a nuisance and if they repeatedly ignored his warnings against sniping at revolutionary government he might come to take a less indulgent view of their activities.

238

Up to now, said Henry, his trouble seems to have been that he wasn't suspicious enough. He believed whatever he was told.

Only if it was a denunciation of someone else, said Ted. The point is, was any of this true? What we want to know is whether he was right – about Proli's gang and the men Chabot denounced.

You've read that article, I said, and you know as much as I do. What do you think?

It's not a matter of what I think. Either they were or they weren't.

That's perhaps an over-simplification, said Henry. There's a whole range of possibilities. X may have been a foreign agent, Y may have followed him in good faith and Z been making a career out of the Revolution, taking money wherever he could find it, without any aim beyond his own power and prosperity. And then there's the question of what they genuinely believed about each other, even if it wasn't true. And if A told B about his mistaken view of C, this could lead B to suspect C, or A, or both.

I was never very good at quadratic equations, said Ted. As a matter of fact, I take your point, Henry, but before we get involved in the higher mathematics we ought to get the facts straight. Never mind the misinterpretations for the moment. People either were foreign agents or they weren't, and J.S. ought to know.

I'll accept that up to a point, I said. Some at least of Ted's questions are theoretically answerable and one day we may be able to answer some of them but we can't answer them now. Lestapis, for instance, in his book on Batz, implies that he believes Chabot's charges against Hébert but he can't prove them and he won't finally commit himself. Take Proli. When he was on the run he asked the banker Perregaux (the man who got that letter from Whitehall) to advance him money to get to Boulogne. Boulogne was convenient for England, but it also seems to have been Batz territory.[30] Were these coincidences and if they were, how many coincidences make a fact?

Fortunately, said Henry, it isn't really our business. So far as Robespierre was concerned, all we need to know is whether it was reasonable for him to suspect the men he did and as I said before, his mistake was that he wasn't suspicious enough.

30. Arch. Nat. F⁷ 4774⁸³.

That was certainly true of his reaction to the campaign launched by the so-called *Indulgents* in December. One or two people, such as the German, Oelsner and Pétion, had already pointed out that Robespierre was vulnerable to flattery.[31] Fabre's report on the Chabot affair was very skilfully written to confirm all Robespierre's previous convictions and it probably strengthened his good opinion of Fabre.[32] But there is more to it than that. Robespierre may have seen where the *Indulgents* were going and endorsed their policies. One *could* interpret the evidence that way.

When he defended Danton in the Jacobins on 3 December some historians say that he damned him with faint praise.[33] That's not my own feeling. After passing rapidly over the issues on which they had disagreed he said emphatically, 'I swear that those are the only things with which I have reproached him', and he repeatedly associated himself with Danton. Robespierre did not often say *nous*. He also made the significant remark, 'If the defenders of liberty were not being slandered the people could give themselves over to rejoicing, the Republic would be established on a settled and enduring basis and there would be no partisans of tyranny left amongst us.' In the context of what he had been saying a few weeks earlier this looks very much like an appeal to wind up the Revolution. Two days later, in introducing his *Réponse aux rois ligués,* he made a curious remark to the Convention. After his usual argument that the Powers were trying to manipulate the revolutionaries into destroying the Revolution and to rekindle the civil war in the Vendée by means of dechristianisation, he went on, 'It is the duty of the Committee of Public Safety to reveal these [intrigues] to you and to propose the measures necessary to stamp them out. It will no doubt discharge this duty. In the meantime it has commissioned me to present you with a draft address . . .'[34] This could be taken to imply reservations about the willingness of his colleagues to expose the guilty men. That night, at the Jacobins, he took up the same theme. 'I could prove conclusively to you the plan that I have just sketched out, if I wanted to expose its leaders. I will content myself with telling you that the men at its head

31. For Oelsner, see Jacob, op. cit., p. 81; for Pétion, *Observations de Jérôme Pétion sur la lettre de M. de Robespierre,* Paris, 1792, p. 29.

32. Arch. Nat. AF II 49; printed in A. Mathiez, *Un procès de corruption sous la Terreur, Paris,* 1920, pp. 145-67. See above p. 217.

33. *Oeuvres,* vol. X, pp. 220-5.   34. *Oeuvres,* vol. X, p. 228.

are foreigners.'[35] This suggests that he was still thinking of Proli's quartet rather than of Batz, Benoît and Delaunay. He went on to stress once again the importance of not harassing '*patriotes* who may have been deceived by treacherous insinuations'. Of course this evidence is very tentative but it could suggest that he was dissociating himself from the Committees and their reluctance to take action against extremists.

On 12 December he treated the Jacobins to a violent denunciation of Cloots as a foreigner and an advocate of both dechristianisation and indefinite ideological war. His arguments, and even some of his language, were taken from Desmoulins's *Vieux Cordelier* No. 2 which had been shown to him in proof.[36] When an attempt was made in the Convention on the 12th and 13th to change the membership of the Committee of Public Safety, he did not intervene and he might well have welcomed the elimination of men like Billaud-Varenne. Garat, you will remember, said that Danton's plan was to eject Billaud, Collot and Saint-Just.[37] Towards the end of the year Robespierre and Saint-Just may have been taking rather different views of the political situation. On 22 December Saint-Just's secretary, Gateau, wrote to Daubigny at the War Office, 'The devil take me if I can help laughing with pity and indignation when I see all the Bourdon de l'Oises, the Fabres who call themselves d'Eglantine, the Thuriots etc. . . . preach morality, *vertu* and disinterestedness.' He went on to accuse them of trying to destroy 'all the *patriotes* of any vigour who are clear-sighted enough not to believe in the *vertu* of certain men who want to force our respect for their immorality itself because they want to wield the mace of the Republic in their own interest, or rather, in that of their base and disgusting passions.'[38]

Gateau was writing in support of the Cordelier, Vincent, secretary-general of the War Office, who was arrested, on the motion of Fabre, on 17 December. Robespierre raised no objection, either to the choice of victims – the arrest of Ronsin and Maillard was voted at the same time – or to the Convention itself exercising powers that it normally delegated to the Committee of General Security. This suggests that he had not been alarmed by *Le Vieux*

35. *Oeuvres*, vol. x, pp. 236-8.
36. *Oeuvres*, vol. x, pp. 247-51; *Le Vieux Cordelier*, ed. Calvet, Paris, 1936, p. 61.
37. See above p. 216.   38. Arch. Nat. F⁷ 4436.

Cordelier No, 3, published on the 15th, which contained a full-blooded denunciation of the Terror. When he had defended Desmoulins in the Jacobins on the 14th he claimed to quote from memory 34 lines of a republican poem of Camille's that he had read before the Revolution. This was a mark of high favour. On the 23rd he told the Jacobins that *modérantisme* had been decisively crushed and implied that the real danger came from 'the Prussian perfidy of those who want a universal republic, or rather a universal conflagration'. He treated Philippeaux very mildly, despite his hair-raising accusation that the Committee of Public Safety had been trying to lose the war in the Vendée and he warned Momoro sharply not to think of trying to organise another 31 May on behalf of Vincent and Ronsin. He claimed that their arrest had been discussed (he did not actually say approved) by the two Committees and contrasted the agitation on behalf of the two Cordeliers with the general indifference to the fate of Chabot 'who has rendered the most important services to the public cause'.[39]

This was the day when the return of Collot from Lyons brought about a major shift in the balance of power within both the Committee of Public Safety and the Jacobin Club. Collot had at one time been very well-disposed towards Robespierre. He even admitted this in March 1795 when Robespierre was everyone's scapegoat.[40] He had written to him frequently from Lyons but Robespierre never replied. This could have had some connection with Collot's links with Desfieux. Any suspicion on that score would be reinforced by Robespierre's abhorrence of the bloody excesses of Collot and Fouché at Lyons. These committed Collot both to the Terror and to Fouché. When he returned to Paris self-preservation drove him to champion both Ronsin, who had been his agent in Lyons, and Vincent, and to attack the *Indulgents*. He soon became one of Robespierre's opponents within the Committee of Public Safety.

When an attempt had been made, on 20 December, to use a petition from the wives of arrested suspects to work on the sensibility of the Convention and persuade it to set up a *comité de clémence* to discover and release those who had been unjustly

---

39. *Oeuvres*, vol. x, pp. 267-71.
40. *Discours fait à la Convention nationale par J-M. Collot*, Bib. Nat. Lb[38] 1309, p. 12.

arrested, Robespierre had denounced what he claimed to be a political manoeuvre but he nevertheless persuaded the deputies to vote for the creation of a secret committee along very similar lines. On the 26th Barère proposed that this committee should be drawn exclusively from the Committee of General Security, to which more members should be added. Claiming that this had been decided in his absence, Robespierre opposed the motion. After a confused debate, Billaud condemned the original proposal (i.e. Robespierre's) as dangerous and induced the Assembly to drop the whole idea. It was rare for members of the Committee to disagree in public and this defeat of Robespierre and the *Indulgents* was all the more significant. Undeterred, he still thought that the main danger came from men posing as extreme revolutionaries. That night he told the Jacobins, 'I am convinced that there are men who regard each other as conspirators and counter-revolutionaries and who have picked up that idea from the rogues around them who are trying to sow distrust between us.' Another version of this speech quotes him as still blaming everything on Proli and saying that the aim of the plotters was to organise another 31 May against the Montagnards, which amounted to a warning to the Cordeliers.[41]

As the Jacobins became increasingly absorbed by the long slanging match between Hébert and Desmoulins and their supporters, Robespierre appealed without much success for a truce in the war of personalities. On 5 January he criticised his brother for joining in the battle.[42] 'Individual grievances are no reason for declaring war on whatever bears the decisive stamp of *patriotisme*. I have tried to stifle [the present dispute] at birth but all my efforts have been made useless . . . I take no sides because I want to find out the truth, but I will say that I think there are fewer guilty men than people seem to think.' An alternative press report says, 'I have already tried to stifle it. Then in friendly discussions and private meetings people would have had no difficulty in recognising their mistakes and proving that they had never had any evil intentions. Nothing of the kind. Pamphlets are published the very next day. So it is intrigue that has brought things to their present pitch.' At the next meeting of the Club, after demonstrating his thesis by exposing a false accusation that Boulanger, of the Parisian National

41. *Oeuvres*, vol. x, pp. 288-92.   42. *Oeuvres*, vol. x, pp. 297-300.

Guard, had been planning an insurrection, he tried to persuade the Jacobins to unite in a discussion of the crimes of the British Government. Fabre's involvement in the East India Company scandal had already been exposed on the 4th and Robespierre must have been beginning to wonder about his optimistic assumption that the warring Montagnards were merely the innocent victims of intrigue. He still pretended that there was nothing seriously wrong. 'The factions exist no more. The genius of liberty and the energy of the Convention have destroyed them. Representatives of the people, do not believe in the power of your enemies – if any real enemies are still left. Your enemies are those who deceive you; the others are too weak to be dangerous.'[43] He then set about the delicate task of persuading the Jacobins not to expel Desmoulins whose increasingly open attacks, both on Hébert and on revolutionary government in general, exasperated most of the members. As a harmless gesture, Robespierre proposed burning the offending issues of *Le Vieux Cordelier*. When Desmoulins had no more sense than to quote Rousseau in his clever retort, *Brûler n'est pas répondre,* Robespierre understandably lost his temper and said more than he intended. 'The man who is so attached to his perfidious writings is perhaps not merely misled.' He went on – forgetting that he had just denied the existence of any factions – to accuse Desmoulins of being 'the mouthpiece of a dastardly faction that has borrowed his pen to spread its venom more openly and brazenly'. Recovering himself, he went on, 'I should not have spoken these truths if Desmoulins had not been so obstinate.'

An interesting admission, said Ted. In other words, the existence or non-existence of factions depended on the state of his temper. He must have had his own view of what it all meant, but what he told the Jacobins was a different matter.

Even if that were true, I said, the fact that he was still telling everyone to trust everyone else tells us quite a lot about the policies he was advocating. With the exposure of Fabre and his own indiscretion, Robespierre could no longer deny that, as he said to the Jacobins at their next meeting on 8 January, 'a new faction exists'.[44] But he was still trying to limit the damage. This speech was to culminate in a denunciation of Fabre and the two surviving versions of it are full of theatrical imagery that was perhaps sug-

43. *Oeuvres*, vol. x, pp. 300-11.   44. *Oeuvres*, vol. x, pp. 311-17.

gested to Robespierre by Fabre's former profession. He now put Fabre on a par with Proli and recognised the existence of two ostensibly hostile factions, the *citra* and the *ultra,* each trying to mislead honest Montagnards. 'Beneath their banners are ranged citizens acting in good faith.' In spite of his previous rebuff, he continued to defend Desmoulins and on the 10th even succeeded, in the face of some resistance, in getting him reinstated when the Jacobins had just voted to expel him. He could not be expected to do any more. His persistent attempts to prevent the Club tearing itself apart, and perhaps the shock of realising how he had been tricked by Fabre, seem to have worn him out. Between 5 and 10 January he is recorded as having spoken on eight occasions. For the next 18 days he was completely silent while the Club – one suspects without much enthusiasm – dutifully considered the crimes of the British Government.

It was probably about this time that he drafted the third and last of his undelivered speeches and the only one to survive in manuscript.[45] The fact that some of the images and expressions in the draft recur in his speech of 5 February provides us with a *terminus ante quem* while the general argument seems to reflect a hardening of his attitude since the speeches of early January. This draft is entirely different from the other two in that it relies on no secret 'revelations' but is based on the evidence of the debates in the Convention. Looking back, Robespierre now decided that the two factions had been at work, one in the Assembly and the other in the popular societies, since the previous August. He had come to see the whole *Indulgent* campaign in these terms. 'Hébert and Desmoulins, Fabre and Proli, Cloots and Bourdon, Lacroix [Delacroix] and Montaut, Philippeaux and . . . alternately slandered and fawned on the Committee of Public Safety.' He still thought the factions were inspired by the foreign enemy but Proli was demoted to a subordinate position and the leader was now said to be Fabre. Almost everyone who had ever criticised the Committee of Public Safety was included, Dubois-Crancé, Merlin de Thionville and the two Goupilleaus in addition to those already mentioned. His only concessions were to Desmoulins ('misled by others' prompting') and Danton ('a proud and indolent *patriote,* in love with both ease and fame, content with cowardly inactivity').

45. Arch. Nat. F⁷ 4436; printed in *Oeuvres,* vol. x, pp. 326-42.

Rather oddly, he left out both Chabot and Basire and the men they had denounced. From now onwards he was to maintain that the main danger to the Revolution came from the *citra* rather than the *ultra*. It is not difficult to see why this speech was suppressed. Taken at its face value, it called for an *acte d'accusation* against the entire cast. It would have united both wings of the Convention and the Paris Commune in a joint offensive against the two Committees. Robespierre, normally a very shrewd political tactician, must have been in a curious state of mind not to see this or to shrink from the consequences.

He took advantage of his speech on the principles of public morality, on 5 February, to include a version of the suppressed speech so enigmatic that it must have been incomprehensible to most of the deputies.[46] The only man he named was Cloots. Since Cloots had recently been unseated, this could possibly imply a veto by his colleagues on charges against deputies. After denouncing the double plot at considerable length, though in very veiled terms, he suddenly seemed to contradict his entire argument. 'We are far from suggesting that there is still in our midst a single man base enough to want to serve the tyrants' cause. But we are farther still from the unpardonable crime of deceiving the Convention and betraying the French people by a guilty silence.' After claiming that a free people had nothing to fear from the truth he concluded with nothing more illuminating than the motion to give wide publicity to his speech, most of which consisted of an appeal to republican *vertu*.

Put yourself in his position, said Henry. There wasn't much else he could do. What I don't understand – but perhaps there isn't anything to understand, in the sense that he didn't face up to things in his own mind – is what he actually thought about the whole business. If J.S. is right, he had agreed to work with men who were generally regarded as corrupt, in order to bring revolutionary violence to an end. At the same time he was ready to take the warpath as soon as anyone denounced a counter-revolutionary plot to him. That makes sense if he distinguished between a little harmless venality – or even a lot – and systematic hostility to the Revolution. But then I can't understand this last speech. It can't have been the exposure of the fact that Fabre had been lining his

46. *Oeuvres*, vol. x, pp. 350-68.

pockets at the expense of the East India Company – there was nothing political in that – which led him to denounce as plotters the men on both sides whom he had struggled so patiently to protect from each other's suspicions. I suppose the sudden revelation that he had been gulled for so long by Fabre – perhaps in the teeth of warnings from his colleagues on the Committees – must have been both a terrible shock and a humiliation. And then his past insistence that the Montagnards were all good chaps, in spite of all the evidence to the contrary, had not been in character. Perhaps he had been refusing to listen to his own suspicions until the day the dam broke and he went to the opposite extreme. But he couldn't really have believed that all those deputies were actually foreign agents. Of course, in the past, he seems to have convinced himself easily enough that opponents like Lafayette were almost *ipso facto* enemies of the Revolution. I suppose we shall never know what he really believed and how far it corresponded to what he said.

I doubt if I can be of much help, I said, but one or two facts may be relevant. At the Jacobins on 7 February he produced a slightly amended version of what he had told the Assembly two days earlier.[47] He confided in the members that some deputies *were* involved in the plot, but his main innovation was to claim that the plot was 'so far developed that within a few days *les conséquences s'appliqueraient aux individus* ', whatever that meant. He was replying to Brichet who had proposed the trial of the 73 Girondin supporters and a purge of the Centre or *Marais*. Robespierre had Brichet expelled for this and although he had been contemptuous enough of the *Marais* in the past he now went out of his way to proclaim its fusion with the Montagnards. This could suggest that he was still thinking in terms of winding up the Revolution and appealing for moderate support.

It still doesn't indicate whether he thought he was faced by conflicting groups that he would conciliate if he could or discredit as counter-revolutionaries if he couldn't, or whether he really believed what he said about foreign plots.

Perhaps both, suggested Ted. If the Committees were in possession of the kind of evidence given in that article – and they must have known a fair amount and perhaps other things too that have

47. *Oeuvres*, vol. x, pp. 369-72.

disappeared – they probably did believe that foreign agents were at work. They were clearly being challenged by ambitious politicians in the Convention and the Cordelier Club. How far Robespierre identified the two may have varied with his mood, but of course he couldn't admit that.

The state of his health may be relevant here, I said. He spoke only twice in the second half of January and four times in early February and then he fell really ill and was absent from both the Convention and the Jacobins from 10 February to 13 March. The attendance register of the Committee of Public Safety, for what its evidence is worth, suggests that he attended very regularly until about 12 February and was then away for the whole of the next month. On the 16th the Jacobins were told that both he and Couthon were ill. We don't know anything of the nature of his illness but it wasn't the first time that he had been incapacitated just before a political crisis broke. He may have felt in a state of utter confusion, unable to see his way ahead, not knowing what to believe and only certain that all his plans for a peaceful return to normality had been wrecked.

I hope you'll excuse me if I don't take my turn with the stethoscope, said Mac. I suppose there's no harm in all this stuff but I was under the impression that the French Revolution mattered and it seems to have disappeared while you weren't looking. Could we leave the spies under the beds for a moment and look at the real issues? Faced with a genuine popular movement of which the Enragés were the spokesmen, the Committee of Public Safety had managed to destroy the leadership without doing anything to dissipate the discontent behind it. This was now expressing itself through the Paris Sections – you see I've been reading Soboul – and it was this popular movement that made people like Hébert important. On the other side, having made their pile, the Dantons and d'Eglantines wanted to stop the Revolution and get off. Naturally this made them the heroes of the wealthy, who were frightened of the sans-culottes, punitive taxation and the threat to property in general. The Committee of Public Safety, while socially belonging to the world of the Dantonists, still thought that to win the war they needed to maintain contact with the sans-culottes. They found themselves pulled both ways so they tried to divert attention from the class war with slogans about *vertu* – which was partly an appeal for wage restraint. Robespierre was only important because he was the man most likely to be able to discourage the sans-culottes from trying their hand at social revolution.

It's a pity you weren't there to tell them what it was all about, I said, because they didn't seem to know. It's true, of course, that the Jacobins complained that the *aristocrates* were reading *Le Vieux Cordelier* and that Hébert's support came mainly from working people. But once you get beyond the general hostility between the rich and the poor and between the producers and consumers of food (which wasn't the same thing at all) you start imposing on them rôles that they wouldn't have understood. The sans-culottes wouldn't have known what a social revolution was, though they did have some ideas about direct *political* action. If this was a class war in which the political leaders were only figureheads, why did nobody fight it? The fact is, that the defeat of the Cordeliers put an end to action in the streets until the hunger riots of 1795. The sans-culottes didn't fight for the Cordeliers and the rich showed no particular inclination to mourn the death of Danton. I'm not denying that the result of the political battles did influence the balance of social forces and that the thermidor crisis left the sans-culottes with continuing war and inflation while it deprived them of the protection of the economic controls of the year II. But what actually happened depended on what a few individuals did. If you want to argue that, in the long run, the Revolution gave a particular form to the way that the industrial revolution developed in France, that's another matter. But I thought you wanted to hear about Robespierre. He would have agreed that the wealthy were putting their money on the *citra* and that the Cordeliers had a good deal of popular support. Anybody could see that but it didn't help him very much when the immediate question was what to do about Hébert and Danton.

That puts you in your place, said Ted. J.S. is obviously right when he says that how a revolution turns out is going to depend to a large extent on how individuals behave. Even Mac isn't going to argue that Lenin made no difference in 1917. Robespierre is certainly worth studying but you two seem to be creating some sort of a mystery out of what was quite straightforward. While he was on the make (trying to bring about a democratic revolution, said Henry) all his opponents were counter-revolutionaries – the Lameths, Lafayette, the Girondins, friend Pétion, anyone you like to mention. When he joined the government everyone was a good chap so long as he supported the government. There were still a few heads to chop off, of course – Roux, Proli, anyone who wouldn't fall into line. When he realised that the good chaps – Cordeliers or *Indulgents* – were thinking of setting up shop for themselves, then of course they became counter-revolutionaries too. Since they were dangerous people to tackle, Maximilien's nerves got the better of him and he took to his bed and hoped that his colleagues would sort it all out for him.

And Hamlet was merely a young man with an unearned income and an inferiority complex, said Henry. I'm always afraid that cutting people down to size means cutting them down to one's own size.

I don't see what on earth Hamlet has got to do with it, I said.

Ted does, said Henry.

He may have something to do with Henry but he's got nothing to do with Robespierre.

Let's be serious, I said. Ted's explanation doesn't fit the facts any better than Mac's. If you remember that article you'll recall that the Cordelier group tried to profit from the illness of Robespierre and Couthon and the absence of four other members of the Committee. Gravier, a friend of Robespierre's and a Cordelier, warned him about this on 10 March.[48] The Committee of Public Safety was probably ready to make concessions over policy and they tried to buy off Vincent with the offer of a post outside Paris but the Cordelier group was out for power and playing with the idea of an insurrection. Robespierre had probably nothing to do with the decision to suppress them. At first sight there is one striking piece of evidence that the government was planning their elimination as far back as January: a letter from Couthon in which he says that Hérault-Séchelles is being sent before the revolutionary tribunal with 'Chabot, Hébert and other villains of that ilk'.[49] But a closer look shows that this letter should clearly be dated 17 March instead of 17 January, or possibly 28 *ventôse* (18 March) instead of 28 *nivôse*. Robespierre probably did not return to the Committee until 12 or 13 March.[50] By this time the investigation had already been set in motion that was to lead to the

48. *Papiers trouvés*, vol. II, p. 195.
49. *Correspondance de Georges Couthon*, ed. Mège, Paris, 1872, p. 283.
50. General Herlaut, in *Le général rouge, Ronsin*, Paris, 1956, p. 225, gives no source for his statement that Robespierre was already back on the 9th.

arrest of the Cordelier leaders on the night of 13–14 March, after Saint-Just had denounced them in general terms and without mentioning any names, earlier in the day. The near-contemporary historian, Gallois, reported Robespierre's doctor, Souberbielle, to the effect that Robespierre said, 'What, still more blood? Is the revolutionary tribunal not shedding enough? They have been wanting me to attack [the Hébertists] for a long time, for I'm always the one to be sent into the breach. All right. I'll take it on once again. Since I have devoted my life to the people I will go through with it to the end.'[51] The sentiments are plausible enough but the story is improbable since Gallois maintains that Ronsin told Souberbielle about his plans for an insurrection and massacre, when Souberbielle was known to be a friend of Robespierre's. So far as the actual evidence goes, Robespierre's only contribution was to tell the Jacobins on 13 March that he was not well enough to play any active part, 'but what I cannot do satisfactorily other *patriotes* will do in my place'.[52] We can possibly infer from the fact that he and Couthon defeated a Jacobin attempt to get the trial fully reported, that he actively supported the attempt of the Committees to keep Pache, Hanriot, Boulanger and Carrier from being included amongst the victims.[53] Fouquier-Tinville had been warned to leave them alone but he had no control over witnesses who blurted out things better left unsaid.

In other words, said Ted, it was a put-up job. They didn't really believe in their plot and they fiddled the evidence to fit the victims they had chosen in advance.

Not quite. There was certainly talk of an insurrection in the Cordelier Club and if the Committees hadn't acted there might actually have been an insurrection. Robespierre may have hoped that his personal prestige would allow him to talk it away without forcing a crisis, but if that was his plan it was spoiled by his illness. Pache, Hanriot and Boulanger seem to have been on the fringes of this movement rather than directly involved in it. Carrier, the terrorist of Nantes, who *had* been involved, was possibly spared because he was a deputy. It would have been rash for the Committees to take on the Paris Commune as a whole, together with the National Guard, but the motives for restricting the num-

---

51. L. Gallois, *Histoire de la Convention nationale*, Paris, 1835, vol. VI, pp. 266-7.
52. *Oeuvres*, vol. X, p. 374.   53. *Oeuvres*, vol. X, p. 388.

ber of victims may not have been purely tactical. The trial itself was indeed a mockery of justice, in the sense that some of the charges seem to have been invented with the main aim of discrediting the accused. Proli's group wasn't involved at all in the plans for an insurrection. It was a political trial and an acquittal would have brought down the government. The Committees had their reasons for taking action and for their choice of victims; they may have been valid reasons but they didn't correspond to the actual charges. What is difficult to explain is why Fouquier-Tinville didn't use Chabot's 'evidence' linking Hébert with Batz and the attempt to save the life of Marie Antoinette. Of course, none of it was conclusive but that wouldn't have worried Fouquier and if the object was to destroy Hébert's reputation, it could scarcely have been more appropriate. But all this is speculation. It's very difficult to understand why the Committees behaved in exactly the way they did and quite impossible to tell exactly where Robespierre stood.

While Hébert and his associates were awaiting their trial, Amar had at last produced his report on Chabot's plot – or at least on part of it. Billaud and Robespierre objected that he limited himself to the *branche corruptrice* and left out the *branche diffamatrice* and they got the report referred back to the Committee of Public Safety. This is a rather mysterious business, unless Amar was hoping to get the accused tried in the ordinary criminal courts and save them from the death penalty.[53a] According to Chabot, the *branche diffamatrice* was the part of the plot that involved David, of the Committee of General Security, and Hébert. It is just possible that Amar was covering up for David. The fact that Chabot's charges against Hébert were not used at the trial of the *Père Duchesne* may have been due to the insistence of the Committee of General Security, which lost the debate on Amar's report but managed to control the trial. At all events, on 18 March the Convention raised the parliamentary immunity of Delaunay, Julien (who was in hiding), Fabre, Chabot and Basire and ordered their trial. Since they were accused of plotting 'against the French people and liberty' this implied another political trial by the revolutionary tribunal.

Once again the government had to decide where to draw the line. If the Committees had followed Amar's lead they would have

53a. Suggested to Robespierre by Payan. *Papiers inédits*, vol. II, pp. 360-1.

restricted the victims to those involved in the East India Company fraud and left out all those responsible for the *Indulgent* campaign, with the single exception of Fabre. Robespierre seems to have been against this. On 20 March, when he persuaded the Assembly to reverse its vote on Bourdon's motion for the arrest of Héron – an agent of the Committee of General Security – his speech was singularly obscure but perhaps hinted at some attempt at political horse-trading by the opposition.[54] 'To consummate this crime they had, little by little, to deprive the Committees and the revolutionary tribunal of cognisance of the conspiracy. To do this they had to spread perfidious insinuations and false ideas throughout the Convention in order to mislead it about the nature and authors of the conspiracy.' He accused the 'conspirators' of themselves clamouring for blood: 'Only yesterday a deputy burst into the Committee of Public Safety and, with indescribable fury, demanded three heads.' Not without a certain prescience, he went on, to warn the deputies that if they failed to eradicate both the moderate and extremist branches of the conspiracy, 'the faction that survived would rally all the survivors of the other faction to its support'. Whatever all this meant, it did suggest that Robespierre was thinking of active political opponents, rather than of the imprisoned Fabre and Chabot. This impression was reinforced on the next day, when he promised that the time to reveal the existence of a moderate faction was at hand. Couthon implied something similar when he wrote, with less than his usual caution, to his constituents on 22 March, 'The day before yesterday, Robespierre and I, with a few words in the Convention, began to force those gentlemen to climb down. A report that will be made in the next few days will finish off the job.' Two days later, he wrote again, 'In a few days we shall make a report that will finish off the business of terrifying the villains of every kind who oppose the progress of the Revolution and would like to prevent it reaching its goal. We are resolved to tear off all the veils and expose all those who have betrayed the public confidence.'[55]

But the report to which Couthon referred was not made until 31 March and between the 21st and the 31st Robespierre said nothing, though he seems to have been present at the Committee

54. *Oeuvres*, vol. x, pp. 392-96.
55. *Correspondance*, pp. 312-13, 315.

of Public Safety every day. If the Committees intended to take action against deputies they would have to ask the Assembly to raise their immunity. This raised the problem of what Danton was likely to do. If he was accused, he might well win the support of the Assembly and overthrow the government. If not, he was still liable to come to the support of his friends and the result might be the same. Robespierre was attached to Desmoulins and he had hitherto said virtually nothing against Danton. Charlotte claimed that he 'often told me that, after our young brother and Saint-Just, Camille was perhaps the man he loved the most among all the leading revolutionaries'.[56] In his unpublished *Vieux Cordelier* No. 7, written in early March, Desmoulins referred to Robespierre, Couthon and Lindet as the three men of integrity on the Committee of Public Safety.[57] Maximilien alone had prevented Camille's expulsion from the Jacobins in January. Levasseur, who thought that Robespierre had quarrelled with Danton, believed that he was reluctant to sacrifice Desmoulins.[58] Vadier, on 9 thermidor, said everyone knew he had defended Chabot, Basire and Desmoulins.

The evidence certainly suggests that Robespierre did oppose the proscription of Danton. The most convincing witness is Billaud-Varenne, who told the Convention on 9 thermidor, 'The first time I denounced Danton to the Committee, Robespierre jumped up like a madman, saying that he knew my intention was to destroy the best *patriotes*.' Danton himself, at his trial, is alleged to have called Robespierre 'the least rascally of the band'.[59] Tissot, who was present when the Convention voted Danton's *accusation,* believed that 'Robespierre did not want Danton's death, but he was easily frightened'.[60] There is a very curious suggestion in a manuscript essay in the Roederer papers, called *Qu'était-ce donc que Robespierre?*[61] This is anonymous but follows the *Portrait de Robespierre* allegedly by Merlin de Thionville, but attributed to Roederer. According to the author, 'Danton was threatened [by

---

56. *Mémoires*, p. 278.   57. Calvet edition, p. 238.
58. *Mémoires*, vol. III, pp. 63-4.
59. J-A. Dulaure, *Esquisse historique des principaux événements de la Révolution française*, Paris, 1823- , vol. III, p. 141.
60. *Histoire de la Révolution française*, Paris, 1839, vol. V, p. 123.
61. Arch. Nat. 29 AP 78. The translation is a conflated version based on two defective texts.

the Committees]. Robespierre, in his perplexity, came to his help but soon, either because he saw that Danton and he were not strong enough to overthrow the Committees, or because he was afraid to give too much weight to Danton and feared that any praise he gave to Danton might accredit the blame Danton might throw on him in the future, joined forces with the Committees again in order to overthrow Danton.'

Whether or not one should give any credit to this suggestion that Robespierre contemplated an alliance with Danton, it seems to be established that the two men met privately. Barras maintained that Laignelot arranged one meeting, at which Robespierre said that Danton's conduct in Belgium was 'perhaps not exempt from blame', but attributed most of the responsibility to Delacroix.[62] Robespierre himself referred to a meeting at which Laignelot was present, when Danton spoke contemptuously of Desmoulins.[63] The evidence suggests, however, that this was probably in January. The reference by Courtois to a meeting at which Danton accused Robespierre of tyranny and Robespierre defended the policy of the Committee of Public Safety, may refer to the same event.[64] Lecointre said in the Assembly that the two men met outside Paris, on the day before Robespierre agreed to Danton's proscription, but gives no details of what took place.[65] There is a much more circumstantial account, by Daubigny, of a meeting arranged by his friends, in the hope of reconciling the two, a fortnight before Danton's death – in other words, about 22 March.[66] According to Daubigny, Danton complained of Robespierre's coolness, which he attributed to the intrigues of Saint-Just and Billaud-Varenne. He said that Robespierre was too ready to believe denunciations and claimed – rather implausibly – to have been impoverished by the revolution. He appealed to Robespierre for a union of all *patriotes* in order to defeat the foreign enemy and make peace at home. 'But with your principles of morality,' Robespierre is alleged to have replied, breaking a chilly silence, 'we should never find any guilty

---

62. *Memoirs* (Eng. trans.), London, 1895, vol. I, p. 191.
63. A. Mathiez, *Etudes sur Robespierre*, p. 135.
64. *Révolution française*, 1887.
65. *Les crimes des sept membres des anciens comités de salut public et de sûreté générale*, Bib. Nat. Lb[41] 1461, p. 25.
66. V. Daubigny, *Principaux événements pour et contre la Révolution*, Paris, an III, p. 49n[1].

men to punish.' 'Would that worry you, Robespierre?' replied Danton. In spite of this unpromising exchange, 'the reconciliation seemed to be complete and the two men embraced each other'. Daubigny's account of the conversation is perhaps too neat to be altogether convincing, although the meeting was probably real enough. But if any serious discussions took place between Danton and Robespierre there were not likely to have been so many witnesses present. Billaud-Varenne said after Robespierre's death that the two men met in the country 'the day before Robespierre agreed to abandon Danton'.[67]

Whatever his reservations and regrets, Robespierre eventually accepted the policy of the majority of his colleagues on the Committees and it was agreed that Saint-Just should denounce Danton, Desmoulins, Delacroix and Philippeaux. Once again, there were curious omissions, such as Bourdon and Thuriot. A new crisis then arose, which suggests that everyone's nerves were on edge. Vadier apparently told Taschereau that Saint-Just insisted on reading his report while Danton was present in the Convention.[68] When the Committees rejected this as too dangerous, 'Saint-Just, in a rage, threw his hat on the fire and left us standing there. Robespierre agreed with him . . . but since he could never resist an appeal to fear, that was the weapon I used against him. "You can risk being guillotined if you like, but I don't intend to." ' Amar and Vadier rushed after Saint-Just and managed to catch him before his report went the same way as his hat. 'An instant later and where would you have been?' commented Taschereau. 'Would you have had the time to draft another report *sur des pièces idéales*, or on the basis of the same notes that Billaud had provided?'

Robespierre supplied Saint-Just with a long commentary on the first draft of his report. This is a rambling affair which opens with an attack on Fabre, along the lines of Robespierre's third undelivered speech.[69] Unlike Amar, Robespierre concentrated on Fabre's political rôle, although even the devious Fabre might have found it hard to recognise his activities from Robespierre's implausible description. He had co-operated with the Cordeliers,

67. L. Lecointre, *Les crimes des sept membres des anciens comités de salut public et de sûreté générale*, Bib. Nat. Lb⁴¹ 1441, p. 25.
68. *P-A. Taschereau-Fargues à Maximilien Robespierre aux Enfers*, Paris, an III, pp. 15-16.
69. Printed in Mathiez, *Etudes sur Robespierre*, chap. vi.

while simultaneously attacking them in the hope of destroying genuine *patriotes* like Pache and Hanriot, who were their innocent dupes. But Fabre's attack was conducted 'in such a way as to enhance their prestige'. Robespierre's references to Fabre's 'frightful reputation' and 'notorious crimes' raised the awkward question of why he himself had supported Fabre in the Assembly. Desmoulins and Philippeaux 'and even Bourdon' were Fabre's agents, but Desmoulins was half-excused as a *patriote* at heart, led astray by his vanity. Saint-Just would have none of this and his own portrait of Desmoulins was a good deal blacker. Robespierre then turned to Danton, offering a critique of his revolutionary career that was a good deal less far-fetched than his charges against Fabre. Danton had been too close to Mirabeau, Lafayette and the Lameths; he had allowed Fabre to enrich himself; he had liberated the Feuillants, Duport and Charles Lameth, and tried to come to terms with the Girondins; he had failed to support Robespierre's campaign against the war or to defend him against the Girondins; he had opposed both the execution of the king and the insurrection of 31 May. All this was more or less true but at most amounted to no more than a charge of political misjudgment that could have been applied to scores of deputies – and to Robespierre himself. He did not suggest that Danton was involved in Fabre's elaborate plots, or even accuse him of being personally corrupt. His only serious accusation was that Danton had been involved in the attempt to stir up a riot on 10 March 1793, to provide Dumouriez with a pretext for marching on Paris to restore order and suppress anarchy. The sneer that Danton kept out of danger on the night of 10 August 1792 was a tactless one for Robespierre to make in view of his own personal record. The charge that Danton and Delacroix had attacked slavery in order to ruin the French colonies was so outrageous that Saint-Just understandably disregarded it. The relative moderation of most of Robespierre's accusations contrasted with the violence of his comment. Danton had a 'black and ungrateful soul'. There was 'not a single *mesure liberticide* that he had not supported'. He had revealed the baseness of his nature by making fun of *vertu* and saying that there was no *vertu* like that which he demonstrated to his wife every night. There was a particularly cruel passage in which he accused Danton of making a ridiculous attempt to imitate Fabre's talent for theatrical tears.

257

Well, Henry, said Ted, how is Hamlet doing now? Even your Christian charity must find that this takes a bit of explaining away. What was it that he had said less than nine months before, that no one had the right to make the slightest reproach against Danton?

He would have done better not to write it, agreed Henry. Saint-Just didn't need any help when it came to that sort of thing. I don't know why he did write it since he didn't produce any important new evidence. One can sense a kind of resentment of Danton's personality, that he'd probably been bottling up for a long time but at least he didn't invent imaginary crimes where Danton was concerned and he did his best for Desmoulins. Perhaps he *was* frightened. One has to try to put one's self in the position of the men involved. If the Committees had decided to try to destroy Danton, Robespierre couldn't stop them and it was going to be such a dangerous business that if he didn't pull his weight they might all go down together. It was a matter of making the best of a bad job and the Committees were certainly likely to make a better job of rounding off the Revolution than Danton and his pirate crew. I'm not trying to justify this thing, but you can't write off a man's whole career by just looking at the black spots.

One can't be sure of the significance of what happened next. Danton and the others were arrested on the night of 30–31 March. On the morning of the 31st there was consternation in the Assembly, where no members of the two committees were present. Danton's friend, Legendre, proposed that the accused deputies should be given a hearing on the floor of the House. Robespierre came in at this point and got the motion defeated.[70] He silenced Legendre with the grim threat that 'whoever trembles at this moment is guilty'. Perhaps unwisely, he went on, 'I too was Pétion's friend; when he was exposed I abandoned him. I had associations with Roland; he turned traitor and I denounced him. Danton wants to take their place and in my eyes he is nothing more than an enemy of the nation.' He twice reassured the Convention that there were not many guilty men and that the Committees had no intention of proceeding against those who were merely weak or misled. Saint-Just was to go further when he read his report and promise that this was to be the last purge. On the face of it, it looks as though Robespierre took the lead but Tissot implied that

70. *Oeuvres,* vol. X, pp. 412-18.

he only spoke out against Legendre because he was the first member of the Committees to arrive and had no alternative but to defend the government. 'From what I knew of the interior of the Committee of Public Safety, and even more from his emotion, the vehemence and the fierce severity of the new accuser, I understood very clearly that he was speaking under the influence of a conviction instilled into him by his colleagues: all is lost if we flinch; the only choice is between Danton and the Committee of Public Safety, between an individual and the nation.'[71]

After this vital, but perhaps reluctant contribution, Robespierre seems to have left his colleagues to surmount the perils of the trial as best they could. They gave Fouquier-Tinville no time to deploy his professional skill: he had had a week to prepare his case against Hébert but Danton's trial began on the third day after his arrest. His case against the East India Company group was carefully pieced together from the results of their interrogation but the evidence against Danton and the other three deputies amounted to nothing more than a hasty summary of Saint-Just's report.[72] This suggests that the decision to include Danton was taken very late – a royalist source suggested as late as 27 March.[73] Fouquier's records include a list of witnesses to be called 'in the case of Chabot, Basire, Fabre d'Eglantine, Delaunay d'Angers and others on the 13th germinal (2 April)' which suggests that the four politicians were added after the date of the trial had already been decided.[74] The only witness who was actually called – Cambon – apparently implied that he did not believe in Danton's guilt. For want of any case of his own, Fouquier read out the reports of both Amar and Saint-Just. Everything went wrong. According to Tissot, the audience was overwhelmingly on the side of the accused.[75] Three members of the hand-picked jury are said to have told David that there was nothing in the charges.[76] Vadier and Amar haunted the court. Together with Voulland and David they were accused of bringing heavy pressure to bear on the jury.[77] When Fouquier had

71. Op. cit., vol. v, p. 133.   72. Arch. Nat. W 173.

73. Historical Manuscripts Commission, *The Manuscripts of J. B. Fortescue*, London, 1894, vol. ii, pp. 555-7.

74. Arch. Nat. W 173.   75. Op. cit., vol. v, p. 145.

76. E. B. Courtois, *Réponse aux détracteurs du 9 thermidor*, Paris, an IV, p. 37.

77. *Dénonciation faite à la convention nationale par Laurent Lecointre*, Bib. Nat. Lb[38] 2175, p. 7.

no option but to transmit to the Convention a request from the accused to cite several deputies as defence witnesses, it was Saint-Just who tricked the deputies into thinking that the public prosecutor was complaining of the riotous behaviour of the accused and persuaded them to vote that prisoners in contempt of court could be excluded from the trial. Robespierre's only contribution to all this was to propose that the decree should be sent to Fouquier-Tinville and to speak against Philippeaux's wife being granted a hearing in the Assembly.[78]

You're not trying to suggest that he didn't share in the responsibility are you, asked Ted.

He himself never claimed anything of the sort and from now onwards he always included Danton in the list of conspirators that he became increasingly fond of reciting to the Jacobins. All I'm suggesting is that, although he accepted the decision to eliminate Danton and Desmoulins, it would be absurd to suggest that this was something he imposed on his reluctant colleagues. It was very much the other way round. I'm also saying that the trial was a nightmare for the victors. They very nearly came to grief and that was something they wouldn't be likely to forget.

As Robespierre had possibly foreseen during the winter, the destruction of the two factions made the Revolution less rather than more secure. To obtain the acquiescence of the Commune and the Assembly it had been necessary to restrict the number of victims to a minimum, so there were plenty of survivors unsure of their own safety and with friends to avenge. The Montagnards as a whole had probably been becoming more and more resentful of the autocratic airs of the Committee of Public Safety. After the death of Danton its rule rested mainly on fear. The revolutionary tribunal had lost all credibility. That meant, of course, from the viewpoint of the back-bencher, that his knowledge of his own innocence offered no guarantee against proscription if he offended the government. Some of this latent hostility may have been directed against Robespierre personally, since he was the most vocal member of the government and the man who claimed to personify the Revolution. But those with any knowledge of what was going on must have realised that he was far from being the most violent member of the government and perhaps even sus-

78. *Oeuvres*, vol. x, pp. 422-3.

pected that he might have been looking forward to the end of the Terror.

They may have believed that, said Ted, but it doesn't mean that they must have been right.

Without necessarily agreeing with him, said Henry, it's difficult to see at what point he could have taken a different line – unless he had supported Danton against the Committees, and then Mac would have accused him of selling out to the bourgeoisie. In a way, what happened confirmed his belief that unless the trouble-makers were eliminated they would wreck the Montagnards and he had tried harder than anyone to prevent this happening. How far any of it was due to counter-revolutionary intrigue and how far it was all a matter of political ambition, is a different question. You couldn't put people in the dock on a charge of ambition so everyone had to talk in terms of plots and there was perhaps enough substance in the plot business to make a lot of people believe it. After all, these were exceptional times and everyone was living on his nerves. What I do resent is people's tendency to blame everything on Robespierre. It was easy for the Prieurs and the Carnots, when it was all over, to say that Robespierre was obsessed by plots. If they didn't believe in them why did they connive in the execution of their fellow-deputies on charges that they believed to be absurd?

Lindet apparently refused to sign the warrant for Danton's arrest, I said.

He didn't resign, did he? And no one else seems to have lost any sleep over it. I'm not holding Robespierre up as an example. I'm not even saying that what he did was defensible, but I think a little humility is in order before any of us asserts that, in the same position, he wouldn't have acted in the same way.

IX The Dénouement

After the great purges of March and April, I went on, everyone lived in a continual nightmare. The fact that Danton, Desmoulins, Hébert, Chaumette and all the others had been executed after trials that were obviously mere political conveniences, meant that no one was safe. The same sort of 'evidence' could be produced against any of the Montagnards. What Baudot said about thermidor could be applied to the whole period: 'Principles had nothing to do with it; it was a matter of killing.'[1] In the new atmosphere of hatred and suspicion any political defeat had come to mean a death sentence. Contemporaries realised, at least in retrospect, how much things had changed. The Montagnard, Choudieu, described the purges as 'an incurable wound; after this blow to the nation's representatives there was no end to the proscriptions.'[2]

Henry seemed to be talking to himself.

> Better be with the dead
> Whom we, to gain our peace, have sent to peace,
> Than on the torture of the mind to lie
> In restless ecstasy.

Aren't you confusing Danton and Duncan, asked Ted.

I was actually thinking more about Macbeth said Henry.

It *was* rather like 'Macbeth' in one respect at least, I said. Everyone felt threatened. As Thibaudeau put it, from the back-bench viewpoint, 'The Terror isolated and petrified deputies as much as ordinary citizens. When he entered the Assembly each member, full of suspicion, scrutinised his actions and his language lest either should be construed as criminal.'[3] Things were no better within the Committee of Public Safety itself, according to Prieur: 'uncertain if the coming hour would see us before the revolutionary tribunal,

---

1. M. A. Baudot, *Notes historiques sur la Convention nationale*, Paris, 1893, p. 125.
2. Quoted in Jacob, op. cit., p. 203.
3. *Mémoires sur la Convention et le Directoire*, Paris, 1824, p. 49.

on our way to the scaffold, without time to say farewell to family and friends . . . There were days so difficult that, seeing no way of dominating events, those in greatest personal danger abandoned their fate to unpredictable chance . . . In the end we became so accustomed to these insoluble problems that, to keep the machinery functioning, we carried on with our daily tasks as though we had a whole lifetime in front of us, when in all probability we were not going to see another dawn.'[4]

That's all very well, said Ted, but in fact Prieur was one of those who sent the others to the guillotine. He may have been frightened but he slaughtered his way through. I've got more sympathy for his victims.

There were plenty of those, for there was a very sharp increase in the Terror. As many people were killed in the nine weeks from 10 June to 27 July as in the previous fourteen months since the revolutionary tribunal had been created. It had now become an undiscriminating murder machine, which had not been the case before. Imaginary prison plots and absurd charges were everyday events. The deputy, Osselin, for example, who had been in gaol since the previous autumn, was executed for his share in a 'plot' to break out of prison, murder the two Committees, tear their hearts out, roast and eat them![5]

How do you explain that, asked Henry, when the Revolution was actually in much less danger than it had been in the previous year.

I don't know. It certainly didn't mean that the revolutionary tribunal had got out of control, since the whole business was very carefully controlled by the Committees. I think this is where the historian's common-sense approach breaks down; it's simply impossible to imagine one's self in the climate of hysteria and fear in which they were working.

You never will understand if you insist on seeing everything in personal terms, said Mac. You only have to look at Colin Lucas's book on the Terror in the Loire to see that the system was breaking down all over the country.[6] Since it had no ideological basis beyond a vague sort of public-school morality – and therefore no social

4. *Mémo'res sur Carnot par son fils*, Paris, 1861, vol. I, pp. 527-8.
5. Arch. Nat. W 397.
6. C. Lucas, *The Structure of the Terror*, London, 1973, chap. xi.

programme – all its criteria were purely subjective. It got by for a time by seeming to encourage social levelling but once the Government put the brakes on, over dechristianisation, and it became a crime to be an ultra-revolutionary, no one knew where he stood any longer and orthodoxy had simply become what the men in power did next.

There's probably a good deal of truth in that, said Henry, but it doesn't explain anything. The situation could have developed either way – towards an amnesty or an intensification of the Terror. After all, what the men in power did next depended on the sort of men they were. In the last resort what's done has to be done by someone.

What was our friend Maximilien doing, asked Ted.

I'll come to him in a moment. He was as much responsible for the savagery of the repression as anyone else. For instance, on 21 July he, Barère and Billaud signed a grim note to Herman, who was a sort of head of the Home Office, 'Perhaps we should purge the prisons at a single stroke and cleanse the soil of liberty of this refuse, these throw-outs of humanity.'[7] At the same time, there's no evidence that he was any more ferocious than the others and the responsibility for most of the bloodshed lay with the Committee of General Security.

It's difficult to know what the Committee of Public Safety was trying to do since most of the evidence comes from those who survived the thermidor crisis and they tried to throw all the responsibility on the dead in order to save themselves. The one thing that stands out very sharply is their policy of extreme centralisation, which reflected their fear of any sort of independent initiative. The 'Hébertist' empire was partitioned. When Carnot had the Ministries abolished, the War Office was split, the most important fraction of the old fief of Bouchotte and Vincent going to Carnot's man, Pille. Robespierre, on the other hand, took over the Paris Commune, putting his own supporters in the key positions there. The revolutionary army was broken up. The Committee as a whole kept the Commune under very tight control, dismissing men who had been elected by the Sections and replacing them by its own nominees.[8] The popular societies that had sprung up in most of the

7. Arch. Nat. F⁷ 4436.
8. See P. Saint-Claire Deville, *La Commune de l'an II*, Paris, 1946, p. 168.

264

Sections were bullied into disbanding themselves, by the chilly disapproval of members of the Committee of Public Safety, expressed through the Jacobins.[9] When some of the Sections began organising fraternal banquets the Committee was immediately suspicious and put an end to this premature fraternisation.[10]

The machinery of repression was centralised. All but one or two of the revolutionary tribunals in the provinces were suppressed and their cases referred to Paris. The *comités de surveillance* in the communes were suppressed too, leaving only those in the Districts – 600 instead of 44,000 – which could more easily be controlled from Paris. One aspect of this centralising process involved the encroachment by the Committee of Public Safety on territory that had previously been reserved for the Committee of General Security. A new police bureau was set up within the former committee.[11] This was originally intended to supervise public officials only, but officials were now so numerous and their status so ill-defined that the Committee of General Security felt that its own powers were being curtailed, especially during the months when the bureau was directed by Robespierre alone. Robespierre and Couthon, who were responsible for the transformation of revolutionary justice by the law of 22 prairial (10 June), seem to have intended it to strengthen the powers of the Committee of Public Safety at the expense of its rival.

Administration as a whole was more and more tightly controlled from the top. Barère's Bill of 11 May, which provided a rudimentary health and public assistance service, substituted central planning for the unco-ordinated activities of the representatives on mission. The latter were increasingly subordinated to the Committees which, as deputies themselves, they were inclined to resent. The Committees also strengthened their hold over the Jacobins. Barère, whose ambiguous record had been criticised in the club in the past, seems to have been foisted on to it by Robespierre towards the end of May. Couthon got him through the scrutiny committee on 1 June and only five weeks later he was elected president. With the single exception of Fouché, who presided from

9. A. Soboul, *Les sans-culottes parisiens en l'an II*, Paris, 1958, pp. 873-917.
10. *Oeuvres*, vol. X, p. 505.
11. See A. Ording, *Le bureau de police du Comité de Salut Public*, Oslo, 1930, and G. Lefebvre, 'La rivalité du Comité de Salut Public et du Comité de Sûreté Générale', *Revue Historique*, vol. CLXVII (1931).

4 to 21 June, every president from 20 April until 9 thermidor (27 July) was a member of one of the governing committees. In the past the Jacobins had been the forum where the Montagnards argued out the policies that they would support in the Convention. By the summer of 1794 all the life had gone out of the club, where ordinary members scarcely dared to risk any initiative. Members of the Committee of Public Safety introduced resolutions which the club duly endorsed and referred back to the Committee!

This intensified centralisation, together with the enmities resulting from the purges, created new tensions within the Montagnards and produced new conflicts within the Committees. At least two groups of deputies began to organise secret opposition to the Government. Representatives recalled from missions where they had discredited themselves by terrorist excesses, notably Fouché, Fréron and Barras, felt that their careers, if not their lives, could only be guaranteed by a change of government. Although, after thermidor, tactical considerations sometimes led them to assert that their target had been Robespierre, there was at first nothing to single him out from the other members of the Government and their hostility was originally directed against the Committee of Public Safety as a whole. Lecointre led a second opposition group. He had prepared a secret denunciation of the Committee of Public Safety which he later re-drafted as a personal attack on Robespierre.[12]

The resentment of the Committee of General Security against poaching by its rival was probably directed from the start against Robespierre, his follower, Couthon, and Saint-Just, who had delivered the reports on 'Dantonists' and 'Hébertists' that would normally have been made by the police committee. It was itself divided, with Le Bas and probably David supporting the Robespierrists. The Committee of Public Safety was also split, over personalities rather than policies. Saint-Just, who spent a good deal of time at the front, resented Carnot's tendency to treat him like any other deputy when he was not actually present in the Committee, to conceal strategic plans from him and to claim credit for victories at which Saint-Just himself had been present. Robespierre,

---

12. L. Lecointre, *Robespierre peint par lui-même*, Paris, n.d., Bib. Nat. Lb[41] 1168; *Dénonciation faite à la Convention nationale par Laurent Lecointre*, Paris, n.d., Bib. Nat. Le[38] 2175; and L. Lecointre, *Les crimes des sept membres des anciens comités*, Paris, n.d., Bib. Nat. Lb[41] 1441.

supported by Couthon, was increasingly taking independent decisions that involved the Committee as a whole in conflicts it would have preferred to avoid.

The result was an extremely complicated pattern of alliances and suspicions that was superimposed on all the other political quarrels. Robespierre's Montagnard enemies in the Convention confided in the Committee of General Security. Disagreement within the Committee of Public Safety was concealed as far as possible from the Assembly but could not be kept secret from the Committee of General Security. Robespierre almost certainly, and perhaps others as well, toyed with the desperate idea of appealing over the heads of the Montagnards to the uncommitted majority of the silent Assembly. No one knew whom to trust and a sudden reversal of alliances might transform a confidant into an executioner. Saint-Just broke off his engagement to Le Bas's sister and left Le Bas behind on his last mission to the front. 'He's such a strange man', wrote Le Bas to his wife, née Duplay. 'I can scarcely confide in anyone but you. One has so few friends.'[13] Until just before 9 thermidor the spies who supplied d'Antraigues with information about Parisian politics insisted that Saint-Just was Robespierre's rival and enemy. This sounds improbable and they were often wrong, but Demaillot, an agent of the Committee of Public Safety, wrote from gaol soon after 9 thermidor to say that on 9 July he had heard Saint-Just criticise Robespierre and say that he might go the way of Vincent and Ronsin.[14]

If the present tensions were almost intolerable, any attempt to escape from them looked even more dangerous. The members of both Committees were threatened by discontented Montagnards. Either Committee might appeal to the Assembly against the other. Lecointre claimed that the Committee of General Security tried to protect itself against its rival by strengthening its links with the Assembly. He thought that the Committee of Public Safety favoured another purge of deputies but dared not act without the other Committee's support. When Robespierre was an obstacle to this co-operation, Billaud proposed getting rid of him.[15] In this

13. Stéfan Pol, *Autour de Robespierre: le Conventionnel Le Bas*, Paris, n.d., p. 254.

14. A. Mathiez, *La conspiration de l'étranger*, Paris, 1918, p. 157.

15. *Les crimes des sept membres*, pp. 14-15.

sort of situation it was impossible for anyone to do more than guess at the intentions and contacts of his opponents – or of those whom he assumed to be his allies. Everyone felt that a crisis was inevitable and no one felt like precipitating it. In view of the fragmentary nature of the evidence it may never be possible to know what those involved really thought, but it seems clear that this nerve-racking stalemate continued right up to thermidor. Even after Robespierre's speech of the 8th had brought things to a head it was still not clear who would be fighting on which side.

This is all very well, said Ted, but I hope you're going to offer us something rather more specific about Robespierre's position.

I'll do what I can, I said, but it's bound to be rather tentative. When I was telling you about his long-term policies I suggested that they seemed to point towards peace and a return to constitutional government, though it's not clear whether he meant free enterprise and the rule of law or whether he had in mind the kind of Spartan constraints implied by Lepeletier's Education Bill. Saint-Just's inclinations were certainly in the latter direction. Several contemporaries believed – at least in retrospect – that Robespierre's relative moderation alienated the other members of the two Committees. His brother, when on mission, had become increasingly outspoken in his condemnation of terrorism.[16] Charlotte maintained that Maximilien had been opposed by Billaud when he wanted Carrier recalled from Nantes and that he eventually boycotted the meetings of the Committee because the others refused to end the Terror.[17] One of Lecointre's charges against the members of the two Committees was that they wanted to proscribe those who had called for a referendum on the fate of the king, and that Robespierre stopped them.[18] His alleged moderation was the subject of a comment soon after his fall: 'What finally confirmed my views about this monster was his protection of the Lyonnais and his hatred of your colleagues, Fouché and Collot. He must have . . . employed every kind of means to ensure that that rebel city escaped the vengeance of the nation.'[19] Courtois, whatever he said in his report against Robespierre, wrote in his

16. A. Mathiez, *Autour de Robespierre*, Paris, 1924, pp. 13-50; C. Nodier, *Souvenirs et portraits de la Révolution*, Paris, 1841, p. 76.
17. *Mémoires*, pp. 263, 273.
18. *Robespierre peint par lui-même*, p. 34.
19. Arch. Nat. F⁷ 4436.

memoirs, 'A short time before his fall Robespierre tried to win some support from the Right in the Assembly. Vadier [of the Committee of General Security] realised this and said loudly enough to be overheard, "If this goes on I'll guillotine a hundred of his *crapauds du Marais* for him." '[20]

If he really wanted to end the Revolution, said Ted, why didn't he say so? What he actually did was to help to intensify the Terror and to increase his personal share in it through this new police bureau. You say that all the subsequent testimony is unreliable. It could be that people like Courtois were merely presenting Robespierre as a moderate in order to attack his enemies. You're not going to get anywhere with this sort of evidence, which is rather hard on you when the question is so important.

You have to speculate, I said. It's certainly true that he did nothing to curtail the new ferocity of the Terror. But, as Henry would say, you've got to put yourself in his position. He was always a cautious man and he knew that one false move would be the end of him and of any hopes of a return to normal government, so far as he could see. His enemies – people like Billaud and Vadier – were certainly more ruthless than he was. I think he realised too that as soon as the Government tried to relax the Terror it would be attacked by all those with scores to settle. Hardly anyone really wanted an amnesty; they wanted to terrorise the terrorists. This had already happened at Lyons and Robespierre was quite well informed about what was going on there. This meant that men with terrorist records weren't going to take any chances and there were quite a few deputies who would oppose any policy of clemency that they couldn't control themselves. So the necessary prelude to an amnesty was to eliminate those who were too heavily compromised.

That's ingenious, said Ted, but it looks to me like the old story: there was always one more lot of victims.

Some of the deputies probably thought like you, but it doesn't mean they were necessarily right. Many years later, Barère seems to have come round to this point of view. 'His dominant idea was the establishment of republican government . . . and as a matter of fact the men he was hunting were those whose opposition put a spoke in the wheels of that sort of government . . . At that time

---

20. *Réponse aux détracteurs du 9 thermidor*, Paris, an IV, p. 38n[38].

we were living on a battlefield; we didn't understand that man.'[21]
Levasseur said much the same thing, that since they couldn't be
sure of carrying the Assembly for a policy of clemency, Robespierre and Saint-Just had to begin by destroying their opponents:
'Before proceeding to establish a constitutional regime, Robespierre wanted to put on trial the commissioners of the Assembly
and the members of the Committee of General Security who were
tarred by too many excesses.'[22] Any attack on terrorist deputies
would have to include Fouché. Collot, who had shared Fouché's
responsibilities at Lyons, was bound to see this as a personal
threat. It looks as though Robespierre called for the execution of
a handful of deputies – probably including one or two of Danton's
friends as well as the terrorists – and that the Committee refused.
They had probably been badly frightened by the fact that Danton's
trial almost went the wrong way and Carnot is said to have carried
a resolution that never again would they demand the trial of a
deputy.[23] Rather than join Robespierre in a risky battle they spread
the story that he was going around with a list of deputies he
wanted to proscribe, in the hope of winning the Assembly to their
side.

They weren't altogether wrong, said Ted. In any case, as you
admitted, this is all more or less speculative. If you look at the
hard evidence you come up against facts like that horrible letter to
Herman about purging the prisons. Didn't Acton say something to
the effect that after the strong man with the sword comes the
weak man with the sponge? You historians will whitewash anyone
if his crimes are on a big enough scale.

Dresden, said Henry.

I beg your pardon.

The thousand-bomber raids. You didn't see anything wrong
with them at the time. If one can be quantitative about cruelty
they make the Terror seem almost insignificant. What did you
expect Robespierre to do? He was caught in the same trap as the
rest of them but at least he was looking for a way out.

Could we have a bit less moralising and a bit more history,
asked Mac. Did anything actually happen?

21. *Mémoires*, Paris, 1842, vol. I, pp. 118-19.
22. *Mémoires*, Paris, 1831, vol. III, pp. 77-8.
23. *Mémoires sur Carnot*, vol. I, p. 369.

Plenty – even if the evidence is hard to interpret. As I said, the Committee of Public Safety was beginning to break up. The first sign of trouble was the fact that Billaud stopped speaking at the Jacobins after his long denunciation of the 'Hébertists' on 14 March and he was generally silent in the Committee whenever Robespierre or Saint-Just was present.[24] There's no obvious reason for this since he got his way, despite Robespierre's initial opposition, in the matter of Danton's trial. The first major row in the Committee happened on a day when the deputy, Niou, was present. The three surviving accounts of this place it sometime about the middle of April.[25] According to the fullest version, written within a year or so of the actual event, Saint-Just attacked both Prieur and Carnot and threatened to have Carnot executed, to which Carnot replied that he and Robespierre were *dictateurs ridicules*. Robespierre was not present but tried unsuccessfully to mediate on the following day. Fits of temper of this kind had not been unknown before. Speaking to the Assembly in the spring of 1795, Collot implied that he and Robespierre had had fierce disagreements which had not interfered with the functioning of the Committee.[26] It was perhaps the heightened tension that made this dispute seem significant and set Robespierre against his colleagues, even though he had not originally been involved. 'From this period the division became clearly pronounced . . . For some time already we had been on our guard, watching each other and no longer discussing things with them [Robespierre and Saint-Just] with openness and confidence. Robespierre had done very little until then. He was always bringing us his worries, his suspicions, his touchy manner and his political moodiness; he was only concerned with personalities and only proposed arrests and dealt with factions, the press and the revolutionary tribunal. Useless in government, useless in war, with never a point of view to put forward or a report to present, he spent his time undermining our courage, despairing of the salvation of the nation, speaking about his slanderers and assassins; his favourite expressions were: *all is lost; there is no*

24. G. Bouchard, *Prieur de la Côte d'Or*, Paris, 1946, p. 447; this was confirmed by Saint-Just in his last speech of 27 July.

25. *Mémoires sur Carnot*, vol. I, pp. 523-4; *Réponse des sept membres*, pp. 104-5; *Discours de C-A. Prieur*, Paris, an III, Bib. Nat. Lb³⁸ 1309, p. 5 n¹.

26. *Discours fait à la Convention nationale par J-M. Collot*, Paris, an III, Bib. Nat. Lb³⁸ 1309, p. 13.

ressource; I can no longer see anyone to save us.'[27] This is obviously a caricature but it does suggest that this quarrel constituted some sort of a turning-point.

There was a second row a few days later, according to Prieur, although his account of what happened includes some matters that had been discussed at the earlier meeting.[28] He claimed that Carnot proposed to arrest Hanriot, dissolve the Paris Commune and put Robespierre on trial. Saint-Just, in his speech on 9 thermidor (27 July) said that it was Billaud who had wanted to dismiss the mayor of Paris and disband the staff of the Parisian National Guard. Once again, no one suggests that Robespierre took the initiative. He had been very active in the Jacobin club from the time of Hébert's arrest until 18 April. For the next five weeks, apart from repeating his speech to the Assembly on the worship of the Supreme Being, and two short interventions, also on religion, he was entirely silent. Such silences in the past had tended to indicate approaching crises.

There are one or two hints that the Committee of Public Safety was preparing the Assembly for a major statement of policy. On 6 April Couthon told the deputies that a report was being prepared on public morality, diplomacy, the rôle of the representatives on mission and a *fête décadaire* to be dedicated to the *éternel*. Billaud's long speech on the 20th was perhaps intended to pre-empt the options open to the Committee. Calling for the regeneration of France, he implied that rigorous action against the corrupt was to continue indefinitely. If, as Levasseur believed, Robespierre had intended to link his proposals for the worship of the Supreme Being with a return to constitutional government, this could have been Billaud's way – not for the first time – of spiking his guns.[29] Billaud went on, 'Every people that is jealous of its liberty must be on its guard even against the virtues of men in eminent positions. Blind confidence begets idolatry and idolatry misleads amour-propre, awakens ambition and corrupts feeble souls that are predisposed to vice. That knave Pericles concealed under popular colours the chains he was forging for the Athenians.' This was a fairly obvious warning to Robespierre but not necessarily a declaration of war. The Committee had too many enemies to go around look-

27. *Réponse des sept membres*, p. 105.
28. *Mémoires sur Carnot*, vol. I, p. 525.   29. *Mémoires*, vol. III, p. 111.

ing for quarrels and though Billaud may have been personally jealous of Robespierre, his colleagues would be unlikely to support him in a showdown.

Robespierre's speech on the worship of the Supreme Being, on 7 May, must have been authorised, in a general way, by the Committee as a whole. But if it was the report that Couthon had announced, Robespierre narrowed its scope and committed his colleagues to a state religion for which some of them had little sympathy. This was especially true of the Committee of General Security whose Protestant members may have feared a revival of Catholicism, while Voltaireans like Vadier would scarcely appreciate Robespierre's championship of Rousseau and his attack on the Enlightenment. He was too good a tactician not to have been aware of this but as the tension increased he seems to have become increasingly fervent in his Rousseauist faith and there was a new urgency in his predictions of his coming martyrdom in the name of his political and religious principles.

At about this time the Committees became suddenly alarmed by the real or imaginary activities of the baron de Batz. Robespierre, of course, had denounced him many months before as the man behind the plot that Chabot revealed, but the suppression of Robespierre's speech at that time suggests that he had not convinced his colleagues. During Danton's trial the speculator, d'Espagnac, and the policeman, Ozanne, who had been imprisoned for allowing Julien de Toulouse to escape, encountered a professional criminal, L. G. Arnaud, who had been connected with Batz. Arnaud, in the hope of saving himself, was prepared to reveal what he knew and perhaps to embroider his story as well. Ozanne got in touch with Fouquier-Tinville, in whom Arnaud confided on 22 March.[30] It was presumably this which alerted the Committees, although Lacoste, in his report to the Convention on the Batz plot, spoke of a denunciation of 9 April that put them on the scent. The 'revelations' quoted by Bonnemain in his survey of the Batz affair, published in the year VI, do not correspond to Arnaud's disclosures and the Committees may have had a second source of information.[31] The new evidence, for what it was worth, linked Batz with Danton, Chabot and Basire and with England. True or

30. A. de Lestapis, *La 'conspiration de Batz'*, Paris, 1969, pp. 241-4.
31. Bonnemain, *Les chemises rouges*, Paris, an VI, pp. 178-85.

false, the Committees seem to have believed it and though most of the members of Batz's organisation were already in gaol, they went to unusual lengths to try to catch the elusive baron himself.

On 22 April the Committee of General Security ordered Fouquier-Tinville to spare no effort to catch Batz. 'Neglect no hints in your interrogations; spare no promises, pecuniary or otherwise; ask us for the liberty of any prisoner who promises to expose him or to hand him over, dead or alive.'[32] On the day before Lacoste's report it was the turn of the Committee of Public Safety to instruct the public prosecutor to offer a free pardon to Batz's secretary, Devaux, despite the fact that he had taken an active part in the attempt to rescue Louis XVI on his way to execution.[33] Devaux, however, refused to say anything. The Committee of Public Safety gave Fouquier careful instructions for the trial of Batz's supporters, telling him to suppress any mention of a note from Louis du Bas Rhin [of the Committee of General Security] and not to disclose any details of Batz's plan to get Marie Antoinette out of the Temple.[34] All this may be less melodramatic than it sounds and the Committee's intention may merely have been to conceal the extent of its knowledge from Batz – who claimed to have been present at the trial – in the hope of catching him off his guard.

Although the real extent of the Batz business may never be known, it is clear that the Committees were taking him seriously. On 22 May a man called Admiral or Admirat, after spending the day in an unsuccessful attempt to find Robespierre, tried to murder Collot d'Herbois. Admiral was arrested and it was soon discovered that he was a friend of Roussel, who was closely connected with Batz.[35] On the following day a young girl called Cécile Renault tried to get an interview with Robespierre 'to see what a tyrant looked like'. Her intentions were presumably unfriendly but she carried nothing more dangerous than a couple of penknives and she seems to have been more or less mad. She, at least, had no connections with the invisible baron. These two *attentats* served as the pretext for a great show-trial on 17 June at which all 54 accused were sent to their death – on the instructions of the Committee of Public Safety – in the red cloaks reserved for parricides.

32. Arch. Nat. W389.   33. ibid.   34. ibid.
35. See Herman's interrogation of Admiral in Arch. Nat. W389.

This is often cited as an example of the Terror run mad and there is an element of truth in this. Cécile's parents were executed with her and the Government even brought her brother back from the front although he was not actually executed. But the great majority of the 54 were suspected, in many cases very plausibly, of having formed Batz's *réseau*, which was effectively destroyed.

The two attempted assassinations probably confirmed the Committees in the policy of intensified repression on which they had already embarked. On 10 May Robespierre had personally drafted the instructions for the creation of a new revolutionary tribunal at Orange, whose judicial procedure was greatly simplified in the interests of the prosecution. The Orange court was presided over by Maignet who had been Couthon's colleague at Lyons and Robespierre may have felt that he could be relied on to use his arbitrary powers with discretion.[36] Four days after Admiral's attack, Barère induced the docile Assembly to vote that no British or Hanoverian prisoners were to be taken. This ferocious decree was disregarded by the army but did result in the execution of the crew of a British merchantman captured in the Mediterranean.[37] On 10 June Couthon presented the Assembly with the law of 22 prairial which reorganised the Parisian revolutionary tribunal along the lines of the Orange court. 'Enemies of the people' were defined in terms so vague as to encompass almost any expression of criticism, pessimism or immorality, and they even included commercial fraud. The accused were denied counsel and witnesses need only be called if 'this formality seems necessary either to discover accomplices or for other reasons of major public interest'. The only penalty was death.

I think even Henry is going to find that a little difficult to explain away, said Ted.

It confirms what I was saying, said Mac. The Revolution had reached a dead end. Since it no longer had any objectives that could be defined in a meaningful way, the retention of power by the Government had become an end in itself. Not being able to resolve the social conflicts, it hoped to repress their symptoms and the more it failed the harder it tried to stifle any signs of opposition – either to the revolution or to the Government. You could

---

36. For a very hostile account of the Orange tribunal, see V. de Baumefort, *Épisodes de la Terreur, le tribunal révolutionnaire d'Orange*, Avignon, 1875.
37. Arch. Nat. BB⁴ 42 (Marine), fol. 215-18.

scarcely ask for a clearer demonstration of the fact that state machinery is essentially repressive.

What makes it so particularly offensive, said Ted, is that it was all done in the name of virtue.

I don't feel under any obligation to defend it, said Henry, but I'm more concerned to understand it than to give way to indignation, however righteous. In the first place, they had probably been frightened, as J.S. said, by Danton's trial when it took them all their time to prevent him calling a dozen deputies as witnesses.

In that case, I interrupted, why did the other members of the Committees always insist that the prairial law was the work of Robespierre and Couthon and that they disapproved of it. Saint-Just's secretary said that he disapproved too – he was at the front at the time.[38]

The widening of the definition of counter-revolutionary activity, went on Henry, seems to suggest that the law was intended for general repression and not for a handful of deputies. But I agree that was not likely to upset a man like Billaud-Varenne. I'm inclined to think there may be a clue in what J.S. told us a long time ago about Robespierre's insistence on seeing revolutionary justice as essentially political and in that advice that Payan gave to the judge at Orange.[39] In a revolutionary situation where the defence of the revolution took precedence over the protection of the individual, the conscience of a *patriote* jury might seem a better guide than legal proof.

Their conscience hadn't got much to go on, said Henry, if all they heard were the charges.

Besides, I added, they already had the law of suspects which allowed them to keep dangerous people in gaol for as long as they liked.

It sounds to me like a bureaucratic solution to a bureaucratic problem, said Mac. They were bringing all the cases to Paris for trial. The ventôse laws meant that when the suspects had been sorted out there would be thousands of them to try too. If revolutionary justice was to look revolutionary it had to be prompt – you couldn't leave a man like Admiral waiting six months for his trial –

38. G. Lefebvre, 'Sur la loi du 22 prairial', *Ann. hist. Rév. fr.*, no. 139 (1951), p. 244.
39. See above, pp. 162-3.

so the only solution was to turn the trial into a formality. It was simply a matter of following up what had been logically implicit in the trial of Danton.

I doubt if we shall ever be sure what Robespierre and Couthon intended, I said. I don't suppose it was what actually happened: an enormous increase in the number of executions of people who were no danger to anyone. But if we get back to the evidence we can at least see some of the consequences of the law. According to Carnot's son, Robespierre had twice persuaded the Assembly to endorse the reorganisation of the revolutionary tribunal but the Committee of Public Safety had done nothing about it, so he and Couthon presented the Committee with a *fait accompli*.[40] If that is true, it was the second time he had done this within a month. In the Convention the Committee maintained a united front – Barère and even Billaud supported Robespierre on the 12th when the deputies proved awkward. The majority of the Committee may have objected to the Bill as a whole or merely to one or two aspects of it. As originally voted it said that only the Committee of Public Safety could reverse a decision to send a man to the revolutionary tribunal. On the 14th this was amended to give the same powers to the Committee of General Security. In the second place, the provision that all previous legislation was superseded could be interpreted as abolishing the parliamentary immunity of deputies. This was what created a storm in the Convention. The deputies were by now in the habit of voting any legislation that was presented to them, but self-preservation drove one or two – especially Ruamps, Lecointre, Bourdon and Tallien – into objecting. When he replied to these objections Robespierre specifically denounced Bourdon and Tallien as men who were trying to divide the Assembly by working on deputies recalled from their missions by the Committee of Public Safety. One of the objectives of the Bill may well have been to give the Committees the means to proscribe deputies, if Robespierre and Cothon were challenging a majority decision not to purge the Convention any further.

The prairial law certainly produced another storm within the Committee of Public Safety – the first since April unless one accepts Baudot's rather improbable account of a quarrel at the end of May when Robespierre attacked Carnot's strategy and Saint-Just

40. *Mémoire sur Carnot*, vol. I, p. 520.

suggested that all power be entrusted to a dictator.[41] Robespierre and Couthon probably seemed to their colleagues to be provoking unnecessary opposition. Besides snubbing the Committee of General Security, Robespierre, on 12 June, had appeared to accuse his opponents of trying to turn the Montagnards against the Government. He had gone out of his way to insist that since the eclipse of the Girondins, the Montagnards no longer existed as a separate group. 'Every deputy who is ready to die for his country is a Montagnard. The only remaining division in the Assembly was that between the virtuous and the wicked.'[42] This sounded very much like an invitation to the Plain to support the Government in a purge of terrorist or factious Montagnards and it was perhaps this attempt to commit his colleagues to a policy they had already rejected, since it risked losing Montagnard support, that provoked their anger. The fullest account of what followed comes from them.[43] When Billaud complained of Couthon's initiative, Robespierre replied 'that up to that moment the members of the Committee had had confidence in each other, which was why he had thought that he and Couthon could act independently'. When Billaud was still dissatisfied, ' "I see clearly enough that I am alone," said Robespierre and entering into a fury he denounced the other members of the Committee, accusing them of conspiring against him. He shouted so loudly that several citizens gathered on the Tuileries terraces. The windows were shut and the discussion continued. "I know," said Robespierre, "that there is a faction in the Assembly out to destroy me, and here you are defending Ruamps." "So you admit," replied Billaud, "that you want to use your law to guillotine the Convention." ' Robespierre is said to have burst into tears and it was from about this time that he stopped attending the meetings of the Committee although he continued his work with the police bureau. Fouché maintained that at this meeting Robespierre demanded nine heads, including Fouché's and that his colleagues refused.[44]

Robespierre's position was becoming increasingly exposed. At loggerheads with his colleagues, he had alienated most of the Com-

---

41. op. cit., pp. 12-14.   42. *Oeuvres*, vol. x, pp. 492-4.

43. *Réponse des sept membres*, pp. 105-8. This seems to be the incident described in the *Mémoires inédits de Billaud-Varenne sur les événements du 9 thermidor*, ed. Vellay, Paris, 1910, p. 19.

44. *Mémoires*, ed. Madelin, Paris, 1947, p. 47.

mittee of General Security and it seems to have been the prairial law that induced Lecointre to try to create an anti-Robespierrist faction in the Convention, in contact with the Committee of General Security. According to Lecointre, Amar and Bayle, of the police committee, told him on 12 June that the Committees as a whole were not responsible for the prairial law.[45] It certainly looks as though Robespierre was intent on the execution of a handful of deputies – Couthon told the Jacobins on 14 June that there were from four to six conspirators – who stood in the way of the policy he hoped to pursue, whatever that may have been. Those who thought they were on the proscription list began a whispering campaign to persuade as many of their colleagues as possible that they too were threatened. Robespierre may have had some justification for saying that men he respected had been turned against him in this way and his policy alienated many Montagnards without going any appreciable way towards cementing an alliance with the Plain.

What makes the situation particularly obscure is the fact that the underground opposition was originally directed against the Committees as a whole. The Committee of Public Safety was aware of this and its spies were following Legendre, Thuriot, Tallien, the two Bourdons and Fouché.[46] Robespierre, in his private papers, jotted down notes on deputies whom he suspected: Dubois-Crancé, Delmas ('as a member of the military commission he is in close contact with Carnot'), Thuriot and the two Bourdons.[47] Some of Robespierre's 'evidence' against these men concerned recent events but he also raked up obscure incidents from the previous autumn, such as the 'counter-revolutionary' proposal of Bourdon de l'Oise, of 2 November, to drain ponds at a time of fish shortage! This suggests that Robespierre was hunting through the records for ammunition rather than still trying to make up his mind about the reliability of his colleagues.

If he wrote that as a personal memorandum, said Ted, and not as a propaganda exercise, it also suggests that he was certifiable.

He noted that Bourdon 'walks about all the time with the air of an assassin contemplating a crime'.

45. *Robespierre peint par lui-même*, p. 3.
46. *Papiers inédits*, vol. I, pp. 366-70. Courtois, in his edited version, tried to suggest that the men were Robespierre's personal spies.
47. *Papiers inédits*, vol. II, pp. 16-21; Courtois, *Rapport*, pp. 189-92.

Even Fouquier-Tinville would have hesitated to accept that as evidence.

He may have been a little hysterical, said Henry, but was he wrong about Bourdon?

Quite possibly not. According to Robespierre, Bourdon had planted an agent in Carnot's administration and Robespierre eventually managed to chase him out.

After the fish-pond business, said Ted, I can't say that his unsupported evidence carries much conviction.

Robespierre's list of suspects is rather an odd one. Of course, it may not be complete. It doesn't include Lecointre, although Robespierre had been warned that Lecointre had written a denunciation of him and was intriguing with Legendre, Thuriot and Bentabole.[48] He didn't mention Fouché or any of the other terrorists. He is generally said to have been an implacable enemy of Fouché, but after his recall from Lyons, Robespierre praised his *patriotisme* in the Jacobins on 8 April. On 11 June he merely called for more information about Fouché's attitude towards dechristianisation when he was at Nevers and he didn't attack him until 14 July, 'less on account of his past crimes than because he was hiding in order to commit new ones and because I regard him as the leader of the conspiracy that we have to expose'.[49] Quite possibly he was prepared to leave the ex-terrorists alone provided that they did not create trouble.

That's not what you suggested a short time ago, said Ted.

One can't be sure of anything, especially when everyone had to act on the basis of what he suspected. Robespierre's suspicions may have been wrong in the first place but the man who felt himself suspected – rightly or wrongly – was likely to start opposing the Government as the means to his own self-preservation. I told you the whole situation was a nightmare. There were said to be sixty deputies afraid to sleep at home. In a situation of this kind one acts on the basis of one's suspicions and turns them into facts by doing so.

The prairial law came just two days after what should have been the triumphal inauguration of Robespierre's religious policy with

48. Arch. Nat. F⁷ 4631. I am indebted to Professor Richard Cobb for this information.
49. *Oeuvres*, vol. x, p. 527.

a fête in honour of the Supreme Being, on what perhaps just happened to be Whit Sunday. David had organised a magnificent spectacle and the weather was perfect. Robespierre, walking ahead of the other deputies as president of the Convention, appeared more as a pontiff than a politician. Greeted by cries of *Vive Robespierre,* he must have felt the contrast between his communion with the enormous and enthusiastic crowd and the less flattering noises coming from just behind him. Baudot describes what happened. 'I heard plenty of curses, spoken loudly enough to reach the ears of the celebrant . . . There were no more than eight ranks between Robespierre and me; I heard all the curses; they came from Thirion, Montaut, Ruamps and especially from Lecointre de Versailles who a score of times called Robespierre a dictator and a tyrant and threatened to kill him.'[50] From Robespierre's point of view it would all fit: a happy people, rejoicing in the repudiation of atheism and eager to welcome the new religion of virtue, and a handful of jealous and cynical Montagnards standing in the way of the triumphant consummation of the revolution. In terms of political tactics, the ceremony was a dangerous luxury that emphasised his isolation, as he emerged from the protective anonymity of the Committee of Public Safety, and gave credibility to the stories that he was aspiring to personal power.

An experience like that, said Henry, which must have meant so much to him, coming on top of all the frustrations and intolerable tensions of the past couple of months, was just the kind of thing to make a man like Robespierre feel that he owed it to himself, and perhaps to his God, to drop his cautious political calculations and stand for what he believed to be right, whatever the cost. There was a noble rôle to play and while he may not have been the elect of Providence, he was the only man who could play it and in a sense his whole revolutionary career had prepared him for it.

It won't do, Henry, said Ted. He's beginning to sound like Eliot's Becket. You can't turn him into what you'd like him to be. Two days after this he was defending Couthon's abominable prairial law that sent hundreds of perfectly innocent people to their death.

I've not forgotten that and I'm quite ready to admit that he's still a mystery to me. But if I recognise one side you have

50. op. cit., pp. 4-5.

to admit the other. That's what gives him his tragic dimension.

I'd like to digress for a moment, I said, to take a last look at his links with Arras. It's not really a digression since it showed how difficult it had become for the Government to control its agents and how any attempt to check the Terror produced an immediate counter-attack on the terrorists. In October 1793 a minute in Robespierre's hand had sent the deputy and former priest, Le Bon, to Arras. Le Bon had written one or two flattering letters to Robespierre during the early years of the Revolution and there may have been other contacts between them. To that extent he was Robespierre's man and when he turned out to be as bloody a terrorist as any, Maximilien found himself in an embarrassing situation. Le Bon's ferocity split the Arras Montagnards and may explain an undated letter to Robespierre from Buissart: 'My wife, outraged by your silence, wanted to write to you to tell you about the situation in which we find ourselves. As for me, I had finally made up my mind to say nothing more to you. I have been warning you for the past four months or more.'[51] Robespierre seems to have continued to support Le Bon and when the revolutionary courts in the provinces were abolished an exception was made in favour of that at Arras-Cambrai. Le Bon eventually arrested the leading members of the criminal court of the Pas-de-Calais and sent them to Paris for trial by the revolutionary tribunal there.[52] One of them appealed for help to Herman, a fellow-Artesian whom Robespierre trusted, while another turned to Guffroy, Maximilien's former colleague on the bishop's court at Arras, and a Montagnard deputy. On 7 May Guffroy saw Robespierre who recalled Le Bon for consultation four days later. He refused to grant him a private interview but Le Bon was allowed to resume his mission at Arras. On 5 June the Committee of Public Safety ordered the release of the men from the Pas-de-Calais, who promptly denounced Le Bon to the Convention. The Committee of General Security then had them rearrested. On 10 July the Committee of Public Safety recalled Le Bon and suppressed his revolutionary

51. *Papiers inédits*, vol. I, p. 253.
52. On this complicated affair, see A. Mathiez, Robespierre et Joseph Le Bon, *Ann. hist. Rév. fr.*, no. 1 (1924); G. Lefebvre, 'La rivalité du Comité de Salut Public et du Comité de Sûreté Générale', *Revue Historique*, vol. CLXVII (1931); and P. Labrachère and G. Pioro, 'Charlotte Robespierre et ses amis', *Ann. hist. Rév. fr.*, n. 165 (1961).

tribunal. A fortnight later they released the officers of the criminal court once again. We cannot be sure where Robespierre stood, but a friendly letter from Buissart, dated 28 June and complaining that Arras was in the hands of priests and lackeys and going on to express reservations about 'your secretary and plenty of other people around you' suggests that Maximilien's rejection of Le Bon may have reconciled him with Buissart.[53] If Robespierre was responsible for Le Bon's recall, the fact that the Committee of Public Safety took his side, even at the cost of a conflict with the police committee, shows that his boycott of its meetings had not destroyed his influence there or produced a final breach.

In the meantime, relations between the Robespierre brothers and their sister had broken down completely. Augustin, in an undated letter to Maximilien, complained that 'my sister has not a single drop of our blood in her veins. What I have heard about her and seen for myself makes me regard her as our greatest enemy.'[54] The fact that he referred his brother for further information to *la citoyenne Lasaudraie,* his new mistress, suggests that Charlotte's objections to his behaviour may well have been more moral than political. On Augustin's suggestion she was sent back to Arras with Le Bon in May. She soon re-appeared in Paris and wrote a rather self-righteous letter to Augustin on 6 July, complaining of his 'implacable hatred' and asserting her own injured innocence.[55] Charlotte, who throws no light on the quarrel in her memoirs, then went to live with friends and her estrangement from her brothers possibly saved her life in thermidor. When arrested, she, like Buissart, claimed to have warned Maximilien that he was surrounded by people who deceived him.[56] The estrangement once again emphasises Robespierre's growing personal and political isolation and his increasing dependence on a narrow coterie of friends who could do little to help him.

The brutal Vadier, of the Committee of General Security – a man who had once described Danton as a fat stuffed turbot he proposed to gut – seems to have taken particular exception to Robespierre's religious policy and tried to exploit it against him. On 12 May the Committee of General Security sent two of its

53. *Papiers inédits,* vol. I, pp. 247-9.   54. id., vol. II, p. 75.
55. ibid., pp. 112-14. Courtois (*Rapport,* p. 178) deleted part of this letter to give the impression that it was addressed to Maximilien.
56. Arch. Nat. F7 4474⁹⁴.

senior policemen, Héron and Sénart, to arrest Catherine Théot, an elderly religious visionary who had been locked up as insane in the years before the Revolution. In the poisoned atmosphere of 1794 the police committee may have seriously suspected that Catherine's mystical gatherings were a cover for more sinister activities. When Cécile Renault was arrested she had been interrogated about possible contacts with Catherine Théot.[57] Further investigation of *la Mère de Dieu* revealed nothing significant but offered an opportunity to discredit Robespierre. One of Catherine's votaries was the former Benedictine deputy of the Constituent Assembly, Dom Gerle, to whom Robespierre had given a political testimonial during the previous winter. What Vadier did not discover until thermidor was that the father of the man whom Robespierre had made mayor of Paris was another of Catherine's devotees.[58] He probably never did discover that both Catherine and Dom Gerle were regular visitors to Duplay's sister-in-law at Choisy.[59] Robespierre presumably knew it and could expect the fact to emerge sooner or later. On 9 thermidor Vadier referred to the discovery of a letter from the illiterate Catherine to her spiritual son, Robespierre, discovered under her mattress. This is generally assumed to have been either a forgery or a pure invention on Vadier's part, but both Héron and Sénart insisted that it was genuine.[60] There was enough material here to make Robespierre, in his new rôle of high priest of the Revolution, look something of a fool and perhaps to do more, since Vadier maintained that there was a counter-revolutionary plot behind all the religious posturing. On 15 June, only a week after the fête of the Supreme Being, he gave the Convention some unaccustomed entertainment with an ironical account of the new plot and persuaded the deputies to order Catherine and her acolytes to be sent before the revolutionary tribunal. Whether he allowed the trial to take place or tried to stop it, Robespierre was equally compromised. It was perhaps sound tactics on his part to assert that Vadier had failed to get

57. Arch. Nat. W389.

58. M. Eude, 'Points de vue sur l'affaire Cathérine Théot', *Ann. hist. Rév. fr.*, no. 199 (1969).

59. G. Lenotre, *Robespierre et la Mère de Dieu*, Paris, 1926, p. 253.

60. *A la Convention nationale par le citoyen Héron*, Paris, n.d., Bib. Nat. Lb⁴¹ 1150, p. 14; *Révélations puisées dans les cartons des Comités de Salut Public et de Sûreté Générale*, Paris, 1824, p. 178.

to the bottom of the plot and to order Fouquier-Tinville, apparently on his own responsibility, to suspend proceedings until a further investigation had been made. When he complained to Vilate, a juror of the revolutionary tribunal, of 'imaginary conspiracies to hide real ones', he was presumably thinking more of Vadier than of Catherine Théot.[61] Fouquier was apparently indignant at Robespierre's interference with what he perhaps imagined to be the independence of the judiciary, but the Committee of Public Safety allowed Robespierre to have his way. This again suggests that they were not prepared to sacrifice him to the rival committee.

Whatever you may think about him, Ted, said Henry, I'd sooner have been Robespierre than Vadier. I think we're perhaps inclined to forget the ruthlessness of the others. I don't know why Danton, with all his vices, is so often presented as some sort of sacrificial victim and Robespierre is made to seem the most cruel and cold-blooded of them all.

It was you who pointed out a long time ago that there's nothing the facts can do to change the myth. It works both ways. I agree that he was neither a paragon of revolutionary virtue nor a political gangster but what he actually was is so complicated and so elusive that it won't fit any popular image. It was partly his own fault if people judge him more harshly than the others – he would have been the first to claim that his standards were higher than theirs.

You're both talking like the first and second courtiers discussing the hero in one of Shakespeare's less impressive historical plays, said Mac. Nothing stopped in 1794, not even the revolution. Robespierre's democratic republic of all the virtues had always been pie in the sky. The Terror had been the only means of saving the revolution from foreign invasion and it had done its job. It never looked like doing any more and there wasn't much more it could have done. There wasn't going to be any New Jerusalem whether Robespierre won or lost and the only problem now was to preserve as much political liberty as possible for everyone while handing the economy back to the owners of property. Danton had possibly stood for something along those lines but his bunch of crooks

61. Vilate, *Les mystères de la Mère de Dieu dévoilés*, Paris, an III, Bib. Nat. Lb[41] 1150, p. 14.

brought him down. Robespierre couldn't do it because he was a moral autocrat. In the end, nobody did manage it.

There's something in that, agreed Henry, but if that's all there is to it then history is one long sum that's always about to add up to infinity but never actually gets past nought.

Of course it's not all there is to it. I wasn't saying you were wrong to put Robespierre under the microscope, only that you both get so absorbed in him that you talk as if the whole fate of the revolution was in his hands. That's rather hard on him since you're bound to conclude that he failed, when he was as much a prisoner of an impossible situation as anyone else and there wasn't any way out. Even J.S. sees that, or at least I think he does.

Events now moved towards a crisis, I went on, but the situation was still fluid. No one wanted to make the first move or to commit himself to a final choice of allies. When it was all over those who thought they had won naturally said that everything had gone according to plan, but up to the last moment it wasn't clear how the sides would be drawn. On 27 June Payan, the *agent national* of the Paris Commune, gave Robespierre his confidential view of the situation in a letter that he asked him to burn.[62] He began by criticising the competence of the Committee of General Security; Amar had failed to appreciate the political significance of the East India Company affair and the Committee as a whole, piqued at not being entrusted with the reports against Hébert and Danton, had tried to turn the Théot case into a *cause célèbre* of its own but made a mess of the job. 'It would be better if this committee were composed of mediocrities who allowed themselves to be guided by the Government, rather than by brilliant men.' After suggesting that Vadier's report might be the product of counter-revolutionary intrigue he added rather unconvincingly that he had no intention of setting the two committees against each other. He urged Robespierre to destroy 'Bourdon and his accomplices' while the memory of their opposition to the prairial law was still fresh, to discipline the press and to enforce his own control over the administration, to 'centralise public opinion – in other words, the moral government – and make it uniform, when you have only centralised the physical and material government'.

62. *Papiers inédits*, vol. III, pp. 360-6; Courtois, *Rapport*, pp. 212-17.

This was dangerous advice, all the more so since it probably confirmed Robespierre's own view of the situation.

Levasseur told the Convention on 30 August that he had been present at a meeting of the Committee of Public Safety on 28 June when the other members called Robespierre a dictator and he and Saint-Just walked out. The incident may be true but the date is unlikely for Saint-Just did not return from the front until that evening and at eleven o'clock Prieur wrote to his friend, Guyton-Morveau, 'Saint-Just [back from the victory of Fleurus] came in just then and we embraced him. I can't begin to describe to you all our *effusions patriotiques*.'[63] Robespierre's semi-confidences to the Jacobins, where he was once again an assiduous attender, suggest that the situation was confused, with everyone feeling his way. On 27 June he seemed to imply that he had resigned himself to accepting the status quo. After complaining of attempts during the previous two months to turn the deputies against the Government and against him personally, he denied that the Committee of Public Safety intended to put any deputies on trial and even called Vadier a faithful representative whose report on the Théot case had been distorted by public opinion. It was a gloomy and pessimistic speech that appeared to announce the Government's capitulation to the extremists. 'If the villains insist that we turn a blind eye to their crimes, we will pretend not to notice them. If they insist that we don't speak about them, we won't mention them. Of course, we shall be lucky if the Republic wins through, but how can we break a law dictated by the base and cowardly Hébert?'[64] Four days later he made a violent but obscure attack on the *Indulgents*. He accused them of turning from an attack on the Government as a whole to sniping at individual members and brought the subject round to himself. Complaining that he was accused of being a dictator, he broke away from the solidarity of the Government: 'These calumnies are repeated in Paris; you would shudder if you knew where.' This confirms Levasseur's story and the two speeches possibly indicate the failure of an attempt to reunite the Committee of Public Safety between 27 June and 1 July. Robespierre went on to confide in the Jacobins that he was uncertain what to do. He paid tribute to the *patriotisme* and firmness of the Committees, but his conclusion pointed in a very different direction. 'When the time

63. Bouchard, op. cit., p. 210.   64. *Oeuvres*, vol. X, pp. 504-11.

is ripe I will explain myself more fully. I have said enough today for those who understand. No one will ever be able to stop me from confiding the truth in the republican Convention . . . If I should be forced to surrender some of my responsibilities I should still remain a deputy and I should fight tyrants and conspirators to the death.'[65] A different report quotes him as saying that he would have left the *Indulgents* alone if they had not taken the offensive.[66]

I see what you mean about no one wanting to make a final choice, said Henry. This was a clear hint to the Committtee of Public Safety that it would be dangerous to try to get rid of him; possibly a suggestion that he would appeal to the Assembly as a whole rather than to the Montagnards. At the same time, since he wanted to deter them rather than to attack them, he couldn't come out into the open and try to enlist Jacobin support against any specific opponents.

J.S. certainly has his problems, said Ted. I don't suppose anyone will ever know what took place in the Committee of Public Safety. He doesn't even know what Robespierre said to the Jacobins since the reports differ. I suppose the editors were terrified of printing the wrong thing and they may all have left out whatever struck them as particularly dangerous. Even if we had verbatim reports they would only tell us what people thought it expedient to say and not what they knew or believed.

It looks to me, said Henry, as though they were all on the defensive. Their little tactical thrusts were only intended to protect themselves.

Collot d'Herbois had been attending the Jacobins very regularly and taking a prominent part in debates. He may have hoped that Robespierre's absence would allow him to win control of the club, where he had always been popular. On 7 July, when Robespierre was apparently away, he took advantage of the unveiling of a bust of William Tell to make some pointed remarks in defence of tyrannicide. After that he seems to have kept away altogether until 8 thermidor. Robespierre attended very regularly from 9 July onwards and kept his hold over the club. He could be reasonably sure of their support but how useful it would prove would depend on the form the crisis took. On 9 July he made another pessimistic

65. *Oeuvres*, vol. X, pp. 511-16.   66. id. p. 517.

288

speech, admitting that revolutionary government was still far from its goal of creating a stable republican regime. He accused his opponents of trying to divide the revolutionaries and said that his own objective was to prevent the emergence of warring factions. One senses a certain weariness that so much should still be left to do, after such prolonged efforts. 'I know that everything criminal is bound to disappear from the earth but it is still true that until now crime has been the curse of the world.' 'The Revolution would end so simply, without any trouble from the factious, if only all men equally loved their country and its laws. But that is still far away.'[67]

During the week that followed he changed his tactics once again and began attacking individuals. On the 11th he denounced Dubois-Crancé, who was expelled from the club at Couthon's suggestion. Three days later it was Fouché's turn and on the 16th Robespierre criticised Pille, Carnot's man at the War Office. This was to provoke opposition without destroying it. Fouché and Dubois-Crancé each persuaded the Convention to order a report on their conduct while absent on mission, which protected them from immediate arrest. In the case of Dubois-Crancé, it was 25 July when the Assembly ordered the Committee of Public Safety to report within three days. It was becoming more and more difficult to avoid taking some decisive step that would provoke a general explosion. Fouché had already written to his brother, on the 23rd, 'A few days more and the rogues and villains will be exposed . . . Even today we may see the traitors unmasked.'[68] By the time his letter was intercepted it was too late to matter. The spies of d'Antraigues, despite a good deal of inaccuracy in their reports, sensed that the crisis was about to break. Their bulletin of 12–20 July described Robespierre's position as desperate. That of the 20–25th claimed that Dubois-Crancé, Billaud and Collot had joined forces with Lecointre and his group of fifteen deputies, while Saint-Just had gone over to Robespierre's side because the others wanted to end the Terror. Robespierre himself was 'a mere shadow'. 'This crisis cannot possibly go on much longer.'[69] They were right about that, at least.

67. *Oeuvres*, vol. x, pp. 518-24.
68. E. Hamel, *Histoire de Robespierre*, Paris, 1867, vol. III, p. 629.
69. A. Rufer, 'En complément des Dropmore Papers', *Ann. hist. Rév. fr.*, no. 153 (1958).

On 22 July the two Committees held a joint meeting which Robespierre did not attend. Some sort of a compromise was worked out and to appease Saint-Just, the other members agreed to complete the organisation of the *commissions populaires* that were to investigate the thousands of suspects in gaol, with a view to the confiscation of the property of those not found to have been wrongfully arrested. This has sometimes been seen as reflecting a 'Robespierrist' policy of economic levelling but Robespierre seems to have been less concerned than Saint-Just and the contemporary evidence suggests that the measure was seen as essentially a means of punishing counter-revolutionaries. Lindet apparently told Lecointre that it was only his opposition that prevented each of the four new commissions being given its own revolutionary tribunal.[70]

Robespierre was induced to attend a second joint meeting on the 23rd at which Billaud-Varenne – according to Saint-Just – told him, 'We are all your friends.' Robespierre is said to have denounced his opponents: Vadier, Amar, Jagot, Collot and Billaud, according to Ruhl (who was there); Cambon and the Committee of General Security as a whole, according to Tissot (who was not).[71] Tissot says that Robespierre agreed to curtail the activities of the police bureau. Saint-Just was commissioned to make a report to the Convention. According to Saint-Just's own version, Billaud and Collot told him not to mention the Supreme Being and Saint-Just insisted that his report must be respectful of the Convention and its members. It is quite likely that no one, including Saint-Just, had any clear idea of what was to go into the report. His own insistence on respecting the Convention could mean that he had rejected the demand of Robespierre and Couthon for a limited purge. The two Committees would have been most unlikely to entrust the report to him if they had thought him committed to Robespierre's point of view.

The relief of the Government at having apparently recovered its unity was given public expression during the next few days. On 24 July Couthon told the Jacobins that if there had been personal disagreements within the Committees, they had never been divided

70. *Crimes des sept membres*, p. 194.
71. R. Cobb, 'Témoignage de Ruhl sur les divisions au sein des Comités à la veille du 9 thermidor', *Ann. hist. Rév. fr.*, no. 139 (1955); and P-F. Tissot, *Histoire de la Révolution française*, Paris, 1839, vol. v, pp. 277-8.

on matters of principle. The members of the Committee of General Security were well-intentioned but they themselves had admitted that this was not equally true of their agents. Couthon went on to repeat his familiar theme that there were foreign agents even within the Jacobins and five or six more in the Convention, 'whose hands are full of the riches of the Republic and dripping with the blood of the innocents they have slaughtered'. Somewhat illogically, he concluded, 'I am not proposing any measures against the basest, but also the most dangerous enemies of public liberty; I am only asking for men of goodwill to unite.' There was perhaps more than a hint here that Robespierre and Couthon, while accepting the truce in the Committees, intended to go on campaigning for a purge. When an unfortunate Jacobin whose good intentions were not matched by his grasp of political tactics, called for an emergency meeting of the club at which Robespierre and Couthon could 'explain exactly what is being plotted against the nation' he must have been thunderstruck by the violence with which the two of them shut him up.[72] An explanation was the last thing that anyone wanted. Barère, on the 25th, assured the Convention that, while foreign plots were still being discovered, they would easily be overcome by the unity within the two Committees. Voulland, writing to his constituents back in Uzès on the 26th, protested rather too much that the Committees had never been divided and were now more united than ever.[73]

Robespierre said nothing and no doubt suspected that his colleagues were insincere. Some of them probably were. Nevertheless, these public protestations of new-found unity naturally alarmed those who felt that their own proscription might be the price of the bargain. Cambon had apparently drafted a denunciation of Robespierre which he and Moïse Bayle had been dissuaded by the Committee of General Security from presenting to the Assembly. When Barère praised Robespierre and announced the unity of the Committees, Cambon understandably assumed that he had been trapped by Bayle. The latter insisted that the Committees were merely 'burning deadly incense to Robespierre', but Cambon may have been only half-reassured.[74] Self-preservation was likely

72. Aulard, *La Société des Jacobins*, vol. VI; *Oeuvres*, vol. X, p. 541.
73. A. Mathiez, *Girondins et Montagnards*, Paris, 1930, pp. 175-6.
74. A. Mathiez, *Girondins et Montagnards*, pp. 166-7.

to keep the Committees united when any other policy represented a desperate gamble.

It was perhaps this suffocating atmosphere of intrigue and suspicion, in which all long-term objectives had to be sacrificed to tactical manoeuvring, that drove Robespierre, most untypically, into decisive action. He may also have felt that if Saint-Just was allowed to deliver a more or less neutral report, he and Couthon would be reduced to impotent isolation. On 26 July he made his first appearance in the Assembly for six weeks, broke the truce of the 23rd and put his case before the deputies. It was not a very good battle-ground for him since many of the Montagnards believed him to be threatening them, and his overtures to the Plain – if that is what they were – had remained very tentative, but if he wanted to get his own way he had not much choice. The Jacobins had lost most of their importance as a pressure-group since the Convention was less afraid of popular movements in Paris. Robespierre had consistently failed to get his own policies endorsed by the Committee of Public Safety and if Saint-Just accepted the compromise of the 23rd he would be more isolated than ever. His only hope of scattering his opponents at one blow was by means of a motion in the Assembly where his personal prestige might still carry the day.

Unfortunately for him, he produced a speech that was vague and disjointed, despite its moments of genuine pathos.[75] Instead of offering the clear lead which the situation demanded, he seemed unable to get away from the sibylline allusiveness of his recent speeches to the Jacobins, parts of which, indeed, he reproduced. He began with the misleading assurance that his aim was to put an end to discord and that he did not intend to accuse anyone. He deleted passages from his original draft that denounced unspecified factions and anonymous enemies, in a painful attempt at conciliation. He presented himself as the defender of the Convention against extremists, reminding the deputies of his protection of the Girondin back-benchers. He told them, as he had previously told the Jacobins, that since the execution of Hébert and Danton the Committees had been on the defensive. This was inoffensive enough, especially since he suppressed hostile references to Amar, Jagot and the agents of the Committee of General Security. He

75. *Oeuvres*, vol. X, pp. 542-82.

appeared at first to be accepting the stalemate and the compromise of the 23rd. 'If there are privileged conspirators, inviolable enemies of the Republic, I agree to maintain an eternal silence about them.' His only aim was to salvage public morality and protect *patriotes* from persecution. For a few moments, his invocation of *vertu* transformed the tone of his speech. 'I swear it exists . . . that tender, impetuous and irresistible passion, torment and delight of magnanimous souls, that deep horror of tyranny, that compassionate zeal for the oppressed, that sacred love of one's country, that more sublime and sacred love of humanity without which a great revolution is merely one dazzling crime that destroys another; it exists, that generous ambition to establish on earth the first Republic in the world.'

This was Robespierre at his best, but after this moment of genuine and passionate eloquence he seemed to lose his way. Complaining that republican government could not stabilise itself, he then introduced a rather milder version of his criticism of the agents of the police committee; he complained of 'being blamed for everything. He had always found it difficult to resist the temptation to self-justification and he digressed to applaud his decree on the worship of the Supreme Being, which he called a revolution in itself. Religion brought him round to the Théot case, but he again suppressed an attack on Vadier and the accusation that the Committee of General Security had been behind all the moves against him.

The tone changed once again as he moved on to attack the *Indulgents* and to make a number of veiled references to his colleagues on the Committees. Three days ago 'they' had been ready to denounce him as a Catiline; now 'they' were all smiles. He gave a thoroughly misleading account of his share in the responsibility for the work of the police bureau and revealed that he had kept away from the Committee of Public Safety for the previous six weeks. His condemnation of those who claimed that all was well with the Republic was a clear repudiation of Barère, but only his colleagues could have understood that the reference to a man who talked about walking on a volcano was aimed at Billaud. A passage calling for the introduction of republican institutions was presumably an overture to Saint-Just, their main champion. He went on to accuse his unnamed opponents of trying to proscribe those who proposed such institutions and then suddenly praising them when 'they' realised their own weakness. This presumably indicated that Robespierre believed that the majority of the members of the two Committees saw the truce of 23 July as a temporary tactical move. It was perhaps also intended to warn Saint-Just that he was being tricked into abandoning Robespierre. Whatever it all meant to him it must have mystified the great majority of the deputies while it aroused the antagonism of his colleagues on the Committees. His general criticism of the recent policies of the Government was more explicit, with obvious references to Barère and Carnot.

After a good deal in this allusive vein, the last part of his speech took on a much sharper and more positive tone, even though it contradicted his initial profession of moderation. 'It is a strange way of protecting *patriotes* to liberate counter-revolutionaries and procure the triumph of knaves! What makes innocence secure is the terror of the criminal.' He then said bluntly that the administration of finance was in counter-revolutionary hands, accusing Cambon, Ramel and Mallarmé of being the successors of Chabot, Fabre and Julien. This was far from amounting to a profession of economic radicalism; on the contrary, he called for a return to a *régime naturel et doux,* in other words, to economic liberalism.

At last he came to his conclusion. 'Let us recognise that there is a conspiracy against public liberty; that it derives its strength from a criminal coalition intriguing in the heart of the Convention itself; that this coalition has accomplices within the Committee of General Security and its bureaux; that enemies of the Republic have set this committee against the Committee of Public Safety and set up two governments; that members of the Committee of Public Safety have entered into the plot; that the coalition thus created aims at the destruction of the *patriotes* and the *patrie*. What is the remedy? To punish the traitors, purge the bureaux of the Committee of General Security, purge the Committee itself and subordinate it to the Committee of Public Safety, purge the Committee of Public Safety itself and create a unified government under the supreme authority of the Convention.'

What an extraordinary muddle, said Ted.

I've simplified it a good deal; the actual speech was much more rambling.

It keeps pointing in different directions and he takes on all comers at once.

294

Not quite all. He never mentioned by name the deputies he denounced in his private notes – Thuriot, Bourdon and so on – and Fouché got only a passing rebuke for his alleged atheism. It illustrates what I said about no one knowing how the sides would be drawn when the crisis broke. In order to get at his colleagues on the Committees, Robespiere concentrated his fire on members of the Committees rather than on the Montagnard back-benchers whose proscription had been one of the main causes of disagreement. The Convention now had to choose between the two factions in the Government. The Montagnards, several of whom had links with the anti-Robespierrist members of both Committees, might well oppose Maximilien but there was always the possibility that they might be out-voted by the Plain, which had been reminded by Robespierre that he alone had saved the Girondin supporters.

It sounds to me like the speech of a tired man, said Henry. It reads as though it was written in several parts. It's a kind of Robespierre anthology: idealism and the vision of a better society, suspicion, the endless denunciation of plots, faith in the Terror and his ability to destroy evil by force. It's as though he couldn't see his way forward any more and fell back on repeating all his old ideas.

He did refer to it as his 'testament' and his conclusion was: 'I was made to fight crime, not to rule over it. The time has not yet come when men of goodwill can serve their country with impunity. The defenders of liberty will always be proscribed so long as the horde of knaves is in power.'

In a way it's logical enough, said Mac; too logical in fact. The only alternative to a social revolution was to go on centralising and increasing the repressive power of the state and the next step was personal dictatorship. But it was rather optimistic of him to expect the Convention to see things that way.

The reception of the speech suggested that no one was quite sure of its implications. Lecointre at once proposed that it should be published. He may have wanted to explore the possibilities of an alliance with Robespierre against the Committees or he may simply have been playing for time. Publication did not necessarily imply agreement. Bourdon de l'Oise, on the other hand, wanted the speech referred back to the Committees. Barère, despite Robespierre's criticisms of him, supported Lecointre and Couthon got the motion carried, with an amendment that the speech should be distributed all over the country – which definitely implied the Convention's acceptance of it. Vadier then made a very deferential defence of the Committee of General Security and of his own report on the Théot case, promising new revelations. Cambon was the first man to challenge Robespierre. Faced with his vigorous defence of his Finance Committee, Robespierre at once retreated and claimed – most implausibly – that he had not intended to cast any aspersions on Cambon's loyalty. This probably encouraged Robespierre's opponents. Billaud called for a showdown and demanded, despite the fact that a motion had already been carried, that the speech should be referred back. Panis joined in with the complaint that Robespierre had had anyone he disliked expelled from the Jacobins and wanted to know if he himself was on Couthon's proscription list. We can't be sure of exactly what happened since the press reports are unreliable, as editors looked to their own safety. The *Moniteur* apparently suppressed the fact that when Panis and Fréron called for the amendment of the prairial law to guarantee the immunity of deputies, it was Billaud-Varenne who silenced them.[76] Bentabole and Charlier opposed the distribution of the speech and Charlier demanded that Robespierre should name the men he was accusing. Robespierre refused. When Amar and Thirion joined in the attack, Barère withdrew to his usual position in times of crisis: on the fence. Bréard eventually persuaded the deputies to rescind their previous vote and have the speech printed but distributed to members of the Convention only.[77]

This inconclusive result meant that Robespierre had lost the first round but the outcome was still unpredictable. The second round was fought out at the Jacobins, between Robespierre and Couthon on the one hand and Collot and Billaud on the other. Although the two ex-Cordeliers were not without their supporters in the club, the majority took Robespierre's side. He read his speech again and Billaud and Collot were shouted down when they tried to reply, and eventually thrown out. Couthon then carried a motion for the expulsion from the club of all members who had

---

76. G. Lefebvre, 'Sur la loi du 22 prairial an II', *Ann. hist. Rév. fr.*, no. 123 (1951), p. 252.

77. A useful, if not very well translated, selection of documents on the thermidor crisis is available in *The ninth of thermidor: the fall of Robespierre*, ed. Bienvenue, London, 1968.

voted against the printing of Robespierre's speech during the debate in the Assembly. The Jacobins seem to have toyed with the idea of trying to organise another forcible purge of the Convention, along the lines of that of 2 June 1793, but this was scarcely appropriate if Robespierre was hoping to appeal to the Plain against the Montagnards on the following day.[78] In the end they did nothing.

Collot and Billaud then made their way back to the Committee of Public Safety where Saint-Just was working on the report that he intended to present on the next day. He does not seem to have spoken a word throughout the day's session and the fact that the Committee allowed him to go on drafting a report in its name – which he had promised to show his colleagues before he delivered it – could only mean that they did not regard him as committed to Robespierre. During the night Lecointre and Cambon tried to penetrate the Committee but were turned away – another indication that the anti-Robespierre forces were still far from united.[79] Collot and Billaud, still furious at their treatment by the Jacobins, apparently attacked Saint-Just. It is impossible to know just what happened since the two surviving accounts – Lecointre's subsequent attack on seven members of the Committees and their reply – naturally present things somewhat differently. No one will ever know what Saint-Just was thinking. His eventual report, which he may have revised as events developed, took the form of a rather lofty exoneration of Robespierre as a man who had been deliberately provoked by his opponents. Disregarding his old quarrels with Carnot, Saint-Just attacked Billaud and Collot for profiting from the absence of their colleagues, away on missions, absorbed by departmental responsibilities or ill, to impose their own policies in the name of the Committee. After accusing them of trying to do away with some of their colleagues, disperse the rest, destroy the revolutionary tribunal and deprive Paris of its magistrates, he concluded rather oddly, 'The members I accuse are guilty of few faults . . . I am not condemning those I have named; what I want is that they should clear themselves and we should become more prudent.' He was possibly hoping to impose himself as the arbiter of the situation. More skilful than Robespierre, he tried to isolate two or three

---

78. See Aulard's *Jacobins* for conflicting accounts of what was said.
79. *Crimes des sept membres*, pp. 16-17.

members of the Committee of Public Safety and to rally the rest of the Government and the Convention as a whole against them. If his colleagues had any idea of what he was writing, this would help to explain the anger of Billaud and Collot and the temporising attitude of the others. Early in the morning of the 27th he left the Committee and the next his colleagues heard was that he had broken his promise and was already speaking to the Assembly.

No one at the time knew what was in Saint-Just's report since he was interrupted as soon as he began to read it. His apparent desertion of his colleagues may have convinced them that they had no alternative but to join forces with the dissident Montagnards whose advances they had repelled during the night. When Tallien interrupted Saint-Just, Billaud came to Tallien's support with a direct attack on Robespierre that Tallien himself would not have dared to make. Barère, more cautiously, defended the record of the Government. He was followed by Vadier who attacked Robespierre. Robespierre – unlike the silent Saint-Just – tried desperately to get a hearing, seeming to appeal in vain to the Plain to defend him against the Montagnards. He was never allowed to say more than a few words and after some hours of shouting and vituperation his arrest was voted, together with that of Augustin, who demanded to share his brother's fate, as he shared his principles. When Saint-Just and Couthon were arrested too, Le Bas insisted on joining them.

If I'd been there, said Henry, I'd like to think I should have had the courage to join them as well.

In spite of everything you know, asked Ted.

On balance, yes, when I think of the alternative.

It was then early in the afternoon, although the arrested deputies were not led away to prison until three o'clock or later.[80] The entire situation was then transformed by a desperate attempt on the part of the Paris Commune to organise an insurrection. The Commune ordered the concierges of the various prisons to refuse to receive any of the arrested deputies. Turned away from the Luxembourg, Robespierre had himself taken to the Mairie, the headquarters of the Paris police, where he was in safe hands but still nominally under arrest. He reached the Mairie about half

80. I have followed the excellent account of the events of the 9 thermidor in Sainte-Claire Deville, op. cit., Part II.

past seven and, despite an appeal from the Commune, it was not until about three hours later that he agreed to join it at the Hôtel de Ville. He probably had few illusions as to his likely fate if he found himself in the hands of Fouquier-Tinville, but as yet the Convention had only voted his arrest and not brought any charges against him. He knew that a law – introduced by Saint-Just – outlawed those who escaped from arrest. He may still have been thinking to achieve something by legal methods or he may have been hoping, if he complied with the law himself, to have it both ways.

Which would be in character, said Henry. It was what he had done on 10 August and 31 May.

You can't blame him for that, said Henry. He had no military experience and he would not have been of much use to an insurrectionary committee.

The Commune seemed to think differently. There's such a thing as moral leadership. He himself had ridiculed Pétion for getting himself locked up on 10 August and I don't see much difference.

How often do I have to tell you, said Mac, that it's the situation and not the individual that counts. It didn't matter where he went. Events had condemned him and he would still have lost, whatever he did.

The Assembly and the Commune each tried to mobilise the Paris Sections and their National Guards. The Assembly won most of the troops but the Commune controlled more cannon and its forces were ready first.[81] At about eight o'clock Coffinhal, a judge of the revolutionary tribunal, led a strong force from the Hôtel de Ville to the Assembly and liberated Hanriot who had been captured a few hours earlier. Hanriot found himself unexpectedly in control of the military situation around the Convention. This was the Commune's only chance – and it would probably have led nowhere. The Convention, which had already committed itself, could not have been 'persuaded' as it had been on 2 June and a successful coup d'état by the Commune would not have solved anything. When Hanriot merely led his forces back to the Hôtel de Ville the issue was settled. Up to a point I agree with Mac: the situation was on the side of the Assembly. All it had to do was to suppress a revolt against the nation's representatives. The only way

81. See A. Soboul, op. cit., pp. 959-1025.

out for the Commune would have been a military dictatorship and it had no regular troops at its disposal. The arrested deputies – who had now been outlawed – gradually made their way to the Hôtel de Ville. Couthon did not arrive until about one o'clock. There they joined the Commune's *comité d'insurrection* and did what they could to muster support. Couthon insisted on drafting a proclamation to the army. 'In whose name?' asked Robespierre, understandably. 'In the name of the Convention,' replied Couthon. 'Isn't it wherever we are?' While the insurrectionary committee debated in a back room the National Guards massed in front of the Hôtel de Ville gradually melted away until the square was quite empty.

You might say that symbolised the relationship between Robespierre and the country as a whole, said Ted.

The Convention put its defences in the hands of Barras who organised two columns for a march on the Hôtel de Ville. Soon after two the leading column, under Léonard Bourdon, entered the city hall without any opposition, to find that Le Bas had shot himself and Robespierre had tried to do the same but only succeeded in fracturing his jaw.[82] Augustin, who had apparently tried to kill himself by jumping from the building, had been no more successful than his brother.

I won't go into the harrowing details of Robespierre's last hours as he lay in pain with his shattered jaw while the Convention went through the formalities necessary for his execution. Since he had already been outlawed there was no trial, merely an official identification. In the early evening of 28 July, he and twenty-one others – for all those who attended the Commune's last meeting had been outlawed too – were taken to execution. The crowd applauded as usual. Perhaps the best epitaph is Carlyle's: 'He had on the sky-blue coat he had got made for the Feast of the *Etre Suprême* – O Reader, can thy hard heart hold out against that?'

Is that the end, asked Ted.

The end for Robespierre but the beginning of the myth and perhaps that was more important. Would you like me to tell you about that too?

I think that will do for the time being.

82. For the evidence that Robespierre himself fired the shot, see Sainte-Claire Deville, pp. 295-7.

Well, I hope I've told you all you wanted to know about Robespierre, I said.

I wouldn't say that, but you've taught us quite a bit about each other.

And ourselves, said Henry.

Bibliography

A comprehensive bibliography of the books and articles about Robespierre would be a monumental work, and one of doubtful value unless it included material on the political background as well. Gérard Walter drew up a list of over 10,000 works on Robespierre in 1936 and the pens have not been idle since then. The following is merely an indication of the sources that I myself have found most useful, omitting well-known general histories. There is a fuller bibliography in J. M. Thompson's *Robespierre* and a useful indication of early works in J-M. Quérard's *Les Robespierre* (Paris, 1863).

To the best of my knowledge, all known Robespierre manuscripts of any importance have been published. There is much still to be learned from the documents in the Archives Nationales about corruption and underground intrigue during the Terror and Robespierre's own activities in the *bureau de police,* which are well documented, have not been systematically analysed. There is always the possibility that important new writings of his will come to light, but no evidence to suggest that this is likely. It is reasonable to assume that new material is not going to provide unequivocal answers to the many questions that are still in suspense.

To compensate for these limitations, the historian has comparatively easy access to printed versions of Robespierre's writings, speeches and newspapers. Almost all of these are available in the ten volumes published by the Société des Etudes robespierristes (Paris, 1912–67). His speeches, in particular, have been edited with exceptional care and the differing reports of them in the revolutionary press fully reproduced. His essay *Les droits et l'état des bâtards* was discovered and published by L-N. Berthe (Arras, 1971). Louis Jacob's *Robespierre vu par ses contemporains* (Paris, 1938) although inevitably incomplete, includes most of the important contemporary comment on Robespierre. His papers were published in three collections. Courtois printed many of them with his *Rapport fait au nom de la commission chargée de l'examen des papiers trouvés chez Robespierre* (Paris, an III). This has to be used with care since Courtois sometimes falsified the text in order to discredit Robespierre. This collection has to be supplemented by the *Papiers inédits trouvés chez Robespierre, Saint-Just, Payan etc.* (Paris, 1828, 3v.). Entirely different material relating to the plots denounced by Fabre d'Eglantine and Chabot is to be found in the *Pièces trouvées dans les papiers de Robespierre et complices* (Paris, an III). There is a certain amount of material about Maximilien in the memoirs of Charlotte Robespierre, of which the most recent edition is that edited by H. Fleischmann (Paris, n.d.) and in Stéfan Pol's *Autour de Robespierre: le Conventionnel Le Bas* (Paris, n.d.). Robespierre's activities as a member of the Committee of Public Safety are recorded in F-A. Aulard's *Recueil des actes du Comité de Salut Public* (Paris, 1889–1911, 21v.).

Biographies of Robespierre are too numerous to mention in detail. *La vie et les crimes de Maximilien Robespierre* by Le Blond de Neuvéglise (almost certainly the abbé Proyart), published at Augsburg in 1795, cannot be neglected despite its ferocious bias, because of its first-hand information about Robespierre's life in Arras and at Louis-le-Grand. J-A. Paris, *La jeunesse de Robespierre et la convocation des Etats-Généraux en Artois,* is also exceptionally well-informed and almost equally hostile. The most exhaustive of the later biographies are E. Hamel's *Histoire de Robespierre* (Paris, 1865–7, 3v.), J. M. Thompson's *Robespierre* (Oxford, 1935, 2v.) and G. Walter's *Robespierre* (Paris, 1936–9, 2v.). Of the more recent brief studies, one of the most interesting is Max Gallo's *Maximilien Robespierre: histoire d'une solitude* (Paris, 1968).

In the following brief guide to the materials on which I have chiefly relied, the division between contemporary and subsequent sources relates to the content of the work rather than to date of publication. All were published in Paris unless otherwise indicated. In the case of lesser-known works, the reference number is that of the catalogue of the Bibliothèque Nationale.

Contemporary sources

Barras, P-F.   *Memoirs.* (Eng. trans.) London, 1895.
Baudot, M-A.   *Notes historiques sur la Convention nationale,* 1893.

Billaud-Varenne, J-N. *Mémoire inédit sur les événements du 9 thermidor*, ed. Vellay, 1910.
Réponse de J-N. Billaud, an III (Le³⁸ 1261).
Réponse de J-N. Billaud, représentant du peuple, à Laurent Lecointre, an III (Lb⁴¹ 1444).

Bonnemain   *Les chemises rouges*, an VI.

Carnot, L-N-M.   *Mémoires sur Carnot par son fils*, 1861, 2v.
Opinion de Carnot, représentant du peuple, sur l'accusation proposée contre Billaud, Collot, Barère et Vadier, an III (Le³⁸ 1305).

Collot, d'Herbois J-M.   *Défense de J-M. Collot*, an III (Le³⁸ 1266).
Discours fait à la Convention nationale par J-M. Collot, an III (Le³⁸ 1309).

Courtois, E. B.   *Réponse aux détracteurs du 9 thermidor an II, an IV* (Lb⁴¹ 3978).

Couthon, G.   *Correspondance*, ed. Mège, 1872.

Danton, G-J.   *Notes de Topino-Lebrun sur le procès de Danton*, 1875.

Daubigny, V.   *Principaux événements pour et contre la Révolution*, an III (Lb.⁴¹ 2105).
Villain Daubigny à Philippeaux, an II (Lb⁴¹ 931).

Desmoulins, C.   *Le Vieux Cordelier*, ed. Calvet, 1936.

Despatys, baron   *La Révolution, la Terreur, le Directoire, d'après les Mémoires de Gaillard*, 1909.

Dropmore papers   Historical Manuscripts Commission, *The manuscripts of J. B. Fortescue, London*, 1894, vol. II.

Dulaure, J-A.   *Esquisses historiques des principaux événements de la Révolution*, 1823, 3v.
Supplément aux crimes des anciens comités du gouvernement, an III (8° Lb⁴¹ 11).

Fabre, d'Eglantine, P-F-N.   *Fabre d'Eglantine à ses concitoyens*, an II (Lb⁴¹ 967).

Fouché, J.   *Mémoires*, ed. Madelin, 1945.

Garat, D-J.   *Mémoires*, ed. Maron, 1862.

Hébert, J-R.   *J-R. Hébert, auteur du Père Duchesne, à
                Camille Desmoulins et compagnie*, an II
                (Lb⁴¹ 3615).

Héron, F.   *A la Convention nationale par le citoyen
                Héron*, an II (Lb⁴¹ 1182).

Julien de Toulouse, J. *Encore un mot à mes détracteurs*, an III (8°
                Le³⁸ 1430).
                Suite à la réponse à mes dénonciateurs, an
                III (8° Le³⁸ 1431).

Lecointre, L.   *Dénonciation faite à la Convention nationale
                par Laurent Lecointre*, an II (Le³⁸ 2175).
                *Les crimes des sept membres des anciens
                comités de salut public et de sûreté
                générale*, an III, (Lb⁴¹ 1441).
                Robespierre peint par lui-même, an II (Lb⁴¹
                1168).

Levasseur, R.   *Mémoires*, 1829–31, 3v.

Lindet, R.   *Discours prononcé par Lindet sur les dénon-
                ciations portées contre l'ancien comité de
                salut public*, an III (Le³⁸ 1304).

Marcandier, Roch *Histoire des hommes de proie*, 1793 (Lb³⁹
                6142).

Nodier, C.   *Souvenirs et portraits de la Révolution*,
                1841.

Pétion, J.   *Discours de Jérôme Pétion sur l'accusation
                intentée contre Maximilien Robespierre*,
                1792 (Lb⁴¹ 162).
                *Observations de Jérôme Pétion sur la lettre
                de Maximilien Robespierre*, 1792 (Lb⁴¹
                2358).

Prieur (de la Côte *Discours de C-A. Prieur*, an III (Le³⁸ 1306).
d'Or) C-A.   *Réponse des membres des deux anciens
                comités*, an III (Lb⁴¹ 1442).
                *Réponse des membres de l'ancien comité de
                salut public*, an III (Le³⁸ 1260).
                *Second mémoire des membres de l'ancien
                comité de salut public dénoncés par
                Laurent Lecointre*, an III (Le³⁸ 1173).

Riouffe, H-J.   *Mémoires d'un détenu pour servir à l'his-
                toire de la tyrannie de Robespierre*, an III.

Saladin, J-B-M.   *Rapport au nom de la commission des 21,* an III (Le³⁸ 1259).

Sénart, G-J.   *Révélations puisées dans les cartons des comités de salut public et de sûreté générale,* 1824 (Lb⁴¹ 36).

Tsachereau-Fargues, P-A.   *À Maximilien Robespierre aux Enfers, an* III.

Tête à la queue (1a) an III (Lb⁴¹ 1451).

Tissot, P-F.   *Histoire de la Révolution française,* 1839, 6v.

Vasselin, G.   *Mémorial révolutionnaire de la Convention,* an V, 2v.

Vilate, J.   *Causes secrètes de la révolution du 9 et 10 thermidor,* an III.

Continuation des causes secrètes, an III.

Les mystères de la Mère de Dieu dévoilés, an III.

(all three works listed under Lb⁴¹ 1150).

Subsequent works

Actes du Colloque Robespierre, 1965.

Batz, baron de   *Les conspirations et la fin de Jean, baron de Batz,* 1911

Bonald, vicomte de   *François Chabot,* 1908.

Bouchard, G.   *Prieur de la Côte d'Or,* 1946.

Chaumié, J.   *Le réseau d'Antraigues et la contre-révolution,* 1965.

Cobb, R.   *Les armées révolutionnaires,* 1961, 2v.

Curtis, E. N.   *Saint-Just, colleague of Robespierre,* Columbia, 1935.

Deville, P. Sainte-Claire,   *La commune de l'an II,* 1946.

d'Estrée, P.   *Le Père Duchesne,* n.d.

Guilaine, J.   *Billaud-Varenne,* 1969.

Herlaut, general,   *Deux témoins de la Terreur,* 1958.

Le colonel Bouchotte, 1946, 2v.

Le général rouge, Ronsin, 1956.

Jacob, L.	*Fabre d'Eglantine, chef des fripons*, 1946.
Labracherie, P.	*Fouquier-Tinville, accusateur-public*, 1961.
Laski, P. M.	*The trial and execution of Mme du Barry*, London, 1969.
Lenotre, G.	*Robespierre et la Mère de Dieu*, 1926.
Lestapis, A. de	*La 'conspiration de Batz'*, 1969.
Madelin, L.	*Danton*. 1914.
Mathiez, A.	*Autour de Robespierre*, 1924.
	Danton et la paix, 1916.
	Etudes sur Robespierre, 1958.
	Girondins et Montagnards, 1930.
	La conspiration de l'étranger, 1918.
	La vie chère et le mouvement social sous la Terreur, 1927.
	Un procès de corruption sous la Terreur: l'affaire de la compagnie des Indes, 1920.
Mortimer-Ternaux, M.	*Histoire de la Terreur*, 1862– , 8v.
Ollivier, A.	*Saint-Just et la force des choses*, 1954.
Ording, A.	*Le bureau de police du comité de salut public*, Oslo, 1930.
Palmer, R. R.	*Twelve who ruled*, Princeton, 1941.
Reinhard, M.	*Le grand Carnot*, 1950–2, 2v.
Soboul, A.	*Les sans-culottes parisiens en l'an II*, 1958.
Walter, G.	*Marat*, 1933.

Articles

(All titles in italics are to be found in the *Annales historiques de la Révolution française*.)

Caron, P.	*Sur l'opposition de gauche à la veille du 9 thermidor*, 1947.
Cobb, R.	*Le témoignage de Ruhl sur les divisions au sein des comités à la veille du 9 thermidor*, 1955.
Cobban, A.	The fundamental ideas of Robespierre, *English Historical Review*, 1948.

	'The political ideas of Maximilien Robespierre during the period of the Convention', *English Historical Review*, 1946.
Eude, M.	*La politique de Robespierre en 1792 d'après le Défenseur de la Constitution*, 1956.
	Points de vue sur l'affaire Catherine Théot, 1969.
	Robespierre a-t-il voulu déstituer Fouquier-Tinville?, 1965.
Jacob, L.	*Robespierre et Villain d'Aubigny*, 1950.
	Robespierre: un mémoire inconnu, 1947.
Labracherie, P. and Pioro, G.	*Charlotte Robespierre et ses amis*, 1961.
Lefebvre, G.	'La rivalité du Comité de Salut Public et du Comité de Sûreté Générale, *Revue Historique*, 1931.
	Sur la loi du 22 prairial an II, 1951–2.
Lestapis, A. de	*Admiral et l'attentat manqué*, 1959.
	Autour de l'attentat d'Admiral, 1957.
	Batz et la liquidation de la créance Guichon, 1952.
	Un grand corrupteur: le duc du Châtelet, 1953, 1955.
Mathiez, A.	*Le Comité de Salut Public et le complot de l'étranger*, 1926.
	Les Indulgents, 1926.
	Les Citra et les Ultra, 1926.
	Robespierre et Joseph Le Bon, 1924.
Reinhard, M.	*La guerre et la paix à la fin de 1793*, 1953.
Schnerb, R.	*A propos d'Admirat et du baron de Batz*, 1952.
Shulim, J. L.	'The youthful Robespierre and his ambivalence towards the Ancien Régime', *Eighteenth-century Studies*, 1972.

Index